Shakespeare, Brecht,

and the Intercultural

Sign

**POST-CONTEMPORARY INTERVENTIONS**

*Series Editors:* Stanley Fish & Fredric Jameson

Antony Tatlow

# SHAKESPEARE, BRECHT, AND THE INTERCULTURAL SIGN

Duke University Press   Durham & London   2001

© 2001 Duke University Press

All rights reserved

Designed by C. H. Westmoreland

Typeset in Dante with Frutiger display

by Keystone Typesetting, Inc. Library

of Congress Cataloging-in-Publication

Data appear on the last printed page of

this book.

For Didi and Clifford

CONTENTS

Preface  ix

Prologue  1

1  Reading the Intercultural: Cultures of Reading  5

2  Intercultural Signs: Textual Anthropology  31

3  Desire, Laughter, and the Social Unconscious  80

4  Historicizing the Unconscious in Plautine and Shakespearean Farce  116

5  *Coriolanus* and the Historical Text  151

6  *Macbeth* in Kunju Opera  189

Epilogue  219

Notes  233

Works Cited  275

Index  287

# PREFACE

Born in Dublin, educated in Ireland, England, and Germany, and living for over thirty years in East Asia, I have been intrigued by the effect of cultural presuppositions upon representation and interpretation. If variations in cultural expression within Europe initially fascinated me, they were as nothing compared with the challenge of grounding the differences between Western and Eastern cultures.

Appointed by the University of Hong Kong in 1965 to teach Western literature, the attraction of intercultural study developed into an incomparable adventure, turning my comfortable assumptions upside down, as I began to understand their relativity, but also helping me to escape deeper frustrations. Encountering other cultures, our "own" is distanced and defamiliarized, the first essential step in really understanding it, let alone any other one. Computing other value systems now assumes different dimensions as they no longer necessarily confront each other from separated, clearly demarcated positions, but begin to interpenetrate. The visual art of theater has benefited from such opportunities. What do these developments tell us about the needs they externalize?

This book develops a preliminary study, *Shakespeare and the Politics of the Sign*, expanding it into topics that have been neglected in discussions of intercultural theater. I am indebted to Jeremy Tambling for earlier criticism and to other colleagues at the University of Hong Kong, above all Ackbar Abbas and Ian McLachlan for their critical friendship. At the University of Dublin I would like to thank the graduate students of my course in cultural theory and, especially, Barbara Wright for all her support.

# PROLOGUE

DIDIER ERIBON: When you gave a collection of your articles the title *The View from Afar,* did you intend to express your distance vis-à-vis the society in which we live?

CLAUDE LÉVI-STRAUSS: The title is taken from the Japanese and came to me when I was reading Zeami, the creator of the Noh theater. He says that in order to be a good actor it is necessary to know how to look at oneself the way the audience does, and he uses the expression "seen from afar." I found that it summed up the anthropologist's attitude looking at his own society, not as a member inside it but as other observers would see it, looking at it from far off in either time or space. —Claude Lévi-Strauss and Didier Eribon, *Conversations with Claude Lévi-Strauss*

The space of observation, of reading, as Lévi-Strauss reminds us, lies outside what is read, even if we are somehow also always within.[1] We cannot read productively unless we simultaneously observe, or think, from outside, from more than one point of view. We can function—or create, and indeed act—without this displacement, but we will not then be able to explain what we have seen or done.

Since distancing is difficult but unavoidable if we seek a wider horizon of understanding, tracing such perspectival shifts is one purpose of this book. Reading that does not stay in movement often settles into ideology that education then disseminates, sometimes disguised by "scholarship" or, indeed, as "theory." Observing others and wrestling with ourselves in a self-distancing practice of interpretation is a precarious task. I call such reading "textual anthropology."[2]

Lévi-Strauss shared an interest with Brecht in Chinese opera. Surprising compatibilities with both reach deeper into Brecht's writing and theater than appears imaginable if we construct that work in terms of a supposedly self-imposed sociometric positivism with which it is so frequently equated. We need an outside eye, an anthropological perspective on that writing and the practice of his theater.

It is a truism that culture is a text that must be read, although the position of anthropologist or reader is never completely clear. Equally, every text, as cultural expression, articulates needs that the writer or performance cannot properly explain. The intercultural sign draws on material and expressive forms across cultural borders. The question is: Why? Much is traceable through that difficult metaphor "the unconscious," often best understood as socially constructed, which is another way of saying the unconscious historicized.

Neglect of the historicized unconscious indicates certain deficiencies in the discourse of the intercultural. This concept is explored more fully through a combination of Foucault's positive unconscious of knowledge and Fromm's social unconscious. There are also obvious links with Deleuze and Guattari's concept of "desire," but I leave them aside because of wider entailments within their writing. However, the following observation indicates why their thought is closer to what interests me in Nietzsche, Fromm, and Foucault than to Lacan's more abstract psychoanalysis: "The set of immanent relations that compose a given social formation actually determine the kind of things of which one can be conscious at any particular moment. For this reason, desire is the social unconscious: it constructs and conditions consciousness, so that images are merely products of the social relations in which one is immersed."[3]

Shakespeare was undoubtedly the preeminent dramatist for Brecht. Engel's production of *Coriolanus* in the 1920s helped to define the so-called epic theater. When Brecht himself reworked that play in the early 1950s, he associated it with what he had begun to call "dialectical theater," preferring it to the earlier term.[4] That much discussed adaptation has not always been well described.

We need to unpick the positivities frequently attached to Brecht in order to appreciate the range of the intercultural sign. I therefore explore the relationship between Brecht and Nietzsche's analysis of tragedy,

Prologue

points of contact with Lévi-Strauss's anthropology, and mention some unexpected compatibilities with Derrida. Such "constellations," to use Benjamin's term for surprising conjunctions, although without its mystical implications, are connected with Brecht's interest in East Asia. He responded more strongly to East Asian culture than is often appreciated, which helps both to complicate our understanding of subsequent developments in intercultural theater and to situate significant Shakespearean productions in East Asia. Poststructuralism and (post-)Marxism both de-essentialize the subject, and their antimetaphysical relationalism is congruent with East Asian forms of thought, especially that Buddhist philosophy for which nirvana, far from constituting an escape into nothing, can only be sought in *samsara,* or the daily "flow of things."

To probe psychoanalytic readings of Shakespeare, and sources of laughter in the Elizabethan and the Roman unconscious, is also to engage with *critical* repressions, perhaps most noticeable when juxtaposing *The Comedy of Errors* and *Menaechmi*, in which nobody is like "himself," where mimesis is apparently axiomatic and collapses. Farce focuses the unconscious more quickly than any other literary form. Contextualizing separates the various historical levels brought into play. In the comparative cultural study I call textual anthropology, a primary function is to show how a culture employs unconscious structuration through the intercultural sign.

Moving Shakespeare's texts, whether into an almost contiguous German, or into a challengingly adulterated English version that has itself passed through German, or into what looks like a geographically and emotionally remote Chinese culture, forces us to question our own construction of those texts. Separating them from "themselves" can also bring them closer. Vigorously externalizing East Asian performance displaces European conventions. In its own performative context, it often resembles contemporary interpretation of Shakespeare that questions mimetic presuppositions. Buddhist theoretical preferences unseat any easy positioning of the text, quickly giving the slip to the official Confucian rectification of names or linguistic social control. This constitutes an East Asian homology and a defamiliarization of the opposition between the powerless conventionalists and the socially powerful semantic naturalists in European Renaissance culture.

The impulse from another culture is sought and absorbed, because it enables an otherwise difficult, if not impossible, engagement with what has been repressed at home. If what has thereby been transformed is later transmitted back, then we can speak of a "dialectics of acculturation." Such practices help us understand how the only way of engaging with "forgotten" aspects of one's own culture can sometimes be this passage through the foreign. Challenging representational conventions, the intercultural sign impedes compliance with strategies of control in the metadiscursive game of power.

An epilogue shows the Noh theater's comedy, not well described in Western criticism, as sophisticated philosophical farce. Rereading this Japanese text suggests affinities with Beckett, and also with Shakespeare and Brecht. The sign becomes problematic when it represses the doubleness of representation, its own unconscious. The Japanese play shows and cleverly deconstructs identity as socially constructed narrative. Apparently eluding this narrative, the characters no longer properly exist and can live forever.

# 1

## READING

## THE INTERCULTURAL

### Cultures of Reading

I

Every engagement with a Shakespearean text is necessarily intercultural. The past really is another culture, its remoteness disguised by language that can occasionally appear as familiar as we seem to ourselves, whom we understand so imperfectly. In considering Brecht's intercultural practices, whose innovations are not fully appreciated, I focus less on what happens to "Shakespeare," than on how such intercultural reading reshapes the conventions of performance and interpretation.

The distinction between inter- and intracultural is itself questionable, implying borders that restrain dissemination, or barriers through which certain kinds of material and mental traffic can usefully pass. Modern Japan, and even China, is in some ways more like contemporary England or the United States than any of them are to their own sixteenth-century selves. To recognize this requires an engagement with linguistic, cultural, historical, and geographical difference. Such a demand is often hard to satisfy. Yet half the battle lies in appreciating its existence, since we so easily fail to recognize how productively it challenges our settled expectations.

A Chinese or Japanese Shakespeare, mediated through Brecht, extends or even contradicts expectations of how a Shakespearean text can be seen through a Brechtian lens. But first we need to know what Brecht learned from East Asian performance. Could such transactions then conceivably impinge on *our* image of "Shakespeare"? Or just widen our understanding of the signifier "Brecht"? Might they change our expectations of intercultural theater? Or even alter our own sense of self?

At the very least, representation and interpretation are defamiliarized. Then we confront the ideologies governing cultural conventions, the natural ways of thinking or feeling that constitute our cultural identity. Particular social cultures of reading predispose us to certain forms of interpretation whose perspective on the text rereads it to the satisfaction of their own presuppositions.

Knowledges and styles of performance now interpenetrate across cultures, and we need to ask why. No matter how well intentioned, hypersensitivity to cultural difference, what has been termed "intercultural angst" in respect of orientalizing, can sometimes constitute the most refined form of condescension, if it assumes a "weaker" Eastern cannot easily withstand the invasions or appropriations by a "stronger" Western culture and should therefore be protected against it.[1]

Intercultural readings question whatever representational paradigm has been conventionalized. Yet we can no longer neatly separate the anthropological sense of culture—geographically distinct, linguistically separate, relatively homogeneous "worldviews"—from culture in the intellectual or disciplinary sense of a preferred, rather than inherited, interpretive perspective. Perhaps this is more apparent to those who have lived within cultures that differ greatly from that of their own origin or who consciously explore the opportunities that increasingly multicultural societies offer.[2] Social, economic, and other pressures now inhibit compartmentalizing cultures in ways that once seemed natural and justified.

For some, this change characterizes the postmodern. It tempts us to an "anything goes," commercially driven, globalized aesthetics that flattens everything into an easy, value-freed version of the culinary impulse Brecht detested—unlike the popular culture he incorporated—but that proliferates because it generates megamoney. Theater is socially marginal, compared with the prime-time culture industry, but there is a danger of simplifying its intercultural practices if alternative aetiologies are forgotten and if the practices are submerged in postmodern eclecticism, perhaps because they seem to coincide with it.

Yet there must be a basis for intercultural performance in the older anthropological sense of employing, in whatever way, material from one culture within the context of another. Defamiliarizing the conventions of representation, the intercultural sign facilitates access to what has, on various levels, been culturally repressed. It speaks through the silence of an *episteme*. The more this disconcerts, alarms, is dismissed or denounced, indicates how a potentially successful, if sometimes temporary, derepression takes place.

Hence another purpose here is to investigate and historicize the effects of those repressions that create a social unconscious as the repository of the hopes and desires whose frustration it locates and conceptualizes. In the longing for liberation from conventionalized representational constraints, we can also observe the expression of an energizing "aesthetic" unconscious when we are released from them. Obviously such processes take different forms in various cultures, depending on the nature of those constraints. I address these phenomena in the context of particular discussions that always involve, from varying perspectives, rereadings of a Shakespearean text.

A consequence of reading texts in terms of how they enable us to historicize the social unconscious, of how they both represent and elide repression, is an interest in the politics of the sign and hence in the effects, within Western cultures, of a predominant mimesis that entails a belief in the efficacy of representation. The attempt by characters within the play to control the discourse, and interpretation's acceptance of the necessity of mimetic presuppositions, may conceal from the proponents of such views the extent of their own investment in the interpretive advantages that accrue from them. These presuppositions are challenged by intercultural performance, by the aesthetically critical politics of the intercultural sign that defamiliarizes and so inevitably questions the often unconscious equation of representation with the structure of reality.

We can speak of a politics of the sign where it also contains an invisible agenda, embodying more than it appears to tell. The texts themselves often show how the unconscious of text and character is concealed and revealed. East Asian dramatic representations are amenable, but not often subjected, to such readings that uncover contradictory impulses. The conventions inculcate Confucian concepts of order and, especially when accepting Buddhist transience, as in the Noh theater, the discipline of the social mask, yet the philosophical culture is uniquely deconstructive. In the West something like the reverse pertained: the absolutes are metaphysical—Platonic ideas and revealed religion—the socialities more relative, perhaps because those absolute ideas implied absolute moral demands that have always been betrayed.

## The Intercultural Sign

The poststructuralist assumption that the "essentialized" subject, or dramatic character, is a theophilosophical or metaphysical social construct clearly relates to East Asian thought since, deep down, East Asian culture never assumed it was anything else. Brecht's work plays across these separations. We might ask in what sense analogies operate through the contradictions of Renaissance ideology that harbored the sceptical and tolerant humanism of a Montaigne within a theophanic Neoplatonism.

The problem of the politics of meaning inheres within language itself as a signifying system and then within all forms of representation that, even when we understand the codes through which they signify in the first place, simultaneously appear to mean and to deny unequivocal meaning. All signifying systems, whether poetry or physics, construct forms of representation whose internal coherence is continuously mistaken for reality itself, or actually constitutes what we take for that reality until something questions it. The politics of the sign obtrudes when representation, and the reality to which it lays claims, slides from an epistemological or cultural into a political agenda. Although these always overlap and often cohere, we can make separations for practical analytical purposes. This is the point where interpretation's complicity with assertions of unequivocal meaning becomes problematic. A surprising number of critics still show their readings to be constructed by one aspect of these always equivocal texts.[3]

A critique written within and for the university does not always penetrate outside. In spite of assumptions to the contrary, there is a real sense in which understanding Shakespeare is still part of a recuperative political discourse and a matter of contention, although this applies primarily in cultures where interpreting Shakespeare can usefully become the subject of public debate.[4] Where there is a national curriculum, its interpretation is contestable; where there is not, radical scholarship does not need to be challenged or faced down, since it can so easily be recuperated as pluralism.[5]

During the last twenty years significant developments in Shakespeare criticism have emerged. These changes came remarkably late: some sixty years after Brecht's radical rereadings of Elizabethan drama through his texts and their performance.[6] Precisely because he is considered politically helpful, Brecht has also been compartmentalized by those critics

Reading the Intercultural

who wished to release Shakespeare from older presuppositions. Yet there are interpretive consequences. Reducing the potential of a Brechtian perspective to constant foregrounding of class struggle may not be the most useful way of enlarging understanding of a Shakespearean text.

Two observations about *Coriolanus* from different critical positions corroborate a common misapprehension about Brecht's response. Assuming "the text itself" will not settle interpretation, Stanley Cavell offers a psychoanalytic reading of *Coriolanus* in terms of the "character" of the main figure. This is used as a carte blanche for a hermetic interpretation that equates Coriolanus surrounded by the three Vs—Volumnia, Virgilia, Valeria—with Christ surrounded at his crucifixion by the three Ms—Mary his mother, Mary Magdalene, and Mary the mother of James and Joses.[7] Cavell gets to this after first envisaging a political argument, but in terms of "whether the patricians or the plebeians are right in their conflict." In that context he assumes Brecht had "little further to add" after showing the viability of choosing the plebeians.[8] This means "the politics of the play is essentially the politics of a given production."[9]

Terence Hawkes shares this assumption, although within a different context: "Of course, any 'reading' of a text can only be achieved by a suppression of the pluralities of which all texts are composed. That is how texts, and indeed language, work. But there is a sense in which this latent plurality is exactly what *Coriolanus* makes overt. As a result, every attempt simply to shackle the play to a specific party-political position must run into crucial difficulties; something which Brecht discovered and which Günter Grass makes the subject of his own critique."[10] Hawkes and Cavell both cite Brecht, despite his usefulness, to illustrate the perils of reductive readings. Neither investigate what actually happened when Brecht contemplated performing *Coriolanus*, how he resisted arguments about "right" or "wrong," and sought to recapture its complexity, so that the text itself could indeed be made to speak. Nor do they separate sufficiently between the different levels of historical engagement with this story from Roman culture. Yet if we do this, we discern a complex intercultural dynamic between the different versions in their specific historical contexts. We encounter a more challenging intercultural sign than is envisaged by historically one-dimensional readings.

## II

It is possible to imagine a Brecht-inflected Shakespeare quite different from what is here virtually taken as a narrowly focused class war correspondent's reduction of *Coriolanus*, appropriately humbled by the tribunes of history. Brecht's texts are now often equated with an inadequate epistemology and a discredited politics, of which the dramatic characters are appropriately superficial representations, deprived of any depth, without real subjectivity, paper creations, algebraic formulations, abstracting from abstractions, flattened by rationality, emotionally eviscerated, lobotomized by doctrine. Perceptions of this nature have a certain social force today and are produced by ideologies that shape those texts into models for disapproval. To see what is at stake for reevaluations, we first need to defamiliarize this conventionalized Brecht.

I begin with Nietzsche, whose impact on Brecht started early, went deep, and lasted long. Certain passages in *The Birth of Tragedy out of the Spirit of Music* read like an uncanny presaging of Brecht's theater.[11] The anticipation of Brecht's methods in Nietzsche's sympathetically critical analysis of Euripidean tragedy is inescapable. For Nietzsche the Socratic infusion into tragedy had a remarkable effect upon the shaping of the texts and the dynamic of performance. It cannot have been entirely bad news, even if he describes it as a form of decline. Utterly opposed to the Dionysiac, the result is closer to "the dramatized epic, an Apollonian form which precluded tragic effect" (77 [83]). Nietzsche argues: "The poet who writes dramatized narrative can no more become one with his images than can the epic rhapsodist. He too represents serene, wide-eyed contemplation gazing upon its images. The actor in such dramatized epic remains essentially a rhapsodist; the consecration of dream lies upon all his actions and prevents him from ever becoming in the full sense an actor" (78 [84]).

Apollonian contemplation alone would not result in tragedy. It needed the wild Dionysiac rapture, its torrent of music, the remorseless and destructive lust for life as an expression of the relentless world will. Yet if Euripides deprived himself of Dionysiac rapture, then he embraced passionate Socratic rationality. Although Nietzsche cannot conceal his dislike of Socrates and what Socrates stands for, he finds him a worthy opponent, not because they are so different but because they are so similar, which naturally reinforces the distaste. Beneath the flood of criticism we can discern a steady countercurrent of admiration. Socrates drives knowledge to its limits, forcing "generation after generation to reconsider the foundations of its art" (91 [97]). That is why, as Nietzsche reports, Socrates told his friends in prison that a voice in a dream spoke to him: "Practice music, Socrates" (90 [96]). In our times such music must be the Socratic, anti-Wagnerian fusion of the passionate and rational in the extraordinary settings of Brecht's texts by Hanns Eisler or Kurt Weill. Consider, for example, this passage from *The Birth of Tragedy* in relation to Brecht's dramaturgy:

> What in Euripidean, as compared with Sophoclean tragedy, has been so frequently censured as poetic lack and retrogression is actually the straight result of the poet's incisive critical gifts, his audacious personality. The Euripidean prologue may serve to illustrate the efficacy of that rationalistic method. Nothing could be more at odds with our dramaturgic notions than the prologue in the drama of Euripides. To have a character appear at the beginning of the play, tell us who he is, what preceded the action, what has happened so far, even what is about to happen in the course of the play—a modern writer for the theatre would reject all this as a wanton and unpardonable dismissal of the element of suspense. Now that everyone knows what is going to happen, who will wait to see it happen? Especially since, in this case, the relation is by no means that of a prophetic dream to a later event. But Euripides reasoned quite otherwise. According to him, the effect of tragedy never resided in epic suspense, in a teasing uncertainty as to what was going to happen next. It resided, rather, in those great scenes of lyrical rhetoric in which the passion and dialectic of the protagonist reached heights of eloquence. (79f. [85])

Nietzsche also had roots in the enlightenment, visible in his identification with Voltaire, in his absolute disdain for anti-Semitism, in his disgust with German nationalism, in his alarm over the destruction of personality in modern culture, over what he called the "Unpersönlichkeit des Arbeiters," which can be translated as "depersonalization of the worker," in industrializing society, over the falsity of the economy.[12] The self-proclaimed *immoralist* was driven by a moral agenda, and this rhetoric, if not his proposed solutions, undoubtedly captivated Brecht. Consider, for example, this passage from *Ecce Homo* in respect of *The Good Person of Szechwan*, but it is also a topic throughout Brecht's work: "I will first consider the psychology of the good person. To estimate what a human type is worth, you must count the cost of preserving it—you must know the conditions of its existence. For a good person they are the lie: to put it differently, on no account wanting to see how reality is fundamentally shaped, namely *not* so as to evoke well-meaning instincts at all times, and even less as to allow the intervention of shortsighted well intentioned hands on all occasions" (368). Nietzsche then argues what Brecht would not have accepted in the later work: since these infelicities cannot be changed, we must learn to endure and rise above them.

Nietzsche describes and criticizes Euripidean drama in the sort of contradictory terms that seem to fit Brecht's theater, although naturally they do not map exactly onto each other. The contexts are too dissimilar.

> Here there is no longer any trace of epic self-forgetfulness, of the true rhapsodist's cool detachment, who at the highest pitch of action, and especially then, becomes wholly illusion and delight in illusion. Euripides . . . lays his plan as Socratic thinker and carries it out as passionate actor. So it happens that the Euripidean drama is at the same time cool and fiery, able alike to freeze and consume us. It cannot possibly achieve the Apollonian effects of the epic, while on the other hand it has severed all connection with the Dionysiac mode; so that in order to have any impact at all it must seek out novel stimulants which are to be found neither in the Apollonian nor in the Dionysiac realm. Those stimulants are, on the one hand, cold paradoxical ideas put in the place of Apollonian contemplation, and on the other fiery emotions put in the place of Dionysiac transports.[13]

Some such combination of cold control and fiery emotions, of passion and dialectic, energizes Brecht's theater where, as in East Asian art, the aesthetic strength in representing those emotions depends upon the intellectual discipline exercised over the process of their externalization. I am also reminded here of Brecht's early comment, "Meier-Graefe says of Delacroix that here was a warm heart beating in a cold person. And when you come down to it, that's a possible recipe for greatness."[14] Brecht's early infatuation with Wagner—he used to conduct *Tristan and Isolde* from a score on his desk—turned, like Nietzsche's, into its opposite, presumably to resist the compulsion of that music, out of fear of its seductive effect upon that "warm heart." Yet what Nietzsche sees as "realistic counterfeits" of emotions may be energized by forces that seem so powerful as to appear metaphysical, but are less transcendentally created. They are more a product of the social unconscious, which is certainly how they are shaped in the texts of Brecht.

What has been termed Nietzsche's "active nihilism" also links him and Brecht with East Asian culture.[15] It becomes part of that restless, driving, de-essentialized dialectic, evident in the Nietzschean "stream of happening" that Brecht quotes in his "autobiographical" poem, *The Doubter*.[16] There it forms the basis for deconstructing Marxist ontology, as part of the only possible development of a more productive Marxist project, probably the main purpose of Brecht's *Coriolanus* and of much else within his work. Ontological deconstruction delineates territory compatible to both Derrida and Brecht, helping to resituate his work, which is also haunted by ghosts.[17]

Many of Derrida's themes are anticipated in Brecht's texts. The following suggestions refer to various theoretical and practical topics:

—the importance of the in-between, of what cannot be univocally established, since the characters are nearly always both inside and outside;

—the emphasis on false oppositions that appear to preclude, but in fact infiltrate and define, each other. An example would be *The Lovers* (Terzinen über die Liebe), sung as a duet in *Aufstieg und Fall der Stadt Mahagonny*, frequently read as lamenting the lost metaphysical dimension in a debased material world, but which deconstructs the oppositions creating those metaphysical suppositions;[18]

—the stress on the inseparability of life and death, almost an obsession in those texts, from the early plays through to that passage in *Me-ti, Buch der Wendungen* entitled "On the Flow of Things" (Üben den Fluß der Dinge), which I relate to the Daoist Zhuangzi and that begins: "And I saw that nothing was completely dead, not even what has died. The dead stones breathe. They change and are the cause of change . . .";[19]

—Derrida's insistence on the permeability of frames whose purpose is exclusion and whose Brechtian equivalent is the unfinished nature of those texts and figures, hence the admiration for Chinese art that lacks a concept of framing;

—the stress on the signifier that alienates transcendental intention or signifieds;

—in both, the phenomenological and phonocentric intentionality of speech is undermined through writing whose postponement of meaning creates a space that enables an engagement with unconscious levels and voices. In contrast to the orality of the dramatic, epic theatre is a theater of writing. Brecht referred to the "literarization of the theater."[20] This must be understood metaphorically, and not as promulgating recipes and slogans. The epic quality of this writing infects representation with its relativizing perspectives and cannot be reliably aligned with its opposite—the claim to omniscience—as so many evidently still believe. The epic theater is an art of inscription, of rewriting, and opposes all *pre*scriptions;

—Derrida's insistence that all writing is plagiaristic and the concept of authorship consequentially always in doubt, something that lies beyond the horizon of a copyright lawyer.

What about the objection that a politically indefinite, even indifferent, deconstruction can hardly be aligned with alienation and interventionary thought? Two points can be made here. First, there are two kinds of alienation in Brecht: on the one hand, a defamiliarizing of all-too-familiar, naturalized appearances by uncovering or explaining the structures behind them and, on the other hand, an alienating confrontation with the unknown, through which the self questions presupposed or reified structures. Second, Derrida's positions have become noticeably more political.

In his recent book, *Specters of Marx,* Derrida stresses the need for "performative interpretation," for which Heiner Müller also argued.[21] Only this can do justice to a text since faithful readings always betray its spirit. It is never a question of *whether* a text is transformed but rather of *how* and *why.* Then we can certainly differentiate. Derrida quotes Benjamin who, very much in a Brechtian spirit, resists the cliché that might always overcomes weakness and, in his *Theses on the Philosophy of History,* compares historical Marxism with a *weak* messianic force.[22] Derrida finds the Marxist critique "unavoidable" for deconstructing every dogmatic ontology and eschatology. But it contains a component that cannot itself be deconstructed, namely "a certain experience of the emancipatory promise."[23] He asserts "that one must assume the inheritance of Marxism, assume its most living part, which is to say, paradoxically, that which continues to put back on the drawing board the question of life, spirit, or the spectral, of life-death beyond the opposition of life and death. This inheritance must be affirmed by transforming it as radically as will be necessary. . . . It remains before us just as unquestionably as we are heirs of Marxism, even before wanting or refusing to be, and, like all inheritors, we are in mourning. In mourning in particular for what is called Marxism" (54).

The specter of Marxism is that "which could not be anticipated" (65), which we can surely call the "unconscious of theory," unforgettably invoked, for example, in the crucial Brechtian poem, *The Doubter*.[24] Earlier deconstruction was a necessary attempt to "question the onto-theo- but also archeo-teleological concept of history—in Hegel, Marx, or even in the epochal thinking of Heidegger."[25] Derrida mistrusted the teleo-eschatological program, but not the desire for emancipation and its "indestructibility," which is "the condition of a re-politicization, perhaps of another concept of the political" (75). This is why deconstruction is a radical form of alienation, or *altérité*, "impossible and unthinkable in a pre-Marxist space" (92) and true to "a spirit of Marxism which I will never be ready to renounce" (89), of which he says, "we cannot not be its heirs" (91).

In a remarkable analysis, Derrida enumerates the ghosts in Marx's texts that are saturated with anxieties, dreams, phantasmagoria, conjurations, invocations of the dead. He concludes the ghost is "the hidden figure of all figures" (120). The Spirit seeks to banish the ghosts of history until it turns into a specter itself and haunts those texts. In your adversary you prey upon yourself and have split in two without achieving the desired outcome. Here I think of Brechtian texts like *Baal* or the early story *Bargan gives up*.[26] In this paradoxical pursuit of a ghostly prey Derrida shows us the radical alienations of Marx: commodities as "sensuous" and simultaneously "supersensible" things; the market as the "dance" of these "specters"; "These ghosts that are commodities transform human producers into ghosts." Marx's texts perform a theatricalization of the phantasmagoric character of the whole commodified social world. Derrida concludes: "Marx has not yet been received."[27]

Brecht's texts cry out for innovative readings to escape the transferential clichés, when we accept, or impose upon them, what seem appropriate presuppositions, although so often the stereotypes of social authorization or what we can call "critical correctness," masked as theoretical necessity. I can, for a start, think of few summary accounts of *Baal, Drums in the Night,* and *In the Jungle of Cities* that can improve on this unrelated passage from Foucault: "From within language experienced and traversed as language, in the play of its possibilities extended to their furthest point, what emerges is that 'man has come to an end,' and that, by reaching the summit of all possible speech, he arrives not at the very heart of himself but at the brink of that which limits him; in that region where death prowls, where thought is extinguished, where the promise of the origin interminably recedes."[28]

Foucault's contemporary countersciences, ethnology and psychoanalysis, suggest the possibility of historicizing the unconscious and of envisaging an escape from Freudian universalist pansexualism. They anticipate Erich Fromm's suggestions for a variable, social unconscious, so to speak in retrospect, because there is no indication whatsoever that Foucault was aware of Fromm's work.[29] These perspectives, so heuristically valuable for reading cultural texts, help to focus much in this study.

"Brecht" can be further defamiliarized by exploring psychomythological territory, conventionally the province of myth and ritual criticism with respect to Shakespeare, and connections between Brecht's work and the thought of Lévi-Strauss. These connections reach deep into that work and can certainly modify Brechtian readings of Shakespeare. Brecht died in 1956, knowing nothing of Lévi-Strauss, who, as far as I can tell, made no use of Brecht. So the compatibilities lie in the structure of their thought. There is, however, an intriguing mutual interest in Chinese theater and distinct, although in the case of Brecht more subtextual, reverberations of Buddhist perceptions that also constitute a link with Nietzsche and can be taken through to the de-essentializing, post-Marxist—which is not the same as anti-Marxist—philosophies of process that characterize what is productive in poststructuralism.[30]

In *The Savage Mind* Lévi-Strauss offers an account of how totemic thought establishes codes for discriminating relationships, establishing dispositions between phenomena through the organization of perceptual space and the correspondences that enable people to make imaginative and practical sense of the world. He recounts a practice among the Hidatsa Indians on the Missouri River who developed a particular technique for catching the elusive eagle, lord of the sky and metaphor of their aspirations. They would dig a pit, a trap, and lie in it, waiting for the eagle to descend upon them. They were, observes Lévi-Strauss, "both hunter and hunted at the same time."[31] He uses this to exemplify the binary—high/low—and triadic—sky/earth/underworld—patterns that organized the Hidatsas' totemic thought and tribal life.

Brecht's early plays constitute an iconographical zoo; they teem with animal metaphors. They are constructed as mythologies of the unconscious, and consequently their plots are labyrinthic. They do not pass, like the well-made play, from incident to incident, but rather wind through uncharted psychographic territory. The other or exotic, no matter how far this mental territory may be placed beyond the Berlin/Bavarian borders, whether in Africa, Tahiti, China, or America, is not a geographical but rather a methodological concept, an ethnography of the imagination, a protosurrealist psycho-collage, rhetorical exploration, all designed to one end: combating the insanity that was the positivist normalization of the actual. Normality, before, in, and after 1918, when he was writing *Baal,* was monstrous. It had to be reinvented.

Like the Hidatsa Indians, Baal, in the provocative song that starts the play, tells how he hunted vultures by personifying their prey. This passage occurs again within the play, in the scene *10° East of Greenwich*.[32] He does so, just as they did, to absorb into himself their soaring immortality. Baal consumes them, swallowing the light of their skies, light enough to hold off the death he embraces, for his whole trajectory is a descent into materiality, the obverse of the Neoplatonic topography that structured the conventions of Brecht's culture.

Nothing is more savage than normality. The imagination resists its own destruction by proposing a counterreality that radically undermines, is simply incompatible with, the whole industrializing post-Enlightenment paradigm, drawing on the metaphorical dispositions of totemic thought because it allows one to reconceive all relationships. But this is no abstract reaction, no simple rejection of indefensible instrumentalization, for it also anticipates realignments of individual positions that refuse the spaces available in modern industrial culture: a constant theme in Brecht.

For Lévi-Strauss myths consist of signs that lie between images and concepts. These signs use images to facilitate a form of conceptual thought. The language of signs in mythical thought is characterized by relationality. By themselves the images mean nothing. They only signify in relation to each other. Hence any form of absolute, so specific to Western culture, is precluded from the start. The method of intellectual production in mythical thought has much in common with practices in modern art and certainly with Brecht's early plays, although not only these, whose alienating methods are apparent yet cannot be adequately explained by the so-called alienation effect.

Much that appears incomprehensible in those plays, or is attributed to the moral failings of their progenitor, can be illuminated by this confrontation with *la pensée sauvage* (untamed thinking). Lévi-Strauss discerns rules of transformation among these myths, where we appear to encounter bewildering multiplicity, as in these plays. Above all, where myth and the psychoanalytic coincide, the stories bring conflicts and inhibitions into the realm of consciousness. They do not provide *specific* solutions; instead, they offer the *form* of solutions. This can certainly be transferred to modern works of art provided we do not search, as the naturalists and psychobiographers always do, for direct applications in both a positive and negative sense.

The shaman not only relates but also incorporates the myth. Lévi-Strauss observes, "But the basic condition remains that the manipulation must be carried out through symbols, that is, through meaningful equivalents of things meant which belong to another order of reality."[33] They function, as a potion or poison works as counterpoison, to change an undesirable state. To this we can relate a series of practical, ritual actions and behavioral patterns that undoubtedly helped Brecht structure his plays, however that may have come about. They consist of forms of engagement, or play, designed to preserve life and delay or banish death, and that work through a contradictory logic that appears to provoke the opposite of what it intends. Lévi-Strauss describes forms of ritual play whose purpose is to lose the game. The opponents are connected with powerful, death-dealing forces that may on no account be provoked by defeat, for their revenge would be catastrophic. They are allowed to win on the playing field, in order that one might emerge the victor in the longer game of life. Such untamed thinking structures *In the Jungle of Cities* and otherwise plays a significant role in Brecht's work.

Shlink issues an enigmatic, almost Kafkaesque, challenge to Garga that threatens his own existence. But Garga must allow him to win the contest, and so he goes to prison for three years. Only through losing has he any hope of deflecting an even greater defeat. He has no alternative. Garga does not go under, because he has "read that soft water can take on whole mountains."[34] "He" had already read that in 1920 in the *Dao-*

*dejing*, a prime example of a sophisticated, textually complex illustration of what Lévi-Strauss described as *la pensée sauvage*, which was focused on *longue durée* (long rhythm of time) and not immediate effects. This is how such thinking reached Brecht and was incorporated into his work, from the early plays and poetry through to the *Buckow Elegies* of his last years.[35]

Other mediating figures in the myths recounted by Lévi-Strauss—and Baal could figure among them—incorporate contrasting realms: they do not unify these; they are ambiguous and embody these contradictions. They are often bisexual or androgynous. They have the capacity to change. Often they occur as twins or siblings. They are both good and evil. If we wanted to moralize their behavior, which would be inappropriate, they appear as unreliable, able to switch positions, changing fronts, avoiding difficulties, always ahead of the hand of death. From the perspective of the developed concept of the individual, as presented in the drama of the enlightenment, they are intolerable figures. Where do we find them in Brecht? The answer is: everywhere, from Baal through Shen Te to Azdak. In the myth of his writing we encounter that chain of tricksters and mediators described by Lévi-Strauss in *The Structural Study of Myth*.[36] The figures in the later plays all contain more than enough of this doubleness, the unreliability that so irritated the cultural bureaucrats and ideologues because such thinking resists prescriptions.

Buddhist ghosts also test the theory-practice relationship, unsettling certainties. The emptiness or silence of Buddha, of *The Doubter*, of Mother Courage, figures relationality and shapes a fundamental *gestus* (externalization).[37] Nirvana conventionally connotes escape from samsara, or illusion, which literally means "being underway," or we could say, in that term of Nietzsche's that Brecht used in *The Doubter*, "the stream of happening," or, in a metaphor that resonates elsewhere in the texts, "the flow of things."[38]

In philosophical Buddhism, nirvana is achieved by embracing, not escaping, samsara, for there is no metaphysical consolation, no redemption through denial or subsumption into a shared, all-embracing, eternal, world substance, as imagined by Hindu metaphysics, no nothing. For Lévi-Strauss, foxing and irritating the Derrida of *Of Grammatology*, Buddhism extends Marxism, since its antimetaphysical relationalism returns to social life, for beyond it there is nothing else.[39]

We notice throughout these approximations and applications that

Brecht de-essentializes or historicizes what first look, to those with more conventionalized expectations as well as to those who view East Asian thought through the prism of Western ontology or theology, like unassailably essentialist and metaphysical absolutes. Yet at the center of this thinking lies a relationalism, sceptical of absolutes, even if it appears to wrestle with them. Thus the energy of metaphysical thinking, as in the philosophical Buddhism of Nagarjuna, is deflected into reimagining nontranscendental relations. We could say that they are reworked in terms of reenergized field theories of the subject and of history. I take it that Fredric Jameson envisaged something similar when he suggestively replaced the "mystery" contained within the anagogic, as the ultimate frame in Dante's medieval hierarchy of values, with "history."[40] At such a dislocating moment the complexly interrelated positions in a hierarchy of interpretive scale can suddenly fall into place, shedding their unearthly certainties or transcendentally focused longings while preserving and secularizing the privileging of meaning.

Brecht shared the linguistic scepticism that permeates Buddhism, since language appears to substantialize concepts, validate metaphysical entities, and protect political power more efficiently than it can describe interrelational processes.[41] The philosophically and morally precarious relationship between linguistic and social order is a strong Shakespearean topic that has implications within intercultural contexts.[42] *Hamlet*, for example, can be read as an enquiry into the problematized, even substanceless, subject as language fails to differentiate between performance and reality.

### III

The tricksters and androgynous figures described by Lévi-Strauss who slip in and out of their own and others' skins, playing against all preconceptions of identity, obviously inhabit Shakespeare's plays, where the role of the trickster is well understood. I am not sure they are given a harder political edge in Brecht, although anachronisms will not help here and none are intended. But this does not mean these repositioned Brechtian figures do not reflect on Shakespeare's and then vice versa. We have been accustomed to judging them in certain ways. In spite of all the substantial differences, setting these plays beside each other reveals the transformative presuppositions that subtend their plots. The differences merely sharpen our perception of what remains analogous. They contain special moments of ideologically shaped action, like knots tying narrative strands together—for example, Prospero's magic and the assumption that it works, or Azdak's "magical" gift for suspending normality and reaching just conclusions out of altercations between unequals. We could relate these moments to what Lévi-Strauss called *mythemes,* or units of meaning, that show analogies at a greater level of abstraction than the constructed or imagined empirical and cultural details appear to encourage or countenance. What finally matters is whether there is an explanatory benefit.[43]

This poses questions about what can reasonably be collated. Richard Hillman, for example, holds a widely shared view of the relationship between *The Comedy of Errors* and its Plautine source: "The fundamental transmutation achieved is of Plautine lead—the slapstick, stereotypes, and petty farce of the *Menaechmi*—into the golden fulfillment of romance."[44] I argue that placing Shakespeare against Plautus need not mean Plautine lead is routinely or providentially transmuted into Shakespearean gold. The juxtaposition produces more subtle alloys and correspondingly differentiated readings—relating those plays to specific cultural molds, suggesting how they are comparably shaped, embodying social mythemes as the expression of a social unconscious—instead of adjusting everything to an alchemistic illusion of greater profit from later transformations.

The plots of those two plays are recognizably connected. What would happen if we juxtaposed *The Tempest* and *The Caucasian Chalk Circle,* whose narratives seem quite unrelated? That depends on what constitutes an acceptable degree of abstraction, on how specific our mythemes, or logothemes, need to be. What if we take them as gestural units, as *analogous* forms of behavior, instead of the *homologous* narrative units they appear to represent for Lévi-Strauss? We would then not seek examples of lame legs or defeated dragons as part of an organizing mythical principle that, somewhat surprisingly, turns a series of disparate stories into illustrations of an argument concerning the autochthonous or nonautochthonous origin of mankind. Instead, we might discern in superficially different behavior, shaped by varying cultural beliefs, examples of comparable attitudes and effects, or gestures of the plot, that are finally determined by their reimaginable relationship to structures of power.

If drama evolved out of ritual after the stories of myth had separated from rites, it retains, perhaps even under the surface of the most banal, naturalist plot, a capacity both to draw us in and to keep us out, to capture and release us, to attract and repel, to overwhelm with its externalizations, exposing us to what Northrop Frye, speaking of ritual, once famously described as a "dialectic of desire and repugnance."[45] Summarizing Jane Harrison's analysis of the origin of drama, Verma concludes it offers both "identification and psychical distance."[46] What energizes the identificatory impulse is probably affected by that residue of ritual, participation in a public enactment, as an expression of what Harrison discerned in ritual as a "collective representation of the needs and desires of life," and that "springs from unfulfilled desire which is the source of art and religion alike."[47] Such "needs and desires" assuredly also activate the social unconscious. Again we are close to Nietzsche's description of the Socratic theater of Euripides, its mixture of passion and rationality, and we understand why alienation and distancing in Brecht's theater only intensifies the emotional engagement, instead of curtailing it, as so many still believe. In short, distancing the emotions renders them more powerful. The topoi or mythemes within and across various plays reveal the contradictions that animate the myth of the work we call Shakespeare or Brecht. As they entice us, the plays themselves offer no solutions but rather, like the structure of myth described by Lévi-Strauss, the form of solutions, as they unfold and think through their contradictions and as we read them in terms of what they can help us understand about our own dilemmas.

In Brecht's play we find several elements of older narrative figurations, plot gestures that have their counterparts in Shakespeare's: the structure of romance; disaster, followed by dangerous journeys and exile; a saved child; moving through renunciation to lovers' union and hope of happiness; the figure of the trickster; masquelike interludes, stage-managed by the trickster, expressing the deepest and frustrated desires. In Brecht, we have the apotheosis of Mother Grusinia who is enthroned almost as a goddess and the emotionally powerful invocation of what she represents, truly the voice of the social unconscious.

We can see some categorical distinctions concerning the shape-changing trickster's social role. If Bakhtin's description of Carnival, embodying the "trickster-archetype," subverts physical and social norms, the figure itself is found to reach beyond social carnival. Hillman criticizes the "inflated claims for the political and cultural implications of carnivalesque social behaviour," seeing the "carnivalesque elements as embodiments of primal energies, which extend to the impulse to challenge political and social power structures."[48] Hence Hillman agrees with William Carroll, for whom "the whole idea of metamorphosis is subversive, for it undermines the traditional belief in a stable, fixed, and ordered self."[49] For Hillman *The Tempest* "problematically combines the supernatural with a controlling human figure who comes closer than might at first be supposed to some of the trickster-like figures of other plays—yet keeps a highly significant distance."[50]

The point of interest, perhaps contention, is the separation of the human figure—the trickster and what we can call ontological shape changing—and the assumption that ontology will necessarily be reduced by the category of the social that is merely a smaller part of it. Belief in a stable ontology is, of course, only "traditional" within Western culture. East Asia views it differently. Recognizing ontological instability, one source of Brecht's interest in East Asian cultures, is a norm, although a point of contention between Buddhist and Hindu philosophy. In philosophical Buddhism, there exists no ontologically fixed self capable of being undermined, since ontology itself offered no self-sustaining stability. Social relations, under those different circumstances, could be differently imagined and cannot become a subcategory within a universalizing ontology. As Brecht and Lévi-Strauss appreciated, they are categorically on an equal footing, one is not primary to the other but, potentially, its other expression, if nirvana must be sought in samsara. By contrast, if the ontological is permanently in flux, then stability can only be sought in imposed social relations, the basis for Confucian hierarchization. During the final dance Azdak skips town to avoid the likely consequences of reimposed hierarchization when his writ will no longer run. How can Prospero figure in such relationships?

The usurped duke, Prospero, is an ambivalent shaman, a good/bad figure, in some respects like, in others quite unlike, the precariously placed Azdak. He is dispossessed and possessive, also constituted by "harshness" (III.i.9), master of that "rough magic" (V.i.50), finally abjured ("I'll break my staff," with which he controls the magical island of his exile [V.i.54]). We have seen that Azdak's power is temporary and he must renounce it. Gonzelo's utopian recipe for "plantation of this isle" (II.i.144ff.) might have been taken straight from the *Daodejing*. Caliban's mooncalf presages the "elephant calf" in the "Interlude for the Foyer," now appended as an epilogue to *Man Equals Man*, for both embody comical and disquieting absurdities, physical and logical surrealities that nevertheless present themselves. Equally, although differently, enslaved, Ariel and Caliban both seek liberty from servitude. The transformations of a differently conducted rough magic turn Galy Gay from *Man Equals Man* into another monster-servant. In the 1926 version of the work his monstrosity is not yet the social disaster, serving an imperial war machine, which it later became. Prospero acknowledges Caliban, "this thing of darkness," as "mine" (V.i.275) even as he seeks the applause, in the role of actor, from the audience who "from crimes would pardoned be."

Shakespeare's and Brecht's plays bear the marks, at the beginning and at what has been thought of as the "end," but is probably at best only the middle, of a historical period of transforming or shape-changing violence. New forms of control over human activities are exercised by those who own "magic" upon those who do not. Their texts manifest uneasiness as they displace these violent events into the realm of temporary romance, a world in which "rough magic" can temporarily change shapes, control events, deliver justice. But if that world is to satisfy desire and promise happiness, then what faces them all when magic's time runs out must be "a brave new world."

Reading one play across another has the effect of differently positioning both. The story of Grusche, the child, and Azdak is performed as entertainment for the members of two collective farms in dispute over the best use of land. This play within a play, expressly located in the world of legend and romance, takes devices from East Asian theater to visualize and structure its narrative. The initial scene, termed *Vorspiel*, or prologue, in which government officials broker the dispute, is often considered an impossible idealization of political reality. Many directors would prefer to shorten or drop it, if they could do so without losing the performing rights.

What matters for my argument is the nature of the relationship between the primary or "real" social world of the prologue and the secondary world of the play, often in dispute when interpreting the closure of

Shakespeare's comedies and romances. In the first version, this play concluded with a short *Nachspiel*, or epilogue, in the primary world that therefore framed the longer story. Brecht then dropped this epilogue for pragmatic political reasons. The old man, representing the yielding and more sceptical goat-herding kolkhoz from the prologue, replies to the agronomist's final prediction of the consequences of giving the valley to the fruit growers—"You will see a garden"—with an observation that concludes the whole play: "God help you, if it isn't."[51]

The implications of this conclusion were simply too obvious for the insecure political culture of the German Democratic Republic. It was not performable. But that prologue should not be read as if it portrayed the political realities of social life as land was retaken from the occupying German armies and redistributed. In its different way, it too belongs to the category of romance. Part of that "romance," expressed within the conditions of twentieth-century culture, consists in the coded political meaning, in saying what otherwise cannot be said, in articulating a hope for what might happen, so that it could not be later said that this hope went unexpressed. If the epilogue had to go by the board—and wait for history to fulfill or deny its prediction—the prologue of a play written when Stalin was in power, praises the poet Mayakovsky and names the kolkhoz that wins the contest: Rosa Luxemburg. That comes straight out of social desire, or political fairy tale, told, like the whole narrative of the prologue, with the same hope, not of sentimentalizing a represented ideality, but of focusing the causes of frustration.

If Brecht's play opens to such contradictory reading of "romance," Shakespeare's closes on a more political understanding of the gap between romance and reality, which is the subtext of Prospero's epilogue. Both plays figure the disproportions between hope and real experience. That was the point of writing them. Hillman has an interestingly provocative comment on such closures. Listing Prospero with Portia and Prince Hal—"theatrical manipulators all"—he concludes, "By recognizing that the ultimate danger of the trickster is to the power of the creator to continue creating, it is possible—as a means of forestalling the reckless projection of ideologies upon authors—to posit an intrinsic need for structural baffles and channels, for agents of order to counter the *agents provocateurs*, if the show is to go on at all."[52] Magic wands, like Azdak's justice, are temporary remedies and must give place, if romance is not to supplant reality and make shape-changing writing impossible.

## The Intercultural Sign

While Brecht wrote *The Caucasian Chalk Circle* in Los Angeles he was reading Shakespeare and Waley's Chinese translations, as well as detective stories, in the evenings.[53] What interests me here is the common ground, no matter how disguised, in the formal structures of writing, connected with popular culture and with ritual. For Northrop Frye, "drama appears when myth encloses and contains the ritual," since myth "is born in the renunciation of magic, and in *The Tempest* and elsewhere it remembers its inheritance."[54] Brecht had always admired in Shakespeare what he once called "that certain illogicality in events," which is true to life, but not to be found in "our" theater.[55] Such inconsequentiality, together with a necessarily episodic structure, does not thereby dispense with explicability, but instead signifies another structural level for the logic of the plot. Myth operates between magic, which promises control, and knowledge, which offers explanation. In such territory certainties are elusive, although patterns recur within narratives, desires are uncovered, preoccupations revealed. Shakespeare incorporated elements of folk ritual from popular culture, and Japanese theater draws on formalizations of ghost placation and shamanistic psychotherapy when identities are shaken, released from their obsessions, and reshaped, as ritual is slowly transformed into performance.[56]

The residue of such universal rituals certainly help, on the level of formal plot structure, to shape several of Brecht's plays. One example would be the ritualistically performed investment of the pope in *Life of Galileo*, which echoes Shakespeare's coronations as enactments of hierarchical ritual in the history plays. Public office consumes all personal space and, in Brecht's play, the scientist-astronomer-cardinal is reluctantly but inexorably transformed into an authoritarian Defender of the Inquisition. Another illustration would be the tripartite structure associated with ceremonies of initiation and identity formation, the stuff of so much ritual and myth, easily discernible in *Man Equals Man*, and elsewhere in Brecht's work. Galy Gay's identity is reinvented after he has undergone a symbolic death, burial, and rebirth. But where initiates must shed their earlier selves, wander through illusion and mystery, so that they may emerge into the truth, Galy Gay is refunctioned, transformed from the gentle messenger, sent to buy a fish for his wife, into a human fighting machine. The process of identity construction is taken out of perennial, mythical time and historicized.

Brecht also adapted dramatized identity formation rituals from Japanese theater when he took the plot of *Taniko,* in Elizabeth Hauptmann's version of Waley's translation, and used it to structure four plays that rework the relationship between sacrifice and social identity.[57] In Brecht's four plays the relationship between sacrifice and victimization is problematized and opened to discussion, so the ritual is both reenacted and made questionable, since attention is focused on the social function of such ritualized behavior. But this invites us to attend to the social function of the Noh theater and its ritual plots and to the relative neglect within Japanese culture of any reflection upon these interrelationships.

Masao Miyoshi fulminates against the application of "First World criteria" in evaluating Japanese texts, which for him exemplify Third World culture. He gives examples of deeply irritating dismissive judgments by ostensible experts from his experience in the United States, for example that Japan has produced "no masterpieces," that its literature cannot endure "sustained, intensive literary criticism."[58] Miyoshi sees this, and who can blame him, as a hegemonic strategy and fears the universal norm of First World culture may represent the future. For me the problems begin with the supposition that there are such universal "First World criteria." They are then compounded when Miyoshi, again understandably, seeks to differentiate the texts of Japanese culture from such allegedly universal standards. But dismissing criteria judged alien and unhelpful to understanding, stressing the great difference in Japanese cultural forms, runs the risk of essentializing views upon them and eliding contradictions internal to Japanese culture. The effect is therefore to replicate the structure of the rejected orientalizing judgment: the discourse is now internally rather than externally monological.

Traditional Japanese theater cannot be evaluated by the standards of Western drama. The performers, he tells us, are not "actors in the ordinary sense," since they sometimes perform two characters in one scene. There is a "denial of a one-to-one correspondence between the actor and the character," marking another difference from Western theater. Finally, the Noh theater "seems indifferent to dramatic representation of human acts." The audience watching a Noh play has "an experience of sheer art, far removed from life."

Here we encounter a formalist fixation with purely aesthetic qualities sufficient unto themselves, which are somehow thought to preclude or impede access to any other category of meaning. In the process, the nature of aesthetic pleasure remains unexamined. To insist that Chinese

## The Intercultural Sign

opera was only concerned with aesthetic experience, and that Brecht therefore completely misunderstood it, to see in Mnouchkine's productions "Far-Eastern gracefulness," where horror "is aestheticized and suppressed by beauty," to separate "art" from "life," all of this means we have not explored the sources and function of aesthetic power and why this creative energy emanates from the juxtaposition and development of East Asian and Western dramatic techniques, as they interrogate each other's silences.[59]

What interests me here are the consequences of Miyoshi's seemingly unexceptional and correct observations. The Noh is compared with standard Western realist drama; of course the differences are apparent. But what of the cultural function of these forms? Western realist drama dwells on the structural surface of events, inhibiting deeper enquiry. The Noh was highly political, even though its plots do not appear so, because of its social function when restricted to the samurai class whose code the plays reinforced as they accepted their evanescence in the service of their lord. What strikes me in these plays is the unparalleled intensity with which human acts are represented as private mental events, as meditations, within their Buddhist context, on the contradiction between substantiality and subjectivity. The politics are played out as metaphysical and psychological contradictions in the minds of the protagonists. This is why Brecht was fascinated by the concentration of signification in Japanese dramatic form. That it is "far removed from life" is an optical, and an interpretive, illusion and replicates the rejected, unsubtle orientalizing judgment. It also restricts interpretation within traditional boundaries, inhibits rereading and the chance of developing the capacity of these forms.

Clifford Geertz concludes his book on the Balinese *Negara* state by observing, "The real is as imagined as the imaginary."[60] In the Noh, the privately symbolic and the political are inseparable, identical even, not because one covertly signifies, but because it has apparently silenced the other, driven it underground into the social unconscious, as the actor unfolds the contradictions that rend the character by lodging them within his body, retreating with them into the mind and slowly dancing into himself, as sure a demonstration of a politics of the body as anything described by Foucault. This in part accounts for the extraordinary aesthetic power of the form. Under these circumstances, we could perhaps reformulate Geertz's phrase and say that "the imaginary is as real as the political." Exploring the self does not amount to its recovery but to a form of "self"-abandonment. The dramatic text only ever speaks in the context of its whole cultural performance, exploring the cultural unconscious as a symbolic embodiment of the psychologically repressed, the culturally meaningful and socially apposite, which cannot be read from the surface of a literary text. A poetics that reads from this surface cannot uncover the formal unconscious and can be nothing but superficial.

We respond to the forms of other cultures because they give us access to the unconscious of our own episteme. In such cases there is no "right" or "wrong" except, on occasion, in a trivial positivist sense. What matters is what becomes culturally possible and why that impulse originally appears to have come from "outside." A response to other cultures meets a lack, of which we are perhaps only partly conscious, in our own. We then must ask why that need, or lack, exists. But to do this, we have to abandon forever the notion of cultural essentialism that still haunts the discourse when East and West meet or analyze each other. We only learn from each other when we question ourselves.

Developing Japanese techniques, Brecht responded to an aesthetic lack in Western forms and found a way of making complex sets of contradictions immediately visible, of concentrating upon the individual and externalizing socially constructed mental states. The later success of Japanese theatrical style in Western culture, resisted by conservatives, also suggests a desire for aesthetic forms judged inappropriate by a dominant realist episteme. If this transforming process then returns what has been transformed to the originating culture, which could not have brought about the transformation of its own, I call it "dialectical acculturation," since a dormant potential unacknowledged by the conventions of reception is thereby uncovered. The forms of the Noh, defended against Western encroachment as purely aesthetic, encode a politics in what is conventionally read as psychological and metaphysical exploration. Brecht's adaptation of a Japanese aesthetic can return to change the Japanese sense of theater.

Such considerations help explain how Brecht's interest in East Asian aesthetics and in ritual forms, which he historicized, in turn enable the quality of response that results in a Japanese or Chinese Brecht, but also an East Asian Brechtian Shakespeare. Meeting an East Asian lack, the Western writers are then reimaged in terms that would not occur within their home cultures. Koreya Senda's best-known production of Shakespeare was obviously shaped by his creative interest in Brecht's theater. Kennedy and Rimer give a good account of his intentions and of the significance of the production, concluding, in effect, that Senda "Japanesed" a Brechtian Shakespeare in his 1964 production of *Hamlet*.[61] They discuss Senda's own notes on the production, show how he historicized the play, thereby breaking with the conventions of Japanese reception, and discern "a Brechtian gestural acting designed to point out Hamlet's complicity in his political fate."[62] They observe political and gestural elements in Senda's reading. Their combination constitutes the Brechtian contribution. My only worry about their analysis of Senda's production, which I did not see, is when they suggest that "perhaps his abilities as an analytical Marxist intellectual exceeded those of a practical skillful director."[63] I have seen something of his work as director. His versions of *The Caucasian Chalk Circle* and *The Good Person of Szechwan* were so subtle and aesthetically sophisticated—producing effects of separation within the characters that are central to Brecht's perceptions and that he admired in East Asian acting, but are so often missed by Western directors without the repertory of externalizing aesthetic techniques—that I cannot believe his *Hamlet* lacked directorial skills.

Senda delighted in Brecht's "great regard for the playful and the fantastic" and sought to realize those qualities in his productions, equivalents for the gracefulness and lightness Brecht admired in East Asian externalizing acting.[64] Such aesthetic values illuminate and enliven the socially focused exploration of identity that characterizes Brecht's theater and Senda's productions of Brecht, and I suspect of Shakespeare as well. Senda well appreciated Brecht's observation that if the theater cannot retain interest through its aesthetic skill, then it will not be able to entice an audience that can be changed.

# 2

## INTERCULTURAL SIGNS

### Textual Anthropology

I

Intercultural performance is on the agenda. The issues fascinate, the topic is divisive, its future as uncertain as it is important. The events are perhaps too close to formulate satisfactorily what is taking place. Patrice Pavis cites Erika Fischer-Lichte's warning: it is "too soon to propose a global theory of intercultural theatre."[1]

But we do have to think globally to make sense of these practices, even if not everything can be encompassed. I cannot offer such a theory. Yet the discussion appears to lack historical dimensions and critical perspectives crucial to developing one.[2] The uncertainties are symptomatic. They also register creative dissatisfaction. I do not seek to belittle them. This material needs a larger frame and a deeper focus than accounts of proxemic innovation. Such perspectives could suggest ways of repositioning the material. I doubt if interculturalism in the theater can be adequately grasped just by describing performance styles, no matter how expertly, because such description, uneasy about its theoretical foundations, widely recognized as difficult, simply begs the question of its own constructing. We need, instead, to connect specific gestural moments to an interpretive strategy, thus binding the particular to a theorizable intention. But we must first situate the discussion.

The widest analysis comes from Patrice Pavis. For him intercultural performance exemplifies a shift: from once analytically confident, textually structuralist or politically Marxist, sociosemiotic paradigms to postmodernism's more diffident investigation of unscripted theoretical and uncharted emotional terrain. "The model of intertextuality," deriving from semiotics, "yields to that of interculturalism."[3] In other words, the intertextual network of Western culture, known cultural quanta within a familiar but restricting frame, give place to wider enquiries into hitherto unknown and unimagined qualities. Within its Western sociocultural context, the frustrated politics of the late sixties and early seventies yields to the explorative aesthetics of the eighties and nineties. This context is also generational. The postmodern intercultural extends its proponents' horizons.

In the theater Brecht exemplified the theoretical high point of abandoned paradigms. Since that work no longer convinces, theory has given way to various intercultural productions that can be described but have resisted adequate explanation.[4] In this analysis, Brecht's work is subjected to a version of that narrow reading that he sometimes appeared to espouse, tying it to a socially authorized "ideological practice" shackled to "norms."[5] I will contend that if we reject such narrow readings, no matter how widely held, we can discover in Brecht's work examples of an intercultural practice that at the very least questions and mostly contradicts those readings and whose analysis contributes to that as yet uncompleted theory of intercultural theater with arguments one might not anticipate.

Moving from political semiosis to "anthropological" territory, Pavis proposes seven inflections to encompass theatrical innovation from the early eighties: inter-, intra-, trans-, ultra-, pre-, post-, and meta-cultural.[6] Two presuppositions obtrude: (1) the intercultural seeks to encompass a human universality, most clearly exemplified by Peter Brook's search for a "culture of links"; (2) these practices, at least qualifying, perhaps even contradicting any presumed universality, are best analyzed through a source/target model that locates them within a specific cultural context.[7]

On the one hand these practices derive from various attempts to devise "an integrating model of all experience," and then the category of the anthropological functions as a means of escape from history by focusing on the supposedly universal; on the other hand, the source/target model, although helpfully inviting concentration on the particular needs of a performance culture, does not really explain its own operations.[8] Pavis uses the image of the hourglass to visualize this cultural transfer: "Only a few elements of the source culture" pass through the "filters" into the target culture, and they are "selected according to very precise norms." These are established by "whatever suits its expectations, reinforces its convictions" (16). Pavis works through arguments,

## Intercultural Signs

familiar from studies of translation, that these processes constitute productive misinterpretations and wonders whether it is not "perhaps Eurocentrist to imagine that a Japanese perspective . . . also implies the imitation and borrowing of elements from outside its own culture in order to further affirm and stabilize it" (2).

Here a crucial question would be whether something within the "target" culture is indeed thereby stabilized, and if so, what; or whether other things are perhaps upset, and if that proves more productive to understanding, why does this take place and how is it accomplished? Although he acknowledges that the purpose of these transmissions, sometimes involving large groups, "often remains implicit or unconscious," such implications remain undiscussed (2). Pavis had earlier called for a "theory of mediation" in respect of these intercultural transfers.[9]

But how can such a theory deal with the following contradictions without falling back on normative, culture-based presuppositions? Pavis takes Mnouchkine to task, firstly by calling the style of her *Twelfth Night* "hypertheatrical and thus false" while still affirming "this theatricality or artificiality reveals an underworld of phantasms that are real enough," and secondly by noticing "a pre-Brechtian culinary way of staging the classics, a refusal to analyze how Shakespearean dramaturgy or a culturalist re-reading of it may be made productive for us here and now."[10] This simultaneously offers insight and refuses analysis, because it rests on presuppositions both in respect to Brecht's theater and of the (in)appropriateness of Mnouchkine's stylizations, while recognizing what they have accomplished. What has been neglected here is the opportunity to explore and situate a cultural unconscious, implied by Foucault's conjuncture of the psychoanalytical and the ethnographic, which constitutes the activity I term "textual anthropology."[11]

In another divided response to Mnouchkine's intercultural style, Dennis Kennedy is impressed yet wary, primarily because she offers an aesthetic rather than a social experience. He describes her style as "Shakespearean orientalism" and relates it to postmodern experience.[12] He contrasts Mnouchkine's performance style with Japanese and with Chinese productions and finds it uncertainly placed in comparison with how they locate Shakespeare in the security of their own traditions, an argument also expressed by Jan Kott.

These comparisons raise fascinating questions. Some will occupy us in greater detail. One issue is this perceived incompatibility between the categories of the ideological, or historical, and the aesthetic. Mnouchkine sacrifices the former to the latter and pays the price, in these readings, of orientalism, of missing that essential grounding of a text in direct or intuitable social experience. This supposition, in turn, asks us to think about how we construct a Brechtian reading, about Brecht's relationship to East Asian aesthetics, and about how that might feed a potential within Western theater for intercultural developments and, just as importantly, how these considerations might mark East Asian receptivity to Western dramaturgy. Mnouchkine's theater, it seems, is either experienced as cognitively productive but aesthetically inadequate, if the phantasms are real enough although the style "culinary," or as aesthetically powerful yet socially and, we could probably say, cognitively disappointing.

Here too we must ask: How do otherwise differentiated dramaturgies interact? Is there not a history of the intercultural, both in performance and discourse, beyond what is generally subsumed within cultural history? It is less a matter of being directly influenced, or even of the source/target model, whose metaphors seem to presuppose influence transmission, since an active source reaches a passive target, so much as a more diffuse and overdetermined sense of cultural possibilities. Did Mnouchkine not respond to externalizing Asian aesthetics, because of internalizations by earlier Western practitioners?[13] If so, then such interculturation is more complex than any source-target model can suggest. What opens up here is a problematic triangulation, between aesthetic satisfactions, or disappointments, social and expressive desiderata, and intercultural possibilities, which on some level implies a reading of the cultural unconscious. This is the territory I wish to explore.

Another issue is encapsulated in the nicely provocative title: *Foreign Shakespeare*. Where the "native" Shakespeare had been invigorated or repositioned by European readings, exposing the paucity of conventionalized English performance, the texts have now opened up to wider appropriations. A Japanese or Chinese Shakespeare no longer seems a contradiction in terms, but rather can open our eyes to readings we would never have associated with those texts, yet which seem entirely justified and hence enlarge our understanding. Some of these performances are simply more exciting and suggestively defamiliarizing, al-

Intercultural Signs

though I will have more to say about this, than anything currently available within a purely Western repertory.

Formulated in respect of Shakespeare, Kennedy poses the crucial questions about intercultural performance:

> We have not even begun to develop a theory of cultural exchange that might help us understand what happens when Shakespeare travels abroad, and so far there has been little interest among Shakespeareans in such an enterprise. A theory that can explain how "Shakespeare" operates in Mnouchkine's orientalism, in Ninagawa's occidentalism, and in what Pavis calls "the politically radical thought of the Third World" may be too much to ask for yet it is the most important task Shakespeareans face. It is much more important than linguistic analysis, textual examination, psychological assessments, historical research, or any of the Anglo-centered occupations scholars have traditionally valued and perpetuated.[14]

## II

Before exploring these questions from the perspectives of textual anthropology, we should first look at a differently aligned project that engages with comparable material, privileges drama, and reads Shakespeare, as well as Brecht's theoretical discourse, as part of the argument. *Comparative Poetics*, Earl Miner's prize-winning study, perhaps the first sustained attempt at an intercultural poetics, is an historical account of how writing has been shaped, or ought to have been and, drawing on intercultural knowledge, a guide to rereading that writing.[15] In this intercultural account, poetic systems derive from "foundational" genres. These genres shape all expression and hence expectations of the culturally possible, implying a universal history of the culturally imaginable. Reading, therefore, depends on the fundamental generic assumptions, but because it is given no space to contest them, reading is thereby functionalized. The major examples are taken from Western (mostly English) and East Asian (mostly Japanese) writing.

Miner does not sufficiently test the foundational, genre-based theories in relation to exemplary writing. So we need to ask two kinds of questions: about the internal consistency of such arguments in an intercultural poetics; and about their anthropological status, their usefulness in describing and interpreting human behavior, this writing and reading of texts.

Another basic argument holds the Western understanding of literature to be the exception rather than the rule in a global poetics. Far from universal and necessarily at the center of explanation, Western presuppositions are marginal in global terms. I find this approach analytically attractive. Marginalizing the presumed center is impeccably deconstructive, although the implications of deconstructive analysis for the security of authorship and of subject positions are incompatible with Miner's own views. Another attractive corollary is that all attempts to justify non-Western cultural practices in terms of Western criteria, considered either universal or representing a desired modernity and hence more prestigious, are based on a shaky premise. This might finally help see off those books and articles that try to prove there is, of course, a Chinese form of tragedy, or pastoral, or postmodernism and so on, all naturally no less worthy of attention than their Western counterparts.

The basic distinction between Western and East Asian poetics occurs because Western poetics are governed by mimesis, derived from as well as constituting the genre of drama and formulated by Aristotle.[16] Most other poetics rest on affective-expressive assumptions that shape the genre of lyric: truth primarily, on the one hand, to an independent and objectifiable external reality and, on the other, to the internal emotions of the reader or writer.

Behind these potentially verifiable propositions—although verification is never simple given the difficulty in establishing the full implications of culturally specific attitudes and terms—lies, however, another agenda. Philosophical realism is a necessary precondition to meaningful writing and reading. I have no quarrel with an abstractly asserted principle maintaining that a world exists beyond writing or the subject, without which neither can be envisaged, but here a doctrine of the real is used to evaluate texts. This agenda becomes visible in assumptions about certain forms and in judgments about individual works.

Mimesis implies a pregiven referent. You can only imitate what is already there. But drama, it is argued, pretends to represent. Its representation pretends to be this referent. An actor embodies a character. Miner cites Brecht's alienation theory as evidence that estrangement is necessarily the consequence of drama's fictionality, since its representations always pretend to be what they are not, namely, reality itself. This stresses the inevitability of mimesis, as the imitation of reality, while assuming it is perpetually condemned to fictionality or mimetic failure, and hence constitutes a Platonizing critique of representation. Yet Aristotle's contradictory mimesis, the foundational genre of Western poetics, can be recuperated because it is based on philosophical realism and thus anchored by an always ambiguous engagement with the real. Drama therefore offers a model for language as representation.

Although Western poetics, structured on mimetic efficacy, may be the global exception, the affective-expressive poetics of other cultures, based upon the lyric, are also characterized by philosophical realism, by a belief in the facticity of reference.[17] Inevitably fictional dramatic mimesis is always related to a theoretically knowable reality, even if failing to be that reality; a transparently fictional East Asian poetics is secured by a necessary relationship with the real.

Drama offers what we know is only fictional, therefore it estranges, even as it represents; it is "a cognitive, potentially pleasurable violation of the real by the fictional."[18] Therefore performance depends upon a preposited reality, not on exploiting its repressed fictionality, since acknowledging this fictionality would destroy mimesis. We connive at this pretense, knowing the representation to be false. Drama, according to these prescriptions, must find its philosophical justification in mimetic realism and offer as exact an imitation of actual behavior as possible. Anything interrupting this dramatic illusion causes potential distress: "The soliloquy, the stage whisper, the aside are perpetually in danger of sounding false. The closer we are to the front seats, the more the paint and wig and saliva are obvious."[19]

Miner knows these suppositions are culturally relative, but supposes them fundamental to Western drama. However, disruptions of the illusion of reality in the theater do not threaten the belief that a world exists beyond our consciousness and can be negotiated through language. Miner here confuses philosophical realism with a particular representational style, with naturalism in the theater, the creation of an illusion of everyday life, the presuppositions of ego-psychology.[20] He argues, "Brecht realized that the conventional estranging of the theatre he inherited might continue to distance audiences from what they beheld and heard" (49). Brecht wanted to see things afresh, and "properly, as he thought" (49).²¹ So Brecht wanted to estrange that estrangement that consists of a fictional (mis)representation of reality, and to distance audiences from the performance in order to show them reality itself, which in his case unfortunately took the form of an erroneous politics.

The media cannot produce the effect of theater. In radio, television, and film "we simply are not in the players' immediate presence, participating with them in the estranged shock of present awareness that 'they' are not who they are but 'we' are who we are" (48). This assumes the position of the audience is secure. If the ontological status of those characters who are really actors is dubious, if "they" perhaps may not be themselves, at least "we" know who "we" are. This security of subject position enables us to place the representation or text and judge its mimetic credibility, put in hazard by its fictionality but ultimately anchored by its truth to an objectively verifiable reality. Aesthetic pleasure or displeasure derives from this tension between fiction and fact. In this mimetic realism fictionality, though offering aesthetic pleasure, always endangers representation, measured against the truth of the represented. The observer's position is secure. Miner fails to see that Brecht's anti-Aristotelianism threatens mimetic representation in order to unsettle the *audience*. A switch of perspective has taken place. At issue is not the truth of the represented, but rather the security of the interpreting audience, of the reader's subject position, itself constructed by the mimetic conventions of representation. Brecht introduces a new dynamic into the static position of the reader whose task, as conceived by mimetic theory, is merely to ascertain the closeness of representation to a pre-established truth and to be rendered more secure in its knowledge. Brecht's plays put the audience in jeopardy, enticed into examining how it is itself constructed by representation.

Applying Aristotelian typology to Japanese literature, narrative becomes "a nonperformed genre" (100). Novels are indeed nonperformed but narrative is not. Storytelling is both narrative and performance. Chinese *ping tan*, Japanese *joruri*, through to Bunraku, can only narrate through performance. Breaking down generic expectations, sustainable only as ideal types, makes representation unsettling and uncertain, engaging its audience. Hence Brecht's interest in East Asian narrative drama and its nonrepresentational, externalizing acting. The actor presents the performance of a role. The effect is to accept the fictionality rather than to connive at concealing it, and hence to uncover the inter-

Intercultural Signs

nalized forces that would have us believe its fictions are true. The character is repeatedly displaced in respect of a mimetics of the surface. Aware of this performative dimension the actor then takes, as it were, the part of audience and performs not just the role but its relativity to interpretation, suggesting its unconscious structuration. Brecht drew on this East Asian aesthetic, which we can also observe in the Kunju *Macbeth*, in order to question the often dogmatic assumptions of an ideologically narrow realism. Here, too, the intercultural sign functioned as the disrupter of conventional signification, not in order to "affirm and stabilize" it.[22]

Discussing Shakespeare, Miner remarks, "Interpolations of lyrics or narratives abate the action of the play, whether we take action to be Aristotle's *mythos* or what the players usually do—act, as opposed to sing or narrate."[23] If the action of the play is so abated or delayed by interpolations and if that action is the mimetic essence that, starting from this dramatic genre, informs the whole of Western poetics, then the thought must occur that these poetics do not perhaps rest on a secure foundation. If mimetic representation cannot easily bear such interruptions because its recognizability suffers, then the credibility of the realist premise must suffer too and its foundation in philosophical realism seems likely to be affected. Alternatively, that philosophical realism may be mismatched with the aesthetic activities it is supposed to ground.

Of course drama contains many such interruptions, and plays embody various levels of action, for example, the several strands or levels in *A Midsummer Night's Dream* that must "retain their distinguishable identities." But these "integral and distinguishable, separate" parts are all "inserted into . . . the general comedy of the highborn people" (101). At that moment we are back with a mimesis that discretely governs the separable parts and a need to integrate the whole work, instead of seeing those levels as questioning the politics of a mimetic coherence and the need of Theseus the Duke to insist on such coherence and to assert his authority over what threatens to dislodge him. In this formal analysis, the audience or readers have been forgotten. Their job in this poetics is to follow the play as it is allegedly unified by that "general comedy" of the highborn, implying a traditional reading, a ruler's view of events, and not to question themselves and their construction of it. But that is precisely what Shakespeare's text invites us to do, as it relativizes the Duke's version of reality, that Puck dissolves into something much

The Intercultural Sign

darker and less comic at the play's end. A nonmimetic reading does not allow the hierarchy of levels.

In Miner's text Beckett best exemplifies a debilitating "antimimetic crusade against the doctrine of the real" (101). To dramatists like Kleist, the world is real and knowable and so they remain within the mimetic fold. Beckett does not, and others have similarly unfocused tendencies: Rabelais, Swift, Lewis Carroll.[24] Compared with Beckett, Miner finds Shakespeare's mimesis reassuring. Beckett's writing, which "seeks to exclude reality by use of meaningless words" (66), may appear reductive and minimalist to Miner's mimetics, but constitutes a whole compendium or memory of Western culture. In Beckett, the lyrical moments are either "all but meaningless" (66), or, compared with the Noh theater, at most "touches of smeared colour" (68). The Japanese Noh plays, with no normative obligations to mimesis in their different cultural tradition, can delight with lyricism and the "lovely little" symbolic theater props. In the Noh theater, "there is a shift from suffering itself to its beauty" (71), for it "transforms the agonies into refinement" (72).

Normative poetics play havoc with cross-cultural interpretation. Which is more important? In *Waiting for Godot*, "the suffering is as real as its meaninglessness is comic" (70). On the one hand, the play is antimimetic; on the other hand, the suffering is "real." But whose suffering? Apparently the author's. Can the text be said to suffer? Are the characters separable from that text? In what sense do the characters suffer? They are effects of writing and performance. These contradictions point to a hidden desire for a particular meaning, the security of something beyond the text provided by an assured mimesis. It is this denial of mimesis that troubles. Where, as in the Noh, it is not even attempted, where we deal not with anti- but with unmimesis, you can relax and enjoy the performance. But why is antimimesis so threatening?

It implies, on a personal level, a repressed fear that Beckett might perhaps be right, that his antimimesis might be the most accurately "mimetic" representation of all. And on the level of conscious analysis, antimimesis upsets the presuppositions of the foundational genre, of the poetics, and of the politics of reading derived from it. The Japanese aesthetic is acceptable because it fudges the issue, and so we do not have to face it. Antimimetic writing denies a secure position for the interpreting subject; it must be rejected or only tolerated to the extent that it breaks with its own presuppositions. Adorno's contextual reading of Beckett as a refusal of commodified language is beyond this interpretive horizon.[25]

Because the Noh does not embody mimetic practices, it can be savored in the form of aesthetic pleasure. My objection here is not to aesthetic pleasure in the Noh theater, but rather to supposing this pleasure mitigates agony. This agony is so compellingly conveyed, it becomes, paradoxically, inseparable from a form of pleasure, the pleasure of discovery. Aesthetic pleasure is a function of the discovery of a truth. Distancing the agony, as in Brecht's theater, intensifies it. Neither aestheticized or "refined" by the sophisticated formal means, it is made visible for the first time. The shock of this estranging but compelling recognition constitutes the pleasure we call "aesthetic": a fascination produced by the concentration into a moment of an experiential truth, the moment of self-discovery. Mere "refinement" is by itself a shallow satisfaction. This self-questioning encounter, provoked by an engagement with the dislocated or intercultural sign, focuses everything, including my arguments. Mimesis seeks to conceal this moment because it calls upon the interpreter to look through the representation at the albeit imperfectly imitated world.

The exposition of this mimetic poetics must be selective. Aristophanic fantasy is as undiscussed as the problematics of representation that characterizes Renaissance drama. It is no accident that the minimalist Beckett so frequently echoes Shakespeare or that the main character in *Endgame* is called Hamm, even though Beckett first thought of Noah's son. Beckett's text is no more meaningless than Shakespeare's, and it is as rich in cultural allusions, even if it seems less certain about the location of a spiritual world. Hamlet inhabits a world where nothing is what it appears to be, and where nothing also is but what is not, where certainty is nothing but an old man's platitude, where all is performance and uncertain representation, as in *Endgame*.

Shakespeare's play turns into a continuous enquiry into its own methods of representation. The language games of the comedies, where the word-breaking clowns and the verbal transvestism of the women challenge the semantic naturalism of the men and their claims to power, now turn into fencing matches with poisoned swords, where the rules of the game are always changing.[26] Hence Hamlet's fascination with all forms of acting, for behind each mask lies another mask and behind each representation another text. Hamlet turns into ever-shifting representations of himself, switching roles and language strategies in an instant, when words give shape to clouds. He becomes a sequence of possibilities and can scarcely distinguish anything that was once "himself." He becomes an actor of his own entanglement.

Hamlet is fascinated by how the actors' roles are more persuasive than anybody's reality. The roles are framed by acknowledged convention, whereas reality has become pure performance. When everything becomes performance, except performance itself, then no value is certain, all knowledge is doubtful. Natural order disintegrates, is revealed as convention, and identity turns into a series of subject positions. Subjectivity becomes a question of discourse. Hamlet has to face the fact that there may be no truth behind appearances, that the only truth is appearance. What matters is control of appearance, the game of power. This is what *Endgame* also shows: nothing is certain except the semblance of control through language.

The acknowledged, not shamefaced, artifice of theater, its nonmimetic imagining, enables us to see the otherwise invisible: the unconscious of a culture and a position's relativities. Imitation of the invisible is mimesis of the repressed, of the surreptitious unconscious, of the apparently unreal or inadmissible, which is why theater, as public event in social space, has always attracted official censorship.

We can trace these effects from Western theater's beginnings in Aristophanes whose fantasies uncover the repressed fear of generative failure and social disintegration, through the farce of Plautus, whose twin brothers in *Menaechmi* externalize one man's invisible repressions, down to Pirandello's denial of mimetic credibility in *Six Characters in Search of an Author,* who does not exist, who has absconded, leaving his characters to fend for themselves, and to Brecht's *Man Equals Man* in which the central figure delivers the oration over his own grave because personality is multiform, identity infinitely malleable, and mimesis once again implements an authoritarian politics. These representations undo the certainties through which we internalize an identity constructed for us. The efficacy of the intercultural sign may likewise depend upon what is unconsciously apprehended rather than consciously affirmed since it undermines the conventions of representation.

Intercultural Signs

### III

The intercultural poetics I have critiqued gives special space to Shakespeare. Earlier, initially unwelcomed, finally influential readings outside Anglo-America demonstrate a curious leap-frogging effect within. Kott's later provocation, superficially contradicting Brecht's largely ignored response but entrammeled with it in ways that can only fascinate, leads to a more adequately complex repositioning of Shakespeare with English-speaking culture. Its impact has certainly been recognized, but its capacity for disintegrating unified personality perhaps not sufficiently juxtaposed. What Brecht was already exploring in the twenties was then below the horizons of Shakespearean theater and related scholarship.[27]

What, after all, could Kott's Beckettian Lear or cyclical human lives have in common with Brecht's historicized Shakespearean characters? The apparently incompatible reaccentuations—history is cyclical; history is specific—need to be contextualized. Then oppositions appear much less certain. Kott argued that, far from consolingly timeless, Shakespeare was alarmingly contemporary, recording the incessant pain of living within a meaningless cyclical history, that "Grand Mechanism which transforms the executioner into a victim."[28]

Brecht took the Shakespearean text differently, not as perpetually contemporaneous, because change is inconceivable and suffering unavoidable, but by putting it back into history and denying its characters' universality. Hamlet does not represent perennial, melancholy indecisiveness in the face of impossibly contradictory political and psychological demands. He does not stand for a "Germany," incapable of realizing itself, as he apparently still did for Heiner Müller.[29] He embodies specific discourses as expressions of Renaissance ideologies, and his behavior, in Brecht's reading, results in the expropriation of his country by foreigners, as Kott himself reminds us.[30]

Kott notices the political force of Brecht's historicizing arguments for a contemporary Polish Hamlet, and, discussing *Coriolanus*, observes Shakespeare "represents Brechtian objective dialectic."[31] This naturally contradicts Kott's stricture, mentioned in the previous chapter, that Brecht is "didactic" and Shakespeare "antididactic," since a didactic style is incompatible with any dialectic that could be thought of as objective, which I take to mean adequate to the real complexity of history, rather than following a prescribed theoretical view upon it. It also helps to situate the "paradox" that a contemporary and a historicized Shakespeare can be simultaneously compelling. Kott observes of Shakespeare's *Coriolanus:* "There is no common system for the polis and the individual," and "that is the bitter drama of Renaissance humanism, of any humanism in fact."[32] This is also the constantly addressed, unresolved problem throughout Brecht's writing, and his version of *Coriolanus* offers a particular and contemporary perspective upon it.

For Brecht, Shakespeare's characters are not the supreme incarnations of unchanging emotions, but rather are constituted by the expressive forms available for the articulation of emotions within specific historical circumstances. To understand this in no way restricts the force of these emotions. On the contrary, they become even more persuasive, and the bearers of their contradictions ever more tragic figures, because we appreciate why they are condemned to incarnate them. Yet Brecht's approach to Shakespeare also makes any easy identificatory extrapolation virtually impossible. This is where the problems, and the possibilities for productive rereadings, began.

Kott and Brecht cannot be compartmentalized, whether as lapsed activist turned existentialist, facing the pain and fatuities of a meaningless history, or as the idiosyncratic expressionist turned socialist apologist for history's victims. Both Kott and Brecht reacted under their own specific and analogous circumstances against politically efficacious constructions of a timeless Shakespeare, either as traditional consolation for the bourgeoisie or, in post–Second World War Eastern Europe, as the undisputed humanist whose work, expressing the vitality of the human spirit, voiced the aspirations of a historically progressive, aspiring, antifeudal, bourgeois, mercantile class that constituted itself within the contradictory framework of an incipient absolutism.

Kott was responding to Stalin's erasure of history that he had replaced with a crash course in forced industrialization, supplemented by the higher morality of the prison camp. The dislocations and pain of those experiences were as specific and contemporary as possible; there was nothing timeless about them. Under these circumstances, his readings constituted an intervention, not a retreat out of history, and they were as political as you could get, never mind the extraordinary personal life of

Intercultural Signs

their author, under the conditions and limitations of speech in the public sphere then prevailing.[33] They figured the unbearable pain of a specific history masked as timelessness.

Likewise, Brecht's *Coriolanus* initially foundered on the intransigence of East German cultural policy, which could not countenance political readings that questioned an uncomplicated universal humanism attributed to the classic text. This official Shakespeare in performance bled the plays of their complexities. Brecht was considered an unreliable writer with a disturbing, potentially subversive aesthetic. Kott's apparently abstract existentialism was, under the circumstances of his day, an inescapably political reading, because to insist on the prevalence of pain was to make a political statement. Brecht's Shakespeare also cut against the grain of expectation, since he was interested in the particularities of the characters' emotional life. Their attitudes were not simple, they could not be reduced to a politically convenient formula. They were constructed by contradictions. To elide those contradictions would deprive the text of its power to move and disturb, hence it would simply illustrate preordained certainties. Seen in the context of the English postwar versions of Shakespeare, locked into their own "timeless" ideology of appropriation, these ideas and the practice they suggested were revolutionary. They revitalized Shakespeare in English theater.

It is only superficially surprising to find the universalizing Kott objecting: "It often seems to me that nowadays Shakespeare is placed in no time and in no particular place."[34] He continues with a specific illustration, raising problems that accrue from perspectives on contemporary intercultural theater:

> I have a great admiration for Ariane Mnouchkine, but when I watch her Shakespearean productions with big Japanese-type dolls and Samurais and a kind of mock Kabuki, I think to myself, "This is fake Japanese and fake Shakespeare." It is quite different from actual Shakespearean productions in Japan, the exact opposite of the work of Kurosawa.... What is contemporary for Kurosawa is terror, the terror of *King Lear* and the terror of *The Throne of Blood*. Kurosawa's Lear is like the *King Lear* of Peter Brook, timeless but contemporary. The one Shakespeare who is not our contemporary is the Shakespeare of nowhere and no time.[35]

Brecht's version of terror, which he called horror (*Schrecken*), is crucial to his theater, and performances that mitigate it have not realized why he found it inalienable, or appreciated how he invoked it, thereby provoking that emotional crisis of perception in the spectator. In 1929, after *The Threepenny Opera*, when he was looking to develop what he called the "great form," Brecht was asked what acting should be like. He replied, "Spiritual. Ceremonial. Ritual. Actor and audience should not come closer to each other, they should move further away from each other. Everyone should move further away from himself. Otherwise we are deprived of the shock and horror which is a pre-condition for understanding."[36] This sounds more like Artaud. At times that shock is envisaged in cognitive terms; at others, it is quite visceral. But it always requires vivid externalization of what is otherwise buried and repressed. Twenty years later they are collecting horses' heads from the slaughterhouse, boiling them in the kitchen and setting the skulls up on poles around the stage for the first production after returning to Europe: Brecht's version of *Antigone*.

When Mother Courage hears the shots that kill Swiss Cheese, she throws back her head in one long silent scream. Brecht had a photograph of a Chinese woman lamenting the death of her child during a Japanese attack on Singapore, and Helene Weigel transferred her gesture in the famous Berlin production. For several seconds the action comes to a complete halt. It is a moment of arrestation, the equivalent of an externalizing gesture in Asian theater. Why? Because we need time to appreciate the complexity of the moment, to realize we are simultaneously seeing the pain and horror she feels upon the death of her son, together with the pain and horror over her own complicity in that death and, in addition, the pain and horror at the unavoidability, the social causes of that complicity.

At this moment of understanding we are both inside and outside the character. What happens is not really so much that the *character* is essentialized, so that we can identify with her, sharing her burden, as that the disparity is revealed, almost objectified, between our initial construction of the character and her structuration, as the complexity of her situation dawns on us. This will not weaken but rather compound our horror and our sympathy. At such moments we realize that our subjectivity, our personality, our very self, is both inside and outside us, that where we think to govern ourselves, we are the expression of forces beyond our individual control. We realize that we are simultaneously self and not-self, the object of structuration that we have not calculated, and that we do not

## Intercultural Signs

even see until it is perhaps too late. Some such experience lies behind the most powerful effects in theater, and Brecht's plays are full of them.

The point is to outwit the defense mechanisms in the spectator anxious to deny anything is wrong. The simplification of Brecht's dramaturgy is one long repressive reading. Brecht did not exclude fear and pity—the Aristotelian criteria supposedly rejected—but rather expanded the opportunity for understanding their function and origin. For example, he expressly said the spectator should feel pity for Mother Courage.[37] And if you are not literally or metaphorically moved to tears, you probably need to see your psychoanalyst. When Kattrin bangs the drum to warn the town and is shot on the roof, Brecht wanted to "outwit convention" and reach "a different stratum of fear," one which the audience otherwise represses.[38] It was a question of breaking through what he called the "ritualisation of despair" (*Zeremoniencharakter der Verzweiflung*) in the response of the peasant woman, so as to get at the fear lodged in a different stratum of the psyche. It is not enough to represent the strategies for repressing fear; the real underlying terror must also be shown. It is lodged beneath the controlling repressive gesture, in the character's unconscious, and has become the object of investigation.

Such considerations are important, even crucial, if we wish to use perceptions of Brecht's work as part of the means whereby we evaluate intercultural theater. We particularly need to bear in mind that rejecting "culinary" theater on no account entails excluding aesthetic pleasure. Indeed Brecht's encounter with East Asian, especially Chinese, culture encouraged him to realize on the stage a defining category of his later aesthetic: gracefulness. I wish to contextualize this in relation to what I call the "dialectics of acculturation."

### IV

Acculturation is normally considered unidirectional, invited by deficit to be made good, either willingly or reluctantly, by adopting more effective practices. The source/target model operates within such parameters. *Dialectics* of acculturation implies a longer lasting reciprocal process of discovery and adjustment between cultures. The second culture absorbs, transforms, and then retransmits. The first culture then encounters its own transformed transmissions, and in turn absorbs and retransforms them. In such a process the encounter is experienced as challenge, not defeat. Where a culture lacks this ability to absorb, change, and transmit, it will eventually succumb, stagnate, or disintegrate. The pressure toward uniformity through rapid globalization threatens, ultimately, the destruction of all culture, for where there is no difference, there can be no identity.

In macrocultural terms, the most challenging encounter is taking place between East Asia and the West. My observations are selective and suppose a degree of complementarity between contrasting cultural forms, the source of the mutual attraction, where critics sometimes see incompatibility, or a presumed universality, either fundamental difference or, deep down, really no difference at all. "Never the twain shall meet" assumes fundamental incompatibility, no matter from what position this is argued. The search for universals takes several forms depending on ideological presuppositions and disciplinary interest. The pursuit of universal religious or psychological impulses can be represented by Rudolph Pannwitz's search for a basis of "world religion," or by C. G. Jung's omnipresent and archetypal symbols. A form of cultural universalism grounds the theater of Peter Brook. The pursuit of generic and thematic-expressive homologies has preoccupied the discipline of comparative literature, either to validate native competence by discovering counterparts for a dominant culture's forms, or to assert thematic or formal universalities. Arguments for homologies are widespread in so-called East-West studies.[39] Complementarity is naturally incompatible with either of these assumptions, since it presupposes that even when absorbing the impulse from outside, for whatever reasons and they may go deep, there exists an ability to transform and hence to resist. Exactly why these processes occur needs some explaining.

A dynamic indubitably exists between Eastern and Western cultural forms. Western practices no longer claim greater sophistication, something the nineteenth century took for granted. The West's absolute cultural security, certain of its modernizing mission, its technological power, is no longer assured. In some respects Japan is technologically more progressive. Given the history of Chinese inventiveness, that culture is unlikely to prove deficient in innovation if it can overcome its developmental problems.

Perhaps we can distinguish between micrological and macrological rearrangements. The former leave the latter unchallenged. Micrological perceptual reorganization might be exemplified by Degas's absorption of Japanese pictorial form that jolted expectations, but in no way challenged the realist aesthetic within which he worked. Whistler's evocation of fin-de-siècle mood through Japanese visual motifs, an analogical perception of the relationship between transitoriness and beauty, likewise presented no violent rearrangement of Western conventions, although incompatible with official art. Where a radical challenge occurs, however, the response is inevitably accompanied by apprehensiveness.

The German reaction to Mnouchkine's acting style was, for example, characterized by such apprehension as a reflex repression of its implied threat, its challenge to perceptual habits. Yet there is an analogy between Mnouchkine's and Brecht's response to East Asian theater, not in visual styles but on the level of underlying structure. There is too a common appreciation of the cognitive dimensions within an East Asian aesthetic, often forgotten in the traditional practice of East Asian theater. To argue this is to imply, as its corollary, that certain assumptions have dominated the understanding of Brecht's theater, and that it is perhaps time to reexamine them. Such a view not only links apparent antipodes—a soberly "ethical" theater and a visually exuberant "aesthetic" theater—but also contradicts the assumption that Brecht's interest in East Asian culture can be counted as micrological defamiliarization. The real challenge, embodying fundamental critique, is macrological.[40]

The processes of response are dialectical. Ignoring the interfiliations, observing only each side's developments, we risk a static analysis that concentrates on the differences, which are naturally important. Critics often assume Brecht's interest in East Asian techniques—he spoke of "transporting" them—was at most superficial and probably misguided, because the respective dramaturgies and aesthetic systems are at opposite poles of intention. They treat the encounter on the micrological level, sometimes accompanied by a reverential attitude toward Brechtian theory. The potential of the work is thus frustrated, together with the aesthetic challenge of the cultural encounter.

Another example of these more complex processes would be Yeats's use of Japanese forms, mediated through Fenollosa and Pound, which freed a potential in Japanese theater of which the Japanese were not then properly aware, due to traditional, unreflecting, to an extent still current attitudes toward theatrical forms. Among other things they were resensitized to disregarded qualities in its language. Such processes show how a culture's self-understanding profits from, is perhaps only possible through, this encounter with the foreign. Forgotten knowledge, the potential of older forms is recuperated.[41] This is true whether we speak of interpreting gesture on the stage or underlying modes of thought. Dialectically transforming incorporation is a question of attaining another, usually repressed, level of perception, never of simple alternation or imposition. The process always involves change but can perhaps also be regressive.[42]

In 1934 Brecht saw a Chinese painting in the house of Karin Michaelis in Denmark. He described it in a letter to George Grosz:

> A little later I saw a large Chinese painting on paper, about 1x3 meters high, apparently representing life in the Golden Age. Trees, old men, girls, buildings. The figures are about [-] cm tall [sic], and there are around 40 of them, and still the painter knew how to create plenty of space between them. Between the groups (there are 6 groups and only 3 single figures) lie whole seas. In addition to this there are tall trees, a small temple flooded with water, a palace, a garden, clouds overhead, and only then does the sky begin. And nothing appears small. Four old men are sitting round a garden table playing a board game, not far away 3 others are examining an architect's plan together. Another is enticing a fish out of the waves, which however—it's about 1 cm long and green—seems to be giving him a negative answer. Half-a-dozen people are sitting on a piece of land in the flood that has been torn away; they are burning incense paper in honour of the gods (enthroned above, busy with their appearance), engaging in discussions, probably about historical materialism, one of them with a fat stomach stands like a dancer on a kind of tub in the waves, holding an umbrella I believe and wearing a beautifully painted crimson coat, a chancer.[43]

This was followed by one of the most suggestive accounts of the potential of his later aesthetic:

*On Chinese Painting*

As we know the Chinese do not use the art of perspective. They do not like looking at everything from one single point-of-view. In their pictures several things are ordered in relation to each other the way a town's inhabitants are distributed throughout the town, not independent of each other but not in a state of subordination which threatens their very existence. It is necessary to look at this comparison a little more closely. The families we are comparing with these things live in a town, represented in our picture, in greater freedom than we are accustomed to living in. They do not exist just by virtue of their connections with a single family. The Chinese composition lacks an element of compulsion to which we are completely accustomed. This order requires no force. The designs contain a lot of freedom. The eye is able to go on a voyage of discovery. The things that are represented play the role of elements which can exist on their own and yet in the relationship which they form on the page they constitute a whole, if not an indivisible one. One can cut the pages into sections without rendering them meaningless, but also not without altering them.

The Chinese artists also have lots of room on their paper. Some parts of the surface appear to be unused; but these parts play an important role in the composition; judging by their extent and their form they appear to be just as carefully devised as the outlines of the objects. In these gaps the paper itself or the canvas acquires a quite specific value. The basic surface is not simply denied by the artist through covering it up completely. The mirror in which something is here mirrored retains its value as mirror. Among other things that signifies a laudable abandonment of the thorough subjugation of the viewer, whose illusion is not fully completed. Like these pictures I love gardens in which the gardeners have not shaped nature completely, which have space, where things lie side by side.[44]

Brecht is clearly not describing an exotic object so much as sketching a utopian aesthetics of daily life. In the second paragraph he refers to the theory of reflection as the extreme form of a dominant realist Western style, imposed in the form of socialist realism, for which art functioned as a reflection of an already theorized reality. This often led to strange consequences. Art did not then produce the complexities of real social life, the imaginings, the silences and repressions, and the social fantasies that they evoked, but merely reproduced reflections of reflections according to predetermined "theoretical" models. Socialist realism, therefore, deprived art of its cognitive function. It was no longer realistic, adequate to reality. Its purpose was abstract and illustrative. That is why he speaks, rather cryptically but subverting the current terminology, of the value of the Chinese painting as mirror, meaning as active agent rather than as passive purveyor of the mirrored.

The nature of the frame is at stake here. Brecht contrasts Western and Chinese use of perspective. Conventional Western perspective imposes a uniperspectival order upon the objects within its frame. According to certain laws of proportion, the painting constrains the objects it depicts through the gaze of a posited viewing subject. Brecht argues, in effect, that this realist aesthetic depends upon a double form of constraint: not only aligned with the eye of a posited dominant subject or viewer, the actual viewer of the painting is also forced to accept the dominance of this perspective. Hence the perspective contained within this frame constrains both objects and viewer. In as much as it includes landscape, it imposes a superficial arbitrary order on the natural world, while through its doubleness accomplishing what he terms "the thorough subjugation of the viewer." In this Western realist aesthetic the natural world is organized for exploitation by the dominant subject, whose perspectival order is imposed over the whole painting.

Such perspective not only subjugates without remainder the whole of the physical world but also guarantees the authenticity of the dominant subject-position, or rather asserts the ideological and power claim to such untrammeled authenticity. Brecht contrasts this mathematization of physical and hierarchization of social space with the multiperspectival aesthetic of the Chinese painting. It eschews any such spatial organization, since its empty spaces remind us of nature's irreducibility, and refuses to reduce the represented human figures to one single point-of-view. They do not therefore depend upon a single perspective. They do not exist in uniperspectival dependency, but rather in a multiperspectival relational independency. "This order," he remarks, "requires no force."

Brecht's Me-ti, a *persona* suggested by the Chinese philosopher Mozi, was "against constructing too complete images of the world."[45] Brecht discovered in Chinese art a way of upsetting the dominant and dogmatically defended Western categories in order to free the potential of the socially responsive imagination. Surely the Chinese painting could be seen as performing, at least potentially, an analogous function, if we see the Daoist Immortals as an expression of the Chinese social unconscious. There can, of course, be no question of a developed theoretical understanding of such phenomena at that time. In this painting they are represented crossing the water on their way to the festival of long life and must therefore embody a longing deeply rooted in that culture. Brecht, in any event, found in Chinese art a means of resisting a positivist, mechanistic thinking prevalent in his day and that was incompatible with creative Marxism. His admiration was not just a matter of personal taste; it rested on deeper congruities.[46]

An intercultural hermeneutics, which Brecht practiced in order to continue thinking, must constantly look for models that question domestic "normality" and draw attention to the dangerous limitations in our understanding of our own practices, in the hope we may eventually succeed in changing those that endanger us. The power of the dominant paradigm automatically ensures that what resists it will be repressed. Access to what is repressed will often come as a passage through the cultural Other, discerned through a process that is perhaps initially largely unconscious—the full implications must certainly remain to a degree opaque—but that occurs because it fulfills a need.

Emerging from the Enlightenment, bourgeois culture and its developing capitalist economic system, turning ever more positivist as it grew assertive and self-defensive, insisted on the independence of its partial systems. These have now become a threat to all of us in the form of a global industrial culture, wastefully parodied in the increasingly dependent Third World as the First World prepares to extricate itself from its local disasters by exporting them. That is why those prebourgeois, protocybernetic, and socioecological models are so suggestive for postbourgeois society and especially in the form of such an aesthetically sophisticated East Asian art.

Justifiably suspicious of lightly asserted compatibility, critics often hold that Brecht misunderstood a sophisticated East Asian aesthetic, deriving from it little more than a means of separating actor and character in order to undermine their unification in a theoretically naive and ideologically grounded realist aesthetic, and that he replaced this conventional, dominant, Western aesthetic with a more or less doctrinal didacticism, where the knowing actor stands in a position of superiority vis-à-vis the unknowing character. The character may be foolish or confused, but the dramaturgy is omniscient, confronting the limited subjective life of the emotions with the clarity of objective historical truth. The audience is, therefore, naturally disabused of any desire to lose itself through identifying with the subjective confusions of the unknowing characters. In such an analysis one form of dominance is replaced by another.

Brecht's passage on Chinese painting demonstrates a way of thinking, stimulated by Chinese ideas about the need to escape perceptual and political forms of dominance. He was not seeking through East Asian theater a method for de-emphasizing the emotions, and thereby misunderstanding the nature of East Asian theater, but on the contrary a method that heightened their importance, raising them to another dimension, allowing them greater scope, and increasing their force as they are both distanced and strengthened, not weakened, by a reflective aesthetic. He observed a principle in East Asian art whereby things are brought closer when they are moved further away. Of course this subverted the realist clichés of thought-impeding emotional excitation, although not by diminishing but rather by increasing the emotional force of the acting. This, in turn, is accomplished by a method analogous to the principle in Chinese acting whereby the intensity of an emotion is best conveyed when it is reduced to its essential features that are not represented, because they cannot be, but rather presented or symbolized. Both methods, with different visual means and with largely, although not wholly, different intentions, sought to convey the essence of an experience by presenting it indirectly.

The conventional Western aesthetic accentuates the character's inner feelings as an essential guarantee of authenticity unavailable to further examination. The emotions are sacrosanct; in them lies the personality of the character, an irreducible individuality. For long periods Shakespeare was virtually equated with such an individualist psychology, and this idea still sustains interpretation in the English theater, as a visit to Stratford-on-Avon will verify.

Brecht wanted to question this subjectivity in its protected secret places. He therefore developed, but never fully elaborated, a method for structuring these emotions, for understanding their provenance and consequences, which was analogous to, and stimulated by, an East Asian systematization of an externalizing aesthetic. Apart from the fact that Chinese theater, although not so much the relatively recent Beijing opera, was often critical of social abuses, an obvious point of contact on the level of plot, the concentration on a stylized presentation of emotion begs the question of its dramaturgical function and psychological origin, as well as of the cultural worldview in which they are embedded. In other words, the demonstration of emotion in East Asian theater cannot be equated with its representation in Western theater, no matter how different the styles, on the basis of the supposition that the emotions are everywhere the same, that their cultural function is identical, that we here encounter a human universal, and that here lies the basis for exchange.

Naturally I do not assert that this East Asian approach to the emotions and their delineation in the theater was identical to Brecht's or fully homologous, for to do this would also refute my argument about the dialectics of acculturation. But there is a significant compatibility, linked with the corresponding anthropology, with the supposition of interdependence or relational independence suggested in the description of Chinese painting, and never of an untrammeled independence grounded in a transcendental claim and authenticated by the demonstration of unique and powerful feelings. Upon such compatibility, upon the combination of like and unlike, depends the whole process of dialectical acculturation.

In substantiation, I select a further example where Brecht's dramaturgy distances the emotions, thus not only raising them to an otherwise inaccessible intensity but simultaneously allowing us to understand their provenance and function, the condition for perceiving this intensity as an interpretive event. At the end of the second scene of *The Caucasian Chalk Circle*, Grusche must decide whether to try to save the abandoned child. The acting method and the textual dispositions inhibit the obvious dangers of sentimentality, unfolding this event's hidden complexity and doing so with unforgettable immediacy. Such sophisticated externalization of the structured emotional moment, the opposite of an emotional outburst typical of realist Western dramaturgy, is an essential characteristic of East Asian theater. After long deliberation Grusche picks up the child. She does not speak. The moment is too strong for speech. "Speech" takes place somewhere else. The narrator speaks on her behalf and also formulates what the baby has not yet learned to say, as well as those thoughts Grusche cannot express and that culminate in the cry from the social unconscious, which Auden could not translate because he did not understand it: "Terrible is the temptation to do good!"

Even in a technical sense this amounts to far more than a simple separation between actress and character, for at this moment the character is also divided between actress and Narrator. A multiple dynamic is established. We realize: this moment is exceptional. Where everything is concentrated upon the person, as in East Asian drama, such a method enables an almost tactile encounter with the character's unconscious and, on several levels, allows us to imagine the force of the social unconscious that it articulates and in which it is embedded. The presentational "East Asian" method encourages the development of such readings.

These illustrations of Brecht's dramaturgy question the authenticity of the mimetically constructed subject, by allowing us to see the field of forces in which that subject inescapably stands and whose articulation it must be. Yet this subject remains at the center of attention. Only thus do we understand the forces that constitute it. The dramaturgy of East Asian theater worked in an analogous way, although outside, or without, the framework of a critical historical consciousness. Although Chinese plots dealt with a largely secular world, unlike Japanese theater, both differed from Western theater in their assumptions about the human subject and hence how it could be visualized. Both theaters typified and abstracted, whether the subject was shown within the structure of metaphysical or secular and social forces.

The codified language of gesture, articulated by an elaborate aesthetic sense, supposed the subject was constituted by such recognizable patterns of forces. There was no Western sense of a uniquely constituted and privileged individuality. In the Chinese theater the counterpart of Western tragedy is interestingly different, accruing from a failure of the social imagination, where the victim is to be pitied, and not from a perversity at the center of the world, challenged by the human spirit, tragically triumphant in defeat.

Hence East Asian theater separates the emotion from the character and demonstrates the separation through elaborate patterns, because the psychosocial subjects are relationally constituted. The pleasure of such artistry was not always a mark of value-free aestheticism or an overindulgence of the emotions, but rather an encoded articulation of a recognizable psycho-cultural structure, of social perception. Brecht, therefore, did not misunderstand Chinese theater when he analyzed it in the mid-1930s, even though his analysis was conducted in part through a contemporary discourse and hence certain facets of that theater were considered unhelpful because seen as deriving from magical thought. This is, however, an intricate matter, since Brecht's own discussion needs to be situated. We have to distinguish, in other words, between any particular analysis and what the dynamics actually shows.[47] To distinguish in such a way also involves realizing the existence of a potential in East Asian traditions that has not necessarily been fully understood, hence, once again, the significance of the dialectics of acculturation.

"Spoken drama" (*huaju*) has a short history in China. In the 1980s there was an upsurge of interest in Brecht's dramaturgy. Coming via Japan, this theater developed in the 1930s among the middle-class intellectuals of the coastal cities. Ibsenian plays served as a vehicle for asserting the rights of the individual against an oppressive social order rooted in feudalism. But this theater was unknown to the mass of the population. The use of the traditional opera as a vehicle for attacking ruling party factions led to its suppression during the Great Proletarian Cultural Revolution. Afterward, the spoken theater reverted to pragmatic productions, propaganda plays in a style termed "Stanislavskian" and loosely connected with his intentions.

The discovery of Brecht's complex, socially focused dramaturgy not only promised a more contradictory view of subjectivity than had been tolerated in the People's Republic, but also a way of recuperating traditional skills without the stultifying political agenda of the eight model revolutionary operas. It may seem strange, but this is how such developments actually happen. So the Chinese absorbing transformation of Brecht could also stand for an attitude toward traditional arts whose position was then difficult and uncertain during the period of rapid modernization. (See Figure 4.) In any event, I have experienced how the use of traditional techniques, and acting styles indebted to them, in productions of Brecht's plays have electrified the audiences, some of whom had assumed, following recent Western critics, that Brecht was that tiresome simplifier, and they have had their fill of simplifications. Instead they encountered in those productions the qualities Brecht himself so admired in Chinese theater, although these have now passed through his dramaturgy: gracefulness and great sophistication in the presentation of psychosocial structuration.

Critical response to Mnouchkine's Shakespeare in Germany showed admiration for its originality and audacity, amazement and even envy of such radical consistency and of a style so antithetical to the often visually impoverished, cerebral German theater, but bewilderment over that

1 Mnouchkine's performance space for Shakespeare's *Henry IV* (Neuschäfer and Serror, *Le Théâtre du Soleil*, 35).

2 Externalizing narrative and ceremony (Neuschäfer and Serror, *Le Théâtre du Soleil*, 35).

3  The duel between Prince Hal and Hotspur (Neuschäfer and Serror, *Le Théâtre du Soleil*, 35).

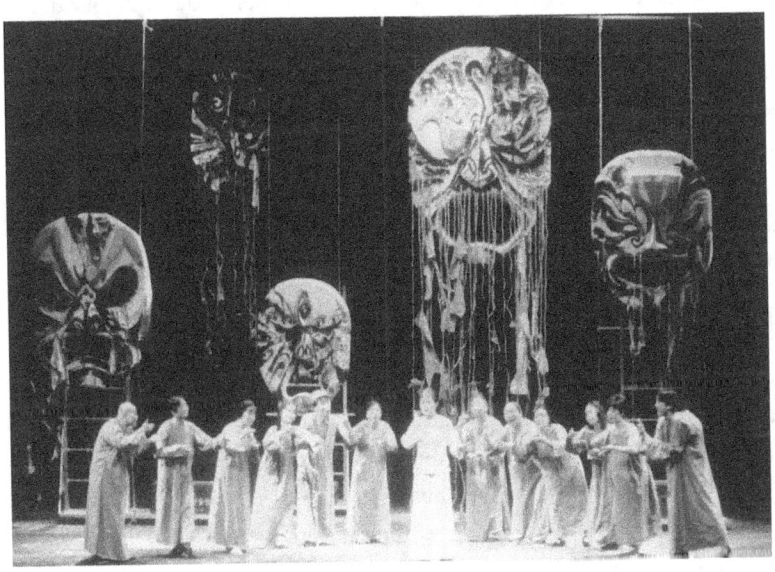

4  Brecht's *The Good Person of Szechwan* performed in a development of Sichuan opera (photo courtesy of Central Academy of Drama, Beijing).

style's deeper purpose. (See figures 1–3.) Yet Mnouchkine really only developed possibilities suggested by Brecht's dramaturgy, although she took them to lengths that he did not then envisage.

## V

The most recent attempts to rethink the battered project of modernity involve theorizing the nature of identity and of political behavior under the new conditions and pressures of economic and cultural globalization. The older categories have crumbled and have not been replaced by more satisfactory ones. Earlier simplicities, theorized by an imperialist, colonialist, or modernist dialectic of self and other have given way to a stronger sense of a shifting difference that is no longer securely and visibly outside but is now unsettlingly located within the self.[48] We have become aware of our own geotemporal complexity for which, like all slogans, the terms "postmodern" or "postcolonial" seem merely to caricature precision. Time is no longer a question of cultural longitude, of where you are, but rather a psychological and experiential category that is now differentially constructed and that we take with us wherever we happen to be, which engages, absorbs, and clashes with or is modified by other times. Anthropologists wrestled with these problems in advance of the current wave of fashionable postcolonial theory, because they became aware of the inadequacy of their own discipline's categories and hence needed to rethink not just the still ideologically loaded self/other distinction but also the extent of ineradicable and multidimensional complexities within the self.[49]

In this new global context, where performances can travel anywhere and videos can substitute for "being there," translated, transtemporal, and transcultural performance no longer takes place or speaks for that other, exotic and geographically remote, ultimately resistant and incomprehensible, alienatingly other cultural space.[50] These appropriations are already within us. So there is a different kind of urgency and need to understand them. When we encounter the exotic we find that it has already responded to, incorporated, and transformed our own experiences. When we now seek it out, we come up against an appropriation of our "own" culture, which we then reappropriate in our act of interpretation, as we could never have done without that passage through the

## Intercultural Signs

foreign. In this new sense the foreign really is already inside us as an aspect of ourselves. One word for this silent companion, this other side of ourselves, is the unconscious.

The performance style that Kott derides as "mock Kabuki" (it has nothing to do with Kabuki and hence cannot mock it) and as "fake Japanese and fake Shakespeare" and that others categorize as orientalist, consists of intercultural signs in a new practice of theater that is responding to, and creating, that postcolonial and postmodern culture as an expression of the reality of contemporary life. Mnouchkine produces a radical alienation of the expectations we bring to the performance of Shakespeare's works. The result is a reinvigoration of the performance texts. The supposition that place and time, or simply, history, have been sacrificed to a superficial and eclectic aestheticization is based on a particular reading of the dynamics of such performance. The attempt to forge an aesthetic by means of cultural bricolage is here understood as a desocialization that removes from the texts their potentially distressing specificity. What is then left, the argument goes, may be visually striking, but it is mere style.

Many critics see Mnouchkine's appropriating development of East Asian style, no matter how aesthetically persuasive it may be, as leading to a desocialization of the plays through a concentration on typifications and the ritualistic, taking them out of history, whereas what interests me is the access they offer to another level of comprehension in respect to how social beliefs shape character and the plot of history. No matter what her subjective intentions may have been, she shows us what we do not otherwise see. Bradby and Williams quote Mnouchkine, "Shakespeare is not our contemporary and must not be treated as such. He is distant from us, as distant as our own profoundest depths." Yet this can just as well be read, not as disinterest in present social relevance, but rather as an enquiry into what shapes behavior on a different level of apprehension.[51]

Furthermore, it is possible to see another connection with Brecht's view of Shakespeare's characters as uncontemporary and therefore more relevant, because we can then appreciate better the forces that have shaped their emotions. Brecht wanted to historicize the characters, not dissociate sensibility. In an otherwise excellent book, Richard Halpern is mistaken in linking Eliot's and Wyndham Lewis's defamiliarizing stress on the "primitive" Shakespeare with Brecht's interest in non-Western theater, if only because it is impossible to think of Brecht's response to Japanese and Chinese theater in the context of colonialist encounters with Third World forms, or of the extremely sophisticated Japanese and Chinese drama in that category. Had this been the case, there would have been no East Asian appreciation of Brecht's response and no dialectics of acculturation. These matters were far more complex and overdetermined.[52]

Mnouchkine appears to essentialize, to concentrate on an extreme externalization of the emotional life that no longer locates and explains it in relation to historical experience. But when these emotional states are so compellingly reimagined and when such performance shatters our perceptual habits, we have the opportunity of reperceiving the misunderstood familiar, because we really are seeing it for the first time. What Mnouchkine does is an extension of what Brecht imagined, partly realized, but largely left undone: the development of an aesthetically compelling style, that gracefulness, which enables us to appreciate a truth obscured by habituation. We then automatically resocialize the gestures that abstract from the conventions of representation. We read them through our own experiences, since that is the only way they can signify for us, and only the alienating enticement of the style can provoke us to this response.

Ariane Mnouchkine's remarkable theater developed possibilities suggested by the Asian stage, by Artaud, and by Brecht's dramaturgy. That she "learned" from Brecht is as obvious as that she abandoned the "Brechtian" dramaturgy that had helped to shape productions like 1789 and L'âge d'or, which employed one form of historicization in shaping the present from the perspective of the future. Letting go of the fashionable "rationalist" dramaturgy was an essential step in realizing its own repressed possibilities, then socially unrealizable. Perhaps this is what she meant by saying Brecht did not offer a form but a "vision" of theater.[53]

These issues are critically divisive, aesthetically delicate, and theoretically important. Brecht's impact on French theater and intellectual life in the fifties is well known and extensively documented.[54] Mnouchkine rightly insisted that aesthetic realism was a perversion of Brechtian realism and was attracted by Brecht's call for developing the art of spectating (Zuschaukunst). In several contexts she refers to the importance of "oriental theater" for Artaud and Brecht, as well as others.[55] Comparing Brecht and Artaud, Mnouchkine finds that Brecht had theorized in a way that often applied to all types of theater but that Artaud, less politi-

Intercultural Signs

cal and more metaphysical, had a deeper understanding of the function of the actor.[56] Artaud is usually invoked, with some justification, as offering the stronger impulse for her later theater, as she moved away from Brecht. But quite apart from the compatibilities between Artaud and Brecht to which I allude, Mnouchkine never read Artaud.

At least that is what she said to Peter von Becker in an interview for *Theater Heute 1984* conducted after her Shakespeare cycle had been shown in Berlin. So we are not dealing with documentable, conscious appropriations on the basis of (theoretical) study of specific texts, but rather with the effect of certain prevalent ideas on the cultural imagination, hence with re-creating. Of course that is what Brecht and Artaud also did. So while Mnouchkine understandably moved away from the (academically) constricted and socially authorized version of Brechtian theater, she developed what it could not then realize. This is partly corroborated by her objections to what she calls the "misinterpretation" of Brecht that consists of thinking he did not want to make theater believable, to create the effects of anger, joy, sensuality, love, hate as something whose representation was credible. Mnouchkine insists that was not part of Brecht's theory. He never said this. He stood for not deceiving people.[57] She developed what Artaud and Brecht held in common, as well as the neglected possibilities of their methods.

The brilliant systematization of gesture in *Le Théâtre du Soleil*, whose codification is not rigid and that faced the same problem of continuance that Brecht scarcely had time to address, rests on a vivid and original presentational style that, far from merely being a contemporary orientalizing aestheticism, probes and externalizes the character's or the situation's contradictions. Such visualization does not lead back to an inviolate, centered self but instead functions in order to help us understand how that self is the product of cultural attitudes and ideological structures.

In the famous battle scene at the end of *Henry IV*, Part I, the culminating duel between Hotspur and Prince Hal is conventionally performed, with more or less fustian, as a credible clash of swords demanded by the dominant realist aesthetic grounded in mimetic convention. In filmed versions of such battle scenes, the imagination is assassinated as horses gallop, blood spurts, and broad swords disembowel. But Mnouchkine's production, like East Asian theater, goes to the heart of the matter (see figure 3, p. 59). Throughout their encounter, Hal and Hotspur are seated opposite each other. They scarcely move. The martial character of the engagement is barely but unmistakably suggested: a red thread held in the mouth. They relate more as lovers than as combatants, stretching out to touch one another.

Such radical gestural defamiliarization, however, instantly reveals not only the otherwise invisible structure of the society within which they exist, invariably elided in conventional productions, and whose internalized ideology they articulate, but also shows how such internalization shapes both character and its unconscious. Although Hal's defeat of Percy may represent the necessary replacement of feudal separatism by incipient absolutism, it is conducted not as an anachronistic revelation of national destiny, the usual schema, but rather as a struggle among equals who are therefore interchangeable and structurally more beholden to each other than to their respective historical positions, no matter on what terms these are subsequently constructed. These are not just opponents, they are also each other's most precious ally.[58]

The historical positions, the whole destiny of history, are beyond their ken. Mnouchkine's style, concentrating upon the person yet refusing mimetic conventions and, instead, externalizing unconscious structures of feeling, enables us to comprehend the ideological complexity of social fact and cultural attitude. This is all accomplished by revisualizing the nature of subjectivity that is disintegrated by defamiliarizing patterns of gesture that then reassemble a differently positioned individual. The audience is compelled to become aware of the conventions that have hitherto structured their own thinking and their subjectivity. Mnouchkine and Brecht have shown that developing a gesturally sophisticated theater on no account need entail the neglect, let alone the abandonment, of speech as the property of conscious individuation, for she preserves the Shakespearean text.

If we allow such a reading of her performance text, something more is involved than a reduction to the aesthetic and, objectively, an escapist preoccupation with orientalist effects. Even if Kennedy is right about the subjective intentions, I still wonder if his assumption holds up: "Mnouchkine was concerned with style, and substituted a powerful aesthetic experience for a social one."[59] Apart from my specific reading of Mnouchkine's production, there remains the question whether or not we can ever separate a powerful aesthetic experience from a social one. I suspect that this is not possible, unless you define them down, whereby

Intercultural Signs

the "social" becomes a specifically targeted political message, and the "aesthetic" is understood as an isolated category of experience, outside history and unconnected to the unconscious. Since that is inconceivable because we cannot lobotomize our socially constructed repressions, we must conclude that what we call "aesthetic experience" is inseparable from the intensity of feeling that accompanies the discovery of a truth.[60] A cognitive gain is always entailed, and it cannot be achieved unless accompanied by an awareness of how the self is positioned. If that does not happen, we are talking about a different order of experience, where the shallower pleasure derives from avoiding an investigation of the self. Although the creators of such self-pleasuring surrogates are handsomely rewarded in social life, the experience should not be confused with the more demanding and disturbing encounters.

Kott's response to Mnouchkine's performance must derive from an antipathy toward what he perceives as an impermissible mixing of styles, from a resistance to the attempt to poach and draw on aesthetic conventions from outside your own tradition in order to extend the available expressive language within it. He differentiates between Japanese directors settling Shakespearean plot into their own representational conventions, although perhaps overlooking the extent to which the consequent performance style can seem disruptive and impermissible to a traditionally minded Japanese spectator, and Mnouchkine's aesthetic eclecticism.

This problem can be considered in two ways: either as a rejection of the possibility of developing culturally hybrid styles, or as a "subjective" reluctance or inability to deal with what is being shown. This second possible objection can only be overcome if the resulting performance appears aesthetically and intellectually convincing by itself, without recourse to any consideration of points of origin for the proxemic and visual devices employed, which it clearly did not for Kott, or if the spectator is sufficiently familiar with how the appropriated aesthetic signs originally function. This seeks something more than a superficial acquaintance with performative styles in other cultures, mere familiarity with their appearance, and presupposes a readiness to enquire what lies behind those appearances and hence how those cultural forms can be reinvigorated. To put the matter directly, if you do not understand enough to reposition what you are seeing, you cannot interpret it. The failure of interpretation then lies with the spectator's lack of familiarity with other cultural codes, of sufficient confidence to reread them and hence to appreciate the purpose of their employment in the different context and the potential intercultural consequences. It is never a question of reading correctly, since reading is as hazardous as writing, but of not foreshortening, of doing justice to these mutual appropriations.

## VI

Let us look at an example of Shakespeare in Japan, where the text is not so much translated, indeed it is more or less abandoned, but rather the basis for an elaboration of a traditional performance style. We can then consider how Mnouchkine's innovations relate to what is accomplished here and in other East Asian productions. I wish to discuss some techniques in a version of *The Merry Wives of Windsor*, loosely based on Shakespeare's plot, by the Mansaku Company, in the style of the comic *kyogen* (wild) plays of the Noh theater, called *The Braggart Samurai*, subtitled *Kyogen Falstaff*, performed during the 1994 Hong Kong Arts Festival and subsequently taken to Europe.[61]

*The Braggart Samurai* transfers Shakespeare's verbal plotting into Japanese visual acting. Played by Nomura Mansaku, Falstaff, a masterless samurai with two servants bearing traditional names from the kyogen plays, Taro and Jiro, has a huge, almost circular black beard, a large backward-pointing conical black hat and a grandiose belly swathed in bright red, a rotund figure on top of black trousered and incongruously nimble legs, as if the head, functioning as path to the belly, and the belly as the incarnation of inextinguishable appetite, were transported by the quite separate agency of the legs. They embody the will to pleasure and have thoroughly understood their only function is to maneuver the belly into the best position for indulging it.

So the body is divided into three parts. Each leads its separate life, but in the service of a central appetite. This is prodigiously imagined. It would be possible to describe this reimagined *Kyogen Falstaff* as a sequence of *lazzi*, because Japanese comic performance, meticulously elaborated, could be analyzed in such terms, provided we appreciate where the differences lie. Shakespeare is not translated into Japanese so much as into this language of gesture that speaks, as it were, with a Japanese accent and is made possible by the imaginative conventions of Japanese theater. It is as if the elaborate lazzi of commedia dell'arte slapstick acting were taken aside, put under the critical microscope, analyzed, disassembled, investigated in their component parts, slowed down, and then reimagined in this other cultural style. Slowing things down, of course, has the effect of speeding them up. The diminution of tempo is entirely relative and in this other choreography everything is intensified. When you slow things down, your attention to detail must be even more meticulous, there is no room for fudging, probably also not much for extemporizing because every gesture is so carefully grafted into and part of a complete choreography.

Falstaff demands sake, usually drunk from a small cup. His two assistants hasten to bring a barrel. He has a huge wooden dish whose contents he swallows as soon as the assistants have poured sake into it. They have to pour theirs onto fans, trying to catch the sake before it runs off. Falstaff has soon emptied the barrel anyway. No gesture is repeated. Every step has a variation as the story unfolds. Such externalization needs no text, although enough of the linguistic code is employed to shape the direction of the plot, but this is no diminution because we are looking at another language.

Falstaff wants to seduce the two women. A husband, Ford, wishes to trap him, so he pretends to be a visitor in love with one of them. He asks Falstaff to test her infidelity and thereby make it easier for him to do so himself. Falstaff writes identical letters. "Mistress Ford" and "Mistress Quickly" receive them and determine to trick him. A laundry basket is brought in by his two household servants, facing each other, imagined pole over their shoulders, miming its weight as they sway into place across the stage. When Falstaff is then "discovered" by the supposedly unknowing husband, he is encouraged to hide in the basket that is then carried off.

Yet how is it carried off, because, of course, there is no basket? Falstaff walks out between the two servants on hands and feet, but with his great belly turned upward, and they move right round the stage, all three miming this action of carrying him off in a swaying basket like an upturned frog, a marvelously coordinated affair, to be pitched into the river, rolling out of the invisible basket until his head is stuck under a curtain and the rest of the massive body upended and in full view.

The second part consists of a masked festival. Omatsu (Mistress Ford) writes that they were regrettably interrupted and must meet again, and he accepts the invitation. She wears a fat-faced comic female mask, and he a very phallic red-faced mask with a huge protruding nose. There is a festival dance and much satirical singing. Finally the masks slip, the roles are unmasked, but Falstaff remains undefeated because, as he says, this belly cannot be subdued by chanting proverbs—that is to say, it cannot be subjugated by morality—and so the play ends with a undiminished celebration of insatiable appetite.

This abandonment or transferal of Shakespeare's primary linguistic code into a performance text, where the proxemic code predominates, can hardly be considered "fake Shakespeare." It is Shakespeare transplanted, rewritten, reimagined for Japanese comic acting that draws on the repertory of traditional theater and develops it beyond what it alone is capable of showing. Its intercultural comprehensibility is unquestionable, provided you have acquired a modicum of knowledge about the conventions of that aesthetic practice. The result is paradigmatic. A Japanese lack is alleviated by acculturating Shakespeare, and the whole point of these transactions is that everything is changed through this process, resulting in a heightened opportunity to envisage new expressive possibilities. This concentration upon acting through the body, repressed in the more verbally focused theaters of Western performance culture, which had gradually disciplined bodies through the device of language, drew Mnouchkine to reinvent these intentions, to uncover an expressive potential, and to suggest buried dimensions of repressed contradiction in Shakespeare's plays. On this level of performance the sophisticated proxemic code "musicalizes" and unfolds a new expressive and interpretive dimension of the play.

Among the most interesting Japanese attempts at developing intercultural performance have been Yukio Ninagawa's *Medea, Macbeth,* and *The Tempest,* also taken to the Edinburgh Festival, and Tadashi Suzuki's Togamura Theater's astonishing *Clytemnestra*. Suzuki has produced three versions of Greek plays: *The Trojan Women,* in traditional Japanese style, *The Bacchae,* in a Western style performance, and *Clytemnestra,* which he describes as "conceived in a contemporary style."[62] Suzuki has rewritten the story of Orestes' murder of his mother, drawing on some of the Greek versions. The result is unsettling, irritating, in a word, productive, and very Japanese, since Suzuki sees problems of contemporary Japanese culture, what he describes as the "decadence" of Japanese society, anticipated in aspects of the Greek plays (122). His play ends with the incestuous, murderous, and suicidal embrace of Orestes and Electra, simultaneously assassinated by the ghost of Clytemnestra who, in the final tableau, stares out across their prostrate bodies holding a blood-stained knife. Like Ninagawa, Suzuki uses contemporary popular songs that really shake up the aesthetic categories. Likewise, if you have heard it, you will not easily forget Ninagawa's dislocating montage of Handel's famous *Sarabande* as an insistent ground bass, sustaining dramatic tension in his Kabuki-style *Medea*.

I will return to Ninagawa, but Suzuki is particularly useful for our purposes because he has also written about his intentions and obviously thought deeply about the compatibility or complementarity of Japanese and Western theater. His view upon Western theater is most illuminating. He observes that in Western theater, "Gesture is tied intimately to the words being spoken; indeed words represent human gesture" (5). The gestural language of Japanese theater, by contrast, is not illustrative of the text, let alone absorbed into and subservient to it, but itself leads to "the creation of a fictional space, perhaps even a ritual space, in which the actor's body can achieve a transformation from the personal to the universal" (12).

What matters here is not any supposed transformation from the personal to the universal. Let us leave that question aside for the moment. Rather at issue is the insistence upon the actor's body as the means whereby, as the site where, any perceptual transformation takes place, which itself creates the special space it then explores. Like Brecht and Artaud, both Suzuki and Ninagawa are unimpressed by the gestural or proxemic codes of Western theater but were, from their position, fascinated by Western plots, which they proceeded to rewrite through, or inscribe upon, the bodies of their performers with astonishing and invigorating results. For these Japanese performers, their traditional acting techniques were self-evidently superior to anything in Western theater except its plots, but these too are then subjected to the primacy of the proxemic code. The results may be initially bewildering, but they are not dull.

How have dissenting Western performance theoreticians and directors reviewed possible relationships between body and space? Eugenio Barba has productive observations about Brecht and, perhaps surprisingly, Ikebana, the Japanese art of flower arrangement. This may not sound particularly promising, especially to orthodox or reductive readers of Brecht, but it will take us straight to Artaud whose ideas about theater are more compatible with Brecht's than most people realize. Artaud also, via Grotowski, leads us through to Grotowski's students, Barba and Brook, although separations and distinctions must be made.

Looking for the principles that might underlie the variety of performance styles in Asian theater, Barba has produced a helpful analysis of how the relationship of body to space is envisaged and practiced in Asian performance and of how these techniques, based on such principles, represent the embodiment of time. He is, of course, continuously looking for what contrasts with the assumptions of conventional Western performance style. Rather like Brecht and Artaud, Barba sees the Western actor as the "prisoner of arbitrariness," working without any real tradition, only with loose mimetic conventions, whereas the Eastern actor is given greater liberty by formal constraints, yet pays a price for them in terms of specialization.[63] One can see immediately that each is riven with the absence, hence the possibilities, of the other. Intercultural enquiry looks into precisely this opportunity, not by imitating anything, but by seeking out the informing principles. They are not especially easy to uncover in East Asian performance because there is no tradition of analysis among the practitioners of these forms.

Barba quotes a passage from Brecht's *Me-ti*, a collection of aphorisms in mock Chinese style that uses this disguise literally to mask his thoughts, for he is writing in the late thirties in Denmark and conscious of what is going wrong politically, but also—typical for Brecht—writing in order to get through to substantial theoretical matters while appearing to underplay their importance. The passage is entitled *The Great Method*, by analogy with the Confucian classic, *The Great Learning*. This is a kind of Daoist joke, which places your own opinions in the mouths of your opponents, because this great method is not that of Confucian moral rectification and preservation of social hierarchization, but rather its opposite, the method of thought in and as social process. Master Hü-jeh—Brecht's Chinese disguise for Hegel—observes, "Thought has great difficulty holding, for example, onto the concept of a flowerbud, since the thing so referred to is in a state of such impetuous change, is so urgently determined, while you are still grappling with the concept, not to remain a flowerbud but to turn itself into a blossom. For the thinker, the concept of a flowerbud is the concept of something which is eager not to be that which it is."[64]

Barba observes that Ikebana faces exactly this philosophical difficulty

## Intercultural Signs

with the use of concepts that appear to stabilize process, but sees the difficulty as a problem of representation, of how to use immobility to suggest movement, of how to turn time into space so that shapes in space are temporalized, unfixed, instead of time being placed, arrested, held down, and rectified. The strategy of the Japanese garden, like the Ikebana flower arrangement, is four-dimensional, exploring the invisible dimension of time.

Acting in Asian theater depends upon a similar principle of dynamic immobility that is achieved through the actor's mastery of the body. What we need to hold onto here is that when movement has apparently ceased, then it is at its most dynamic. I could cite as an example a performance of Noh plays by the Kita Noh company during the 1990 Hong Kong Festival of Asian Arts. One play, *Hagoromo*, a source for Pound and Yeats, contained one of those slow dance sequences during which the *shite* almost lapses into immobility.[65] But when he does so, the music begins to whirl around him. The dancer appears to stand still, yet everything is now in motion, and then the mind is most intensely moved. Barba has a nicely extreme example from the perspective of an eighteenth-century Kabuki actor who describes, in effect, how compression, restriction, what the Japanese term "holding back" or "accumulating" (*tameru*), how absence of movement is always thought of in terms of its capacity to produce the opposite effect. This actor was required to stand with his back to the audience during another's dance. "I do not relax," he said, "but perform the entire dance in my mind. If I do not do so, the sight of my back is not interesting to the spectator."[66]

What happens in all these techniques is, we may surmise, that the vestibular system is reorganized in order, sometimes literally and sometimes metaphorically, to refunction conventional or natural balance, to put normal corporeal dispositions into jeopardy. When this is accomplished, no matter in what particular performance style, the body is no longer just in space; it is, it has itself become space, the space of the imagination and of the unconscious. It has pulled spatial dimensions into itself and is thus transformed into an extraordinary means of representing dynamic tensions, oppositions, or contradictions.

The Noh theater, which appears statuesque and solemn to the untutored eye, is actually riven with tensions beneath a deceptive serenity. The musicians bounce their rhythms off each other, improvising syncopations, cutting in just ahead of time, as in a kind of slow-motion jazz performance, and the actors always move just out of time with the music. To a Japanese sensibility, dancing in time to the music must sometimes appear clumsy and dull. The figures in the play, who flow through these actors' bodies, are simultaneously dispersed across unsettled time, and times can be drawn together into one unbounded moment when multiple states of mind are simultaneously displayed and everything is seen at once. These are the effects that Mnouchkine seeks to achieve in her Shakespearean plays.

This simultaneous multiplicity is what Artaud meant when he spoke of the metaphysical force of these East Asian forms that disturb the boundaries of an accepted self—for that is what he wanted to do—and that unbalance all conventions of normality.[67] We have seen that Brecht used similar externalizing techniques, moments of apparent arrestation where a dynamic concentration pulls together psychic states that are normally compartmentalized and so kept apart, and then we are simply forced to consider the connections between them. In Chinese opera, movements always start in the direction opposite to the one they will finally take. In Balinese dance, codified gestures are classified as either strong or soft (*kras* or *minis*) and simultaneously set beside or against each other, the energy turning inward, the dance unfolding in the body, and never spreading in leaps and bounds across the stage as in a Western aesthetic. The contradictions are internalized and then unfolded, they are placed within.

Artaud is usually thought of as advocating a theater that makes a radical demand upon the psyche, producing extreme emotional states. We think of his metaphor of the plague that he associated with the East, calling it an oriental virus. Half-ironically claiming the authority of St. Augustine, the moralist Artaud also saw plague and theater as synonyms, engendering equally incurable infections.[68] But Artaud also welcomed laughter. He loved the Marx Brothers and of course admired Brecht, and he played Filch in the French film of *The Threepenny Opera*. When he speaks of Balinese theater, he is anxious to undermine the contemporary evaluations that stressed its religious origins and soothingly spiritual effects. Instead Artaud sees it as a "non-religious theater" (39) and stresses what he calls its "active metaphysics" (33) or, referring to the whole ensemble of performance, "this gestured metaphysics" (38). He also marks with such terms its distance from contemporary Western theater's concentration on ego-psychology. So it was neither religious

## Intercultural Signs

and consolatory, nor psychological and individually therapeutic. Instead, he saw Balinese theater as profane ritual. He welcomed it not just, or so much, as a form that concentrated upon exploring the emotions, but as one whose "gestures are always ultimately aimed at the clarification of a state of mind or mental problem" (43) and by which "we are led along intellectual paths towards reconquering the signs of existence" (45).

Brecht's plays are full of emotionally powerful moments because of the skill with which he takes the mind apart, uncovering, in a flash of unforgettable insight, the repressions lodged in the social unconscious. Artaud's theories called for a theater that would not merely frighten its audience but also explain, through a profane ritual and a systematic depersonalization of the individual into gestures, why such depersonalization has taken place (40). Although they do this with decidedly different emphasis, both theories, and contrary to common belief also at times the practice of Brecht's theater, advocate a gestural language that shuns or discounts representational convention, that comes from within the body, is expressed through it, and uncovers the forces that have structured it, and that is intended to create viscerally disturbing effects.[69] What Suzuki describes as a move from the personal to the universal, and Artaud explains in terms of a metaphysical force that disturbs the accepted boundaries of the self, can be seen as an escape from the preoccupation with conscious ego-psychological mimetic representation in order to envisage what lies beneath the surface of appearances, shaping what our language calls our "self."

What so impressed English critics in the Japanese Toho Company's *Macbeth*, directed by Yukio Ninagawa, was the emotional force of an acting practice that draws on a repertoire of formalized but not standardized gesture. It employs a gestural language whose strength depends on its consciousness of body as the primary site for exploring the emotions, but that has been able to shed, or escape from, the standardized conventions because its engagement with a "foreign" text encourages it to reimagine its own tradition's proxemic conventions. Ninagawa's production, in terms of a Japanese aesthetic, is as revolutionary and distressing to traditional minders of Japanese acting conventions in the old, and on their own terms still wonderful, theatrical forms as Mnouchkine's was unsettling for Western lovers of "Shakespeare" even, as we have seen, rattling Jan Kott.[70]

Likewise the Chinese version of *Macbeth* in the style of kunju opera was so disruptive of that opera's conventions the performers encountered considerable technical difficulties in stretching or reimagining their techniques to accommodate the unfamiliar material.[71] There are suggestively different Buddhist resonances in both Ninagawa's and the kunju versions of *Macbeth* that, especially when dealing with Shakespeare's witches but also on a more abstract interpretive level, result in what, particularly in the context of the Chinese performance, suggests a Buddhist-accentuated, or repositioned, philosophical materialism that some might associate with the "postmodern." Efficacious intercultural performance, what I am calling the intercultural sign, is most noticeable by the distress it causes, by its ability to disrupt "aesthetic" conventions that themselves mask ideologically protected presuppositions.

Brecht's *The Good Person of Szechwan*, performed in the "style" of Sichuan opera also constituted something like a revolution within the conventions of that form. Chinese critics described this extraordinary 1987 production as nothing less than a new stage in the development of Chinese drama.[72] Knowledge in China of Brecht's response to Chinese theater has the effect of challenging directors and dramatists to reimagine the potential of their own traditional forms, so that aspects of the traditional opera can be brought to bear on "spoken drama," which is associated with Western theater, has a problematic status, and is still in development. This happens because the transactions include and move through Brecht.[73] The term "dialectics of acculturation" seeks to encompass such interactive processes.

In Ninagawa's production Lady Macbeth was played by Komaki Kurihara, and she fascinated English critics.[74] They were particularly impressed by the intensity of her performance, by her ability to figure apparently contradictory emotional and psychological states, thus bringing to light the invisible repressions that energized the figure. Leonard Pronko has drawn attention to specific qualities of this production, of the effect of the text in performance, crucial to intercultural theater and that literary scholars, focused on their readings of purely textual events, tend to forget. He remarks how Kurihara performed "the sleepwalking scene one has dreamed of but never seen in the West."[75] Pronko also observed a particular effect in Mnouchkine's Shakespeare that he correctly relates to a Japanese practice. He remarks of the unconventional speech patterns in *Richard II*: "Meaning is communicated by music of speech as much as it is by denotation of words. This cannot happen, I think, in a realistic context where psychological concerns are foremost."[76]

Here we find another point of contact with Brecht, although Mnouchkine herself was in all likelihood unaware of it. The third production of *Man Equals Man*, which Brecht directed in 1930, is recognized as one of the defining events in the development of his theater. This production was unquestionably shaped by his response to Kabuki aesthetics as demonstrated in performances he had just seen in Berlin. One of the estranging effects noticed by critics who did not necessarily appreciate its aetiology, and merely registered its impact, was how Peter Lorre, playing Galy Gay, heightened certain sentences by calling them out against the normal rhythms of speech. This drew attention to another level of awareness, to what the "character" does not know about himself, to what is no longer certain, to what "character" cannot clearly encompass as it changes and adapts to the pressure of events, to what, in other words, can be located in his unconscious as it is constructed and constrained by his acquiescence to the demands of social character, to becoming what his culture requires him to be.[77]

This capacity for visualizing contradictions and externalizing states of repression was the main reason Brecht found East Asian acting so suggestive. If this is also held to demonstrate, as is constantly asserted of Brecht's theater, that "psychological concerns" are not foremost, then that only applies to the egopsychology, which is amenable to realist or naturalist acting. It does not apply to externalizations of the unconscious, for which a precondition is escaping, at some level or other, from the constraints of realism.

So it is not a coincidence that Kurihara, almost at the same time she was performing Lady Macbeth, gave the best performance of Shen Te / Shui Ta in *The Good Person of Szechwan* I have ever seen. Koreya Senda brought his Haiyuza Theater's production to the 1986 International Brecht Festival in Hong Kong. What she did was allow the spectators to sense the repressions that finally result in the invention of that other self and that are reversed when she embodies the other role. She showed each figure as riven with the contradictions that are brought to the surface in the other, without recoursing to the simple binary oppositions that ruin the sophistication of Brecht's play in so many thoughtless productions. She made sense both of the imagined figure and of the play's dilemma, through this ability to show how it is possible to be constructed as both gentle and violent at the same time, because in its other dimension the "silent" language of gesture reveals the shaping force of the social unconscious, which the "character" can only express or experience but cannot "herself" understand.

The invasion of cultural material from another culture can, in the hands and minds of artists of this calibre, produce such a creative revolution. But why does it take place and what does it accomplish? In all of these examples, the conventions of representation are surely alienated and reimagined. This is no less the case with Japanese and Chinese productions of Shakespeare, or Brecht, within the conventional paradigms of their traditional forms. What looks to the Westerner like an adaptation of a much admired classic into an unfamiliar, externalizing East Asian performance style, and is then either appreciated or dismissed, seems to the East Asian spectator like an assault upon the conventions of traditional theater. So what Mnouchkine does is not greatly unlike what Ninagawa or Suzuki do. Kott is mistaken in thinking Japanese performances are more authentic, or less "fake," than her so-called orientalist imitations. Kurosawa's marvelous *Throne of Blood*, which draws so successfully on Noh theater techniques, is a film, using the resources developed in that Western invention, and not a Noh play. In terms of traditional Japanese theater, he has decisively shifted or alienated its procedures, and the music often sounds as Western as Japanese, offending purists. Kurosawa was notoriously unable to find Japanese backing for his provocative films, eventually only gaining support from Western directors such as Coppola and Spielberg. The result is indeed compelling, but it is accompanied by methods that are not fundamentally different from Mnouchkine's procedures.

The new material enables these artists to reimagine their familiar forms or texts and get through to what representational conventions have repressed, to their buried potential, to the aesthetic repressed, to what may not be shown or even acknowledged. In this context, Brecht's rejection of "psychology" must itself be understood as a partly repressive gesture, necessitated by contemporary ideological rhetoric, for what he in fact rejects is egopsychological theory, and what he appreciated and adapted from East Asian theater was a means of getting behind mimetic

Intercultural Signs

representational assumptions and revealing the invisible shaping force of social character and the social unconscious.

The solemnity and tempo of Japanese acting is defamiliarized for its audiences and something of an earlier impact recaptured. At issue here is not "just" performance, a matter of performance style, but the whole question of how we read what is shown to us. The conventions for reading Japanese and Chinese theater need to be challenged.[78] In the epilogue I give an intercultural reassessment of the capacity of the Noh theater, through a rereading of a kyogen play, that departs from a conventional Japanese practice of interpretation, but sees it within a Buddhist context. At least by the Tokugawa period this theater had been refunctioned as a form of social ritual, part of whose meaning lay precisely in its exclusivity. Interpretation of these plays was ritualized as well, and that is how they are still largely read in Japanese criticism.

In Western performance these reimaginings, as a result of an encounter with an East Asian aesthetic of performance, enable the spectator to escape the all-too-familiar Western expressive conventions and to uncover the buried potential of the text, what can no longer be so easily seen because we have been habituated by style. In East Asian performance, the primary, gestural language is reimagined because it is interrogated by the foreign text and is challenged to prove adequate to it. Kennedy observes of Ninagawa's *The Tempest* that it did not just accommodate Shakespeare to Japanese sensibilities but also challenged "Japanese spectators to question both codes."[79] The result is a disturbing gain in expressivity. In each case the process of acculturation occurs because it gives access to a buried potential in the self, to what has been culturally repressed, because it uncovers the force of the social unconscious. The intercultural sign, at its most suggestive, is a function of the unconscious. The answer to Kennedy's call for a theory of cultural exchange must be sought in explanations of this kind.

In 1979 in Beijing, Brecht's *Life of Galileo* accomplished what no Chinese play could possibly have done. In simple political terms it was, for the audience and the participants, not about "us" but about "them" and therefore not really our responsibility, while in psychological terms the alienatingly unfamiliar eases the painful process of self-examination. The real shock, however, is not caused by an encounter with the disturbingly unfamiliar but by an encounter with the far more disturbing, all-too-familiar and half-acknowledged repressed.

A further refinement of this process, and a further explanation of its efficacy, occurs when this encounter with the alienated self through the foreign also involves an encounter with cultural forms or ideas that originated or flourished in one's own culture, were transmitted to and transformed by a foreign culture, and then returned as an alienating echo or transmutation of undeveloped inherent possibilities.

Sometimes the only way of engaging with one's own cultural past lies in its alienation not just by but through the foreign. So the response to striking, alienating cultural forms from another culture is not necessarily a formal matter, an extension of the range of expressivity, but rather is interwoven with the unconscious of one's own culture. We can observe such a process within one culture alone, as it discovers unfashionable aspects of its own past, but when this process occurs between global macrocultures, such as developed in East Asia and the West, we face potentially significant discoveries about developments in those cultures that offer us the opportunity of reevaluating the extent of their compatibility.[80]

Such appropriations and reappropriations challenge cultural self-understanding. Successful intercultural performance occurs when it helps to overcome a cultural or aesthetic lack or repression. The intercultural sign releases a potential within the performance text that has been dulled by convention or elided by ideological preference. Because it derepresses, it challenges our cultural presuppositions.

Those performances will be most successful where the reimagined performance style or the appropriated text resonate with a neglected capacity. Mnouchkine's appropriations of East Asian style feed this desire, even hunger, reinforced by the predominance of linguistic conventions in Western theater, for aesthetically sophisticated visualization. The language of gesture, its wordless eloquence, speaks through the performers' bodies and shifts the mimetic presuppositions that so often govern the linguistic code, undermining or contextualizing the ideologies through which we read it, hinting at structures that frame and transgress or control the extent of the characters' self-comprehension.

Suzuki calls the transpersonal, "universal"; Artaud speaks of "metaphysical" forces. Such terms metaphorize structures that both shape us and escape our understanding. We can "materialize" these metaphors and speak of an internalized social or historical unconscious, which

## Intercultural Signs

Erich Fromm would call "social character." This unconscious allocates the space for acceptable identity, thus producing the repressions that such internalization necessitates, and helps to explain the embodied contradictions that textual anthropology can uncover, as the intercultural sign challenges these processes.

# 3

## DESIRE,

## LAUGHTER, AND

## THE SOCIAL UNCONSCIOUS

### I

If reading is text- and self-construction, then we must attend to the psychoanalytic. Interpretation is relational, conducted through transference and countertransference. Preferences must be justified, since mutually exclusive theories compete. These position: the text's relation to author and reader; interpretive needs; the psyche as primarily drive- or desire-oriented, impelled by instinct or drawn by longing; the personal, the social and familial, and their interaction; the metaphors "unconscious" and "conscious"; the unconscious as textually mediated.

Reading Malinowski on the Trobriand islanders, or Mead on Samoa, or Geertz on the Balinese, or Lévi-Strauss on the Tupa-Kawahib, or Brecht's construction of Shen Te / Shui Ta, or Shakespeare's construction of Theseus and Hippolyta, or Mozart's of Don Giovanni, our interpretations will reveal predilections, even if these are uncertain to us.[1] Gary Waller observes, "If either (or a mixture of) bio-psychological and cultural layering makes up what Freud called our unconscious, then Shakespeare's comedies are among those works of literature that draw most deeply on what that often contentious term stands for."[2] Psychoanalytic readings proliferate, yet inflections I find productive are not widely employed. Without trawling through all the arguments, I wish to differentiate, relating them to various theoretical possibilities. Some descriptions will briefly sketch, or simply allude to, relatively familiar positions. Other discussions will be more detailed, where arguments are less well known.[3]

In *Shakespeare's Personality*, Norman Holland introduces what looks empirically and theoretically like the unverifiable: the Shakespearean texts manifest a personality structure that energizes them.[4] In classic Freudian symptomology the text externalized and worked through, in

## Desire, Laughter, the Unconscious

more sophisticated versions displaced, the author's problems. Here two moves differentiate the earlier Freudian argument, recognized as inadequate to the dynamic of a literary text, even before critical theory began to reshape our understanding of textuality.

On the one hand, the author is replaced by an author function, hence the reader's wishes construct the text (3). Furthermore, personality, once a "unified self," and for Freud still "bounded by the individual's skin," is now seen as "more like the Renaissance concept in being inextricably involved with its social surround" (4). So analysis is potentially displaced onto the cultural formation, read through the socially focused personality as well as the reader's preferences, although just how these connect remains unclear.

On the other hand, Shakespeare's personality, projected into the plays, is read as constructed, not by an author function or a declared reader's preference, but by an empirically evidenced familial dynamic. A younger brother interrupts the closeness to his mother. Hence early relationships with women result in complications, later overcome. Together with the father's financial and social failure, this creates an intense object hunger. Fixated by anxiety over betrayal, Shakespeare "justifies and defends his aggression by idealizing the established social order, although not without ambivalence" (7ff.). He "shared the aggressive male-male values of his society" and "construes his world as split between male and female, parent and child, private and public, love and war, word and deed, theater and polity, play and reality." Yet, he overcomes personal fracturing "by imaginatively being on both sides" (15).[5]

Although specifically located in familial relations, it is not immediately evident how such a personality structure really elucidates the texts. Its self-construction, also textual and circular, seeking corroboration in what it presupposes, has become virtually contentless because these universalizations or abstractions seemingly extend to everything. Consider another example, presuming a firmly located authorial "personality" and structure of belief, which is perhaps more easily inspected since it is closer to us. Contesting what she considers a standard reading of *The Good Person of Szechwan*, Elizabeth Wright constructs the author as a fiction of the interpreted text.[6] Brecht's one-dimensional figures—the woman is idealized, the man not—depend on reductive Marxist presuppositions inattentive to the culturally and linguistically constructed subject within patriarchy, especially as explained by Lacan. Illustrating the values of such an author, the plot reveals an underestimated problem. Wright does not examine the text. She discusses views about it. The behavior of the good person represents the necessary masquerade of the dissembling woman in patriarchy, as described by Joan Rivière, who must conceal her "male" ambition by "female" coquetry if she wants to be successful.[7] The good in the good person exists only in the imaginary of a split subject, itself the product of the symbolic order. The play, in this reading, shows no understanding of the relationship between the sexes outside class. Motherhood is not alienated by Brecht; it is simply presupposed. Goodness is represented as naturally female. The man may be rational, decisive, and nasty. Such gender-specific attribution of character is a form of sexism. What more could be expected from the macho Brecht? The author's sexism, reinforced by the master knowledge of Marxism, dominates all forms of alternative discourse, reducing the constitution of the subject to a particular historical dimension, instead of the universal process revealed by Lacan.

Yet the role division in *The Good Person* is not naturalized, since it represents historically produced fictions. Even Brecht remarked in his *Work Journal* that Shen Te is not stereotypically good, nor is Shui Ta stereotypically bad, that merging the two figures, their disintegration into each other is reasonably well conveyed.[8] This implies something evident in the text, namely, that each "figure" embodies the other's repressions and is always double. "Shen Te" has at least five voices, although lazy productions frequently sacrifice all of this to simplistic binary oppositions.[9] The play figures the social unconscious, enabling us to understand why it is unconscious. The rhetoric in Wright's text reveals her presuppositions. She says time and again that "Brecht" sees or misses this or that. But the name of the author is merely a metaphor justifying the fictional figure needed to authenticate a particular interpretation. Speaking with Foucault, the author simply functions as a device to justify the exclusions that are then practiced in his name.[10]

Wright accuses Brecht of practicing a male essentialism with Marxist characteristics. Could we not just as well say, with Lacan, that in this play knowledge only progresses so long as the questions of the hysterical woman prevail over the answers of the master?[11] This is why the patriarchal representatives of the symbolic order, the Gods, finally force Shen Te into the role of the hysteric, and why the play then concludes with a catalogue of questions.

## Desire, Laughter, the Unconscious

Constructing a character's unconscious is recognized as problematic. If characters are effects of writing, how can we treat "them" as real people? If the aesthetic or dramaturgy apparently restrains us to the level of individual character, we miss other opportunities for discerning an unconscious of the text or of the culture. The metaphorical density of a Shakespearean text seems to create a weave of meaning beyond the consciousness of the character. By convention a naturalist play cannot use language outside the character's capacity. An unconscious is differently suggested, as an effect of the necessary subtext, hence as an interpretive choice. Information is sometimes contained in stage directions or produced by evaluating what the character does: how Nora dances the tarantella, or what the macaroons variously signify. Reading such texts, we are caught up in a game of transference and countertransference that we must both play, if we are to read at all, and practice suspiciously. In the naturalist plays, Ibsen implies and Strindberg more directly formulates unconscious material.

The unconscious of the text, however, is constructed by the reader on the basis of textual evidence excessive to credible mimetic readings or internal consistency. Here the text shows more than it seems to know about itself. With the benefit of historical and cultural distance we can see what the characters and the author could not because they were too close to their problems. The moral solutions Ibsen favors will not solve his culture's problems. It is not enough for Torvald to improve his manners and be a nicer man. Critics who take Torvald to task, or observe the role is insufficiently realistic, are still caught up in that culture's problematic. The problem is not individual but structural and therefore not soluble on the level of individual morality. It points beyond the level of contemporary awareness, hence, we can speak, using this provocative metaphor, of the "unconscious" of the text. Macherey suggests readings of a work's unconscious where the narrative undoes the suppositions of its own plot. Conan Doyle's Sherlock Holmes stories exemplify how a text displaces cultural anxieties into a plot that appears to control them, because it does not comprehend their extent, probably thereby revealing the unconscious of his culture.[12]

In Strindberg's *The Father*, husband and wife have developed a way of living together, a compromise that covers up their problems, a form of coexistence that breaks down over their daughter's future.[13] The most striking characteristic in the relationship is that between wife/mother and husband/child. The Captain is fixated on mothers and mother substitutes.[14] He says this fixation derives from his "lack of will" (60). An unwanted child, he had no will. He was rejected by the loved mother. (In dyadic analysis, the mother is a powerful but ambivalent figure. She possesses a good and a bad breast.) For Schopenhauer, "will" is a metaphysical principle, the life force, blind energy, desire, libido. We can read this word "will" as code for desire and sexual drive.

Will Shakespeare's sonnets metaphorize the word and also show the psychological difficulties. Sonnet 135: "Whoever hath her wish, thou hast thy *Will*, / And *Will* to boot, and *Will* in overplus"; above all, Sonnet 143, which describes a sexual relationship and imagines it in terms of a child seeking his mother's protection:

> Lo as a careful huswife runs to catch
> One of her feather creatures broke away,
> Sets down her babe and makes all swift despatch
> In pursuit of the thing she would have stay;
> Whilst her neglected child holds her in chase,
> Cries to catch her whose busy care is bent
> To follow that which flies before her face,
> Not prizing her poor infant's discontent;
> So run'st thou after that which flies from thee,
> Whilst I, thy babe, chase thee afar behind,
> But if thou catch thy hope, turn back to me,
> And play the mother's part, kiss me, be kind.
> So will I pray that thou mayst have thy *Will*,
> If thou turn back and my loud crying still.

The abandoned lover, figured as frightened infant in Shakespeare's sonnet, seeks protection from the fear of this separation, of this loss of unity with the mother, of a compelling source of desire or pleasure whose strength only a sexual metaphor, satisfaction of the *will*, can adequately convey. But this feared loss of unity simultaneously and irrevocably constitutes the self, in an act of separation or alienation the self unconsciously longs first to obviate and then to overcome: "So will I pray that thou mayst have thy *Will*, / If thou turn back and my loud crying still." In Shakespeare's sonnet, just as in psychoanalysis, the child is also figured as the desire of the mother, as the mother's *Will* or, to use the Freudian technical term especially as developed by Lacan, as the *phallus*, the symbol of her own desire. This mother embodies the desire of others. To reembody her desire is the boy's wish after physical separation and the development of self-consciousness. This psychological loss—the forfeit of its comfort—is his greatest fear. To "satisfy" the mother's desire is, metaphorically, to refuse both individuation and maturation and to reject the Law of the Father that forbids this desire in the name of the social order.[15]

Reading *The Father* through a Shakespearean sonnet starts from a verbal "coincidence" and assumes both texts displace a problematic mother/child relationship, amenable to various theoretical explanations. The textual evidence is transparent—I have only cited a fragment, not intending a fuller analysis here—and the psychoanalytic theories are well known. Some would locate the explanation in the authors' private experiences and see the text as working through earlier inhibitions. Others might find these representations metaphorical displacements of overdetermined dissatisfaction.[16] Although one can argue which analysis is most satisfactory, and thereby reveal an element of personal choice, the connections are not themselves farfetched. My focus reveals a theoretical predilection, but it does not display an interpretive need. Violence is not done to the text. The references derive from it. In other words, the person of the reader is not, at least not predominantly, involved.

Another model of psychoanalytic reading differently constructs an unconscious for the character. Here the justification finally lies in the desire, more or less ironically acknowledged, for what satisfies a personality structure in the reader.[17] We would then have to decide whether reading from such a structure sufficiently elucidates the text. Holland offers an illuminating reading of Hermia's Dream by constructing the character as if she were a real person who, unfortunately, cannot be taken out of the text and questioned on the couch: "We have no way of knowing how much Hermia has heard through her sleep of Puck's talk about the charm of Lysander's eye . . . but I am willing to assume that some of this talk has percolated into her dream." Yet he concludes, "Hermia is working out with Lysander a much earlier, more formative relationship with a figure never seen, never even mentioned, in this comedy: her mother."[18]

Acknowledging and relativizing the presuppositions, as if this were the "clinical study of an adolescent girl" (85), he offers something like a "new critical" psychoanalysis, where computations of the latent and manifest and of developmental levels establish and balance out intrinsic meaning within the play.

He then explores the play, through a "transactive criticism" (86), not as an objective, separate reality but in relation to his own identity structure. Her dream figures his own puzzlement over "large questions of fidelity and possession between men and women" (86), or, more abstractly, "separation and fusion" (83). Holland detects a personal, unconscious need for an uncompromising love beyond sharing, and a fear of the loss that sharing might entail. These problems are expressed when the dream, and the play, figure a total demand on love or, as indicated by Lysander's distressing smile, tolerate change and infidelity. In what must surely be a truly unconscious move in this analysis, he, like the play, rejects "that kind of possessiveness—at least I consciously do" (88) while maintaining this moral theme is introduced by Egeus.

In other words, he aligns the "possessiveness" of love with the paternal claim over a daughter's future, something entirely different, especially if love takes the form of mutual sharing. For Egeus the kind of ownership entailed in money and class relations is more at stake than sexual "possessiveness," since the daughter is a pawn in a bourgeois social contract. Evidently such a psychoanalytic reading has little room for the cultural effect of socioeconomic structures on identity formation. The play shows "the lovers learn fidelity through their infidelities" (89), and Holland wonders how. Out of the mother's "first infidelity, most of us made the most basic fidelities" (89). Needing "coherence and unity in human relations" (90), he finds the play silent on this point.

This reading through "psychoanalytic identity theory" (91) and a personal identity structure finally turns out to be uncannily like, virtually identical with, the first "unmediated" reading that treated the characters and the world of the play as real. In both cases separation from the mother problematizes loss of fidelity. Although the characters may not be real, the reader transfers his reality onto them instead of asking, for example, what cultural needs these representations reveal. One conclusion must therefore be that what earlier masqueraded as psychoanalytic scientific objectivity was itself derived from a projected identity structure. Furthermore, psychoanalytic readings taken out of history and the culturally specific, and which do not seriously consider the variables of social character and the social unconscious will, like repressions, constantly repeat themselves.

If we would ground a psychoanalytically inflected reading in something other than a personal identity structure, as private as it is unassailable, we must locate that identity in relation to what is socially and culturally specific. Because of cultural difference, intercultural theater anyway renders this more problematic, or challenging. Those who retain a psychoanalytic interest more commonly take another route, assuming their model valid in all cultures and historical periods. Search for a lost mother substitute is considered a perennial phenomenon. Here we are close to Jungian archetypes, whose symbols have universal meanings.[19]

We need, in other words, a theory of the unconscious that starts from different presuppositions and moves into less familiar, perhaps more contentious, territory. Foucault's concept of the "positive unconscious of knowledge" offers a starting point, although it may at first seem psychoanalytically tangential. If we equate psychoanalysis with discerning and removing or obviating emotional or neurotic impediments to psychic health, then Bachelard's obstacles to the steady acquisition of knowledge, those blockages Foucault thought of as a *negative* unconscious, impeding better understanding, might at first seem a better analogy.[20] Starting from another model of knowledge acquisition governed by paradigm change across disciplines instead of gradual accretion within them through overcoming obstacles, Foucault's *positive* unconscious refers to what invisibly structures such paradigms in the first place. His epistemes are defined by these macrochanges on an "archaeological" level. If taken, or takable, into the territory of psychoanalytically inflected readings of texts, this would question or problematize direct transference and countertransference, unless we assume a level on which human nature does not change—hence a sixteenth-century textual effect explains a twentieth-century identity structure and vice versa—and rest our reading at that point. Most psychoanalytic theories of reading do make such assumptions.

Foucault's project implies other ones. He proposed to counter what could be called the steady state view of human nature in the human sciences through a combination of what he termed the countersciences of "psychoanalysis" and "ethnology." He cannot speak of anthropology because, in his terminology, that word has been affixed to the problematic that first arose after the collapse of the classical age: the discourse of the sovereign subject who believes himself ideologically and idealistically in command of his material, even though it is partly formed by what he cannot know about himself. Psychoanalysis and ethnology address this problematic because both engage directly with the unconscious, with what seems to lie beyond the representable and is therefore viewed as mythological.[21] Foucault appreciates how they reinforce each other's insights. His approach offers a way of rethinking the relationship between individual and cultural experience, so I wish to describe it.

Concerned with the dimension of the unconscious, psychoanalysis "disturbs from within the entire domain of the sciences of man," and ethnology questions them "from without" because it challenges our understanding of history. He argues we do not normally associate ethnology with historicity, which means the concept of an unfolding history, because ethnology is thought of as studying societies without history. This presumed absence of chronology, the assumed *ahistorical* nature of primitive or earlier cultures, is a value judgment from within modern culture.

Psychoanalysis and ethnology, together, cover the whole domain of the human sciences: "It was quite inevitable, then, that they should both be sciences of the unconscious: not because they reach down to what is below consciousness in man, but because they are directed towards that which, outside man, makes it possible to know, with a positive knowledge, that which is given to or eludes his consciousness" (378). Not a unique personal unconscious in its undivided inviolability but what underlies or lies outside it is the issue. This, in turn, suggests a more sharply focused view of historical material, a more productive way of reading it, by interweaving the perspectives of psychoanalysis and ethnology. When we attempt this, we can begin to see "the double articulation of the history of individuals upon the unconscious of culture, and of the historicity of those cultures upon the unconscious of individuals" (379).

If we can practice systematically such a procedure of reading, we will not be simply interpreting a text; in other words, we will not be uncovering a latent meaning of which the author was perhaps only partly aware but which is a kind of latent *intention* of the text. We will be reading it in light of how its unconscious structure establishes the conditions of its possibility. Then the thought occurs that such a procedure could be applied to any cultural material, not just to an individual in psycho-

Desire, Laughter, the Unconscious

analysis or to an apparently closed and delimited, ahistorical culture that is artificially isolated by the theory you apply to it. Then:

> One can imagine what prestige and importance ethnology could possess if, instead of defining itself in the first place—as it has done until now—as the study of societies without history, it were deliberately to seek its object in the area of the unconscious processes that characterize the system of a given culture; in this way it would bring the relation of historicity, which is constitutive of all ethnology in general, into play within the dimension in which psychoanalysis has always been deployed. In so doing it would not assimilate the mechanisms and forms of a society to the pressure and repression of collective hallucinations, thus discovering—though on a larger scale—what analysis can discover at the level of the individual; it would define as a system of cultural unconsciousness the totality of formal structures which render mythical discourse significant, give their coherence and necessity to the rules that regulate needs, and provide the norms of life with a foundation other than that to be found in nature, or in pure biological functions. (380)

Here Foucault naturally addresses the issues of his whole project; but he also proposes what we can call a method for historicizing the unconscious. The implication is that *every* culture has its unconscious that must be historicized, and *every* text needs to be read in terms of what structures its possibility of signifying, for what it does not directly say, for what it does not know about itself but makes available anyway. We would then be looking not so much at its hidden meaning, which can be teased out of it by interpretation, but at what creates the possibility for such hidden meanings in the first place.

It is not a question of seeing the individual as the place of expression for a group mentality; it is not a question of "cultural psychology" (380), just as it was not, to reiterate his term, a matter of psychoanalytic anthropology. Rather, the group and the individual

> intersect at right angles; for the signifying chain by which the unique experience of the individual is constituted is perpendicular to the formal system on the basis of which the significations of a culture are constituted: at any given instant, the structure proper to individual experience finds a certain number of possible choices (and of excluded possibilities) in the systems of society; inversely, at each of their points of choice

the social structures encounter a certain number of possible individuals (and others who are not [let's say this means the impossibility of other ones])—just as the linear structure of language always produces a possible choice between several words or several phonemes at any given moment (but excludes all others). (380)

Foucault's third counterscience is, therefore, linguistics, which investigates the structures available for thought through language. This explains why modern and contemporary literature is fascinated by language. A literature that takes language as its reality, rather than reality itself, draws attention "to the fundamental forms of finitude" (383), because it tests the limits of meaning. Such propositions offer productive methods for reading modern texts. The following passage quoted in chapter 1 to suggest a searching reading of Brecht's early plays could equally illuminate Beckett's *Endgame*, although intended in respect of neither author: "From within language experienced and traversed as language, in the play of its possibilities extended to their furthest point, what emerges is that 'man has come to an end,' and that, by reaching the summit of all possible speech, he arrives not at the very heart of himself but at the brink of that which limits him; in that region where death prowls, where thought is extinguished, where the promise of the origin interminably recedes" (383).

Leaving aside the preoccupation with "linguistics" and the theoretically self-conscious concern with structures of language, we can appreciate how such proposals, enabling us to historicize the unconscious, can apply across genres and aesthetic conventions and give us another purchase on historical material, acknowledging its unconscious yet not needing to hear or reach it through a resonance with the personal unconscious of the reader.

Texts that bridge epistemes are particularly revealing. For Foucault, *Don Quixote* and de Sade's novels mark the transitions, respectively, from the Renaissance to the classical, and from it to the modern episteme. In the first part of *Don Quixote*, the world obeys the commands of language because Don Quixote sees it through the texts of romance and tilts at windmills instead of opponents. In the second part this misrecognition becomes inescapable. Things no longer obey words. They must be differently described and organized. In de Sade's novels, "It is no longer the

## Desire, Laughter, the Unconscious

ironic triumph of representation over resemblance; it is the obscure and repeated violence of desire battering at the limits of representation. . . . Sade attains the end of Classical discourse and thought. He holds sway precisely upon their frontier. After him, violence, life and death, desire, and sexuality will extend, below the level of representation, an immense expanse of shade which we are now attempting to recover, as far as we can, in our discourse, in our freedom, in our thought" (210).

We could just as well place Mozart's *Don Giovanni* of 1787 in Foucault's episteme transition from the classical to the modern. De Sade's extraordinary texts were *prison* literature. Hence the violence of his desire, and the "outrageous" forms through which he expressed it, derive, both symbolically and in reality, from desire's systematic and enduring frustration, because it is in chains. And because it is enchained, the imagination rages. The mutual interference between the erotic and the political, and the practice of metaphorizing the latter through the former, and then confusing political and erotic freedom, especially in the Sadist version of the freedom of men to dominate women, and vice versa, characterizes this whole transition. De Sade's *Philosophy in the Bedroom* (1795), published as the work not only of the *anonymous* but also the *posthumous* author of *Justine*, contains within it a political pamphlet, felt apposite enough to be separately republished in 1848, entitled: *Yet another effort, Frenchmen, if you would become Republicans!*

Lovers of Mozart may be scandalized by this alignment with the notorious Marquis de Sade. They seem temperamentally, socially and culturally, utterly incompatible, as personally unlike each other as their work but, as contemporaries formulating the obsessions of their age, they share, although it was differently expressed, a fascination with the erotic and a sense of its investment in the political, as well as the topos of the conscienceless seducer perpetually in pursuit of self-pleasuring in defiance of all moral and social decorum. For de Sade, therapeutic cruelty within the home should moderate the violence of political life. His arguments, if unwisely abstracted from the texts, are specious and imply a domestic fascism. But his texts act out, in obsessionally physical terms, what *Don Giovanni* accomplishes psychologically: the right to abuse and abandon another person for the sake of one's own pleasure. Mozart's *Don Giovanni* offers more, but it is a fascinating embodiment of the most violent contradictions. To follow the variations of this story down the centuries is to understand how the frustrations of an age are similarly repressed but differently externalized. We can see both how the social unconscious is shaped and how it is historicized.

Don Juan's story has the status of a modern myth, a defining narrative, capable of endless reinvention. Like magnets to fantasy, Don Juan and Faust drew into themselves the dreams and frustrations of successive generations. They trace a history of the European unconscious. Tirso de Molina's educative dramatic narrative of 1632 concerning the wages of sin—where the offending transgressant is dragged into hell fire as an unquestionably satisfying physical solution for moral evil—transferred to Italy and the commedia dell'arte, for which there are scenarios.[22] Molière's *Don Juan or The Statue at the Feast* was first performed in 1665. He played Sganarelle.

Felt as a political play and subject to public, and probably self-censorship, Molière's work was not published until 1682. One hundred and twenty years before *Don Giovanni*, it also distances itself from the less complex, purely moralistic, earlier dramatic narrative. It works with a range of comic effects, from knockabout farce to sophisticated ethical questions, confronting a series of contradictions: between master and servant, man and woman, aristocracy and peasantry, morality and hypocrisy, religion and free thought, superstition and rationalism. This Don Juan is a *divided* figure with positive as well as negative qualities. The self-obsessed aristocrat *opposes* aristocratism's archaic defense of honor and position. He believes in *mathematical*, not revealed, religion. Challenging all convention, he recognizes no rules and none are capable of binding him. Sganarelle fears his power as a nobleman and his own dependence, his amorality and freedom from constraint. Breaking with previously unquestioned attitudes, this Don Juan represents a disturbing new phenomenon. Disruptive, unpredictable, dangerous, perceptive, frightening, obsessive, narcissistic, energizing, and attractive, he represents a new principle of self-interest that will guide and energize the emerging bourgeois class. He also incarnates untrammeled libido. He will not take "No" for an answer. In the end he is dragged into hell, but the world he leaves behind has been stood on its head.

Don Giovanni's erotic obsession begs to be psychoanalyzed: the great lover, pursuing women with such energy, is Narcissus wielding a rapier and only in love with himself. The consummate actor of only one role preys on the desire of women to be loved and so also plays to a secret masochism that he understands intimately. He can only overwhelm and then abandon them. Since there is no question of equality, love is not on his agenda. The Oedipal situation in Freud's favorite opera is obtrusive.[23] Don Giovanni slaughters the intervening father who returns to haunt him as a ghost, or stone statue, or internalized superego that, because it is defied, drags him to his death. This can be read in individual psychological terms as a perennial father/son conflict, or as marking always painful historical and cultural change. To kill the father is to escape from the past that can return to haunt you. This can be read as ideologically positive or negative, depending on the position within a power structure. When to invent or imagine the future involves rejecting the past, we can speak of revolution.

In the classical Freudian paradigm the opera encodes Mozart's troubled relationship with his own father who tried to control him. Guilt over symbolic patricide explains the suicidal defiance, the absolute refusal to repent. Unconscious wishes are externalized and exorcised in dramatic form, perhaps in an act of symbolic restitution. We can also see in Don Giovanni *another* aspect of the Oedipal problem. His inability to love is a defense against the fear of rejection, hence he can never stay long enough to risk it. The story of Oedipus began, after all, when he was abandoned, and the fear of such abandonment can produce the carapace of character armor that renders a person too difficult or obnoxious for others. Locked within himself, he has always been in hell and must sublimate this personal terror by punishing others. Elvira, Don Giovanni's nemesis, the unrestrainable woman, pursues him relentlessly because she hates herself for still loving him. Mozart's music articulates her complexity superbly, both to herself and others, exposing the agony of her wounded unconscious.

For Kierkegaard *Don Giovanni* epitomized the aesthetic consciousness for whom "the genius of sensuousness . . . is the absolute subject of music." His *Either/Or*, written in 1843, lies midway between Schopenhauer's and Nietzsche's vision of music as the purest expression of the will or Dionysiac spirit. The romantics had begun to amalgamate Don Giovanni with Faust, seeing in him a frustrated, inward-looking, *romantic* rebel, and then some of the sharper, more abrasive and difficult contradictions begin to soften. In *Mozart auf der Reise nach Prag* Mörike shows his death as a merging with nature, an illustration of the romantic sublime. E. T. A. Hoffmann's novelle *Don Juan* (1813) turns him into an idealist. Don Giovanni becomes more heroic, isolated by a curse, a less problematically representative figure. In other words, he becomes less political. That is how we encounter him in Richard Strauss, whose magnificent *Don Juan* (1889) celebrates the energy and the romantic yearning for fulfillment, evident in the protracted post-Wagnerian search for a resolution of the musical key, but does not register the complexities of the dramatic encounters, which is why, as Peter Conrad observed, the dramatic opera has been transformed into a tone poem.[24]

If we historicize it, Mozart's *Don Giovanni*, like Foucault's episteme-bridging texts, faces both ways. Representing aristocratic libertinism, provocatively parodied by the servant Leporello, it simultaneously externalizes a libertarian social unconscious. At the end of act I, the outrageous invocation by Don Giovanni, taken up by all the participants in this social dance, "*Viva la liberta*," like the whole opera, is multiply encoded. Compared with the static and spatializing *opera serie*'s elaboration of sentiment, the sonata form *dramatizes* music, freeing its kinetic potential, allowing complex, contradictory representations. Where the classical opera spatialized and hierarchized emotions, Mozart dramatizes time, and history permeates music. Contradiction and conflict are no longer socially and musically separated, but rather embodied within the same musical form, simultaneously differentiating character positions.

No matter what material they engage, such readings are not negotiated through a personal unconscious. They reveal an historical unconscious in operation that speaks through the characters and the form. It is indeed a combination of the psychoanalytic and the "ethnographic" that makes this palpable for us. The personal is not thereby obliterated, or exonerated, but situated, both in respect to the reader and to the read, by questioning all presuppositions and by inviting us to understand how, for example, libertinism and libertarianism can be articulated within the same music.

## II

A quite different approach to this problem of understanding identity formation as an historicized function of the social unconscious lies in Freud's celebrated analysis of laughter and its relation to the unconscious. Precisely because the "personal" is inextricably involved in "read-

## Desire, Laughter, the Unconscious

ing" jokes, we have a special opportunity to recognize how our personality, or identity, is structured for us. Perhaps I can put it like this: the more "personal" and automatic the response may appear, or the funnier the joke, the more culturally determined it will probably be. Freud's analysis, so remarkably specific, is sometimes overdetermined in ways he could not appreciate since he lived within the culture that shaped both material and analysis. Looking at this evidence again, with the sympathetically distanced eye of the anthropologist-critic, affords insight that helps us appreciate the complex dynamics of reading and of reader construction.

Freud quotes Shakespeare to illustrate the dynamic between told, teller, and listener:

> A jest's prosperity lies in the ear
> Of him that hears it, never in the tongue
> Of him that makes it. (*Love's Labor's Lost*, V.ii.861)[25]

Interpreting jokes tells us much about reading a play's performance text. The larger joke can only be appreciated by the audience in the precarious space of interpretation. We observe teller and listener on the stage, constructed wit and butt, and must remain aware of our own role as potentially incorporated witness and victim of this apparently objective mimetic event, distinguishing between imposed social character and our own half-recognized experiences of the resisting social unconscious. Whether this is perfectly theorized in everybody's mind, that is how the theater, at its most critical, actually functions as a medium for social self-perception.

Freud tells a famous joke:

> Two Jews meet on a train in Galicia.
> The first says: "Nuh, where are you going today, Samuel?"
> The other answers: "I'm going to Cracow."
> The first replies: "Look what a liar you are. You tell me you are going to Cracow, because you want me to think you are going to Lemberg. But I happen to know you are going to Cracow. So why do you have to lie to me?"[26]

What do we make of this? First of all, we laugh at someone who is unable to hear the truth when told without subterfuge. In many comedies, the humor derives from a congenital inability to see the obvious, even when it stares you in the face. Thus the servant constantly outwits the master, blinded by predisposition: to vanity, power, greed, or whatever. Eventually, he is unmasked and humiliated. Then we reach for a social correction theory proposed by many, particularly by Bergson.

But this joke pushes beyond any so easy a reading to something more convoluted and disturbing. Freud calls it a "sceptical" joke that questions the possibility of certain knowledge. His interpretation therefore naturalizes, or universalizes, this specifically Jewish joke through a philosophical or abstract reading, not so surprising perhaps, given his own background and the climate of his culture. It seems to show a first speaker congenitally unable to trust that the second speaker will ever tell the truth. He must always assume everyone is lying. Only thus can he protect himself and his interests. He therefore thinks everyone must behave exactly like himself. The joke suggests a state of moral anomie. It is a particularly Jewish joke because of the degree of self-deprecation, of course a form of psychological self-protection. The Jews laugh at themselves, at their "Jewishness," at what appears characteristic in their behavior. They should trust each other, but they know better. They have learned not to trust anybody.

Yet to tell such a joke is to show people who have utterly internalized the conditions that make such behavior necessary. To be a Jew, the joke shows us, is to be a plaything of forces beyond your control. To be a Jew is, therefore, also not to be a Jew, to be yourself and not to be yourself. The joke makes a demand—the impossible demand—to fulfill simultaneously two mutually contradictory obligations, a version of the double bind. It is not so much the uncertainty of all knowledge that is involved here, Freud's "scepticism," as the certainty of a specific contradiction within knowledge. Under the circumstances that have produced such a joke, a Jew can never be a Jew.

If we have not internalized the conditions that produce the structure of this joke, we will not really laugh at it. Of course we can appreciate it and, standing aside, laugh, as it were, vicariously. But if we have internalized its structure, if it provokes us to unpremeditated laughter, we must also, in the process of laughing, internalize its surrogate or false satisfaction. And Freud has surely done this too, for he absolutizes its meaning, instead of historicizing it, thereby softening its stinging particularity. His own reading shows that he is caught within the frame of the

## Desire, Laughter, the Unconscious

joke, living its historical specificity, part of the performance, even as he appears to transcend it through his analysis. This is his version of the double bind. In his reading, the joke appears to free us through laughter, but it quickly ties us up again, because it reimposes the conditions that make it necessary. Knowledge will always remain uncertain, and to say so helps us laugh at the consequences. For some, that is the fate of humanity, an inescapable existential reality. Whatever position we take, we can surely say: here lies one problem for evaluating the dynamics of reading.

Asserting an homology between the structure of jokes and of plays, I do not mean plot structures or "character" construction, but rather how that dynamic entices, traps, and draws us into itself, compelling us to make sense of its text and of ourselves as well. The joke does this involuntarily, almost instantaneously. That is why it is so revealing. We do not have to "read" a joke, in the sense of engaging with a text. Our unconscious does this for us. It happens the other way around. The joke reads us. Therefore the joke is a model for an interpretive practice; it is a form of epigrammatic drama. As a corollary, the joke may read us in quite different ways. We may laugh together but interpret the joke differently. And showing this on the stage is one source of comedy.

I alluded to a double-bind theory of the joke. The double bind operates upon the figures, characters, types *within* the joke, caught in contradictions, making impossible demands upon each other, as in the sadist and masochist joke, or as in *Endgame*, where Hamm and Clov can neither live without nor with each other.[27] The double bind also functions as a structural dynamic *between* listener or audience and joke or play. We encounter a dialectic of liberation and repression, where the joke / play uncovers a moment of freedom, only to cover it up again, releases in order to recapture, where the temporary release of tension into laughter depends upon retaining and reinforcing the repression that necessitates relief. This process allows us to understand the relationship between internalized social character and the workings of the social unconscious.

In this context, Bergson's theory of laughter is interestingly contradictory.[28] If laughter functions as social correction, his text undermines or deconstructs its own arguments, because this laughter is a double surrogate: firstly, as a substitute for, and maybe an impediment to, the most valuable form of knowledge, not available in second-level comedy but only through "drama," by which he means serious drama or tragedy that brings us "face to face with reality itself" (162); and, secondly, as an activity that purports to cure social inelasticity by correcting deviant behavior but which may, in fact, merely function as a means of imposing once again "something mechanical encrusted on the living" (84), since it corrects deviance to a social norm, whether it be good manners or common sense or convention.

So its claim to free from rigidity can be refuted by imposing another kind of rigidity. Bergson uses as an example of correction the practice of "social ragging" (148) by military cadets. Laughter should awaken our attention but, instead, seems to slacken it. This is, of course, Bergson's version of the double bind, which implies you have somehow accepted the conditions that make the joke funny and necessary, so your release from them is only temporary and they are reimposed. Freud's "mis"-reading of the Cracow joke shows he has unconsciously, or realistically, accepted those existential conditions, hence the impossibility of absolute certainty in knowledge does not address or disturb them. Laughter promises release but can actually tie us up again more tightly. It makes a demand upon us while simultaneously ensuring we cannot fulfill it because it is contradictory: we should both derepress and repress. The laughable figure corrected to the social norm may also constitute an unacknowledgeable challenge to it. The force of that contradiction, Bergson intimates only at the end of his essay, which he takes no further because it would undo his whole argument, will be felt "below" (189). We can take this both as psychological and as social metaphor.

Powerful inhibitions in relation to change ensure conformity to social character. This is subtextual to Freud and can be related to Bergson's social correction to a norm. Erich Fromm's analytic social psychology offers a way of thinking about, perhaps around, this problem. It "seeks to understand the instinctual apparatus of a group, its libidinous and largely unconscious behaviour, in terms of its socioeconomic structure."[29] His concept of social character describes the space of subjectivity in terms of socially required and therefore sanctioned values, which can be internalized to the point of absolute self-identification. We identify, often to our detriment, with what our culture validates for us. Consider, to take an extraneous example, how the *Daodejing* complains about the unthinking embodiment of Confucian values, which is why Mother Courage observes that only a bad general needs heroic soldiers. Contesting the orthodox Freudian position, Fromm maintains that instincts are a modifiable biological given, that the individual is more affected by socializing influences mediated within the family, and that both individual and family respond to pressures from a more general socioeconomic state of affairs.

This more flexible libido is not that relentless, almost mechanical, instinctual Freudian engine. Although its energies are deflected, the process is less a direct confrontation between ruthless individual desire and socially imposed repression. The repression, in Fromm's model, is more mediated, less punitively confrontational than in Freud. It is not so much a question of disciplining the instincts into obedience as of creating another space within the unconscious, of differentiating the repressions that shape it. Hence Fromm's concept, social character, is accompanied by that of the social unconscious.

In *The Social Unconscious* Fromm questions Freud's topography, where the unconscious, identified with the id, is relegated to the cellar of the house, the ego placed on the ground floor, between the id and the superego, which is installed as the voice of internalized conscience on the floor above.[30] Freud did not "examine the specific structure of a society and its influence on repression" (88). For Spinoza, whom Marx studied, human bondage resulted because men "are conscious of their own desire, but are ignorant of the causes whereby that desire has been determined" (96). For Marx, false consciousness identified an ideologically determined set of beliefs equated with reality or desirability. The bourgeois consciousness equated its interests with that of humanity and installed them as the voice of reason. Fromm argues there is also a Freudian false consciousness, the rationalization of unconscious desire, exemplified by the moralist punishing those who do what he must deny himself.

But Fromm stresses that the unconscious is not just the repository of repressed instinct, it also absorbs what is associated with the superego. Therefore, he suggests separating "the concept of archaic content and that of the state of unawareness, or unconsciousness" (93). Such an unconscious is no longer merely the repository of repressed instinctual drives but also of repressed, because frustrated, hopes. Since they are frustrated, they will unconsciously energize, affect the psyche deeply, and also turn outward into aggression if circumstances allow this to happen.

Social character is maintained by repression, which is preferable to the loss of love, to social isolation. Hence identity tends to conform with the current "social clichés" (119). But beyond or behind or surrounding identity or social character is this other side of the self, the cause of such powerful emotions, the source of our tears of sadness and of joy, the repository of all we secretly long for ourselves but also for others, the origin of that participatory, altruistic delight in others' happiness: the social unconscious. For Fromm, "It always represents the whole man, with all his potentialities for darkness and light. . . . Man in any culture, has all the potentialities within himself; he is the archaic man, the beast of prey, the cannibal, the idolater, and he is the being with a capacity for reason, for love, for justice" (120f.).

In Fromm's model there is no human essence, but there is a "universal psyche" as a psychological potentiality. The "essence" he attributes to the human species "is not a substance," but rather consists of an awareness of the contradiction between nature and culture and of the realization that man has somehow "to overcome the split between himself and the world outside of him" in order to achieve a new harmony "with his fellow man and with nature" (165). Like all his generation Fromm, an Austrian Jew who emigrated to the United States, had to confront xenophobic nationalism, fascism, and anti-Semitism. Behavior is learned and the judgment can go either way. We are *given* instincts. Values have to be argued for, and the conditions imagined, and then realized, in which such values can be shared. The social unconscious is produced by a repressive society and constitutes "the socially repressed part of the universal psyche" (108n). Experience in the form of awareness depends upon a shaping conceptual or moral system, which we could see as something like Foucault's "positive unconscious of knowledge," which functions as a "socially" and culturally "conditioned filter" (109).

Since a "universal psyche" does not entail a human essence, when Fromm speaks of humanism, he means a freedom from the illusion of believing in essential values that presuppose a fixed identity and a pre-established human nature. Fromm's humanism is not an anthropocentric defense of any status quo, but rather is more related to Marx's idea of "species being" and seeks a realization of Marx's call for a reconciliation between man and nature, one of his definitions of communism. What we are prevented from being or incapable of realizing in ourselves, both good and bad, because of internalized, no longer noticed social inhibitions, demands, and conventions, lies dormant as potential within us until it springs its surprises and shames or delights us. It is probably useful to connect this concept of the social unconscious, which Fromm does not idealize, both with Hegel's "struggle for recognition," one of the animators of history, and with Deleuze's concept of desire that arises when the sense of meaning has collapsed.[31]

Arthur Koestler stresses unconscious processes in all forms of discovery, assuming the long-sustained equation of the mind with conscious thinking to be a Cartesian catastrophe. He sees laughter in the context of a psychology of creativity where the joke bisociates two otherwise incompatible matrices. The resulting surprise enables a cognitive gain and the previous tension is released into laughter.[32] He finds a sort of downward mental traffic to stereotypes and an upward creative surge from underground. Zen calligraphy is a virtuoso method of allowing the unconscious to release its creative potential (376). Koestler attempts to theorize self-transcendence, obviously crucial both for laughter, with its apparently opposite move toward self-assertion at the expense of others, and for the emotions normally associated with tragedy rather than comedy. We can probably connect this enlargement of the capacity of laughter with Fromm's inclusion of aspects of the superego in the social unconscious.

My argument looks toward intercultural perspectives, in relation to an adequate theory of laughter in all its particular psychosocial complexity, one which will take account both of laughter in Shakespeare's comedies, or the farces of Dario Fo, and also of Buddhist kyogen jokes. It is probably true, for most instances, that we laugh off inhibitions, usually sexual / social and concealing aggression, in order to accept their reimposition, to accept the definition of imposed social character. We dissipate the energies of the social unconscious that resist social character. This is my double-bind supposition. Otherwise we would have to act, and to act is often impossible, sometimes undesirable. Laughter and the joke are forms of surrogate action. They appear to render other activities unnecessary.

But we also laugh, not because we are frustrated, but because we are capacitated. In such creative laughter, the laugh stands for symbolic, not surrogate, action. The laugh itself, as physiological phenomenon, still results, as Freud supposed, from a saving of energy, but it accompanies a different psychological event. Cognitive laughter, or the laughter of self-transcendence, does not accompany the reduction of others, which is what sudden glory actually entails, but rather an extension of ourselves. The pleasure of the joke can also derive from an expansion of understanding, not just from the release of an inhibition. Laughter need not be the expression of a discharge of cathectic energy on the temporary loss of inhibition; it can perhaps signify the release of unconscious tension through a sudden extension of the self through a gain in understanding. This is not sudden glory because of the misfortunes of others, but because of the fortune of the self, the loss of its constrictions.

Here, surely, we can see how the psychology of aesthetic perception loops back into the psychology of creativity and laughter. In *Life of Galileo*, Brecht calls laughter the physicist's equivalent of ringing church bells. In earlier decades or centuries, this laugh might have been called cosmic or orgasmic laughter. Such a laugh will not function as a reinforcement of social character, but rather as its analyst and critic. It will be a sign of a breakthrough in understanding how social character is formed, in realizing that the processes whereby we define ourselves in terms of its requirements need not bind us forever. In such laughter, we validate ourselves relationally. We free ourselves from the restraints of imposed social character and redefine our relations with others. But this laugh can also constitute a double bind. If the cognitive gain is forgotten or lost, it reverts to the level of surrogate rather than symbolic action. Like the joke, reading comedy also decodes the critic.

### III

Freud's Shakespeare quotation reminds us that speech is directed at somebody for particular ends, the basis for speech act theory. *Love's Labor's Lost*, in particular, focuses on the uses of speech. Yet speech act theory offers no room for the unconscious. However, the dramatic context within the play cannot really explain the argument, which must be situated within a wider cultural context, unless dramatic and cultural context appear identical, as in mimetic reading, which reveals an unconscious ideological position. The cultural context is, of course, the effect of another reading and stands in a dialectical relationship to the play and any speech within it, because the play is part of what enables us to understand that context. Since laughter signals the release of a repression, we need to observe how the jokes are told:

## Desire, Laughter, the Unconscious

> Touchstone: Then learn this of me: to have is to have. For it is a figure in rhetoric that drink, being pour'd out of a cup into a glass, by filling the one doth empty the other. For all your writers do consent that ipse is he: now, you are not ipse, for I am he.
> William: Which he, sir?
> Touchstone: He, sir, that must marry this woman. (*As You Like It*, V.i.40)

Not everyone gets results as quickly as Touchstone who "proves" by means of rhetoric that he must have his own way and so imposes his will on William's reading.

Historicizing interpretation, we observe ideological preference, mostly unconscious of its origin. For Schlegel *As You Like It* meant "dreamlike carefreeness."[33] He stated, "It seems to be the poet's design to show that to call forth the poetry which has its dwelling in nature and the human mind nothing is wanted but to throw off all artificial constraint and to restore both to their original liberty."[34] "Poetry" stands for a utopian, visionary capability hindered by social and political restraint. We can understand this concept of poetry as an expression of the social unconscious, repressed by internalized social character, while observing a voluntarism, once more noticeable within Shakespearean studies.[35] Schlegel supposes that removing such restraint uncovers an innate capacity that can then be transferred from the natural to the social or from the secondary to the primary world, by virtue of its own preexistence, bending social discourse and reality to its will by the simple process of enunciating it. This reading, seeking to restore the natural right of freedom, made provocative cultural and political sense in Berlin in the first decades of the nineteenth century, even if Schlegel was not so certain how soon the primary world could be transformed in the contradictory postrevolutionary and later post-Napoleonic era. These expectations were less nostalgic, part of an intellectually credible cultural politics. That we can know anything about what might happen after the marriage dance in Shakespearean comedy, once an interpretive commonplace, is a revealing delusion, which supposes the play's apparent resolution, in reality a particular reading, can then imprint itself upon reality, thus eliding the contradictions of the text.

Within the extensive feminist debate on Shakespeare, Kathleen McLuskie criticizes the mimetic model employed by essentialist feminism that argues dramatic representation is an accurate reflection of real nature and ideas and does not find such representation divided in itself nor sees the need to locate it historically. Shakespeare is thereby enrolled in defense of, or criticized for opposing, an appropriate view of women.[36]

In *Twelfth Night* Feste describes himself to Viola as Olivia's "corrupter of words" (III.i.36). The verbal quibbles, puns, and homophones give a voice to the social unconscious and contest a belief in meaning stabilized, and social character shaped, through correct appreciation of the use of words and rectification of names. This incessant playing with words is only understandable in relation to a deep sense of existential crisis, evident in Shakespeare's day, for which there are social and religious frames of explanation. These, in turn, surely depend on the transition from feudalism to a developing, still insecure bourgeois culture, both of which are threatened, although differently, by an incipient absolutism representing the state's temporary, and contradictory, negotiation of the difficult historical passage. The plots are propelled by an engagement between two opposing attitudes aligned according to contemporary epistemological theory, to a belief that if only you understand words properly, you can control things and people.[37] That fits with Foucault's Renaissance theory of resemblance, whereby knowledge derives entirely from the correct understanding of words.[38] Since the conventionalists dispute naturalism's right to impose meaning upon reality through control of language, these plays mark the breakdown of that Renaissance episteme. Like *Don Giovanni*, they face both ways.

In *Love's Labor's Lost*, a group of aristocratic Platonists endeavor to isolate themselves in an academy in the belief, which Berowne challenges, that knowledge of names can secure adequate control of reality. No matter whether, or to what extent, Shakespeare was parodying Raleigh's School of Night, later examined publicly for propagating atheism, what they set out to assert, and utterly fail to achieve, is a version of the axiomatic belief in mimetic or semantic naturalism associated with Neoplatonic doctrine.[39] This doctrine of the sign supposes an exact correspondence between words and things, between sign and referent, between language and reality. There is here no room for doubleness. It is a magical theory where possession of the word ensures, by imposing, proper understanding. The comparable Confucian doctrine, the *rectification of names*, usefully defamiliarizes the mystical assumptions in Western linguistic theory by drawing attention to the direct political

## Desire, Laughter, the Unconscious

benefit from this assertion of equivalence between linguistic and social propriety.[40] Social relations necessitate learning the proper use of language that protects structures of power. In this Orphic thought lower and higher correspond, so that one stands for the other. Kott refers to this belief when suggesting a compatibility between the Platonic and Saturnalian code, which then translates the Saturnalian ass Bottom into the realm of higher spirituality. So comic reversal, according to this reading, signifies mystical knowledge and power. Such reversal could also be given a strong political reading in terms of recuperating the lower social or Rabelaisian body for the higher social and spiritual world. We can surely now conclude that this amounts to an attempt to excise the social unconscious.

Pastoral takes the form of an extreme and often obscure cult of language, resisted by the women and impervious to the harsher facts of life that escape the control of any naturalist language. Perhaps because the language strategy is much less absolute or principled or academic, it meets with less resistance in *As You Like It*, which nonetheless transfers pastoral, and its claim for untroubled control, into drama. This is why Goethe's poem *Ilmenau* describes the behavior of the Duke of Weimar and his entourage in terms of the forest pastoral in this play, also critically drawing attention to the supposed connection between bad harvests and bad government, a version of Confucian phenomenalism that held that proper social practice would regulate nature. Jaques's melancholy feeds on his reluctance to accept the Duke's sentimental but politically astute rectification of names. That the Duke imposes his lesson upon nature, and has not perhaps learned much from his enforced holiday in the pastoral forest—except a way of talking about it—is suggested by his final allusion to the primary world to which he will return, which promises *unequal* recompense, awarded strictly on the basis of social rank (state):

> And after, every of this happy number,
> That have endur'd shrewd days and nights with us,
> Shall share the good of our returned fortune,
> According to the measure of their states. (V.iv.172)

Meanwhile the play reverts to "rustic revelry," which they must celebrate while they all still have the chance.

Tamsin Spargo suggests the epilogue to *As You Like It* questions or at least opens up the issue of gender position since the speaker plays with the idea of gendered roles: "This final speech can be seen to invite the audience to think about how sexual difference is constructed, which may in turn disrupt the apparently patriarchalist vision of the happy ending of the play."[41] Perhaps we can indeed see in this epilogue an invitation to transcend, in the imagination, the conventions of gendered roles, hence that the comedy offers this opportunity for that temporary self-transcendence that accounts for the satisfaction of the genre. However, that opportunity was limited in real life and followed by the socially demanded reimposition of the repression, released primarily, but not solely, from the female social unconscious. This incipient reacceptance of the repression is perhaps also marked within the text by the Duke's qualification of any desired "happy end."

Such a return of the repression at the end of *As You Like It* suggests once more the analogy, even possible homology, between joke and dramatic performance. In both, the reality principle is suspended only to be reinstated again at the end. Although neither theater nor jokes have the power to alter the forceful realities of social life, we can distinguish between what I have termed "surrogate" and "symbolic" solutions: the former accept and the latter reject the reimposition of social character and the consequently constructed social unconscious. Spargo looks to a symbolic solution in respect of gender role construction. The text seems to imply its conclusion is closer to the surrogate, realistically representing, although not exactly advocating, the Duke's "back to normality" and the reality principle.

The alternative to this strategy is that other, "forward-looking" view of laughter, especially as developed by Koestler, linking it with creativity, rather than seeking its origin solely in the release from a socially sustained repression, which can be thought of as "backward-looking," especially when the effect is temporary. Koestler astutely connected his view of laughter with Zen's ability to release the mind from the constraints of conventional perception and to stimulate creativity. We no longer shed the emotional load by laughing it off; we laugh at the extraordinary insight that capacitates us to reimagine reality. I call this "cognitive laughter."

The Noh play, discussed in the epilogue, does not suspend "normality" by creating a twice fictional secondary world as a temporary counterweight to the primary world of the play to which it must return. Instead it deconstructs all narrative and representation. It shows all human existence, real and possible, as verbally, aesthetically mediated, the result of differently imposed narratives. It is therefore more aesthetically and philosophically radical. This happens, perhaps, because there were no real, credible alternative spaces available in traditional Japanese society, no New Found Land, no America. So a potential social critique is transferred to the philosophical and absolutized.

*A Midsummer Night's Dream* invites us to go more deeply into problematic laughter, as an expression of a desiring social unconscious, rather than the reader's personality structure or any temporary lifting of a repression. The amateur theatricals appear clumsy when contrasted with the court's sophistication and with the intransigent logic that governs the apparently fanciful world of the fairies. Yet it looks as if they will not get to perform at all. It depends, like so much else, upon the judgment of the Duke, because three other plays are ready for performance. Theseus does not like the sound of the first three and so chooses the fourth possibility, although his Master of Revels steadies himself for a disaster. What are those other plays? Theseus reads from the list handed him by Philostrate, and unsurprisingly chooses the "comedy" (*Midsummer* V.i.44ff.). What is unexpected is that he has such a choice. The first two plays he dismisses, not as unsuited to the occasion but because he knows them already. Indeed he participated in one of their events. They are both stories of violence, of explicitly sexual violence. And this is not all that is strange about them. In the pause between the public celebration of marriage and the private pleasures of the bed, the three happy couples are first offered a story about centaurs, phallic man-animals, marking in the Greek imagination the link between conscious and unconscious forces, between animality and spirituality, breaking into a marriage ceremony and carrying off the bride—a kind of attempted mass rape. The second story tells of the violent, drunken female followers of Dionysos who tore the poet Orpheus to pieces in an outburst of sexual frenzy.[42] That the first story is to be narrated by an "Athenian eunuch" adds particular injury to sexual insult.

It is no coincidence that Theseus prefers instead "the most lamentable comedy and most cruel death of Pyramus and Thisby" (I.ii.11). Not that it seems entirely suitable either, since it laughs at a problem that might have ended tragically in the play itself: lovers separated by parental displeasure. When they begin to rehearse this comic-tragic play about lovers' double suicide, which parodies Elizabethan dramatic language, maybe the plot of *Romeo and Juliet*, Bottom asks: "What is Pyramus? A lover or a tyrant?" (I.ii.17). Shakespeare makes fun of such categorizations. Either you have plays about lovers, or you have plays about tyrants. Bottom would have preferred a play about the strongman Hercules, a play about tyrants therefore, but he gets the other category. We are reminded how love-making, violence, and tyranny are happily bedded together.

Catherine Belsey writes about this play's evocation of an unconscious. Bottom's inability to communicate his experience, the failure of language, indicates the energy invested in the indescribable dream. She quotes Derrida's observation that the unconscious offers a "radical alterity," adding that this makes psychoanalysis "only a sophisticated instance of all interpretation, just as dreaming is a common instance of all inscription."[43] While this alterity is indeed radical, from the perspective of a consciously sustained "normality," it is surely anything but abstract, no mere function of an *inherent* instability or multiple interpretability in language. It rather results from the *particular* repression that creates this need or desire within the social unconscious. Although about the exercise of power, the politics of gender, and sexual violence as a social commonplace, the play does not reveal "this universal madness of Nature and History."[44] Rather, it uncovers particularities in the specifically Elizabethan unconscious: the inevitable underside of the pastoralized May or Midsummer festival of love, its ostensible instigation serving for Theseus to ideologize sexual relationships within the sacramental social institution of marriage, which he as Duke upholds, no matter what it might signify to the mythological figure.

Theseus's celebrated speech—"Lovers and madmen have such seething brains" (V.i.4ff.)—presents the doubleness of his function. As public figure, he must deny the insights whose truths he has unconsciously acknowledged by his private behavior. The imagination of the poet enables us to sense the sources of lovers' madness, which Theseus may only apprehend because he must dismiss its implications, that is, the possibility of really tracing it to its source and comprehending it.

Earlier interpretive traditions had no sense of the specific resonance with the Elizabethan unconscious. References to love's perennial irrationality scarcely explain the rationalized sexual violence and its de-

## Desire, Laughter, the Unconscious

liberate invocation.[45] In 1986 I saw a Royal Shakespeare Company production at Stratford that perfectly encapsulated the confusions of this abstraction. Titania was fashionably tough and dressed in leather trousers, arms akimbo, but otherwise surrounded by dock leaves and the flora of "children's" fairyland. The play was treated as ballet, spectacle, and performed to Mendelssohn's trivializing music. The New Cambridge Shakespeare edition shows how this visual tradition persisted at least until Peter Hall's 1959 Stratford production, sustaining a repression some thirty years after Brecht had questioned the whole process.[46] Britten's mannerist opera virtually eradicates the primary world, hence any dynamic relationship to the secondary world, since Theseus appears only as a master of the final ceremony of love. Long considered particularly suitable for children, its obsessions are beyond their horizon. Furthermore, the section of the play they are encouraged to read and enact—the story of the fairies—is the most difficult passage for them.

The editor of the Cambridge Shakespeare found a "delicate English beauty" in Oberon's description of the "Warwickshire countryside":

> I know a bank where the wild thyme blows
> Where oxlips and the nodding violet grows
> Quite overcanopied with luscious woodbine
> With sweet musk-roses and with eglantine. (II.i.249)[47]

Before we get carried away by nostalgia, we ought to read on. We discover other vintage English sentiments:

> There sleeps Titania sometimes in the night
> Lulled in these flowers with dances and delight;
> And there the snake throws her enamelled skin,
> Weed wide enough to wrap a fairy in;
> And with the juice of this I'll streak her eyes
> And make her full of hateful fantasies.

The naming of flowers has a function in the play's metaphorical strategy. In Freudian language, it is decidedly tendentious. The relationship between tendentious metaphor and "hateful fantasies" depends on the cultural context that produced them both.

Theseus expects to exercise social and linguistic control over his sur-

## The Intercultural Sign

roundings. There are two acts of rebellion against the social control he incorporates: within his court, and in the night world of the fairies. The second is a projection of the female social unconscious and the more disturbing one. But the acts of rebellion are related. Theseus appears to mitigate the extreme demand of Hermia's father, Egeus, who would have her marry Demetrius or put to death. Faced with the prohibition of their love from both father and sovereign, Lysander flees with her into the forest. Although Theseus offers Hermia the softer alternative to death, life in a convent, and so perpetual celibacy, a standard threat to recalcitrant daughters, he sets out the argument for paternal authority in terms not open to misunderstanding:

> What say you, Hermia? Be advized, fair maid.
> To you your father should be as a god;
> One that composed your beauties; yea, and one
> To whom you are but as a form in wax,
> By him imprinted, and within his power,
> To leave the figure, or disfigure it. (I.i.46)

The mother had an irrefutable claim to her maternity. The claim to paternity was not so obvious, in part because of the state of physiological knowledge. The father was therefore more crucial, imprinting himself upon his child. The assertion goes back to Aristotle, but social formations were changing. A mythical physiology served as a means of control. The endless edgy jokes about cuckoldry were never simple ribaldry, but instead implied the undermining of social structures. Paternity was a social metaphor.

In the forest the lovers are transformed. Friends become enemies. They threaten violence: of combat, of rape. The forest's monsters prey upon their minds. The counterpotion resolves the confusions and they are reincorporated, on their own terms, into the primary world. Theseus overrides Egeus's impetuous claim to exercise his own will. Since Demetrius no longer wants to marry Hermia, the dilemma is resolved. Conveniently, it is the man who has changed his mind.

Titania, the other rebel, is punished through the same love potion that Puck mistakenly uses on the wrong Athenian lover, Lysander instead of Demetrius. She is inflamed by the ass Bottom's sexual energy, well

Desire, Laughter, the Unconscious

described in Kott's *Shakespeare Our Contemporary*. Only when Titania has been thus exposed and humiliated, and her rebellion exaggerated and contained, is she released from her fantasy. Kott elsewhere offers another reading of this symbolism in terms of Renaissance Platonism.[48] He proposes two codes for interpreting the play: Saturnalian reversal, where the plebeian ass becomes king, and Platonic reversal, where the ass stands, in the words of a contemporary translation of the passage from 1 Corinthians 2.10 for the "bottom of God's secret which the spirit searcheth." We could therefore see Bottom as a comic Minotaur whereby Titania is confronted with her own social and physical grotesque.

The symbol of this rebellion is the "changeling child," which Titania has steadfastly refused to hand over to Oberon. When she does agree to do so, she is released. But what does the child signify? It is related to a symbolic paternity claim, hence to the plot in the primary world. The story between Oberon and Titania encodes the fears, and therefore the warnings, that accompany Theseus's marriage to the violently won Hippolyta and that function as a problematic within the Elizabethan unconscious. Through Oberon, Theseus exercises control over Titania who is in love with him and, therefore, symbolic control over his future wife. Titania refuses Oberon the child in a strange and suggestive passage:

> The fairy land buys not the child of me.
> His mother was a votress of my order,
> And in the spiced Indian air, by night,
> Full often hath she gossiped by my side,
> And sat with me on Neptune's yellow sands,
> Marking th' embarked traders on the flood;
> When we have laughed to see the sails conceive
> And grow big-bellied with the wanton wind;
> Which she, with pretty and with swimming gait,
> Following (her womb then rich with my young squire)
> Would imitate, and sail upon the land
> To fetch me trifles, and return again,
> As from a voyage, rich with merchandise.
> But she, being mortal, of that boy did die,
> And for her sake do I rear up her boy;
> And for her sake I will not part with him. (II.i.122)

# The Intercultural Sign

5  The purple wounded love-in-idleness and chaste Dian's bud
(de Bray, *Fantastic Garlands*, 107).

If Theseus, in Athens, asserts the absolute claim of paternal discretion upon the shaping of his child, then Titania, in the forest dream of the Elizabethan social unconscious, does the reverse. That, after all, is hardly surprising. There are no fathers in her story, only women and mothers, sustaining, and maybe even producing, male progeny without the help of any husband. This will have to be the ultimate, feared, imagined act of

Desire, Laughter, the Unconscious

> ... we have
> the receipt of fern-seed, we walk invisible.
> Gadshill – *1 Henry IV*, II. i. 95

> Yet mark'd I where the bolt of Cupid fell:
> It fell upon a little western flower,
> Before milk-white, now purple with love's wound,
> And maidens call it love-in-idleness.
> Oberon – *A Midsummer Night's Dream*, II. i. 165

> Be as thou wast wont to be;
> See as thou wast wont to see;
> Dian's bud o'er Cupid's flower
> Hath such force and blessed power.
> Oberon – *A Mudsummer Night's Dream*, IV. i. 76

| | |
|---|---|
| Fern<br>1 MALE FERN<br>*Dryopteris felix-mas*<br><br>2 POLYPODY<br>*Polypodium vulgare* | There are very many old legends about ferns. It was believed that 'Fern-seed' (which cannot exist, because ferns have no flowers) could confer the gift of invisibility to the finder. He or she must seek the seed on St John's Eve (23 June), and if the proper ceremonial is not observed the seed will vanish on the way home. It is possible that the stories referred to the spores that are found on the back of the fern-fronds after midsummer. |
| 3 LOVE-IN-<br>IDLENESS<br>(Heartsease)<br>*Viola tricolor* | The Wild Pansy or Heartsease is still called 'Love-and-Idleness' in Warwickshire, and 'Love-in-Idleness' in the next-door county of Gloucestershire. The old names for this annual flower of the cornfields are not used as much as they were. There are less flowers among the corn now, and so this so-pretty wild Pansy is almost forgotten except by gardeners who cherish the wild flowers as well as their pedigree relatives. |
| 4 DIAN'S BUD<br>(Wormwood)<br>*Artemisia absinthium* | It is generally believed that Wormwood is the plant that Shakespeare called 'Dian's Bud', because the scientific name of Wormwood comes from Artemis, the Greek name for Diana, goddess of the hunt. This silvery-leaved plant was much used in early medicine, though later physicians discarded it for more effective herbs. Its only certain use in the home was to discourage fleas. |

6 A gloss upon these flowers (de Bray, *Fantastic Garlands*, 107).

subversion. Not only that, but their sisters mock the activities of men whose merchandise cannot compete with theirs and whose activities are a parody of their fecundity. These women seem distressingly independent of any men.

We can see an illustration of the flower from which the love potion is produced.[49] Oberon describes it as:

> ... a little western flower,
> Before milk-white, now purple with love's wound,
> And maidens call it love-in-idleness. (II.i.166)

How suggestive is that popular name given it by the women: love-in-idleness. The potion's antidote is "Dian's bud" (IV.i.70), the silver-white wormwood, associated with chastity, the moon, purity, and the visual opposite of the purple "love-in-idleness" that figures unsatisfied female sexual desire.[50] (See Figures 5–6.)

This "gossamer" play harps on passion, defloration, sexual violence, and the appropriate control of female desire. Thomas Laqueur has described contemporary physiological knowledge that helps us understand the response to female sexuality.[51] Conception would only occur, such was the belief, if the woman experienced orgasm. The future of humanity, in a period when life was short, therefore depended upon men pleasuring women. No wonder that female sexuality produced anxieties in men, for to "control" female desire must also have implied that you were trying to defy nature. The fuller passage from which I have just quoted performs a defloration on the flower of love:

> Yet marked I where the bolt of Cupid fell.
> It fell upon a little western flower,
> Before milk-white, now purple with love's wound,
> And maidens call it love-in-idleness.

Theseus "won" Hippolyta in a manner, drawing blood, whose description suggests his fear of what it might produce: "Hippolyta, I wooed thee with my sword / And won thy love doing thee injuries" (I.i.16). Is it not significant that alone of the stage audience, Hippolyta does not like the performance of Pyramus and Thisby?

Theseus incorporates the control that produces the Elizabethan unconscious. Louis Montrose has suggested this problematic is in part produced by the ambiguous role of the Virgin Queen Elizabeth.[52] Particularly for her male subjects she embodied the contradictions of the cultural discourse, using her powerful and inviolable female body to dazzle and manipulate them. To question her virginity was to commit an act of treason. But in addition to any such provocation the replacement of feudal concepts of order in a society rapidly aligning itself ac-

## Desire, Laughter, the Unconscious

cording to mercantile bourgeois values now turned every daughter of that class into an essential object of economic exchange. This must have greatly increased the fear of ungovernable female sexuality and the need to control it, thereby shaping a specifically "Elizabethan" unconscious.

After Theseus has disappeared, Puck returns us, if only in the space of an epilogue, to a real and troubled nature, which the imagination cannot appropriate as easily as Theseus rules Athens and, through Oberon, the wood:

> Now the hungry lion roars,
> And the wolf behowls the moon;
> Whilst the heavy ploughman snores,
> All with weary task foredone.
> Now the wasted brands do glow,
> Whilst the screech owl, screeching loud,
> Puts the wretch that lies in woe
> In remembrance of a shroud. (V.i.368)

No matter that Oberon and Puck may then try to mend the audience's humor, that society's unconscious has been uncovered. These plays voice the female and social unconscious, what gets repressed and silenced but still resists within the social game of power. They appear to offer an escape from constraint into pastoral or imagined worlds: the Academy's maze of words, the pastoralized Forest of Arden, the forest dream of the Elizabethan social unconscious. The women and the fools, turned into conventionalists by social circumstance, challenge the mimetic naturalism of the powerful and not-so-powerful men whom they instinctively resist. A mimetic strategy of reading, criticized in recent Shakespeare studies but still practiced, identifies with positions within the play, rather than historicizing them.

# 4

## HISTORICIZING THE UNCONSCIOUS IN PLAUTINE AND SHAKESPEAREAN FARCE

### I

One way of situating Plautine farce is to ask what criticism makes of it. Plautus is ritually situated in accounts of the development of comedy between extravagant Aristophanic fantasy and the more sophisticated Renaissance comedy of character. Although Plautus was an important source, after Terence, for the Renaissance, his writing is often presented as a cruder anticipation of later subtleties, while also offering something flatter and more conventional than Aristophanes. Either way, his work seems to stand for a more slack attention to the possibilities of comic form, a lower level of perception, and a lesser quality of entertainment.

One "problem" in reading Plautus is perspectival, as well as ideological, created by looking at his writing through the prism of a particular construction of Renaissance comedy. To break away from this convention of reading, we first need to ask how Plautus has been placed in the Greco-Roman world, starting with the basic philological and generic assessments.

Titus Maccius Plautus (c. 254–c. 184 BCE) represents the less secure, more marginal Roman comedy that drew on richer Greek sources, translating, adapting, and rewriting them to suit Roman circumstances.[1] Aristophanes may have been the culmination of a longer comic tradition—too little is known about his precursors—or his work may have been as unique as it appears to us. His last play dates from 388 BCE. The next body of writing is markedly different, although this change is already anticipated if we compare *Wealth* with his earlier plays. There are plays and fragments of this New Comedy's surviving representative, Menander, who wrote in Athens about sixty years after Aristopha-

Historicizing the Unconscious

nes. Scholars have found fragments of Menander that Plautus later reworked.

Aristophanes had turned the normal upside-down or inside-out, rearranging perceptual or behavioral expectations, and then working out the consequences episodically. His plays only needed a loose structure, because the radical fantasy holds everything together. Plautus, by contrast, constructs elaborately balanced plots, a comedy of manners, a recognizable, down-to-earth, urban world going about its daily business, in some respects so "typical" that aspects of these plots can be almost effortlessly transferred into Molière's society 1,800 years later. Yet Plautus offered Shakespeare what is usually considered his most improbable plot, although what looks like an objectively verifiable judgment about the empirical limits of probability, hence to be itself free of presuppositions, could imply another kind of misrecognition. But it is generally held that Plautus supplied the models for a certain kind of comic plot construction, for the intricate intrigues in which servants outwit masters, pry victimized lovers from powerful clutches, and win freedom for themselves. To this comedy of manners, easily assimilable to a Bergsonian social correction theory of comedy, is added the element of knockabout farce.

In Plautus we find, the explanation runs, domestic plot rather than radical fantasy and, when compared with later comedy, typification rather than the exploration of character, low farce rather than high comedy. Later Renaissance and post-Renaissance comedy therefore constitutes a transition from the relatively crude to the more sophisticated, based on an accretion of experience, offering necessary differentiations, where an essentially simple, although often technically elaborate, plot can be retained to enable a more developed investigation of personality.

Since so much of this seems incontrovertible, more a matter of ascertaining historical fact, we should step back for a moment and take account of the later trajectory of thought, of its hidden, hence unquestioned, parameters. Our perspective on Plautus may be to some degree determined by an inadequately examined supposition about cultural development, by an aesthetic ideology that constrains us to see only what we are predisposed to expect, to misrecognize the complexities of the form, to judge ahistorically, because we assume a particular transcultural standard, because we have not properly analyzed our own.

## The Intercultural Sign

A little more than one hundred years ago, Nietzsche debunked a widely held view of Greek culture, developed by eighteenth-century German intellectuals, its construction as an idealized incorporation of humanism. Much literary and dramatic criticism is still caught up in presuppositions about a developed and self-sufficient subjectivity in terms of which everything is measured and either found wanting or approved, but that in fact derive from an internalized ideology associated with the changes that accompanied the rise of the bourgeois class. The necessary claim of that emergent class for conscious control over its economic, social, and then political affairs, later made in the name of reason and humanity, implied the assertion of an independent consciousness as an absolute and inviolable, moral and psychological fact. The transition from the Greco-Roman Mediterranean world to Renaissance and then to post-Enlightenment Europe could be seen as one from communalist, ritualistic, and economically relatively primitive cultures to civilizations resting on assumptions of personal autonomy and developing an increasingly efficient scientific culture.

The necessary ideology of individualism within the sphere of religion produced the Protestant revolt against systemic hierarchization and ecclesiastical mediation between the individual soul or conscience and God. Theologically, individual responsibility became an absolute demand. There could be no mitigating intercession, no confession of sins and guaranteed absolution. Such unmediatable singularity always entailed the risk of failure. The merchant's transaction might be a gamble, but he alone had to face the consequences of failure or could profit from its success.

Aesthetic forms developed in the context of these major psychological and social realignments. Choral antiphony and interweaving polyphony yielded to melodic singularity, as the musical line was rearranged in homophonous support of subjective melodic and textual expression. All such developments overlap, but in Shakespeare's day, the popular communal ballad gave way to the singular art song.[2] In painting, portraits emerge among the late-fifteenth-century German merchant class, unmistakably individualized features, faces you can see today in Nuremburg.

Of course, the conflict between competing bourgeois and absolutist ideologies, in which a claim for individual rights is set against an assertion of hierarchical or mediating power, can be traced back through the centuries. We can ascertain homologies within earlier forms of Western culture. Christianity had both hierarchical and revolutionary implications. It was harnessed initially to justify a social gospel or the ideology of kingship and later to legitimate both a centralizing papal infallibility in the interpretation of metaphysical and social doctrine and the worker priests and liberation theology.

Yet Christianity's claim for irreducible and inalienable survival rights, for immortality and social justice, originated in the world described by Plautus. His Roman world was the social reality in which it first took root, to which it constituted a response. There could well be a more troubling and unconscious preoccupation with a deeply problematic identity, underneath the surface of an apparently harmless, even innocent, knockabout, farcical entertainment that, in spite of some clever plotting, seems to lack any sense of a developed individuality that would secure and then hold the attention of more developed cultures.

Furthermore, in the Greco-Roman context the change from Aristophanic to Plautine comedy, from politically alert fantasy to steady domesticity of plot and the intrigues of a mundane horizon, does not necessarily imply a complete regression, an abrogation of political interest, a retrogression to a smaller, more circumscribed, less troubled and hence less interesting world. The cultural circumstances were quite different. The obviously different response to these changed social and political circumstances has been conventionally and reductively explained in their terms. A brief account is necessary here in order to show why such explanations are not really adequate.

There are analogies between life experiences in relation to the larger historical events during the lives of Aristophanes and Plautus. Aristophanes reacted to sociopolitical changes as Athens became ever more involved in the Peloponnesian Wars. The increasingly intractable problems dominate his plays. Similarities appear to exist between the Roman republic and the Greek city-state, so that we wonder why Plautus did not show a comparable interest in public life. After all, his lifetime was dominated by the Punic Wars against Carthage, and their resolution was by no means certain. Probably the different ethos of the cultures was already discernible. Athens and Rome were moving in different directions; one contracting and the other expanding.

But the political structures must have been the major reason for the lack of any direct sense of political urgency in Plautus. The Roman republic ruled itself through its Senate, a highly restricted body of men, and through its appointed and governing officers. In Rome no equivalent for the Athenian *demos*, or assembly of citizens, existed. Hence, there could never have been a comparable sense of responsibility for public affairs or the ability to participate in influencing them. The theater was a relatively late development in Rome, where the main public entertainment was horse racing and gladiatorial combat. Theater buildings as permanent stages in stone only existed from 55 BCE.[3]

The more domestic plots seem to meet the more diffuse, less urgently focused needs of the different urban communities. We must therefore ask how Plautus addresses these different needs. At this juncture, the question of presuppositions becomes important. One noticeable difference between Plautus and Aristophanes is the predominance of slaves as key figures in Plautus's plays. Aristophanes gives the major roles to citizens. In contrast, Plautus's slaves often take control of events, although not in *Menaechmi*, even if one brother has been freed. Although Athenian democracy depended upon an imperialist expansion and the institution of slavery, the incorporation of institutionalized slavery within the Roman state was on an incomparably greater scale. Early Roman peasant farmers could no longer compete with imports from subject territories. Their holdings were organized into large estates that depended entirely on slave labor. The difference was largely one of scale; hence, there was greater dependency upon, as there was greater differentiation between and among, slaves in Rome.

Athenian culture rested upon its citizens, freed by the institution of slavery from the need to do manual labor. In Rome, the citizens often acquired their culture from the captured slaves. The role, the identity, of these slaves was therefore different in Rome. Because Rome developed into an imperium and a complex, stratified society, the danger from a disaffected population was also greater, as the celebrated slave revolts make obvious. The slaves in Rome were a source of both culture and rebellion. Their "identity" was provocatively complex.

Two main arguments have undergirded my discussion here. First, a process of aesthetic change, seen here in different plot structures, exists not just as an abstract, formal, autonomous, inevitably differentiating and improving development, but rather in relation to historical needs. Therefore we must take account of these needs, which are not always easy to discern because we are often guided by our own presuppositions.

Historicizing the Unconscious

Aesthetic forms must be historicized. This does not mean reducing them to a direct function of a presumed social context, itself perhaps an anachronistic abstraction of human needs related to the march-of-history argument, but rather seeing interrelationships between history and desire and appreciating the force of the social unconscious. Second, ideologies of interpretation hierarchize aesthetic forms which a critical discourse sometimes takes for granted without our fully understanding why.

II

Shakespeare used the *Menaechmi* plot for *The Comedy of Errors*. Juxtaposing the two works reveals the presuppositions behind generic description. A standard opinion, expressed in the 1988 New Cambridge Shakespeare *Comedy of Errors*, is that Shakespeare "enlarges" a "heartless farce" into comedy.[4] It is odd, yet strangely symptomatic, that a recent play-by-play account within a study of Shakespeare's comedies, conscious of "the problem of closure" and of psychoanalytic and contemporary critical positions, simply omits *The Comedy of Errors*.[5] The silent assumption must still be that it is too tainted by relative immaturity, less well-constructed than the festive comedies, less rewarding for analysis. I suggest interpreting Plautus affects our reading of Shakespeare, although not as this is commonly assessed. How do some critics measure the distance between them?

We start with the conventional attributes of farce. The *Oxford English Dictionary* defines it as "a dramatic work, usually short, which has as its sole object to excite laughter." The implication is clear, and typical: farce, and laughter, comes in short, sharp bursts. These cannot be sustained, their interest is limited. Of course, this begs the question about the origin of laughter, let alone its value. When juxtaposed, farce is frequently described as simple and crude, and comedy as more developed and sophisticated. Comedy investigates "character," farce does not move beyond the type.[6]

Comedy is more concerned with truth than exaggeration, with unfolding the moral values of the inner life, rather than visibly punishing gross breaches of social decorum. Where farce concentrates on evoking mere laughter, comedy has a deeper purpose. Physical or, at most, physicalized psychological buffoonery gives place to philosophical and moral investigations of identity. In farce we encounter a blind and implacably self-centered incorrigibility that must entrap or unravel itself, exposing its logical contradictions, and be hammered back to the acceptable social norm so that the necessary Bergsonian social self-correction occurs. But the figure in comedy, capable of self-reflection, will be able, through questioning his or her identity, to adjust to these discoveries and to grow in stature. This leaves us with the contradiction, noticed but left unresolved by Nelson, between comedy that closes in harmony, unity, and celebration, and its agent laughter that separates and divides.[7]

Disagreeing with earlier critics and citing Coleridge, Barton argued in the 1970s that there is more to *The Comedy of Errors*, at that time considered Shakespeare's earliest, least sophisticated comedy, than mere farce, in which "by special agreement between dramatist and audience, even the widest and most coincidental plot structures become acceptable."[8] Behind such a judgment lies the old assumption that farce has no deeper purpose than mere entertainment, although what such entertainment might actually involve, what needs it might meet, remains unanswered. Barton admired the clever construction of the *Menaechmi* but concludes, "It would be difficult to claim that it has any object or concern other than to turn the normal world upside down and to evoke laughter of a simple and unreflective kind."[9] Its characters are simple and rigidly typecast: Menaechmus's wife has no name and is shrewish as all wives are; she bears no marks of difference, and there are "no feelings to be considered." Death is never a serious possibility in the *Menaechmi*, "or in most of Roman comedy," whereas it hangs as a threat over the whole of *The Comedy of Errors*, since Egeon is condemned to die if the fine cannot be paid. Yet we can see, for example in *Miles Gloriosus*, how death is not merely a serious possibility but rather an omnipresent threat, in the subtext and the text of that play. We can safely assume it was also in the minds and unconscious of actors who were themselves slaves, as well as for the audience. Death constituted a far more pressing and vicious reality than it ever was in Shakespeare's not very gentle society. If it is not a topos in the *Menaechmi*, death is subtextual to the culture of Plautus. The escape from an imposed, arbitrary identity that can, upon a whim, be just as arbitrarily curtailed or obliterated, energizes the slaves in all these plays.

Identity in Menander is "psychologically more complex" than in Plautus, but it is still a matter of establishing parentage and social class, whereas later Renaissance drama lays "stress upon the inner life." We can read this as asserting the existence of an essential integrity beyond and beneath the necessities and vagaries of social character. The struggle between temptation and nature or conscience is what dignifies the comedies of the Renaissance; and its absence marks the comparative shallowness that qualifies the otherwise ingenious Plautine plots and undermines their claim for greater attention or any aspirations toward moral seriousness.

Plautus focuses on the twin who is at home in the city of Epidamnus and hence on the "perversity of a familiar world," whereas Shakespeare concentrates on Antipholus of Syracuse, on the traveler and visitor to the city of Ephesus. The other Antipholus, at home in this sinful city, does not make his appearance until the beginning of the third act. Shakespeare probably changed the name of the city because of St. Paul's *Epistle to the Ephesians*, which contains a discussion of the nature of Christian marriage, while Ephesus was also associated with magic and witchcraft, with temptations and delusions. Shakespeare's Syracusan Antipholus is, for Barton, a "traveler in an alien city of reputed sorcery." We can more firmly situate this culturally determined rhetoric of witchcraft and sorcery, since it shows how he no longer feels sure of himself when faced with the bewildering and apparently gratuitous enticements in this bustling, modern, commercializing and palpably venal world of London that turned upside-down the moral simplicities of normal life in a rural Stratford-on-Avon.

Leah Scragg notes the greater attention Shakespeare gives to the wife in comparison with her role in Plautus. Whereas in the earlier play we see her as

> contributing through her pursuit of status and goods to the image that the drama projects of a competitive, economically oriented society . . . Adriana extends the disruption that the comedy enacts from the public to the private sphere, highlighting the emotional trauma that the play's errors involve. Rather than seeking to protect her possessions, Adriana is struggling to preserve her marriage, and though the means she employs are prejudicial to her own ends, the ends themselves are far from unworthy.[10]

The "stereotypical" scold has given way to "a highly original representation of her as an agent of renewal" (68). The final comments of the

Abbess are taken straight, as moral reprimands to an inadequate wife in not sufficiently disciplining her errant husband. Scragg misses entirely the subversive force of Shakespeare's bawdy for idealizing "character," which permeates and undermines this forthright mixture of practical ethics and high moral tone.

Mimetic assumptions shape such judgments and depend on a series of critical dispositions whereby "the play world" can be separated from the spectator and then evaluated according to presuppositions that rest on universal values. Scragg, therefore, considers that "where the Roman play deals with a specialized incident, the Shakespearean drama has a universal application, and is consequently relevant to those outside the play world" (18). Shakespeare shows these spectators "the cataclysmic events that beset man in his progress from the womb to the grave" and "the upheavals to which every human life is subject" (18). Therefore, in Shakespeare's play, "It is not merely the humorous aspects of mistaken identity that are brought home to the spectator" (22). In the face of "a diabolical force" (21) and in the context of "a metaphysical dimension to the action that has no part in the Roman play" (23), Shakespeare's plot reconstitutes the temporarily disordered world. In sum:

> Where the meeting between Plautus' brothers brings a series of misunderstandings to a close but leaves their society unchanged, the reunion between the members of Egeon's family restores order in the social, economic, intellectual and spiritual spheres, giving rise to both joy and wonder as each individual "finds" himself in the fullest possible sense ... the later dramatist has thus transformed a drama designed to amuse its audience by presenting the improbable consequences of an improbable situation into one in which improbability is deployed to explore an aspect of reality. (23f.)

The concept of the individual remains as unquestioned as the nature of the universalized "family group" (15), whose harmonious reconstitution is seen as the antidote to the "fragility of man's sense of selfhood, and the pain that social dislocation entails" (35). These infelicities characteristically accrue from "the interaction between main and frame plots," the story of the brothers framed by Egeon's postponed death sentence. They do not refer to the challenge posed by the unsettling of individual identity that is, in such readings, capable of recuperation since it is anchored in universal values beyond the text. In such judgments, nothing is historicized and the text is presumed identical to itself, the function of a mimetic imposition that disregards any engagement with the unconscious. Judgments beholden to a strictly mimetic view of theater or to an essentialist or even metaphysical view of character have naturally not gone unchallenged in recent criticism.[11]

First we need to corroborate this reading of Plautus. In an authoritatively placed essay, *The Comedy of Greece and Rome*, Michael Anderson, referring to the "farcical knockabout of a Menaechmi," all but dismisses Plautus from serious consideration as too improbable and inconsequential, as lacking mimetic credibility:

> The extended joke of the play depends almost exclusively on the fact that two individuals, identical in appearance and both answering to the unusual name of Menaechmus, are abroad in the streets of Epidamnus. Accordingly the main job of the Prologue, after a few jokes to capture the audience's attention and a summary account of the story of separation, is to hammer home the point that the twins have the same name (l.43); it is repeated for good measure a moment later, "so that you won't go wrong" (l.47). Throughout the Prologue, delivered in direct address to the audience, there is no pretence that the performance is not a performance, that the stage setting is not a stage setting . . . that a noisy audience, capable of impatience and bad behaviour, is not a few feet from the stage; in short, the whole story of the separated twins and the confusion awaiting them is cheerfully accepted as a fiction expressly designed for entertainment.[12]

Plautus, in this reading, is also the ingenious man of the popular theater. His plays therefore lack sophistication. The audience is not yet ready for it. The Penguin edition, a good translation, offers a similar, surprisingly dismissive opinion. The play "has gained a special place in the attention of English readers, a place of privilege perhaps rather higher than is justified by its merits."[13] Once again, the plot's improbability is criticized and "the merely farcical possibilities of the impossibly identical resemblance" between the twins. Yet this is perhaps justified because "any serious reflection would make the improbabilities of the affair all the more conspicuous." Furthermore, it is "something of a weakness in the comedy that both the brothers are equally callous in their treatment of the women; there is no hint of censure upon the infidelity of Menaechmus, and Sosicles first appears as a staid and virtuous young man, only to be easily tempted into debauch and theft."[14]

In his interesting discussion of identity as a form of role-playing, where *The Comedy of Errors* figures the loss of identity as the greatest possible misfortune, hence, the true subject of the tragedies, Thomas van Laan also draws the line between Shakespearean sophistication in the exploration of identity and the simpler Plautine plot: "Shakespeare has brought into central focus a type of activity that Plautus has shown surprisingly little interest in . . . the attribution of identity to one who does not correspond to it."[15] Thomas MacCary offers a psychoanalytic reading of *The Comedy of Errors* in terms of a narcissistic pre-Oedipal search for self and wholeness in the form of an idealized other ego, represented by the brother. He finds Shakespeare's quest for wholeness "more satisfying than the oedipal comedy" available in New Comedy.[16]

A number of studies argue for the importance of Roman comedy in the Renaissance and in particular for a more sophisticated analysis of Plautus. Indebted to Frye's and Barber's views on ritual and festive comedy, Erich Segal proposes that Plautus's plays address the contradiction between public and private values, between *industria* and *voluptas*. The superego is thereby distracted and a notionally displaced "Greek" indulgence enables the repressed Roman to "escape the toga."[17] He argues the pleasure overcomes the reality principle within the play, hence the audience is enabled to indulge a "vicarious prodigality."[18] But Segal treats such liberation of the (male) psyche as relatively straightforward and does not envisage a more complex relationship among text, plot, and social or familial structures. Robert Miola stresses the impact of the sophisticated comedy of Terence and Plautus in the Renaissance but still differentiates, observing "Shakespeare translates Plautine confusion into moral folly, and romanticizes classical eros, particularly by expanding the role of women."[19]

Wolfgang Riehle makes an even stronger case for the significance of Plautus to Shakespeare and Renaissance drama, arguing what has been attributed to the "native popular tradition" (by Robert Weimann) or to romance is already present in Plautus.[20] *The Comedy of Errors* "is solely concerned with a young man's search for his social integration in his family and especially for his male counterpart. Finding each other, the twins become a symbol of male friendship because they best embody the way in which true friendship is defined by classical authors, above all by Cicero as well as by Renaissance humanists" (204).[21] Together with the play's labyrinthine "mythological associations" this points to "a universal, symbolic significance" (206).[22] Yet in Shakespeare the knot of the action is also tighter than in Plautus, producing "a certain 'cogency' completely lacking in Menaechmi" (89).[23] What needs are satisfied by such a judgment?

By now some positions must be clear. I want to argue from the other end: not how did Shakespeare improve on Plautus, but what can Plautus teach us about Shakespeare? If Roman farce is not characterized by the psychological verisimilitude expected of later comedy, it is nevertheless governed by a rigorous internal logic. Far from resting on intricately plotted but inherently improbable coincidences, defying mimetic credibility, and stretching the attention of an audience, farce is aligned with another persuasive account of human behavior, following a logic that links it with surrealism and the unconscious. Let us formulate the distinction between integrative, identity-settling, harmonizing comedy and disruptive farce by saying: farce is the comedy of the unconscious.[24] Such a narrative logic infiltrates Shakespeare's play, trenchantly subverting the plot's ostensible romance closure. Why do so many critics fail to see this?

The Plautine farce, integrated into Shakespeare, troubles conventional representations of identity. This assault on identity produces a critical repression. Critics find the brothers *dramatically* insufficient. They have no distinguishing characteristics. They are interchangeable, differentiated only by the situations they encounter. Yet such characterological defects make quite different sense if they are not supposed to represent discrete, individual personalities, indistinguishable only because the restricted farcical plot requires it. Rather, they show normal and abnormal, conscious and unconscious, quotidian and repressed facets of the same "person" who, because he is so misunderstood, releases contradictory readings of his character in the minds of those who have the best reasons to mistrust him. Such misunderstandings allow the "other" brother to indulge fantasies without social or psychological cost. He then represents uncensored, unrepressed, guiltless, and unfettered appetite, those facets of the self that a developing comedy of "character" cannot countenance, which it must dispose of and relegate to subsidiary and ludicrous figures. Inventing an identical servant may appear to create space, at the other end of the social scale, for a comedy of developing character, but it has the opposite effect, reinforcing the unconscious dynamic.

Barbara Freedman has made the most sophisticated enquiry into Shakespeare's play as paradigmatic of the divisions in all psychological and textual constructions, constantly eliding each attempt to pin them down and produce harmony out of an incessantly unfolding diversity. "Being," she finds "a function of splitting."[25] Arguing the text resists any ideology that structures it, she also maintains "the superposition of a religious narrative of Christian redemption on a simple Plautine farce of physical mishaps works to contain the splits and repressions incurred by debts and so to limit rather than disseminate meanings" (97). She rehearses probable Elizabethan readings: long-lost brothers reunited in the family; a dissociated self; Everyman's warring spiritual and physical parts; romantic comedy; a morality moving from self-division and bondage to penance and redemption (100f.). In a subtle discourse Freedman argues Shakespeare

> offers a model of how the mind and so how meaning works: we no sooner assert the unity of identity than unconscious splits proliferate and doubles appear; we no sooner loosen ego boundaries and open ourselves up to different points of view than the mind organizes, privileges, represses. What *The Comedy of Errors* finally puts on stage are such basic principles of psychological functioning as splitting, projection, denial, and repression as they haunt our quest for meaning. Since subjectivity is implicated in and predicated upon otherness, identity is itself a product of projection, transference, repression, and internalization. Neither self nor text is ever stable, continuous, or self-present. (111)

Hence "in farce, plot is more disturbing than content" (105). Her impressive psychoanalytic and deconstructive enquiry, therefore, tends toward the ahistorical and abstract, so that we finally find no other explanation for those plots except that they stage the impossibility of any settled reading, evading attempts to pin them down. This has the salutary effect of also unsettling critical positions, but it inevitably also elides what is historically specific, and similar or different, in the structure of those plots.

Farce sets normality aside and vividly exposes social repressions. We should therefore ask what the repressed of that culture might be. The

## Historicizing the Unconscious

answer must be ascertainable in its plots, its texts, which reveal social self-representation. Observing how a culture deals with unconscious structuration, such interpretation exemplifies the comparative cultural study I call "textual anthropology."

If we are to relate *The Comedy of Errors* and *Menaechmi* we ought to beware of assuming the play written 1,800 years later must have improved on the earlier one.[26] The differences and similarities cut across such assumptions. Shakespeare reworked the *Menaechmi* plot, adding the complication of identical servants and the impersonation of a husband from Plautus's *Amphitryon,* as well as other characters. This results in a more complex plot. Another order of difference and similarity exists between them, not because Shakespeare is a "greater" dramatist than Plautus, with "deeper" insight into human nature and "richer" intellectual resources, the familiar arguments, but because of differing cultural needs. Instead of supposing Shakespeare's "first" comedy is tainted by a crude Plautine plot, we can investigate both plays, not in terms of their relatively unsophisticated treatment of "character," whether compensated by farcical qualities, but in terms of what this farce shows us about the underside of events, something both concealed and ill-concealed, something that "character" is expressly designed to deny, about the contents of the Roman and Elizabethan unconscious.[27]

It is possible, although not especially profitable, to read the plots of Plautus and Shakespeare from the standard of representational verisimilitude: as a series of increasingly improbable misrecognitions. However, when the twins—either two or all four—eventually appear together, the inexplicable misinterpretations are finally explained and confusion ended, the family unified and the wholeness of identity finally established. In Plautus, I have suggested that the twins represent the shadow or other side of each other, that it is more helpful to think of them as facets of one person, and that what most interests me is how mistaking "identity" uncovers both "hidden" aspects of that imagined person as well as repressions in whomever misidentifies him. The play does not depend on a series of incredible misidentifications, taxing intellectual patience, but rather moves through ever greater differentiations whose real cause lies outside the improbable plot that can therefore only offer a spurious closure and the illusion of reconciliation. Can we observe a comparable process in Shakespeare's play?

## III

We need to ask whether, or to what extent, *The Comedy of Errors* probes that "inner life," not accessible to Plautus, but attributable to the more developed later culture. When the twins appear together for the first time, the bewildered Duke exclaims:

> One of these men is genius to the other,
> And so of these which is the natural man,
> And which the spirit? Who deciphers them? (V.i.335)

This implies two levels of perception and a body / spirit dichotomy consistent with a Platonizing theology. Finally persuaded that Ephesus is a dangerous place, Syracusan Antipholus determines to flee before it is too late:

> There's none but witches do inhabit here,
> And therefore 'tis high time that I were hence.
> She that doth call me husband, even my soul
> Doth for a wife abhor. But her fair sister,
> Possess'd with such a gentle sovereign grace,
> Of such enchanting presence and discourse,
> Hath almost made me traitor to myself;
> But lest myself be guilty to self-wrong,
> I'll stop mine ears against the mermaid's song. (III.ii.156)

S. Antipholus resists temptation. His soul is not enchanted by the first female witch, but her sister is another matter. Mermaid euphemizes prostitute, and her song entices him. Luciana, the sister, sings a different tune from Adriana, the wife who makes demands upon her husband. Luciana argues women should subject themselves to men, that is the way of nature:

> Luc.: O, know he is the bridle of your will.
> Adr.: There's none but asses will be bridled so.

Historicizing the Unconscious

> Luc.: Why, headstrong liberty is lash'd with woe:
> There's nothing situate under heaven's eye
> But has his bound in earth, in sea, in sky.
> The beasts, the fishes and the winged fowls
> Are their males' subjects and at their controls ... (II.i.13)

The self he might have betrayed, or might yet betray, given this enticing humility, and if he were to stay longer and be afforded greater opportunity, is constructed by a moral ideal not further argued for but, by implication, under permanent threat. The endless misrecognitions provoke a sequence of revealing misreadings. We need to ask: What do they see, fear, assume, and do as a result of these mistakings? Nothing is as it seems to be. The play is a parody of mimesis.

The conclusions the characters jump to, when normal expectations are deflected, reveal contemporary anxieties, the pressures of the day. These anxieties show a fear of being unable to exercise self-discipline, of losing control, in other words of an inability to summon up the moral concentration required for the necessary social and psychological transformations, the contradictory movement toward a puritanizing but liberating, developing bourgeois urban culture that creates the wealth and temptations, now self-evidently destructive of patrimony, which must therefore be resisted. It is ultimately the contradiction between spending and saving, between postponing or taking pleasure, between calculating and difficult self-control or its abandonment for self-indulgence. The two brothers' behavior splits uncleanly along this issue, but this is an invisible stratagem of the text, its ideological subtext, the unconscious of the plot.

That pleasure is problematic, offered or withheld, to be indulged in or refused, to be mutually negotiated in marriage, is more than suggested by the text's metaphors. This pleasure is above all sexual. The play is a compendium of lubricious allusions or "dirty" jokes whose effect has been underestimated, especially by those critics for whom Renaissance romance purifies and spiritualizes Plautine farce. Language is as double as the characters, and puns are made to be mistaken. Where the woman represents temptation, her sexuality always threatens to escape control and overwhelm the men. The sexual jokes are a means of linguistic control and of excising the existential fear on this linguistic level.

The story of the separated family, deprived by Fate of its wholeness and searching to reconstitute itself, the substance of romance, is played out within the context of trade wars in which you can lose not just your shirt but your life as well. In order to survive not only the temptations of the flesh and the devil, but also the slings and arrows of outrageous bourgeois fortune, you must have the strength to withstand and contain, to *transform,* yourself. This is what is meant by the following passage:

> S. Antipholus:
> There's not a man I meet but doth salute me
> As if I were their well-acquainted friend,
> And everyone doth call me by my name;
> Some tender money to me, some invite me;
> Some other give me thanks for kindnesses;
> Some offer me commodities to buy.
> Even now a tailor call'd me in his shop,
> And show'd me silks that he had bought for me,
> And therewithal took measure of my body.
> Sure these are but imaginary wiles,
> And Lapland sorcerers inhabit here.
> *Enter S. Dromio:*
> Master, here's the gold you sent me for. What have you got the picture of Old Adam new apparell'd? (IV.iii.1)

These blandishments are not simply the result of being mistaken for your look-alike brother, they also constitute the temptations that beset the formation of this newly energized and money-centered economy where everyone, for a while, extends seemingly magical credit. Welcome to bourgeois (Renaissance) Britain in the (15)80s offering guiltless credit until the crash. But the economic reality principle requires that the Old, innocently lascivious and lackadaisical Adam must transform himself into a New Adam, if he is to survive in this disturbingly and enticingly energized Elizabethan world, where money may not be misplaced, where squandering it will catch up with you in the end, where everything must be accounted for, where money alone confers the material substance of identity, and its absence deprives you of it or even condemns you to death. In his Epistle, St. Paul had urged the Ephesians to shun lasciviousness and to "put on the new man," a lesson for the (15)90s.[28]

Historicizing the Unconscious

The temptations of the flesh are so omnipresent, they must be disciplined or disparaged. First, the overdemanding wife cannot discipline herself and must be constrained by the husband's withdrawal, and by the surprising refusal of his misrecognized substitute to take his place. Second, we encounter an uneasy and contradictory comical disparaging of gross sexuality and bodily functions, instead of their unregrettingly provocative Rabelaisian celebration. In this Elizabethan world, the earlier garden of delights is now going to seed, turning rank or foul. Metaphors of disgust proliferate, the innocent medieval bathhouse is turning into a psychologically tendentious and theologically precarious witches' cauldron. A cultural transformation is now required. Sensuality must be transformed; it must be split and either spiritualized or animalized. That is why the play is so edgy about sexual pleasure. It is no longer innocent, it now constitutes a threat. It has become tendentious. Repression is the new order for a different day. The play explores the infelicities and vicissitudes of this contradictory demand, of the new social edict that is so palpably and frustratingly *contra naturam*.

The family has been torn asunder and wishes to reconstitute itself. S. Antipholus seeks his brother and his mother. Is there not an unconsciously regressive moment in this Shakespearean addition to the plot? This Antipholus wonders at times whether he is dreaming what happens to him, the dream of unsolicited pleasure being of course the sign of a desire that the repression or inhibition upon its fulfillment might be permanently lifted. The implication in the cited passages is not just that what is happening can only be a dream but also if only this dream were true. Since it cannot and may not be true, it must result from witchcraft. But the longed for, elusive wholeness of the previously dismembered family—dispersed by Fate, dislocated by forces beyond its control and, as the play unfolds, unknowingly set against itself, as the continuous misrecognitions produce ever more serious consequences, leading through arrest, possible financial ruin, and evident loss of emotional and mental control, to madness—is finally and quite miraculously restored.

The comic denouement reconstitutes this family that has, unwittingly, been competing with itself. So a whole series of tensions are symbolically resolved in what we can call a surrogate solution. The commanding mother, as Abbess a superb authority figure, saves her misguided sons, physically protecting one of them in the sanctuary of her abbey. We do not have to be Kleinians to give this gesture a strong reading as regression to maternal protection from the dangers of the unsociable world: the play's resolution in fantasy, dream, or comedy, of the invisible because incomprehensible tensions that cannot be properly named or placed but can be glimpsed through the figurations of the writing. The Abbess, however, is a contradictory figure.

Searching for this mother and his brother, and they are mentioned in that order, S. Antipholus "confounds himself." He fears he may even "lose myself" (I.ii.40). He is the ingénu or guileless traveler who must strengthen himself to resist the temptations that might otherwise smother him. On one level, the brother, Ephesian Antipholus, therefore stands for his dissolute other self, for the one that must be kept in check, for what he secretly would like to do but may not. E. Antipholus lies, he cheats on his wife. Shut out of his own house, he hammers on the door. To S. Antipholus and Dromio inside, he sounds just like someone demanding entry to the brothel in which they believe themselves to be (III.i).

The reversal of positions also applies to E. Antipholus. When he hears from E. Dromio allegations about his behavior, although his twin was mistaken for him, he angrily and correctly denies saying what is attributed to him. The point, however, is that this apparently false attribution reveals an inner truth or inclination, alleging that, in spite of his superficial protestations, he does indeed "deny my wife and house" (III.i.9). When he is shut out from both, he knows exactly where to go.

The play is a catalog of transformations, of what can happen as you negotiate your identity in this bewildering world. How are these transformations figured? S. Antipholus is lodged at the Centaur, a potent metaphor in a play that so obsessively investigates sexuality, marking the transition from animal to man. The mythological figures had a man's torso to the waist, and below, the body of a horse. They were ambiguous, unsettling creatures, liable to burst into a wedding feast unbidden and carry off the women. E. Antipholus lives at the Phoenix (I.ii.75). This bird signals a spiritualizing transformation, dying in the flames and rising from the ashes, hence the opposite of the Centaur. But E. Antipholus cannot be so monstrously tempted as his brother, because he has little inclination to resist. He need not protect himself; instead, he must transform himself. There is a joke here too: the phoenix is a unique creature, there is only ever one of them.

E. Antipholus betakes himself to the courtesan and asks the goldsmith

Historicizing the Unconscious

to bring the chain to her, "to the Porpentine" (III.i.116). This constitutes another complex and suggestive pun, setting up a series of associations that lead us into the double and duplicitous language of the text. Porpentine is a version of Porcupine, and porcupine stands for hedgehog. The words all marry pig and spine or prick. So the porpentine or hedgehog, home of the courtesan, metaphorises animality, gross or beastly sexuality. In *Macbeth*, witches and hedge-pigs (IV.i.2) will associate buggery, sodomy, "a deed without a name" (IV.i.49), and similar associations surely hover in this witch-ridden comedy's subtext.[29]

Let us look a little further into the nature of these transformations, into the language that figures them. Adriana entices S. Antipholus, thinking him her husband, saying to herself:

Come, come, no longer will I be a fool,
To put the finger in the eye and weep,
Whilst man and master laughs my woe to scorn.
Come, sir, to dinner. (II.iii.203)

As so often occurs in this play, the meaning here is double. Eye stands for sexual organ. So the line's second meaning is: masturbate to orgasm. Listening to this, S. Antipholus is understandably perplexed:

Am I in earth, in heaven, or in hell?
Sleeping or waking, mad or well-advis'd?
Known unto these, and to myself disguis'd?
I'll say as they say, and persever so,
And in this mist at all adventures go. (II.ii.213)

S. Dromio has just exclaimed, "I am transformed" (II.ii.195), which has the connotation of sexual mutilation or change into the other gender. This was a slippery business, and precariously easy, since the Elizabethans believed in the absolute homology of the sexual organs, the female being an inverted mirror image of the male. Gender was not so soundly marked by sexual difference. Consequently there was a real possibility that one sex could suddenly change into the other.[30] Of course that also constituted the basis for a catalogue of anxieties about the need for men to control women. Otherwise women might simply turn into men, metaphorically, politically, and biologically, if brought to a sufficient condition of heat. The Elizabethans believed that conception only took place after female orgasm. Female sexuality was infested with male anxieties, and the daughters of the bourgeois family were rigorously protected. Transformation is given an anxious and comic reading:

> S. Ant.: Thou hast thine own form.
> S. Dro.: No, I am an ape.
> Luc.: If thou art chang'd to aught, 'tis to an ass.
> S. Dro.: Tis true she rides me and I long for grass.
> 'Tis so, I am an ass, else it could never be
> But I should know her as well as she knows me. (II.ii.198)

Ride is a metaphor for fuck, and to graze, here expressed as to "long for grass," means to prostitute yourself. So S. Dromio is joking that unless he is transformed, he'll never get to "know" her properly, that is, have sex with her.

The word "transform" occurs at least twice more in this double context. Each time it is given a different reading. At the end of the long conversation between S. Antipholus and S. Dromio, a whole catalog of the fat servant, of the gross female body that terrifies him, Dromio concludes:

> ... this drudge or diviner laid claim to me, call'd me Dromio, swore I was assur'd to her, told me what privy marks I had about me, as the mark of my shoulder, the mole in my neck, the great wart on my left arm, that I, amaz'd, ran from her as a witch. And I think if my breast had not been made of faith, and my heart of steel, she had transform'd me to a curtal dog, and made me turn i' th' wheel. (III.ii.140)

He fears she will sexually overwhelm, curtail, or castrate and enslave him. Halfway through the elaborate description of the terrors of her body, S. Antipholus asks him, "What's her name?" He replies, "Nell, sir; but her name and three quarters, that's an ell and three quarters, will not measure her from hip to hip" (III.ii.109). Once again, meaning is double. On the surface she is simply very fat—"she is spherical like a globe" (III.ii.114)—but the tendentious joke concealed in the innocent pun reveals more. An ell is a unit of measure. My scholarly Riverside edition correctly informs me in the annotation to this passage that it equals 45 inches and plays on the name Nell. Now 45 inches is one and a quarter yards, since one yard measures 36 inches. But one yard and a quarter, or "her name and three-quarters" together makes 2 yards. Yard is one of the most common Elizabethan terms for penis. Dromio is also saying that two penises at once are not enough to satisfy her. This is, of course, sexual gross motor joking.

My final example of tendentious transformation comes from the Platonizing language of S. Antipholus. Luciana tempts Antipholus because she encourages him, thinking he is Adriana's husband, to dissemble and practice a double morality. She too has a double identity and is incompatible with herself. It is worldly wise advice to equivocate and pleasure yourself, and he will finally resist it. But at this moment he tells her:

> Against my soul's pure truth why labour you,
> To make it wander in an unknown field?
> Are you a god? Would you create me new?
> Transform me then, and to your power I'll yield.
> But if that I am I, then well I know
> Your weeping sister is no wife of mine,
> Nor to her bed no homage do I owe:
> Far more, far more to you do I decline. (III.ii.37)

It is an invitation to be dominated by the woman, to be resexed and yield or physically decline and bend to her power, but made to the woman who resists his advances, not the one who seeks to bind him.

At the end of the play, the holy Abbess, trying to understand the behavior of anyone called Antipholus, remonstrates with Adriana for treating her husband badly. The exchange, a sequence of sexual puns, implies she has neglected her husband's desire. Adriana, in turn, complains he has been unheeding of hers and has strumpeted her with his contagion (II.ii.144). The Abbess lists a number of possible causes for the apparent madness and then asks:

> Abb.: . . . Hath not else his eye
> Stray'd his affection in unlawful love—
> A sin prevailing much in youthful men,
> Who gave their eyes the liberty of gazing?
> Which of these sorrows is he subject to?

> Adr.: To none of these, except it be the last,
> Namely, some love that drew him oft from home.
> Abb.: You should for that have reprehended him.
> Adr.: Why so I did.
> Abb.: Ay, but not rough enough.
> Adr.: As roughly as my modesty would let me.
> Abb.: Haply in private.
> Adr.: And in assemblies too.
> Abb.: Ay, but not enough. (V.i.50)

This exchange also suggests that sexual punning must have been more important for the contemporary audience than the simple telling of tendentious jokes. Assembly, or meeting, stands for coitus, reprehend has the meaning "hold fast," and private connotes sexual organ. So the Abbess is telling Adriana she has not masturbated her husband vigorously enough, nor slept with him sufficiently. In other words, she has not done his bidding. The fault in the marriage must be hers. The project of the bourgeois marriage, which has to do with constraining wives and daughters, and controlling the self and its capital assets, is launched in a contradictory flood of holy ribaldry. Throughout the play this bawdy is at war with the moral project of self-containment and harmonious reconciliation.

This play negotiates, or simply shows, the anxieties in private and public life that accompany the repressions and disturbing transitions in late-sixteenth-century culture, as it reveals the force of what must be overcome if the moral bourgeois subject is to constitute itself successfully. Shakespeare's "inner life" is far more problematical, the issues sharper and more riven, identity more difficult than we might have assumed. In a word, identity is more "farcical" and complex, more consistently undermined by an edgy self-questioning, as a consequence of the confusions literally embodied in the misrecognized other, here so transparently a projected construct of the self, than anything envisaged by the proponents of a spiritually elevating struggle for unified character, or any reconstitution of a holy family, let alone a case of mistaken identity. For all that, the plot finally brings them together. The supposition of a potentially, but imperfectly, integrated self, sustained by a transcendental and ultimately religious value system, allows Scragg to view the "errors" in the characters of *Twelfth Night* as self-generated, com-

Historicizing the Unconscious

pared with the externally generated errors in the earlier play and its source. This sense of a selfhood within one's grasp, as a form of moral choice, integrates identity.[31]

## IV

What can be said of Plautus? How is *Menaechmi* positioned?[32] What strikes me about Plautus is not the farcical inconsequentiality of his ingenious plot, but rather its psychological credibility. The fundamental argument linking these two plays is now emerging. Shakespeare's farcical comedy of character draws its energy and interest from the *cognitive* capacity of farce, not in spite of its characterological deficiencies. Plautus's ancient farce offers insight into the psychological structuring of identity, because his texts enable us to reach different assumptions about the representation and formation of character than those made by most of his critics.

The prologue tells how the brothers were separated, and how the stolen child was given a new identity in the city of Epidamnus.[33] It anticipates what we think of as a Renaissance topos, that the theater can represent anything in the world, the whole panoply of characters, which therefore seem as insubstantial as their representation in the theater. Epidamnus is also a city in which you can be damned if you are not careful: there is such wordplay with the name (112).

Peniculus the parasite then tells us his name is Sponge, or one could say Little Brush, because he sweeps everything off the table. But the name also has another meaning: Little Penis. Menaechmus's "mistress," Erotium, is called Erotium Meretrix, which means harlot or courtesan and clearly fixes her social status. Peniculus tries to compete with Menaechmus for her attentions, so the parasitic Little Penis is not just an ever hungry stomach. He tells Menaechmus "The day's already dead down to the waist. What are we waiting for?" (108).[34] He wants to light the flame that burns at night and below the waist. But Erotium briskly tells Little Penis, "You don't count" [*Extra numerum est mihi*].[35] Menaechmus says there will be a drinking competition between the two of them, and the better fighter or drinker will become her "conscript" (109). She will have to choose with whom to spend the night. The Latin word here is *legio*, or legion, meaning a choosing or chosen body, hence army. The text's sexual punning seems less fraught, more innocent than Shakespeare's, as we might expect of the Greco-Roman world, but I doubt we can say this about its representation of other aspects of psychic identity.

Menaechmus ($M^1$) has a "nagging" wife. The relationship between this husband and wife is revealing. When the wife's father is later called to mediate between them, he gives her the standard advice about treating a husband properly. The problems are an arranged marriage (131) and the husband's behavior. She complains he is "making love to the harlot next door" and "drinking there too" (132). The father remonstrates; he cannot "be your slave"; you'll be asking him "to do the housework next." She pleads, he's stealing "my clothes and jewels." Whereupon the father responds, "He has no right to do that." So the wife, it seems, has vicarious domestic and legal property rights. The father thinks women with "good dowries" often make unreasonable demands on their husbands (131). This attitude indicates that Roman women have a greater degree of independence than women in Renaissance England. Erotium also behaves decisively, throwing Menaechmus out when she thinks he is lying. In Plautus, Menaechmus is barred from *both* houses. In each case he is denied entry because he does not have the stolen gown. The gown has become a fetish, of rights and power, of something stranger.

To understand what is happening here, we need to appreciate the social, economic, and cultural issues as well as an historical perspective upon them in the Roman republic after the victorious conclusion of the Second Punic War in 201 BCE, fifteen years before Plautus produced this play. These matters range widely, and the theoretical basis for the arguments reach beyond this particular period. There seem suggestive analogies, even homologies, with later cultural formations and, if this can be demonstrated, implications for evaluating the function of comedy and assessing the relationship between these plays by Plautus and Shakespeare.

Since the plot of *Menaechmi* betrays obvious anxieties about the role of women and reveals them as a source of paranormal or comic behavior among men, hence that such behavior is unconsciously produced, we need to look at the interrelationships between domestic and public life. Both respond to and are a function of rapid social changes that question the economic structures and the ethical basis upon which Roman society had hitherto reproduced itself. Two relevant issues must be investigated: the changing nature of economic and social life, and the role of women along this interface between the public and the private or domestic spheres, since the comedy appears to represent this role as troubling.

First we need to discuss briefly the nature of marriage and the regulation of this social institution during the period that concerns us—the mid-third century to mid-second century BCE. There were three forms of marriage recognized by civil courts whereby the woman passed into the authority, into the hand (*in manum*), of her husband. She did so, and this is crucial, under different circumstances and conditions: *confarreatio, coemptio,* and *usus*.[36] Under these three forms of marriage, *manus,* or marital authority, was negotiated differently. In the oldest and patrician form, confarreatio, marriage and manus were established simultaneously through the ceremony. With coemptio, the acquisition of manus by the husband was conducted through a separate legal ceremony, which was not part of the wedding. The major difference lay in the third form: usus. Here manus was only acquired after a year's cohabitation, but if this period was interrupted by three nights' separation (*trinoctium*), then it did not come into effect. This resulted, therefore, in a relationship that was tantamount to a marriage without manus, and it is known to have been practiced by the time of the First Punic War.[37] Marriage without manus meant the wife remained under the authority of her "father or of his legal representative" (15). In practice this meant the husband had no rights to her property and that she, therefore, enjoyed considerable real independence.

What from one perspective must have been experienced as a breakdown of authority in marriage, a retreat from customs and ethical standards linked to the ethos of the state and its prosperity, the necessary self-sacrifice to community that created the so often reinvoked ethical Roman state, must have come about as a result of the changing nature of that state. The elder Cato, an exact contemporary of Plautus, deplored the alteration in these traditional relationships: "All nations rule their wives, we rule all nations but our wives rule us" (25). The changing position of women produced considerable anxiety among the men, but this emancipation also related to the changing social structures produced by different opportunities in economic life.

By the end of the Punic Wars two decisive developments were taking place. Large estates, known as *latifundia,* were created out of small holdings bought up by the rich; and the labor of the free peasants was replaced by slaves. The small holdings could not compete with these relations of production, and the farmers moved to the cities, creating a proletarian class. At the same time considerable imperial expansion gathered pace, leading to cheap imports and to economic opportunities in the cities that had not previously existed on this scale. Some of the displaced small farmers transformed themselves into merchants and then into financiers, gradually rising into the class of knights (*eques*), creating an aristocracy of money and eventually forming a new oligarchy. The old patrician families that constituted the administrative elite were not theoretically allowed to participate in business and finance, but the demand for these new services grew ever stronger as the Roman territories expanded.

This new money led inevitably to social tensions and, finally, to civil war. But that, for the time being, lay in the future. Old families began to break up, ceding power to a new commercial class. This appears much like what was to happen in the European Renaissance with the breakdown of the feudal order and the creation and expansion of the power of bourgeois merchant capital, and so of new forms of economic and social life. It must, therefore, finally explain why Shakespeare could write *The Comedy of Errors* and base it on Plautus's *Menaechmi*. The anxieties these comedies addressed were homologous, even if the cultural circumstances were different.

The gradual breakup of this old order created opportunities for women, a process reflected in the passing of laws. One such law decreed that no woman related to a knight was permitted to sell herself (38). The laments for lost chastity seem to begin at about this time in Roman culture, although that particularly male song may well be perennial. During the Punic Wars, aristocratic women prostitutes were banished. A *Lex Voconia* was passed in 169 BCE, forbidding women to receive legacies, indicating the prevalence of what was perceived as a disturbing social practice. There seems to have been a degree of real economic and sexual emancipation for women, which must have depended upon the creation of this new wealth among the merchant and banking class. Women in Rome had no political rights but wielded much greater personal independence than Greek women. There are references to an *ordo matronarum*, or women's meeting, where women could articulate their views and draw the state's attention to their demands. In 215 BCE a *Lex Oppia* was passed, restricting the use of ornaments and displays of wealth by women. Women agitated for its repeal and the law was eventually overturned in 195 BCE. Livy's account of this argument is telling:

> The tribunes Marcus and Publius Junius Brutus defended the law, and said they would not allow it to be repealed; many distinguished men appeared to back it or oppose it; the Capitol was crowded with its supporters or opponents. Neither influence, nor modesty, nor their husband's commands could keep the married women within doors. They beset all the streets in Rome and all the approaches to the Forum, imploring the men who were going down to the Forum that they should allow their former luxuries to be legalized, now that there was general prosperity in Rome. (52)

A debate took place between Cato and the liberal tribune Valerius, in which the two argued about the position of women in social life. Cato stated:

> Our ancestors laid down that women might carry out no business—even private business—without supervision from her guardian, and they confined them to the authority of their parents, brothers, and husbands. But we ... are allowing them to take part in the government of the country and mingle with the men in the Forum, the meetings, and the voting-assemblies. What else are they doing at this moment, in the highways and byways, except supporting a bill sponsored by the tribunes and voting for a repeal of the law? Give rein to that headstrong creature woman, that unbroken beast, and then hope that she herself will know where to stop her excesses! If you do not act, this will be one of the least of the moral and legal obligations against which women rebel. What they wish to have is freedom in all things—or, rather, if we are to tell the truth, licence in all things. (53)

Opposing him, Valerius did not advocate freedom from patriarchal authority for women; rather, he believed this authority should not be too restrictive: "As long as her kinsmen are alive, a woman is never free from her slavery, and she herself prays that she will never have the freedom brought about by widowhood and bereavement. They would rather that you should decide on their adornment than the law. And you ought to keep then under your authority and guardianship, not in slavery to you, and you should prefer to be called fathers and husbands than masters.... In their weakness they must accept whatever decision you make. The more powerful you are, the more moderately you should use your power" (54).

Their rhetoric reveals both the uneasiness of these proposals and the fact that women with money could achieve a degree of freedom, legally sanctioned only by the state of widowhood. It seems a small wonder, under these circumstances, that a decisive woman in this Roman society could easily cause severe psychological problems for her husband.

The play depends upon a sequence of misrecognitions that grow ever more complex as the story unfolds. To mimetic literalists they become increasingly improbable. Once we appreciate that the brothers embody each other's repressed side, that they therefore signify the character potential of *one* person, that they represent levels of constructed social character and hence uncover the accompanying social unconscious, it becomes important to realize how their identities are both constructed and mistaken by the other characters. We need to grasp the sequence and logic of these misreadings in their complexity. Tracing this has nothing to do with demonstrating abstract ingenuity, with an unproductive semiotic or structuralist obsession. On the contrary, it enables us to understand the dimensions of the psychological space within which representation occurs and that is shaped by the social pressures of the culture.

$M^1$ appears to have a problem with his identity. He steals his wife's gown to give to Erotium, but he is actually wearing it. To make the point more clearly, he poses first as the catamite Ganymede and then as Venus seducing Adonis. This concealed dress implies another, repressed identity. $M^1$ is afraid of his wife. She is as dangerous as Hippolyta, Queen of the Amazons.[38] One would need the psychological strength of a Hercules in order to stand up to her. Although $M^1$ fears and dislikes his wife, he wears her dress, as his mistress quickly observes (110), indicating that he cannot escape her. She gets under his skin. She is a constant unconscious presence.

He also needs to disparage her femaleness, here the smell on the dress, hence his fantasy of love with a perfumed courtesan. The dress also smells of "stolen goods, secret amours, and a free lunch" (109) or "theft, a harlot, a feast."[39] That is, of course, a complete illusion. The courtesans, Messenio says, are as dangerous as pirates who capture and sell you into slavery. There is precise information about how they capture their customers (115). The dialogue also moves from "normal" to "abnormal" in this episode. Little Penis tells M¹ that he should dance. The implication is an erotic dance, before taking the gown off:

M¹: Me dance? Are you out of your mind?
P: One of us is, I'm not sure which. (110)

The language is also double when M¹ hands the gown to Erotium and she says, "You set an example to all true lovers" (110).[40] She is professionally concerned with money and careful with it, ordering an appropriate feast, "not too little, not too much" (111). She uses M¹ as a source of income. Prostitutes in Rome were slaves, but there was unquestionably common anxiety about the behavior of independent-minded, married women who took lovers against payment for pleasure.

Enter Sosicles, whom I call M², and Messenio. The slave always is, and must always be, someone else. For the slave, identity is constantly threatened, so it must always be shiftable. We see this clearly in *Miles Gloriosus*. The well-named Cylindricus, Erotium's cook, approaches M² and immediately turns him into someone else, his twin. He says to the audience about M¹, "He can be ever so amusing—when his wife's not there" (114). So M¹ has at least three personalities: his apparent public identity; his behavior in the absence of his wife; and what is suggested by his fetishization of her power through his wearing of her dress. These incompatible identities will lead to metaphorical schizophrenia or "madness."

Let us look again at the critically literalist mimetic objection that the plot is impossible because nobody could consistently misrecognize for so long. Of course M² ought to realize sooner that he is being taken for M¹. But in comedy the normal rules are suspended in order to question them by showing what lies below the surface of normal daily life. This used to be called aesthetic license, where the demand of verisimilitude is suspended. Yet this is what actually happens all the time. We constantly misrecognize ourselves and others. Therefore he cannot see the difference. So *actual misrecognition is best conveyed by apparent theatrical mimesis*.

M² wants to be literally and metaphorically "taken in" by Erotium, while asserting the opposite. On a simple level, this can be read as temptation of a susceptible man by a professional woman, but given the relationship between the twins, something more interesting is taking place. We cannot simply think of them as two quite separate and different people.

Erotium is a professional dissembler. She sells fantasies to men. She makes a profession of double identity. The superficial point about the encounter is that she is mistaken in thinking $M^2$ is $M^1$ (115). But her love or friendship is itself a pretense; it too is mistaken. $M^2$ thinks she is pretending love to ensnare him, and we may think he is mistaken because we know she thinks he is $M^1$. But, in reality $M^2$ is correct, since her love for $M^1$ is itself pure pretense. The question—"Who is the woman talking to?" (115)—is absolutely accurate, for who *is* $M^1$, whom she confuses with $M^2$?

For Erotium, $M^1$ is not the person he believes himself to be. The answer to that question—"She is talking to you, of course" (116)—carries this doubleness, for who, under these circumstances, is "you"? $M^2$ thinks Erotium must be either "insane or intoxicated" (116). Both are alienated states. But she is perpetually alienated and always playing a double game. For the sake of Erotium, $M^2$ decides to become $M^1$. He seizes an opportunity and indulges a fantasy. He becomes $M^1$'s fantasy of his role for Erotium. He does not become that role, which is double, because he does not pay.

But $M^2$'s role as $M^1$ is also as real, or as unreal, as $M^1$'s. Stepping over the doorstep (117), or threshold, or border, is to step through the looking glass, to enter into fantasy, to participate in the mysteries and to parody their search for identity, to pursue what later scholarship will deny Plautus and attribute to Shakespeare.[41] On another level, Messenio tells $M^2$, "You're done for if you cross that doorstep" (117).[42] The slave Messenio stands for the necessity of a reality principle in a dangerous world. Yet $M^2$ believes he can dupe and profit from Erotium.

$M^2$ leaves satisfied and is going to steal the dress, which is already stolen, already a purloined identity. He is given a bracelet as well (121). $M^2$ does not, of course, recognize Peniculus, but then $M^1$ never did either, for Peniculus is unknowable, another meticulous dissembler (120). $M^2$ thinks his sexual identity is questioned, because $M^1$ wore his wife's dress and Peniculus thinks he is $M^1$ (121).

The wife accosts, we expect, $M^2$, but no, it is $M^1$, whose hidden identity will be revealed because it has been impersonated, or in part

## Historicizing the Unconscious

usurped, by $M^2$. When Peniculus sees $M^1$ and says, "Here he is too . . ." (123), he is superficially wrong, but he is also right because they encounter $M^1$'s *concealed* identity revealed by $M^2$. From the subsequent soliloquy (123) it appears $M^1$ is a patron or protector of his clients' interests, which involved defending them in lawsuits, and so he is also a lawyer who lives by pretending bad is good. That profession rests on systematic deception.

Peniculus tells lies, assuming $M^2$ to be $M^1$, and thus uncovers the truth about the stolen gown (126). The wife then bars $M^1$ from the house until he brings the gown back, which $M^2$ has taken. Peniculus says, "It's obvious I'm no longer a friend of the family" (127). This lie is a truth as well, for he never was. The confusion $M^1=M^2=M^1$ then reveals Erotium's concealed identity (128). $M^1$ is locked out of both houses.

$M^2$ is now taken for $M^1$ by the wife. Previously she thought $M^1$ was $M^2$ whom she had confused with $M^1$. The false husband reveals that husbands play roles (129), even though and because $M^2$ is not the real husband. The real husband, $M^1$, is himself a fake. The false husband uncovers the reality. This false husband therefore is the reality. He represents the hidden or repressed identity. On one level, as throughout, it is all simple though bewildering confusion. On another level, it is complex psychological and social reality. One thing, however, we can be sure it is not—namely, a play which can only provoke "laughter of a simple and unreflective kind."

For the wife, $M^2$ is "just like you too" (130), that is like $M^1$, so he reveals the socially structured personality, the expectations of a man in such a marriage. Nothing is more like somebody else, who is not actually there, than the same behavior in another person, because it shows the same structuration that we anticipate. The father then sides with the husband against the daughter (132). But if I does not equal I, then "I" have not lived there (133), and this is no lie. It is the truth.

Messenio's other self is discovered by $M^1$. The terms "slave" and "freedom" exist on different levels, simultaneously in two matrices. But then identity and individuality also adhere to different matrices. $M^2$ then asserts absolute ownership of Messenio (142). And Messenio confuses the two brothers, one who wants to free him and the other who does not. This is a typical comic confusion, but it also shows that Messenio recognizes the generous man, in this case $M^1$, as master. Messenio then turns M² into M¹. He says to M², "That man, sir, is either an impostor—or your twin brother" (143). He is both at the same time, for the man is an impostor of himself.

M² tells Messenio, if M¹ is my long-lost brother, "you are a free man" (143). M¹ tells him, "I am willing to serve you as your bought slave" (143). What, then, is a slave? M¹ was himself kidnapped. He could just as well have become a slave, but was lucky and did not, eventually inheriting the merchant's money. The play ends with the discovery of the other self or lost identity, and M¹ asks M² to free Messenio "for my sake" (145). So M² frees him for the sake of his lost and restored self. M¹ then sells off his property, including the wife, if he can find a buyer, since he no longer needs to be "himself." This constitutes the final misrecognition or joke, since his wife and her property are not his to sell. The play has centered "identity" on this contradiction.

For Messenio, however, the troubles are only beginning. Freedom is not enough. He needs an income (146). It seems that identity is arbitrary, complex, and if it is secured by anything at all in a society that is obviously no longer sure of its own stability, then perhaps by the strength of one's financial position.

## V

Both societies that Plautus and Shakespeare lived within and shape for us by their texts were shaken by changes in economic and social relations, deriving from the creation of new wealth, then in the process of being distributed in ways that were disturbingly different. These new relations therefore also unsettled the conventions that had hitherto organized appropriate gender roles, so that these new possibilities were creating different experiential spaces and they, in turn, expressed themselves most vividly in representations of dispositions between the sexes.

This, precisely, is where Plautus must now surely seem to us more "modern" than Shakespeare, and why his questioning of identity seems as radical and convincing as Shakespeare's does not, in spite of his formidable rhetorical skills. Antipholus may be troubled by witchcraft and sorcery, or rather, these are the historically provocative and contradictory terms available within Shakespeare's world to explain and neutralize the temptations that must be resisted if the self is to be constrained and capital, both moral and financial, successfully accumulated. The temptations are figured primarily in sexual terms. They serve to entice the characters, in the process of being shaped by these larger events without understanding what has produced them or where they will lead. They also simultaneously register or unsettle the wider repressive project enabling social development, which will eventually triumph through a combination of successful economic policy and the accompanying internalized pressure exerted through the social unconscious, here in the form of a desire for hitherto inaccessible ways of living.

Yet Antipholus seems less psychologically disturbed than Menaechmus. He may be bewildered and tempted, but he does not get into his wife's dress. The dress is something of a fetish. It is described in interestingly different, even divergent, ways in various texts. In what may have been one of the direct sources for Shakespeare's play, William Warner's translation of Plautus, this dress is referred to as "a fine ryding cloake," and none of the Plautine associations survive such a superficial transferal into a more decorous moral environment.[43] It is probably symptomatic of this shift that Scragg evaluates the crucial initial episode simply in terms of an "estrangement between this brother and his shrewish wife, whom he proposes to spite by giving one of her garments to a courtesan."[44] Again there is no consideration of how this "garment" functions in psychological or physiological terms, except as a superficial mark of his anger. Shakespeare omits it.

Shakespeare's ending celebrates the unification of the family. Critics tend to register this as a decisive advance on Plautus, whereas we might reflect that the lack of any such resolution in Plautus makes his play more interesting. Because the restitution of the family effectively situates, or restores and reasserts, a particular power structure that remains quite unresolved in the Roman play. Even though Menaechmus may talk of selling off his wife, this does not affect the distribution of economic power in the marriage.

In Shakespeare, the wife's power is humanized and transformed into a neglected potential for private affection. It becomes part of that mysterious "inner life." In this process, the woman is contained and left with the privilege of displaying the strength of her finer emotions in respect to her husband. In Shakespeare's culture, there is nothing else she can do but represent this moral claim. In Plautus, from the perspective of the men, the woman remains distressingly powerful. The economic question, the ownership of wealth, is not resolved, no matter how much Menaechmus may wish to ignore it.

What is often considered as a civilizing advance into the private sphere of the emotions out of the merely economic sphere, thought of as the essential advantage of Shakespeare and his advance over Plautus and evident, for example, in the demonstration of the greater importance of the emotional life and of how the wife is prepared to struggle "to preserve her marriage," in fact depends on the presupposition that this wife has no other weapons with which she may greet or confront her husband than her tears or a display of her frustrations.[45] We could therefore conclude that the movement from the public into the private sphere, far from being an unequivocal sign of a more developed moral and emotional sensitivity, stands as a surrogate satisfaction for the lack of real economic power and represents, if we look back at Plautus, a considerable political retreat.

# 5

## *CORIOLANUS* AND

## THE HISTORICAL TEXT

I

An author rewrites. A critic (re)interprets. Brecht's adapted *Coriolanus* shows definitively why we must historicize the intercultural sign.¹ How do the plays relate to their respective historical moments? They both represent and undermine narratives of history. Do we not always "replace" the Shakespearean text, especially if we merely wish to reproduce it?

The arguments reach in various directions. The principle is simple. The subtexts of these historical, cultural, and critical narratives relate Roman, Tudor/Jacobean, and twentieth-century European political and social history. We must bring these moments to life, feel their contradictions. Only then do we understand why these representations can be read so differently.

Where should we start? "With the politics," says Michael Bogdanov. "Identify the social structure, the protagonists, the status quo."² He is speaking of *The Wars of the Roses*, his adaptation of *Richard II*, *Henry IV*, parts 1 and 2, *Henry V*, the three *Henry VI* plays (shortened to two), and *Richard III*, played more or less nonstop, with occasional breaks for eating and sleeping.³ At the end of his book Bogdanov has amusing examples of the effect of this enterprise, lasting from 1986 to 1989, an aggressively contemporary production, disrespectful of convention, taken on a world tour. France was invaded by an army of English football supporters, waving banners proclaiming "Fuck the Frogs."

Michael Billington, for many years drama critic of *The Guardian*, was disenchanted by the "dubiously Marxist readings of the Histories."⁴ He wrote of the *Henry IV* and *Henry V* plays in terms that take us through, and back, to central issues not only in respect of Shakespeare but of the engagement with all dramatic and "literary" texts, whether conducted in the form of readings or productions or replacings or rewritings or whatever we want to call the process of interpretation: "I find Bogdanov's interpretation of England's National Epic willful, vain and historically dubious. I take Shakespeare's three plays to be complex, ambiguous works about the education of a king; about Hal's immersion in the life of his country in order to become an ideal governor.... Mr. Bogdanov often seems to be overlaying Shakespeare with a play of his own invention.... Henry V also looks forward to the Tudor world in proving that kingliness can be achieved ... dynastic succession vindicated.... But my real objection is to the bias that constantly emphasizes Hal's ruthlessness at the expense of his humanity."[5]

These objections are instructive. Some issues are familiar in their English context: Hands off the National Treasure! Read Shakespeare as he read himself! Anything else is "historically dubious." We notice the presupposition that Hal's "humanity" takes precedence over his ruthlessness, or is equally important, but my central point here is that what helped Bogdanov to this reading of Shakespeare was his knowledge of Brecht and of those "dubiously Marxist readings."

How did Brecht enable such directors to read Shakespeare so differently, and thereby disturb conventional expectations? He historicized. He modernized by historicizing. He put the plays back into historical contexts by distancing them from contemporary conventions. Distancing often brings something closer because we then begin to see it clearly for the first time. This historicization is not that historicism that believes it can recapture the past's self-understanding, and that accumulating such moments amounts to the narrative of history, because it always extrapolates from its own epistemic values. Neither does it abstract from history into an eternal present, as if the protagonists of the plays somehow transcend the humiliations history offers them.

It is not an escape out of history nor a flight back into it. Nor does it mean reading the plays in terms of a presumed authorial intention—Shakespeare longing for a return to the comfort of disappearing feudal values—or as fixed by clarified historical meanings or dominant ideologies.[6] Instead, Brecht saw them in terms of unfolding historical perspectives, as dialectically related to the debates and ideologies of their day that they both embody and encompass or transcend, but from which they cannot be separated. Through these texts we can therefore

*Coriolanus* and the Historical Text

see history moving and glimpse the historical unconscious that is not transparent to the characters.

We could, therefore, say Brecht understood the real complexity of Shakespeare's writing, refusing to share the conventions of contemporary interpretation, blind to their own ideological presuppositions. Hence he rediscovered the issues to which that writing responded as it both represented and elided them. In other words, Brecht was acutely aware, particularly sensitive, to the contradictions in Shakespeare whereas much Shakespearean criticism and, for that matter, criticism of Brecht has instinctively simplified them, privileging one set of values over another, an ideological choice often rationalized in the belief that this uncovers an evident authorial intention. So in juxtaposing Brecht's and Shakespeare's versions of this story, I want to open up a few of these questions and consider some of the relationships between the narratives of history and literature.

II

Why did Brecht object to contemporary productions of Shakespeare? He adapted *Coriolanus* in the 1950s, but in the 1920s he developed his own theater in part as a response to what he so disliked in those interpretations of Shakespeare. What Brecht then took exception to in German productions was still widespread in English culture, indeed it represented the norm until a few years ago. Even today the assumptions are still active.

In Germany, Shakespeare is virtually considered a national author due to the success of the early-nineteenth-century Schlegel-Tieck translations. Greatly admired by Goethe, he was idolized by the generation of romantics through whom the questioning definition of "German" cultural identity began again, as they freed themselves from the disadvantages and benefits of French cultural and political dominance in the post-Napoleonic era. Shakespeare is by a wide margin the most frequently produced author on the German stage, in marked contrast to France. For a while he was overtaken in the 1970s and early 1980s by Brecht, but he has now pulled ahead again. These translations inevitably flattened ambiguities in the original language, and so encouraged romantic readings, seeing the plays' singularity in the representation of great individual destinies, isolated from common life by the force of their imaginations and the grandeur of their language.

The language of these translations has a particular flavor. They had to adapt the less flexible German sentence structure, which places verbs at the end of relative clauses and infinitives and past participles at the end of sentences, to the demands of the iambic pentameter line by often inverting normal word sequences. This gives the verse a certain stagey quality that separates it from everyday speech. The translations lack that frequently devastating directness that Shakespeare's language has for contemporary English-speakers once you have overcome the problem of unaccustomed words. These translations also embody a smaller sociolinguistic range than Shakespeare allows the language of his characters.

Another crucial factor, accounting for the particular quality of the German Shakespeare, is the convention the translations respect, whereby a uniform tone of speech that eliminates regional accents—called *Bühnendeutsch* (literally, stage German)—predominates in performance. This is a standard or elevated form of speaking that requires that, for example, the gravedigger in *Hamlet* will literally speak in accents very like the king. The range and reverberations of Shakespeare's language are thereby narrowed and the consequence, of course, is a different body of writing, a different "author." The differentiations tend to fall away and one of the major casualties is the silent subtext. Another effect is to concentrate attention on the main personages or the hero and this, in turn, affects the dynamics of the plays, encouraging us to take them out of history into the perennial present of the isolated, larger than life, romantic individual. Sociocultural attitudes are involved here, the constructing of a unifying national cultural ideology under different historical circumstances at the turn of the eighteenth and nineteenth centuries, which we must leave unexamined since they take us too far from our topic.

Brecht responded in the 1920s to contemporary representations that took these views as axiomatic, as the common sense of bourgeois culture, in two ways: a sharp criticism of the prevailing ideology that required such interpretations of Shakespeare; and a fascinating assault upon the conventions for dealing with translated Elizabethan language. He understood that the audience, just as much as the character, was constructed by the conventions of performance, even as their culture accepted those conventions. He saw that the audience expected to iden-

## Coriolanus and the Historical Text

tify and empathize, to suffer with the feelings of a character responding to the demands of fate, and ultimately transcending those demands in a spiritual triumph over a crushing physical and historical force majeure.

The consequence of this concentration upon the protagonist's singularity is, paradoxically, the loss of identity's specificity. All sense of historical difference disappears, and play and audience are swept off by the passion of the language, not as it is "given" us in the text but as it is unconsciously interpreted, into a state of mind that traditional criticism equates with an aesthetic state of grace. In fact this depends upon a superficial and self-endangering suspension of thought and so prevents the attainment of that more complex aesthetic experience that is actually the goal of Brecht's theater.

By such a process of abstraction, Othello became the incarnation and benchmark, the synonym of jealousy. When that happens, the emotional force of the play is not increased, which is the conventional assumption, but actually lessened, and that is also disadvantageous to a full appreciation. Yes, this is what Brecht really means, and it is a far cry from the caricature of his as a narrowly rationalist theater, anxious to avoid emotional depth and obsessed with teaching a set of misguided socioeconomic lessons. The clearer we are about precisely how the exceptional Othello is historically and socially positioned, the more powerful will be the effect of the play. These relationships can only be clarified if we distance ourselves from the performance, instead of disappearing into it, allowing it to overwhelm and in effect annihilate us in our difference from him, because we then see the specific differences in Othello's positioning and not just the apparently universal similarities. These characters, therefore, are not "our contemporaries," in Jan Kott's popular and evidently still provocative phrase.[7] They are, in Brecht's view, different from us, and they are "impermanent."[8] But it is this knowledge of their impermanence that guarantees their actuality and the persuasive force of Othello's emotions: "The passion of jealousy, if we show all this, is not narrowed down but on the contrary increased."[9]

To raise such objections to contemporary styles of performance is a precondition for getting through to the complexity of the interpretable text that has been sacrificed to an easier and reductive universalization. We need to focus on its contradictions, its difficulties, on those aspects that resist such easy readings solely in terms of a reconstruction of the emotional life of the central figure.

The other step Brecht took in the 1920s was to rewrite the texts. In a famously innovative production of Marlowe's *Life of Edward II* that he adapted and himself directed in 1924 and that flabbergasted his generation, he also roughened up the all-too-smooth and predictable iambic pentameter by reorganizing the rhythms in a way that stopped the experienced actors in their tracks, leading to resignations and nervous breakdowns, where the language created a continuous sequence of rhythmical and perceptual shocks, drawing constant attention to its own, and the speakers', strangeness.

Brecht later associated this technique with what he called his "gestural aesthetic," which clarifies relations by breaking down and rearranging the conventions of social and linguistic communication into striking audible and visual externalizations that define the position and attitude of the characters. By such means he put the play into crisis with radical methods that were unthinkable and certainly unthought of and unimitated in English theater, which only began to respond to Brecht's ideas and activities about forty years later. The text of his *Coriolanus* does not perform this complete rout upon convention, and in a sense did not need to, because by the 1950s the old perceptual habits had been transformed in Germany, although other problems had replaced them, if not yet in the English-speaking world.[10]

### III

Such fearlessness in the face of great works of art is, in a way, the rule rather than the exception, as we quickly discover if we reflect on attitudes to Shakespeare's texts over the centuries. The idea that a text could be fixed in its meaning is relatively recent and developed with the nineteenth-century historical science of philology. *Coriolanus* was simply not on the program for a couple of centuries. We can also think of the fearlessness with which a work of art is ignored because it appears too unruly or abstruse, out of sympathy with contemporary cultural norms.

In 1682, Nahum Tate could only deal with this play's troubling implications by a large-scale adaptation, called *The Ingratitude of a Common-Wealth*. In his dedication he refers disparagingly to "those troublers of the State," the plebeians, whose loyalty could and should not be trusted.[11] There is far more violence in this adaptation than in Shakespeare. The Tribunes are assaulted. Virgilia is captured by Aufidius and collapses self-slaughtered. Her son is mangled by an introduced character, Nigridius, who kills Menenius. Volumnia enters with the boy in her arms. She strikes down Nigridius. As in a Senecan tragedy, everyone expires. Rebellion has no defender in Nahum Tate's restorationist adaptation and leads only to utter chaos, self-evidently detrimental to the state. We could take as another, celebrated example of ideologically necessitated adaptation, Olivier's 1944 film version of *Henry V*, made in wartime as a patriotic contribution to that conflict. He too interpreted radically, by cutting 1,400 lines, including Henry's instructions to take no prisoners, but leaving in the subsequent French slaughter of the boys in the baggage train that could be seen as a response to Henry's earlier behavior. Foreigners, it seems, are wicked, the home side patriotic.

There is a sliding scale, from critical responses to an established text, or to its interpretation in performance, and on to a major adaptation, rewriting or reworking and recreating of its story. Of course, I could also say there is not necessarily that much difference between these activities in the sense that, like a dull analysis, an apparently more innocuous or respectful interpretation of an unamended text, which is unaware of its ideological position, can produce a reading that undoes or misappropriates a work more thoroughly than extensive or performative rewriting could ever accomplish.

Such critical (re)readings are always instructive. Bradley found the treatment of the common people in *Coriolanus* "amusing": "When the people appear as individuals they are frequently more or less comical. Shakespeare always enjoyed the inconsequence of the uneducated mind, and its tendency to express a sound meaning in an absurd form."[12] What is missing here, as in many other more recent critics, is any appreciation of the pressure of events in Shakespeare's play, in which people are hungry and frightened, or of any pressing relationship between the circumstances of its plot and the historical moments to which it is related. Instead, we have a much more leisurely and gentlemanly contemplation of the text from the perspective of the socioculturally untroubled pre–World War One generation of critics.

Another familiar judgment from the early 1970s is based on a political position that is assumed to be close to Shakespeare's own, distinguishing between the "wholeness of the state" and the aloofness of Coriolanus, the fact that he stands "alone."[13] We find no sense here of the politics of that state as a developing entity, as something in a state of change or as a matter for contention. These politics are rather seen as factored by established and indisputable ideology. Coriolanus is considered a "Roman" hero, and there is little sense of the relativity of that position, of how it is socially constructed and why this was happening in the first decade of the seventeenth century.

In what looks like a step toward a more differentiated reading but does not sustain this expectation, Kermode believed, in 1974, that Shakespeare did not see the story "with the sentimental republicanism of Plutarch but with a predisposition to deplore the attribution of power to the people."[14] Persuasive examples of this ideology in later productions, and in criticism with a specific focus on *Coriolanus,* can be found in an illuminating contribution by Richard Wilson to a discussion of the question: "Is Shakespeare a Feudal Propagandist?"[15] These debates continue. They are by no means laid to rest. It is unwise to assume the issues are settled, because an academic peer group may have reached a consensus.

As a chancellor of the Exchequer once explained, some things really do not change at all.[16] This is what Brecht objected to, but it is not why Brecht was fascinated by Shakespeare. How did Brecht approach the Shakespearean text? What can we learn from his response? Such a comparison throws light on Shakespeare's sources, Plutarch's "sentimental republicanism." It also helps us understand how Shakespeare dealt with those sources, and in turn, how Brecht reread all these relationships.

### IV

Brecht set about adapting *Coriolanus* in the early 1950s.[17] There is an interesting discussion in 1953 with his assistants, Palitzsch, Rülicke-Weiler, and Wekwerth, about the problems he envisaged with the first scene.[18] He wavered between rewriting the play or reproducing it and would have been content enough to reinterpret Shakespeare's text in a production, if he could thereby get at what interested him. It was not absolutely essential to rewrite it. We need to bear in mind the interposition of the Schlegel-Tieck translation. Brecht is more tolerant of Shakespeare's text than his assistants who tend to criticize it in terms of traditional readings, equating that text with Shakespeare's presumed position

## Coriolanus and the Historical Text

toward it, as if the compromiser Menenius adequately embodied the author's Tory values.

Brecht never finished the adaptation. It was rearranged after his death, and first performed in 1962 in Frankfurt, and in a "definitive" Berliner Ensemble production in 1964, which was taken to London in 1965. I saw this astonishing production in Berlin, one of the strongest theatrical performances I have witnessed. It made the hopelessly conventional English Shakespearean productions appear vacuous, abstract, and theatrical, merely rhetorical, dramatic fashion shows for superficial flourishings of language, lazy stylizations lost in histrionic rodomontade. There were, I believe, two reasons for this achievement in the Berliner Ensemble: first, the meticulous attention, a hallmark of Brecht's work, to all the physical and visual aspects of performance, where the smallest detail was part of a design, and the battles, directed by Ruth Berghaus, were themselves physical works of art with echoes of the "military" gymnastic performance in Chinese theater although, as always, nothing directly imitated; and second, clarity in presenting the dynamics of the plot in all its necessary complexity.

We can get a sense of what is at stake here, of the relationship between translation and text, performance and visualization, by reading a fascinating account Brecht wrote of cooperating with Charles Laughton in translating his *Life of Galileo*.[19] Laughton's private readings of Shakespeare stimulated Brecht, and he played Galileo, performed first in English in August 1947 in Los Angeles where they both then lived. We should notice their meticulous attention to the details of performance as the text the audience will read, something academic scholars often overlook in their preoccupation with the literary text, which is why drama best teaches us the basic lesson that all reading is interpretation. Brecht stylizes slightly but basically describes his own approach to theater as he observes Laughton at work. We can also see how they learned from each other.

What do we find there? Primarily a discussion of the play's ideas? Of the famous alienation effect? Of the politics in Rome or Venice or Florence? Not at all! Instead, they talk about the texture of performance, its appeal to the senses, its externalizations, how to make everything visible. Brecht was a great director and a perfectionist, obsessed by the creation of aesthetically powerful effects. That is why his plays were so forceful. The allusions to avoiding the psychological should not be misunderstood. Brecht's theater, like Laughton's, looked for ways of externalizing behavior, not internalizing in the manner of imitation Stanislavsky. Such externalization was meant to show the forces that construct the psyche, hence the unconscious, but not the assumptions of an inward looking ego-psychology concentrated solely upon the isolated self.[20]

Brecht's approach to *Coriolanus* is finely adjusted to the needs of the 1950s in the German Democratic Republic, but he accomplished this by looking hard at Shakespeare's text, by seeing it as historically positioned and asking how and why. When we investigate all of this, we discover that what look like occasionally embarrassing anachronisms, reading modern attitudes and positions back into a supposedly "Shakespearean" text, or an adaption of one, in fact recourse to what is actually there in Shakespeare's text, but has been ignored by other readings, or to attitudes more active in the sources than in that Shakespearean text.

Early on Brecht saw Shakespeare's plays as "unclear," a term of endearment indicating they were characterized by necessary complexity, as offering "absolute material," frequently flattened in performance when the tensions are permitted to relax into an apotheosis for the protagonist's singularity, whereas those plots are "tempestuous, passionate, contradictory, dynamic," and the plays "as rich as life."[21] He is arguing in 1927 that Shakespeare's plays are unsuited to contemporary theater, because they capture the truth of life itself, which that theater cannot adequately convey, because it is fixated by ideas about life.[22] In 1953 he makes the same distinction between the richness of these texts and their inadequate representation in "bourgeois" theater.[23]

In approaching *Coriolanus,* Brecht did not want to diminish the sense of his pride but, as with Othello's jealousy, to situate it, to historicize it, which has the effect of making the figure more comprehensible, in a degree more sympathetic to us, not less so, and hence more tragic. What we then see is not the singular figure brought low by a combination of his own arrogance and the comic and incompetent people's selfish ingratitude, but rather the forces that produce these responses, the doubleness and contradictoriness of all the reactions, historical experience itself, and not its simplification to suit a narrow view upon it. This invaluable sense of history in the raw, this clash of intransigent contradictions, was what Brecht most admired in Shakespeare whom he called, in his highest term of praise, "a great realist."[24]

We need to remember that such an adequately complex apprehension of history was deeply troubling to the political authorities in the German Democratic Republic who wished for nothing more strongly than those idealizing simplifications of history, the great heroic figures that Brecht was unwilling to supply. They wanted representation untroubled by complexity, clear-cut figures, heroes or villains, gods or monsters, in accordance with the Stalinist demands enshrined in the aesthetic of socialist realism.

What did Brecht give them instead? Something much more troubling that addressed the issues of the day, instead of following the politically correct view upon them: the struggle between claims for absolute power and rebellion, in other words a continuing struggle between classes, and the inevitable dependence of the plebeians on military technocrats as a consequence of their own weaknesses. Not something the real-existing Stalinists wanted to hear. We can surely see this dictatorial Coriolanus, the indispensable, heroic enemy of the people, who equates his person with the state, who is so ruthless in pursuit of his own interest that he naturalized it and cannot recognize it as a function of anything beyond himself, as a figuration of the man Brecht once called the "honoured murderer of the people": Stalin.

In editing down the text and sharpening some of the issues, Brecht appears to modernize the play. For example, he shifts the balance of power toward the tribunes. The play ends with them in control of affairs and able to ignore the pressure from the patrician families, giving them a much stronger role than they appear to have in Shakespeare. Brecht also seems more sympathetic to the political interests of the common people. Coriolanus is a less heroic figure. By cutting down the play, the social and political dynamics between the groups appear more prominent and more sharply observed. Some of the introduced material seems anachronistic, like the man with the child at the beginning of the first scene who is starving, does not want to fight rich men's wars, and says he wants to emigrate if, as he believes, the citizens will not achieve much in their battle with Coriolanus. But if we look again at the historical records, we may find them surprising.

One reason why we are perhaps surprised stems from the consistency with which this play is read from an opposite point of view, one that flattens out these differences along the familiar lines, and in the belief that to do so is to follow the author's intentions.

A performance of Shakespeare's *Coriolanus* in September 1990 in Basel showed the plebs as either comic in distress or vicious in revenge. The age of heroes is done, but they are then replaced by comic incompetents, scornfully caricatured, banging spoons on tins, wearing hats too small for them, stabbing Coriolanus to death at the end. This appears to echo Shakespeare's presumed distrust of the fickle mob in sore need of a governor, perhaps also to reflect a desire to distance the production from what may have been perceived as Brecht's idealization of the people's representatives, and to comment on the collapse of the unsustainable so-called People's Democracies.[25]

But a more conventionally angled 1977 Royal Shakespeare Company production by Terry Hands in Stratford sums up the problems this play creates. It was a pre-Thatcherite response to the perceived demise of socialism, equated with the lazy trade unionism of the Labour Party. The program printed part of an attack upon it by Paul Johnson, a former editor of the *New Statesman,* who had moved to the political right. The tribunes were played as cowardly clowns and Coriolanus as the apotheosis of the heroic individual, brought down by envy and the isolation of his own grandeur. Everything was pointed to evoke sympathy for the psychology of the extraordinary hero, clothed in gold and red, a free-market Henry V taking his revenge on Parliament, and the real historical arguments were swept into the wings.[26]

What falls away in such productions is a sense, that can be easily discerned in Shakespeare's text, not to speak of his sources, of the social and political precariousness of life and of events. Western European culture has largely lost this intrusive sense of alarm, all-pervasive to the play and without which the dynamics of its plot must shift decisively. In respect of this endemic social insecurity, Shakespeare's Elizabethan or Jacobean England was probably closer to the republican Rome of two thousand years before than it is to us nearly four hundred years later.

V

The three curses in Rome were dearth or famine, plague, and war.[27] In Shakespeare's day the three great judgments upon humanity were dearth, plague, and the sword.[28] We could add debt as a fourth disaster, and all four were intimately connected with social structures, a fact well recognized in both historical periods. The plebeians in *Coriolanus* complain about the burden of "usury." In Rome the punishments for the mostly plebeian debtors were draconian. Ceres, the goddess of the sufficient corn, was worshipped by plebeians. One longs for what one has not got. As Ceres descended from the Greek goddess Demeter, she was associated with Greek ideas about democracy. From Greece also came knowledge of the understandable, and often imitated, attempts to sustain a plebeian autocratic dictatorship to alleviate their desperate condition. We can surely see aspects of the rules of Hitler, Peron, Stalin, and so on as contemporary analogies of this social phenomenon.

These apocalyptic visitations were rationalized by conservative churchmen and Tudor apologists as punishments for sinfulness, for which the recommended cure was obedient repentance. They were in actuality produced by social and political change, as the economic order went through the traumatic period of reorganization, with nascent capitalism and an emerging bourgeois society replacing the old feudal system. The contradictory political absolutism initially asserted its absolute right to power. Thus securing social order, it therefore also protected, as it tried to exploit, these economic developments. As always, these developments hung together. Obligations and customary rights were giving way to the right to individual profit. The land enclosures directly deprived people of their earlier rights and swept beggars and so-called masterless men off the land and into deeper penury. These enclosures, the hoarding of grain, and the consequent fear of dearth, led to the Midland's Rising of 1607. There are accounts of customary gleaners of grain being prosecuted for theft by landlords, one of whom was "almost pulled in pieces by the poor."[29] The public records of the day tell how these events made "the people arrogantly and seditiously to speake of the not reformeing of Convention of errable land in pasture by enclosing."[30]

When the plague struck, its victims were contained and enclosed, locked up in their houses. The connection between plague and poverty was noticed, and this fearful contagion perceived as dismembering the body of society. Such treatment, as well as a visceral fear of infection, was protested in metaphors that reverberate in *Coriolanus*. "A commonwealth is a body, and one member methinks should nourish another," wrote Benjamin Spenser.[31] But equally, one such member could infect another. The disease was spread through miasmas, such was the as-

## The Intercultural Sign

sumption, that the wealthy could escape. The London theaters were closed. Coriolanus harps on the omnipresence of disease. He hates and fears the breath of the plebeians, the infection of the people, as the reek of the rotten fens (III.iii.121). Shakespeare's plebeian citizens, meanwhile, are obsessed with hunger and the price of corn. *Coriolanus* is a play about the realities of daily life on the streets of London in 1608.

The metaphorical fable of the threatened body politic comes straight out of Plutarch. It is instructive to see how Livy and Plutarch describe the republican Rome of 490 BCE, and tell the story of Coriolanus.[32] Shakespeare's fellow citizens were very much aware of the contemporary political implications of their accounts, and his text appears to evaluate them within this context of public discussion.

After the Tarquin kings had been removed in 509 BCE, Rome established a unique and uneasy republican political system. Administration was conducted by Consuls, members of a patrician Senate, the legislative body, and appointed with the support of the plebs that they had to solicit. A quasi-democratic political system was established but did not rest on any real social or legal equality. The Senate needed the loyalty of the plebs and, above all, of the army, and it feared with good cause to lose it. The plebeians were oppressed by moneylenders and haunted by famine. In his history of Rome, Livy recounts how the army simply left the city, when sufficiently irritated by their living conditions.[33] Physical departure, temporary secession, withdrawal of service—Brecht's emigration—was a regular form of protest. The office of tribune, or representative of the plebs, was granted by the Senate to placate them and preempt such refusals. There were insurrections over the price of corn. There was enough. But the plebs had insufficient money to buy it. They demanded that corn should be imported from Sicily for free distribution, a proposal Coriolanus vigorously opposed.

There is a fascinating story in Livy, a glimpse into the plebeian social unconscious and how it is represented to us. A householder had apparently beaten his slave, under a yoke, to the circus on the morning of the Great Games, although Livy says their sanctity was thereby untouched. A plebeian called Titus Latinus then dreamed that Jupiter had said the leading dancer at the Games—the slave who had danced ahead under the blows of his master—had not been to his liking and they would have to be repeated because their sanctity had been violated.[34] The narrative tells he was first ashamed, but finally insisted on reporting this dream to the Consuls. The games are then indeed repeated. Like foreign football club supporters, the Volscians attend, and Coriolanus announces that they are harmful to the city and should be expelled. This is done. But they are offended and return to take revenge. This accomplishes Coriolanus's purpose because it unifies the Romans under their military leader, putting an end to possible insurrection. The senate wanted to appease the plebeians by sacrificing Coriolanus, but then he disappeared to the Volsci. The subsequent story, the substantial plot in Shakespeare's play, is more or less the same in Livy and Plutarch.

Shakespeare used Plutarch extensively. Volumnia's famous speech to her son, begging him to break off his attack, is a more eloquent and impassioned, versified version of North's prose translation of Plutarch's account. We can observe how Shakespeare conveys a standard Elizabethan reading of Plutarch in several places. When Coriolanus sought support of the plebs, they had been ready to give it to him as an individual who had been wounded in defense of his country. But Plutarch describes how they later had second thoughts when they saw him coming "to the market-place with great pomp, accompanied with all the Senate, and the whole nobility of the city about him." They saw him then as their political enemy, "being a man somewhat partial towards the nobility, and of great credit and authority amongst the patricians and as one they might doubt would take away altogether the liberty from the people."[35] In the margin to this passage North comments, "See the fickle minds of common people." In Shakespeare, Aufidius describes the attitude of Coriolanus in metaphors that also made better sense in aristocratic England than republican Rome:

I think he'll be to Rome
As is the asprey to the fish, who takes it
By sovereignty of Nature. (IV.vii.33)

There is another instructive example of differences in perception between Plutarch and Shakespeare. The Volscian army, led by Coriolanus, is approaching Rome. In Shakespeare the Romans are united, if only by their misery and helplessness. Coriolanus has been thwarted and is returning to take revenge upon them all. Shakespeare does not, in this respect, differentiate between the big and the little fish. They merely argue about who bears most responsibility for what has happened. Here

Shakespeare seems to see events in more of a social vacuum, whereas Plutarch is surprisingly explicit, describing how Coriolanus in his march on Rome is careful to spare the property of the rich: "For his chiefest purpose was, to increase still the malice and dissension between the nobility and commonality: and, to draw that on, he was very careful to keep the noble man's lands and goods safe from harm and burning, but spoiled all the whole country besides, and would suffer no man to take or hurt anything of the noble men's. This made greater stir and broil between the nobility and the people than was before" (30).

North comments ironically again, "A fine device to make the commonality suspect the nobility." Many of Shakespeare's late plays are concerned, obsessed even, with ungoverned governors and the dangers they constitute for the commonweal. Coriolanus tries, and fails, to behave "As if a man were author of himself/ And knew no other kin" (V.iii.36). Plutarch also says the senators promise the plebeians a fair price for corn as they attempt to pacify them in the face of Coriolanus's behavior, a detail likewise not found in Shakespeare, but this could also be read as sharpening the contradictions between them (19).

## VI

Knowing other views in Shakespeare's culture upon these issues helps us locate the difference between his play and Brecht's, even though Shakespeare's Roman play is no less focused on contemporary political crisis than Brecht's is a reworking of it. These issues were socially vital and politically difficult. Therefore, in both plays, they had to be distanced into remote Roman history. But there was a lively sense of the appositeness of that history for thinking about experience in the Renaissance.

Let us start with Machiavelli, whom Shakespeare is supposed to have read. We associate him with a cynically realist view of human behavior and strong advice to authoritarian rulers how they may govern successfully through the efficacious use of power untroubled by considerations of morality, but it is clear that Machiavelli preferred republican to aristocratic government. In *The Discourses on the First Ten Books of Titus Livius*, written at the same time as, and in conjunction with, the better-known *The Prince*, Machiavelli describes the advantages of republican government.[36] The fundamental question is: How can it be sustained?

He praised the institutions established by republican Rome and the role of the tribunes in making them work to the benefit of the whole state. I quote from book I.4, *How Necessary Public Indictments are for the Maintenance of Liberty in a Republic*:

> This can be shown by numerous examples, and especially by one that Titus Livy adduces, namely, that of Coriolanus. Livy tells us that, when the nobility were annoyed with the plebs because it seemed to them that the plebs had too much authority owing to the appointment of tribunes to protect them, and when, besides this, there was a great scarcity of provisions in Rome and the senate had to send to Sicily for corn, Coriolanus, who was hostile to the popular faction, suggested that the time had come to punish the plebs and to deprive them of the authority they had assumed to the prejudice of the nobility. Hence he advised that they should be kept hungry and that the corn should not be distributed among them. When this came to the ears of the populace indignations against Coriolanus grew so intense that, as he was leaving the senate, he would have been killed in the tumult if the tribunes had not cited him to appear in his own defence. One notes in this incident what has been said above, namely, how useful and necessary it is for republics to provide a legal outlet for the anger which the general public has conceived against a particular citizen, because when no such normal means are available, recourse is had to abnormal means, which unquestionably have a worse effect than does the normal method.[37]

Far from seeking to do away with political conflict through exercise of administrative power, Machiavelli found such conflict beneficial to a republican state, for example, from the heading for book I.4: *That Discord between the Plebs and the Senate of Rome made this Republic both Free and Powerful*. In these disputes, he was on the side of the tribunes. They were right to oppose Coriolanus as they were right to resist the senate's attempts to encroach upon their powers.

The political arguments conducted in London during the first decade of the sixteenth century explain why Shakespeare used this celebrated story for his play. They took the form of an emergent and increasingly vigorous political struggle between Crown and Parliament. The end of the foreign threat from Spain enabled criticism of Tudor ideology, which was then reasserted with arguments for the absolute and divine right of kings. Medieval theory had allowed a right of rebellion, presumably because feudal rulers were interchangeable, whereas this emergent absolutism was directed against a feudal replaceability and was welcomed, when not overbearing or tyrannical, by the growing merchant class, since a system of political order protected their pursuit of wealth.[38] Where some political theorists even made allowance for electing kings, James I took a much tougher stand than Elizabeth, claiming the right to the untrammeled exercise of power in his *The Trew Law of Free Monarchies* (that is, nonelected) written in 1598.[39]

After he took the throne, James became embroiled in a public argument with parliamentarians over the rights, or abuses, of purveyance, that is, requisitioning, for the Court. Things came to a head in 1605–1606. *Coriolanus* was probably written in 1607–1608. Most political theorists supported the monarchist position absolutely, which is presumably why they were published. But there were enough warning or protesting countervoices. Robert Parsons (1594) argued, in terms that would have been widely supported, that God or the law was more powerful than any king but that monarchy was the best form of government.[40]

William Fulbecke used a variation of a familiar metaphor in 1602: "Democracy I have always taken contrary to the ancient division of Monarchy, aristocracy, etc. to be no form of a commonweal, if it be properly taken for the equal sway of the people without any superiority. For the heel cannot stand in place of the head, unless the body be destroyed and the anatomy monstrous. It is against the nature of the people to bear rule; they are as unfit for regiment as a mad man to give counsel."[41] Two members of parliament, John Hare and Lawrence Hyde, had introduced a bill in 1594, vetoed by Elizabeth, censuring the practice of purveyors. They returned to the problem with James I, writing an Apology of the House of Commons, made to the king, touching their privileges, in which they said, "Let your maj. be pleased to receive public information from your commons in parl. as to the civil estate and government; for private informations pass often by practice: the voice of the people, in the things of their knowledge, is said to be as the voice of God" (326).

James replied when opening the second session on 18 November 1605, and I quote from Zeeveld's account that draws on contemporary sources:

> "Diversities of spirit" were to be expected in parliament . . . some of them "more popular than profitable, either for that council or for the

commonwealth." But particularly offensive were "some Tribunes of the people, whose mouths could not be stopped, either from the matters of the Puritans or of purveyance" . . . "if any such plebeian tribunes should incur any offense . . . [the Commons] would correct them for it." Meanwhile, they should "judge themselves, as St. Paul saith, that they be not judged, and that the whole body receive not a wound by one ill member thereof." (327)

The Treasury is attacked in another speech as "a royal cistern . . . a continued and remediless leak." Salisbury, Lord Chancellor, replies on the king's behalf that he is on the contrary their *fidus depositorius* (faithful depository) (327). It is easy to understand how London was full of the talk of these disputes; indeed, they were described by contemporaries as the best entertainment in town (325). In Coriolanus's rage in Shakespeare, we can see something of the king's anger over the impudence of these tribunes. He is the dripping cistern, or faithful depository, wasting or, as Menenius will argue, best guarding and processing the wealth of the commonwealth. The arguments in Shakespeare's play were exceedingly topical, the issues were highly political, the metaphors implied many allusions that reverberated in contemporary discourse and debate.

### VII

How, then, may we now read Shakespeare's *Coriolanus*? The play is named after its central character who stands in some need of explaining, or at least many critics think so. A recent example would be this systematic commentary on the play that attempts to get inside his mind. I quote typical comments from the account of act IV and the aftermath of his banishment: "It is impossible to fathom his feelings or his plans at this point. He is free, that is all, and it is an elation that he recognises. . . . It is difficult to believe that he feels no pain in the severance from his family, his friends and his city, but this kind of pain is what he is used to. He is used to leaving his city and his loved ones. The pain of such departures is swallowed up by the pleasure of anticipation at being and doing out there, beyond the city walls."[42]

This critic does not find it easy to understand his hero but perseveres in this attempt to second guess the tribulations of the professional soldier's life. Yet such psychologizing is both unproductive and methodologically suspect. An actor must have a sense of a subtext, but speculation of this kind takes us too far from the text and, as a practice for reading the whole play, subtly dissuades us from paying attention to the plot and the nature of Shakespeare's dramatic discourse, how the dialogue is crafted and the language of the characters juxtaposed. This reading constitutes a contemporary and more differentiated version of precisely what Brecht objected to: a naturalist essentializing of the central character, since it assumes too comfortably the efficacy of a psychological mimetics.

I want to take the opposite tack and start with the heuristically useful supposition that Coriolanus is incomprehensible, enigmatic, impenetrable. He represents an extreme of behavior, metaphorized as a fearful and irresistible natural force, therefore as a kind of innocence. He compels others to define themselves in response to his behavior. In other words, we need to attend to what a character does and what others say about his behavior, and how they then behave, and not to what we surmise he might be thinking silently. Shakespeare shows the character's "singularity," and with a vengeance, but the text also unfolds the political, social, and dramatic dynamic that enables us to place it. In looking at the structure of this plot, we need to beware of privileging any of the characters, of siding with their positions, let alone of assuming the author wants us to share what we assume is his own predilection for any of them, finding the common people always comic, the mob inevitably fickle, Menenius invariably right as he speaks for rational social compromise with the voice of invaluable common sense.

Coriolanus finally offends everyone because he who would be his own "author" cannot control himself. In politics, whoever controls the public discourse has the most power. In this most political of Shakespeare's plays, or at least where social conflict between classes is most graphically represented, we learn how the loss of control of appropriate language leads to disaster. Coriolanus cannot control his tongue. He explodes when goaded by language; nothing more is needed. The "play" does not side with any of the speakers, it merely situates their speech. Here speech is always public speech or related to its control. At the end, after assassinating Coriolanus, Aufidius publicly promises, "Yet he shall have a noble memory" (V.vi.153). Just before the murder, his coconspirator warns him:

## Coriolanus and the Historical Text

> Therefore at your vantage,
> Ere he express himself or move the people
> With what he would say, let him feel your sword,
> Which we will second. When he lies along,
> After your way his tale pronounced shall bury
> His reasons with his body. (V.vi.53)

The public profession of honor and the secreted reasons for murder together bury the opponent's version of the truth of history. All these transactions are fully "visible" in the text, so there is no need to speculate on the contents of the private mind. This is the essential assumption for reading Shakespeare's play.

The "singularity" (I.i.278) of Coriolanus requires ever more extraordinary epithets to describe his behavior. We can disregard the speaker's implied attitude—for example, the tribune Sicinius observes this singularity—and simply notice how these epithets and metaphors accumulate. He is imaged as a great vessel under sail whose stem pushes all men aside like water weeds (II.ii.106), as a celestial force who strikes his enemies "like a planet" (II.ii.113), as a "lonely dragon"[43] (IV.i.30), as a winged dragon, an engine of war, a god who only lacks eternity (V.iv.13ff.), as someone who can no longer be named, who will recreate himself, who has put himself beyond the reach of normal speech, whose violence is silent:

> Coriolanus
> He would not answer to; forbade all names;
> He was a kind of nothing, titleless,
> Till he had forged himself a name a' th' fire
> Of burning Rome. (V.i.13)

The anticipation of warfare is as pleasurable to him as that of making love (I.vi.29). When Aufidius greets Coriolanus in his house, he tells him he is happier than on his wedding night (IV.iii.113ff.). His servants remark that he treats Coriolanus like his mistress (IV.iii.195). This self-loving solidarity among the warrior caste could be understood as a narcissistic feudal respect for your adversary who is equal in rank. But, as we well know, it is accompanied here by Coriolanus's inexhaustible disdain and hatred for the plebeians. The play turns on these differences of class, and the trouble with Coriolanus is that he represents an ideologically unbending assertion of patrician values, although we should probably also see this as partially figuring the new singularity of bourgeois economic power and narcissism. He cannot compromise until his mother forces him to see that his final choice can only be between degrees of ignominy. He chooses the lesser and his own death.

His scorn of the common people is absolute, yet other members of his class express their hatred just as forcefully. The metaphors express fear of their numbers, of their proximity. They are likened to animals and are the source of frightening infection. "The beast with many heads," he tells his mother, "butts me away" (IV.i.1). To which she replies, "Now the red pestilence strike all trades in Rome, / And occupations perish!" The Tribunes she greets with, "The hoarded plague a' th' gods / Requite your love" (IV.ii.11). But banished Coriolanus will not distinguish between his opponents and determines to "fight against my cank'red country with the spleen / Of all the under fiends" (IV.v.90). In Shakespeare, Coriolanus refuses to recognize the class distinctions observed in Plutarch's account, as he prepares to attack the Romans, a catastrophe for his own class that he is ready to sacrifice to his anger, as they are only too aware. Coriolanus therefore also represents a new stage of social behavior, although here appearing as an unnatural renegade: radical self-interest that we can read in terms of new forms of competition that ignore all the old and waning feudal courtesies.

Coriolanus forces everyone to define their own position, and although this wavers and changes, in part for tactical reasons, under the pressure of events, the fundamental attitudes are determined by class structure. Although this is well known, I want to ask how the play actually shows these attitudes. There are some nuances here that I have never seen adequately described.

In the famous first scene, the citizens are at the point of revolt. They complain the patricians have too much food that they are hoarding, support usurers or moneylenders, and pass laws that "chain up and restrain" the poor, who are eaten either by war or by the rich (I.i.84ff.). Menenius trots out the contemporary conservative counterarguments. The gods are responsible for the famine, therefore the Romans should pray to them, the patricians have most charitable care for the plebeians, and, anyway, the "Roman state," which he automatically equates with the interests of the patricians, must prevail (I.i.69). "What is the city but the people?" the tribunes will later argue (III.i.198). Menenius answers this in advance with the fable of the belly from Plutarch. This wonderfully apposite and elaborate metaphor of the body politic does not, like Fulbecke, contrast feet and head, although Menenius will make abusive use of the contrast when speaking to the First Citizen, but belly and the rest of the body that feeds it. The citizens calls this "cormorant belly . . . the sink" (sewer, cesspit) of the body (I.i.121). Not so, replies Menenius, it is the body's "store-house" (I.i.133). This does not so much echo Plutarch as the use of Plutarch in contemporary political debate. We can see an exact correspondence between the speeches in parliament and the metaphors in Shakespeare's text. And what is the city but its people whose voice, "in the things of their knowledge," as parliament and the king had been told, is as the voice of God?

The mob is constantly derided as fickle by all the patricians and chided by Menenius as infantlike (II.i.37), yet his own behavior is not so very different. He's "honest enough," says the First Citizen, "would that the rest were so" (I.i.53). Brecht will change this to: "He has a weakness for the people." But this easy assumption of his "honesty" is contradicted by his opinions and his behavior. There is no question of any real neutrality. The intransigence of Coriolanus is politically impractical and dangerous to the patricians, so Menenius attempts to mollify the plebeians. But this apparent sympathy is motivated by political interest and entirely fickle. He professes the patrician's care for them but is quite unable to conceal his own contempt from the First Citizen: "Rome and her rats are on the point of battle / The one side must have bale. Hale noble Martius!" (I.i.162). Menenius thereby completely contradicts his attempts at mollification, because he sees Coriolanus approaching. He is a weak man, automatically seeking the protection of Coriolanus's strength, and dares not risk his displeasure by appearing to conciliate them in his presence. He immediately concurs with everything Coriolanus then says. He is easy-going, more addicted, as he says, to the buttock of the night than the forehead of the morning (II.i.52), but his class position is crystal clear and devoid of real sympathy for anything else. He lacks independence. He lies to the tribunes about Coriolanus—"He loves your people, / But tie him not to be their bedfellow" (II.ii.64)—thus breaking the fundamental rule for any mediating conciliator: to win confidence by telling the truth. But at that moment he is speaking in public with Coriolanus right beside him.

His own behavior becomes positively childish when he hears from Volumnia that Coriolanus is returning home from battle:

> Men.: Ha? Martius coming home?
>
> Vol.: Ay, worthy Menenius, and with most prosperous approbation.
>
> Men.: Take my cap, Jupiter, [*tosses it up*] and I thank thee. Hoo! Martius coming home?
>
> Two Ladies.: Nay, 'tis true.
>
> Vol.: Look, here's a letter from him; the state hath another, his wife another, and, I think, there's one at home for you.
>
> Men.: I will make my very house reel tonight. A letter for me?
>
> Vir.: Yes certain, there's a letter for you, I saw't.
>
> Men.: A letter for me! it gives me an estate of seven year's health. (II.1.102ff.)

Menenius will not do as a serious mediator. He is simply too lightweight, too biased, and the clash of social attitudes too severe. Mediation is not possible. There is no middle position. The clash must run its course to the catastrophe. But the story is extraordinary and only ends with the death by assassination or suicide of the would-be dictator. And given the identificatory implications in contemporary politics, Coriolanus standing for James, this is strongly plotted, even if the story can be blamed on Plutarch.

There is one other significant factor in the plot of Shakespeare's play that repays attention and has, I believe, received little. I refer to a sequence of scenes, the effect of a particular juxtaposition. In act IV, the servants in the household of Aufidius comment on the amorous behavior of the generals as they plot their revenge on Rome. The scene provides an example of how an absent evaluating narrative is dramatized when distributed among contrasting character positions. These servingmen then discuss the relative merits of peace and war before rushing back in to their work. They conclude with comic paradoxes, which Brecht will explore, that peace makes men hate one another because they have less need of each other than in time of war (IV.v.220ff.). Cut, immediately, to Rome under the tribunes and in the state of deepest peace, an idyll of course, which cannot last, the people among themselves, singing at work, contented, relieved of their tyrannous rulers. It is an extraordinary little scene, very short, the voice of the contemporary social unconscious speaking through Shakespeare's text because

*Coriolanus* and the Historical Text

he can imagine it. I do not find Shakespeare favors certain voices. These voices simply speak as they are disposed to, and we have the chance of placing them.

## VIII

To place these voices, we need to be able to read and "see" the text. In that interesting discussion with his assistants, Brecht observes that the stage directions in Shakespeare's text were added later, which is to imply they don't necessarily indicate reliably how certain passages ought to be read according to any original intention. These stage directions are, of course, often crucial to the text as performance, and since performance constitutes the most exacting reading of any dramatic text, the stage directions, just as much as the main body of the text, must be read for their subtext as well, which therefore needs to be evaluated and interpreted.[44] But unless this is done arbitrarily and irresponsibly, any necessary "replacing" of stage directions must be justified from a reading of the whole text.

Brecht was fascinated by the complexity and concentration of Shakespeare's plot, by the sheer range and tempo of his play and the way it displays interdependent contradictions, its sense of how history gives and takes at the same time.[45] This is subject matter that can only fascinate someone who has looked deeply into the texture of lived and imagined lives and appreciates the space they are allotted by the unfolding historical forces that encompass them.

So it is interesting to observe a difference between Brecht's response to Shakespeare's play in this discussion and that of some of his young assistants. One of them assumes the plebs must be united in their opposition to the patricians, an attitude that is presumably governed by the ideological presupposition that they must or ought to have a clarified understanding of their class position in this struggle between the classes. This, the assumption must run, should at least be the basis for their modern reading that would be useful for a contemporary audience in Germany in the early 1950s and that would furnish the justification for their production.[46] But Brecht quickly disagrees and does not see the plebs, even in this opening scene, as particularly united or that it would be desirable if they were so represented.

Instead of any such simplification of their position into what at that time might have appeared a proper consciousness of class, and all that would then be entailed by such presuppositions, the idealizing ideology and aesthetic that together force representations and then real people into a mold that suits a view upon them beneficial to certain power structures, Brecht draws attention to the complexity of the situation:

> B: . . . neither we nor the audience must be allowed to overlook the contradictions that are bridged over, suppressed, ruled out, now that sheer hunger makes a conflict with the patricians unavoidable.
> R: I don't think you can find that in the text, just like that.
> B: Quite right. You have got to read the whole play. You can't begin without having looked at the end. Later in the play this unity of the plebeians will be broken up, so it is best not to take it for granted at the start, but to show it as having come about. (253; 380)

Brecht understood and therefore saw in Shakespeare what his assistant here did not, and what we need to be clear about: in theater the written text is always and only the basis for the performance or interpreted text, and it rests on a view of the dynamic that constitutes the structure apparent in the whole play. His fundamental point about Shakespeare is that the realized text of his play contains these complexities. It is up to us to unfold what is actually or potentially there, even if it is not always apparent to someone who has not yet learned to think visually. These plebeians exist in a contradictory unity. They are united by their misery, and they are also divided by it. To stress, let alone only see, the unity is to miss the divisions under the surface of events and so to misunderstand and then misrepresent their complexity.

The existence of the office of tribune also depends upon a fundamental contradiction of interest between plebeians and patricians. Therefore it should not be looked upon as a simple gain, something that has been achieved, and hence as something that can be idealized analogically as a necessary stage of historical progress. The main reason the office of tribune was granted the plebeians by the senate is the Volscian attack on Rome, as a way of buying their loyalty (259; 387). But this attack also turns their main enemy, Marcius, into the national hero Coriolanus. Republican Rome without the patriotic patrician hero is also indisputably weaker (260; 288). So the plebs are both weakened and strengthened through the assault from the Volscians. They may hate the person of

## *Coriolanus* and the Historical Text

Coriolanus, but they cannot deny his patriotism and usefulness to the state.

If we look at the position of Coriolanus, he too is divided against himself, not just, as they argue in this discussion, because his pride drives him to join his nation's enemy, with the potentially impossible personal and familial consequences that his patrician mother then points out to him, but because, as they observe, he believes himself to be "irreplaceable." Palitzsch then remarks:

> P: Isn't that because the play only comes to life for us when interpreted like this, since we find the same kind of thing here and feel the tragedy of the conflicts that result from it?
> B: Undoubtedly. (264; 393)

In other words, they are beginning to see the possibility in this play for a contemporary reading that would explore the tragic consequences that can ensue for a state when it is weak and so has apparent need of heroic figures. Such figures then assume the right to dominate it, asserting or even believing their actions are sanctioned by divine grace or historical necessity. In the end they are prepared to destroy the state rather than forego their self-abrogated right to dominance.

Such men cannot control their once necessarily forceful and state-protecting subjectivity. The consequence can only be personal or social catastrophe, and usually both together. This seems to fit the figure of Coriolanus in republican Rome, as it fits the history of Tudor and Stuart England from Elizabeth to Charles I, as it would fit many other political conjunctures, and as it also most assuredly fits that implacably self-assured, pipe-smoking ex-seminarian, Uncle Joe Stalin. This patriotic catastrophe "saved" his now-collapsed state from a vicious enemy, whose attack so nearly succeeded partly because he had already slaughtered most of his own generals and murdered millions, virtually anybody he wanted to, in the name of a dogmatically asserted, trickle-down scientific socialism and fortified by his belief in the inevitability of theoretically sanctioned historical progress. Marx, whose favorite slogan was *de omnibus dubitandum* ("everything must be called into doubt"), and who was also highly conscious of the temporary nature of his theoretical models, would have been horrified by what was done in his name. Dictators are seldom interested in thought or able to appreciate why its results must always be provisional; they are simply preoccupied with control—Plutarch remarked that Coriolanus "lacked education"—and their power derives from the weakness of the people.

In Shakespeare's *Coriolanus* Brecht saw a familiar, intertwining social and political problem and suggested using Mao Zedong's theoretically unexceptional but pragmatically useful short essay *On Contradiction*, which had just been published in German, as a way of understanding the issues. The battle between the Guomintang and the Communists was put on hold by the Japanese invasion of China. The class war and the national war were understood as main and secondary contradictions respectively (261; 390). If war unites a people, then it does not necessarily thereby do away with the divisions between and among them. These are merely suspended. We can extrapolate, as Mao does not but as Brecht would have been disposed to, that an equally important corollary is that war, or the threat of war, can always be used to justify strong or dictatorial leadership that then papers over the real and perpetuating social divisions between the leaders and the led. So the "class war" also unites but simultaneously divides and weakens the people.

Brecht's *Coriolanus* would have reached right into contemporary life, which is probably one reason why it was not finished in 1953 when they were working on it: far too political for the time. But how does this text relate to Shakespeare's? What do we finally learn about "replacing" Shakespeare from this juxtaposition?

A statement by Brecht in that discussion achieved a certain notoriety. It has been quoted over and over again and nearly always misinterpreted, which is scarcely surprising, since anything that is continuously quoted must eventually be misunderstood. Wekwerth asks:

> W: Can we amend Shakespeare?
> B: I think we can amend Shakespeare if we can amend him. (259; 387)

I should like to amend Willett's translation at this point:

> W: Can we make changes to Shakespeare?
> B: I think we can make changes to Shakespeare if we are able to.[47]

This has often been represented as implying that Brecht thought he was big enough to rewrite Shakespeare, and that meddling with an authentic text is a tricky business, thus returning to the question of the authenticity of original texts and their authorized readings. But a more fruitful, and probably accurate, reading of what was then meant, would

## Coriolanus and the Historical Text

be something like the other way round for all of these suppositions: "If you want to rewrite the text, you had better be sure you are able to, and anyway it probably is not necessary, also because every interpretation is a rereading." Brecht then continues, "But we agreed to begin only by discussing changes of interpretation so as to prove the usefulness of our analytical method even without adding new text." His assistants make other suggestions about changes to the Shakespearean text and Brecht resists them. He was more interested in reading it. There is a very nice, precise formulation of the issues involved in one exchange at the end of their discussion, as they summarize what they have learned:

> R: Do you think that all this and the rest of it can be read in the play?
> B: Read in it and read into it.[48]

Arguing from a German text alone, the individual points would be slightly different but the arguments substantially similar. Brecht worked largely from the nineteenth-century Schlegel-Tieck translation, amending it when necessary, but he did not finish his version. The production, after his death, went back to Schlegel-Tieck, adjusting it to the exigencies of their performance. The English edition of Brecht translates his version and where that text, printed in 1956, long before the performance of 1964, incorporates Schlegel-Tieck, the translator Ralph Manheim supplies not so much a simplified as a clarified version of Shakespeare's "original" text. The consequence is, naturally, that we have another text, yet one that sensitively and cleverly captures the purpose of Brecht's interventions. The effect of all this is that we read Shakespeare differently, we see his text afresh, because Brecht brings to life the issues that animated it. The purpose of changing or alienating is clarification, in order to get through to what has been obscured by convention and the passage of time.

The effect of these language changes, of passing through these versions, of this extensive and complex rewriting, is to desacralize the otherwise sacrosanct Shakespeare, and so to sharpen, rework, reaccentuate, reimagine his text, in order to get through to what is central to it. Two methods are employed: ruthless cutting down, shortening of speeches, and removal of scenes; and reformulations of the obscure, lexically and grammatically difficult passages. This is no more or less than what every energetic production will do: clarify its text so that the audience can understand it. The only difference is that in this case the emendations reach into the verbal formulation and remain open to inspection as writing.

When we examine what has been amended, it almost invariably turns out to be the result of such a clarification and is fully justified by something in Shakespeare's text. One of the surprises in approaching Shakespeare through Brecht is how much of what we think surely must be "Brecht," since it seems so adjusted to his interests, so modern, and must therefore be anachronistic, turns out to be nothing of the sort and instead to derive from something in Shakespeare's text.

Many changes rewrite Shakespeare's early-seventeenth-century English into contemporary language, where the intention is to preserve the full sense and impact of the original words, which are lessened for us today because the usage has changed. Such passages can be simply archaic, or virtually incomprehensible to a modern audience. Even if people are familiar with the text, these expressions no longer have the same force. The effect of the accumulation of such archaisms is the all-too-familiar self-distancing of the text, then of the plot. Then, especially if you hold other presuppositions, you may find the plebeians merely amusing. So modernizing the language can also have the effect of historicizing the play, putting it back into its historical context. The consequence of doing this is that you are able to actualize its meaning. We may find the amended text sometimes goes too far, or not far enough, but the interventions unquestionably wake us up and start us thinking.[49]

In the first scene, Menenius asks the plebeians with what can only be half-hearted concern, but that is not the point here: "Citizens, my good friends and honest neighbours / Are you determined to destroy yourselves?"[50] The First Citizen replies wittily and perhaps with a sarcastic edge, if he has the measure of Menenius who is so outspokenly rude to him later: "We can't do that, sir. We're destroyed already" (61). This takes Shakespeare's "Will you undo yourselves?" and "We are undone already" (I.i.63) and translates it into their exact modern English equivalent. Even if we know this other, by now archaic meaning, and thus what these words meant to speakers in Shakespeare's day, their force is lessened for us because they have not retained this sense into contemporary speech. Their original impact is therefore restored by the modern word. Indeed, the phrase, as an exclamation from a young lady in dire straits, "Oh, sir, I am undone," now interrupts Shakespeare's sense with

*Coriolanus* and the Historical Text

associations from Restoration comedy and Victorian farce that are potentially fatal to their connotations in this passage.

Menenius immediately replies in just one passage that I want to compare exactly with Shakespeare's text:

> I tell you, friends, the senate has for you
> Most charitable care. For your grievances—
> The rising cost of food—you may as well
> Strike at the heavens with your staves as lift them
> Against the senate; you see, the soaring prices
> Come from the gods and not from man. Alas
> Your misery is driving you to greater
> Misery. You remind me of a babe that
> Bites at the empty breast of its unhappy
> Mother. You curse the senate as an enemy
> And yet it cares for you. (61)[51]

Shakespeare's equivalent for this passage:

> I tell you, friends, most charitable care
> Have the patricians of you. For your wants,
> Your suffering in this dearth, you may as well
> Strike at the heaven with your staves as lift them
> Against the Roman state, whose course will on
> The way it takes, cracking ten thousand curbs
> Of more strong link asunder than can ever
> Appear in your impediment. For the dearth,
> The gods, not the patricians, make it, and
> Your knees to them (not arms) must help. Alack
> You are transported by calamity
> Thither where more attends you, and you slander
> The helms o' th' state, who care for you like fathers,
> When you curse them as enemies. (I.1.65ff.)

Brecht's is shorter, but only by three lines. Some of the language is clarified; Shakespeare's sinuous, longer, and often elliptical sentences are replaced by more gestural ones in Brecht's understanding of this term. They are easier to act, closer to the gestures of speech, the language therefore becomes more visible as gesture and so less rhetorical and less metaphorical. This has the effect of clarifying the position of the speakers, who are then not so much performing through language, somewhat in the manner of opera singers, but rather are constrained and able to show where they stand. Profusion then gives way to precision of metaphor.

In this general context, there is also an interesting specific shift of emphasis in this passage away from an attempt to intimidate the plebeians with the power of the Roman state, with the threat of force, with arguments from the divine right of state, or patrician, violence. Such threats of course make better sense in Tudor and Stuart England, which made short shrift with rebellious subjects, than in republican Rome, where the senate had to win the plebeian army with bribes and smiles and could not threaten it with violence. Brecht's version, in any event, shifts away from these threats and focuses on the hunger of the plebeians. After all, that is why they are at the point of rebellion. His Menenius replaces the patriarchal metaphors in Shakespeare's text. The senate is now no longer the fatherly but stern and, above all, irresistible helmsman of the state. It has become the distraught mother who is no longer able to nourish her hungry child. Biting the empty breast is doubly painful; it hurts both physically and emotionally and is fruitless as well, if only the child could understand this. Like the mother who has no milk, the senate cannot be blamed if there is not enough corn—it is an effect of nature. This reinforces the suggestion that the senate is both caring and helpless and thus accomplishes Menenius's deceptive purposes.

Shakespeare's Menenius tells Coriolanus the plebeians are cowardly, but Brecht's tells him they gave way not to "The sword of my voice but rather the voice of your sword" (64). This is one example in which Brecht appears to change Shakespeare and take sides with the plebeians, but it is also a reading of Shakespeare. Here, Menenius can be thought of as ingratiating himself with the more powerful Coriolanus by drawing on his power and flattering it. There is a distinction between the two representations of Menenius, yet Brecht's "anachronism," building up the class strength of the plebs, is based on a reading of Shakespeare's play. Where in Shakespeare the plebeians, as Coriolanus reports, "sighed forth proverbs" (I.i.205), in Brecht they "bellowed slogans" (64). They have become better organized. This whole first scene in Brecht is a sharper, tauter statement of the central issue for his play: Coriolanus as an essential but dangerous asset to the city.

Brecht's second scene is a vigorously cut version of Shakespeare's act I, scene iii, in which the three women reveal their attitudes to Coriolanus. The method here, as throughout, is similar to Ezra Pound's editorial practice: a ruthless pruning out of elaborations, of narrative passages, of what merely embellishes the core of the dramatic text. What is then left are the essential gestures that advance the dynamic of the plot and uncover the core of the character's attitudes, what we could call the politics of character. Pound and Brecht both had spatial, dramatic imaginations and their extensive translations, adaptations, reworkings, and replacings observe an interestingly comparable practice, in spite of the disparity of political and intellectual interest.[52] Otherwise Brecht's text gives modern equivalents for less accessible Shakespearean phrases: "... she will only spoil a pleasant evening" (69)[53] for "she will but disease our better mirth" (I.iii.104).

The battle scenes (I.3a–g) follow Schlegel-Tieck more closely, since Brecht did not work on them, wanting to do it when the play reached production and the text could be adjusted to rehearsal and performance. They are, however, simplified and easier to follow. There is one nice example of an improving clarification at the end, when Aufidius retires to contemplate his losses:

> I am expected at the cypress grove. I pray you—
> It's south of the city mills—to bring me word
> How the world goes, so I may adjust my step
> To its pace. (84)

Shakespeare had written:

> I am attended at the cypress grove. I pray you
> ('Tis south the city mills) bring me word thither
> How the world goes, that to the pace of it
> I may spur on my journey. (I.x.30)

Brecht's version, where the voice is audibly running out of steam, is demonstrably more gestural and less rhetorical than Shakespeare's, closer to the emotions of the moment, since the defeated Aufidius must now slow down and not "spur on" his journey.

In this gestural method of rewriting, the shifting dramatic positions and emotional states of the speakers are conveyed in sharpened images and breathe through the specific rhythms of their language. The plot becomes concentrated around its essential steps. The politics, unquestionably there in Shakespeare, sharpen. Brecht, perhaps, clarifies the interest and this appears so mostly because of how the text is sharpened. In act II, scene i of Brecht's play, this is done to stress the appeal of Coriolanus to the plebs as the conqueror of the Volsces. This double process entails a clarification that concentrates what was already there. One example would be the use of the term "dictator," when Sicinius in the English text says to Menenius, "Yes, he aimed to make himself dictator" (126),[54] in the sense of calling a spade a spade and in place of Shakespeare's "And affecting one sole throne, / Without assistance" (IV.vi.32). Shakespeare's "crafts" (IV.vi.118), who were the artisanal plebs, become the "working class" (129) with the loss of Shakespeare's pun when Menenius plays on making and intriguing.[55] Coriolanus's disdain of "Rome's bricklayers" (141) is now for "Rome's mechanics" (V.iii.83), which again means artisans. When Cominius hears Coriolanus is descending on Rome with the Volscian army, he turns on the tribunes: "Now you can take your precious bill of rights / And stuff it in a mousehole" (128).[56] In Shakespeare's text the equivalent passage reads: "Your franchises, whereon you stood, confin'd / Into an auger's bore" (IV.vi.86).

I doubt if this can be understood today without a gloss and in performance it will, therefore, remain incomprehensible. "Franchises" means "political rights." "Whereon you stood" means "which you insisted on," and "an auger's bore" is a tiny hole drilled by an auger, with which a carpenter drills tiny holes! This Brechtian version, once again, finds a graphic equivalent for an archaism. The mousehole comes from Tieck.

Reading Brecht's more modern and therefore apparently sharper formulations often suggests that he is changing Shakespeare's plot. At the end there is one fundamental alteration. What we first think must be anachronisms—surely Shakespeare did not say this—often have their justification in his text. The citizens are puzzled by Coriolanus's behavior as he solicits their votes, and one says to himself: "If I had to give again . . . But never mind" (96).[57] What does Shakespeare's citizen say? "And 'twere to give again—but 'tis no matter" (I.iii.83). Not only is this

*Coriolanus* and the Historical Text

semantically exactly the same, but it also gives the lie to the view of the people in Shakespeare's play as simple and unreflective. It is one example for the opportunities offered by Shakespeare's text for a more political reading that Brecht then develops. In its context, this man is immediately having second thoughts.

Brecht concentrates Shakespeare's more prolix text into an unforgettable metaphor. Shakespeare writes:

> Sic: We charge you, that you have contriv'd to take
> From Rome all season'd office, and to wind
> Yourself into a power tyrannical,
> From which you are a traitor to the people.
> Cor: How? traitor?
> Men: Nay, temperately; your promise.
> Cor: The fires i' th' lowest hell fold in the people!
> Call me their traitor, thou injurious tribune!
> Within thine eyes sate twenty thousand deaths,
> In thy hands clutch'd as many millions, in
> Thy lying tongue both numbers, I would say
> "Thou liest" unto thee with a voice as free
> As I do pray the gods. (III.iii.68)

In place of this, Brecht's text has:

> Sic: You are accused of trying to overthrow
> The tribunes of the people and to seize
> A tyrant's power. Hence of treason
> Against the people.
> Cor: Treason!
> Men: Easy now!
> Com: You promised!
> Cor: Let the fires of bottommost hell
> Swallow up the people.
> Sic: Did you hear that?
> Cor: Call me a traitor! Why, you dog
> Of a tribune, you tribune of dogs. You lump
> Of filth! You scoundrel hungry for my death!
> You throat clogged fast with lies! (111)[58]

185

Brecht's Coriolanus chokes with anger on his final line. His invective is starker than Shakespeare's, more injurious, more gestural, less carried by the rhythm of the verse. However, Brecht's text changes significantly the ending of the play. Volumnia's long speech is shortened (141f.). In Shakespeare, it is not so much the metaphorical power of her language that carries this speech as the drama of the extraordinary encounter, which Brecht diminishes or rather reinterprets. Shakespeare stays unusually close to the language of his source. He versifies Plutarch. Volumnia pleads with Coriolanus to reconcile the Volsces and the Romans. In Brecht, however, Volumnia explains to Coriolanus that Rome has changed, that he is no longer indispensable, that the plebeians have turned decisively against the patricians. The contradictions for the patricians are sharpened, since they must either remain indebted to the plebeians for saving them from the Volscian army, or lose the national war with the Volsces who will save them from their own people. Brecht added a seventh scene in which the republican senate learns of the death of Coriolanus and refuses his family the right to wear mourning for ten months.

The play ends in dishonor for his family, an apparently opposite conclusion to Shakespeare, where Aufidius proclaims Coriolanus's nobility. This happens, of course, in Corioli, not in Rome, and as a mark of respect for his "feudal" adversary. Here Brecht's reading of the political dynamic was not possible in Shakespeare's day.

In surveying all the evidence, it is striking how little Brecht read *into* Shakespeare and how much of what he did depended on simply reading *in* Shakespeare. Comparing the two, Brecht's version seems to move toward a film script and scenario, because it is crafted with a sharp eye on performance. Although he decisively changes the end, Brecht distances conventional interpretations of Shakespeare's play by going back to its politics and reviving the sense of their importance for a contemporary reading. Historicizing so intended. The closer Brecht looked at Shakespeare, the less he felt a need to rewrite. Interpretation would probably be enough. But then interpretation necessitated rewriting, because he saw how apposite Shakespeare's play was for his own culture.

Because Brecht has been taken to task for tampering with Shakespeare in the first place and distorting Shakespeare's view of the political dynamic, or for anachronistically idealizing the plebeian faction to suit a contemporary political preference, I seek out the compatibilities and locate them in a dramatist's sense of living contradictions. The Brechtian text is also authorially overdetermined in an almost exemplary manner: composed by various hands at different times and finally reaching the stage some years after his death in a pathbreaking production, inconceivable without the impetus Brecht gave to the whole as yet unfinished project. The text he left behind, which was expanded and reworked for the later performance, certainly contained elements of idealization but these do not so much contradict "Shakespeare," although obviously departing from what he had written, as certain readings of his text that, for example, presupposed his sympathy for the compromiser Menenius. A more "impartially" forensic scrutiny of that text reveals a more evenly displayed dynamic and hence the ideological presuppositions of such critical preferences.

The other political critique of Brecht's version, associated above all with Günter Grass—that its idealizations aestheticized, theatricalized, and betrayed the actual working-class rebellion in the streets of the city of Berlin—misunderstood and perhaps underestimated the political thrust of Brecht's project. To put this plainly, the enemy for his plebeians was not their class antagonists, graphically institutionalized in the (West) German Federal Republic, and hence implying the need for a phony contrary solidarity within the East German state that the actual workers should embrace, but their own weaknesses and the quality of political leadership within their state that such weakness therefore permitted.[59]

There is an instructive difference in the response of a Marxist critic like Eagleton on the question of the relevance of *Coriolanus*. Eagleton sees *Coriolanus* as "perhaps Shakespeare's most developed study of a bourgeois individualist."[60] This makes sense when the person who threatens the whole places his own interests before everything else. But Brecht saw something more in the figure, more contradictory and more problematic, a link between earlier and modern systems of governance that rely on self- and socially destructive, heroically energized autocrats. Eagleton shows too little appreciation of the fact that the "bourgeois individualist" in Shakespeare's day was also a positive, if contradictory, historical force. More disturbing was the autocratic impulse, with links to patrician psychology in Rome and to the authoritarian personality of the twentieth century.

The utopian impulse in Brecht's reading is that the both necessary and destructive authority figure will prove a tragic personal failure, if the people develop the capacity to dispense with him. Where they do not and cannot actualize their democratic desires, they will be compelled to repeat the catastrophic pattern. Does "Brecht's" text, therefore, "replace" Shakespeare? Yes, with another reading of the Shakespearean text.

# 6

## MACBETH

## IN KUNJU OPERA

I

The kunju version of *Macbeth* radically defamiliarizes Shakespeare's so familiar play. Understanding what this courageous intercultural version implies could well compel us to relocate ourselves as readers of texts and interpreters of culture. An encounter with the Chinese production at least offers such an opportunity. The issues range widely. We may expect a few surprises.

Kunju, the oldest surviving form of Chinese "opera," developed in Jiangsu Province near the remarkable city of Suzhou at the time Shakespeare was writing his plays. The main difference between kunju and the more familiar "Peking" opera lies in the character of the music. Kunju adapted Indo-Asian melodies. According to the Shanghai Kunju Theater, the melodies originated among tribes in the Kun mountains near the Burmese border, hence the name "Kun theater" (*kun ju*). Other scholars associate the name with a place near Suzhou. Whichever version you prefer, the music sounds quite distinct. There is also a greater range of character-types than in the later Peking opera and a more expressive style of dance that accompanies the emotions expressed through song.

The kunju *Macbeth* raises fundamental questions. One approach that would close all questions down would be to assume our understanding of Shakespeare's text is secure; that the capacity of Chinese "opera" is in some degree familiar, depending on our cultural positioning, and that the juxtaposition invites us to ascertain how much, or how little, the kunju version recaptures of Shakespeare's play.

My argument unfolds in three stages, instead of abstracting straightaway from the discoveries of my analysis in a more theoretically forthright manner. This approach has certain advantages. I saw the production in 1987 and found it fascinating. I followed some of the responses to this performance in Britain and Ireland and will refer to part of that reaction. I wish to show: first, that this performance does not drive us back to the original "Shakespeare," which in fact does not exist, but instead compels us to question our reading of his play; second, that it therefore contributes to the contemporary reappraisal of Shakespeare's work; and third, that it forces us to look again at the differences and possible conjunctions between Western and Chinese theater.

I should mention a personal interest in this production and all it stands for. The artistic director, Huang Zuolin, was a friend.[1] Both he and the stage director, Li Jiayao, visited Hong Kong with productions during the Seventh Symposium of the International Brecht Society in 1986. In some sense, they came to their staging of Shakespeare through Brecht. This had a subtle effect on their work and results, although the process is intricate, in what could be described as a Chinese Brechtian Shakespeare. In any event, something is working its way through these processes that the practitioners themselves do not necessarily explain very well.[2]

Shakespeare's *Macbeth* is mediated in standard sourcebooks, in a popular encyclopedia, in the introduction to my Riverside edition, and in others for which the Arden edition is symptomatic.[3] I want to contextualize some criticism and argue the kunju *Macbeth* reappraises Shakespeare's play.[4] It is not typical "British Council" Shakespeare, but more usefully aligned with contemporary rereadings than with many still influential critical positions. Although some of these now seem transparently dated, scarcely worth dismissing, they keep returning in slightly different guises. Their assumptions underlie quite common responses to Shakespeare's plays. We need to recall them in order to appreciate how the Chinese production defamiliarizes conventional Western essentialism and to situate the artistic director's own discussion of his production.

We encounter a classic example of constructing, and then identifying with, the character as a real person, when R. S. Crane, in 1952, wanted Macbeth to stop committing horrors "not only for the sake of humanity and Scotland but also for the sake of Macbeth himself."[5] For Campbell, Macbeth's death, because of what we can learn from it, is an "important moment in the march of human destiny." We can also learn a thing or two from watching Lady Macbeth. Her death is "due to the revolt of her woman's nature, which has been forcibly suppressed." The strain of unsexing herself at first fills her with "febrile exaltation" and, alarmed by Macbeth's behavior, "she sinks under the strain and swoons." She is, we are told, "a victim of utter devotion to her evil husband," although we have just been also told that she is stronger than him and that he is not simply "evil." In comparison, the other characters "reach only the threshold" of Shakespeare's "creative imagination."[6] We witness in this reading how the supernatural powers of evil triumph over a mortal man too weak to resist them and over a woman who allows this to happen because she denies her own nature.

This all assumes the reality of the character beyond the pages of the text; an identification with the moral universe in which the characters are thought to move; the existence of evil as a supernatural power; and essential human qualities that the misguided or wicked character consciously rejects. Kermode's reading is based on similar assumptions. Although he finds it "difficult for us to credit the supernatural manifestations," his rhetoric actually replicates the conventional ideology shared, as he believes, with Shakespeare's text, so that this ideology is therefore apparently read out of the text and then read back into and imposed upon it. For Kermode, the play reveals, "the human predicament," where "evil" is the "common enemy of man" and witches or demons embody that "equivocal evil in the nature of things." Unlike "angels," they are "produced by nature" and can "see some distance into the human mind." Although "the evils within and without Macbeth's mind are subtly twinned," they cannot touch his "soul." Since there is free will, choice becomes fate. The temptation to which he succumbs will "unman" Macbeth. His is an "unnatural act" and "he sinks below manhood."[7]

Lady Macbeth is "even less aware of the spiritual crimes and penalties," and therefore perhaps "casts off her womanhood and so loses her mind in guilt." Her unsexing is a form of demonic possession. The man is unmanned; the woman is demonized when she too is separated from her nature. If he were prepared to fudge a little on the issue of the supernatural, Kermode could have had a good conversation about the play with James I, before and perhaps for whom it was first performed. For Kermode's is still a theological reading, and although the supernatural may manifest itself in an unseemly fashion, it is an independent real force. Really, we have not moved out of the medieval universe. And neither has Kenneth Muir who, in 1984, still sees Lady Macbeth as a "second Eve."[8] Female nature is thereby predestined and delimited by religious myth.

Likewise, in 1986, Germaine Greer reads the play in terms of a representation of the personal morality of the characters who are "exemplars of the human struggle for salvation."[9] Although she enjoins us not to psychoanalyze them, "what shakes the heart" is "the gradual revelation of the sublimity of the moral universe in which (the tragic hero) moves" (67). This heart is more likely to be shaken if it beats in a British breast. For "the quintessential British hero, King Harry" is the center of the history plays (70), suggesting an empathy still accessible to inhabitants of the former colonies. Shakespeare's plays show "the kind of organic unity which could keep disparate elements in his own version of the Heraclitean dance," the "pluralism and tolerance," the "freedom from aggressive certainty," which "makes possible the emergence of consensus, the art of compromise" (86) and all those qualities that "characterise English political thought and institutions." Shakespeare's "belief" in "Merrie England" recalls a "way of life essentially British," yet "something enduring in human nature," or "an anchor in human goodness" that is "our best corrective for the cruelty and inequity of the human condition" (102f.). Such readings are still pervasive in education, even though Brecht, for example, was arguing more than seventy years ago that contemporary readings of Shakespeare constituted anything but perennial wisdom, let alone efficacious British antidotes for the human condition, but were ideological through and through.

The American new historicist critics read Renaissance literature in relation to other cultural texts. The forces that construct the characters can be sought in the needs of contemporary political ideologies and not seen as expressions of perennial salvationism, whether theological, existential, or just plain national. For Tennenhouse *Macbeth* exemplifies a Jacobean theme, the reassertion of patriarchal power after the unsettling of patriarchal imagery under the Virgin Queen Elizabeth. Lady Macbeth is the unruly aristocratic woman unnaturally challenging the king's male body, threatening his power, inverting patriarchy and sovereignty, as Macbeth usurps the kingship, which is then resanctified and resexed through the virgin male heir to the throne, Malcolm.

Recent criticism in Britain, sometimes referred to as British materialist criticism, takes issue with the assumptions of traditional Renaissance studies in English. These studies are partial in their reading of Renaissance texts and overlaid with ideological expectations and do not do justice to the argument and thought available in the Renaissance itself, which helps us appreciate the complexities of Shakespeare's plays. Such criticism is then taken through to poststructuralist readings of the texts.

The target for attack is the still powerful notion that for two reasons these plays offer the experience of reintegration: either they naturalize order, degree or, social hierarchization—by means of the famous Elizabethan world picture—and so function as a form of ideological control by state or class power, hence the rebellious head is severed from its provocative body; or through the workings of mimesis, we identify with the represented and imagined characters and seek our salvation after their mistakes. Dollimore, however, shows that Machiavelli, writing on power, and Montaigne, on the law, both argue these are based on interest, not nature, that they are determined by what Montaigne called "custom," while fearing the radical consequences of such understanding. Burton, Bacon, and Montaigne all analyze the process whereby custom is internalized and structures consciousness, which is therefore ideologically constructed. Perry Anderson even argues that Althusser's best ideas derive from Spinoza.[10]

This all rather puts paid to the essentialism that supposedly constructs the depiction of human nature in Renaissance texts. You can choose to believe in such essentialism, but you ought to be aware of what you are doing, and that it was not the only choice even within Renaissance culture. When we relate such thought to Renaissance language theory, the clash between Platonic naturalism and demystifying linguistic scepticism, and the preoccupation with the duplicity of all representation, an obsession in *Macbeth*, the unequivocally essentialist salvationism begins to appear like an unconscious defense against the evaporation of its values.

If the texts are freed from constrictions put upon them, something of their complexity is recovered. We can then look at textual and performance language or codes, not at dramatic characters who embody perennial truths and essential qualities, at relations not at essences. We then realize, to take the programmatic title of a book, that Macbeth's "signifying nothing" can be allowed a greater range of meaning than any construction conventionally put upon it. Far from indicating his moral collapse or bemoaning the loss of transcendental truth, "signifying nothing" can be read as denying the usefulness or reality of a metaphysical something, and so as refusing a transcendental signified or signifier.[11] In turn, this can be seen in terms of a possible relationship with the Buddhist concept of "emptiness," which does not signify "nothing" either, but rather encodes the complexity of relations in process. This analytical step moves beyond the Western conventions of poststructuralist thought and onto the subject of Shakespeare in East Asia.

The kunju version of *Macbeth* interrupts the empirical and conventional readings of the play with a constructed, stylized performance that stops these automatic and familiar Western responses dead in their tracks. Some modern criticism is just as traditional as the much-maligned Bradley and is also based on the supposition that the figures in the play possess unified character and embody perennially human qualities so that the readers can share their dilemmas and learn from their experience: how to be a man, how not to be a woman. Other contemporary readings reinstate the fundamental uncertainties or equivocations embodied in Shakespeare's text. What look like poststructuralist or post-Marxist readings can in fact be seen as reiterating possibilities for interpreting language and positioning texts available within Renaissance culture. Finally, there are productive analogies between such readings and the kunju performance, which has more in common with them than with conventionalized Shakespeare.

## II

Taking Shakespeare into Chinese culture is not simple. The repositionings focus our attention yet again on what we take for granted. This applies to both sides of the encounter. The intercultural sign is most productive when it unsettles all conventions. Both cultures have the opportunity to question their own presuppositions, to test what ideologies of representation have conventionalized, to engage with their own cultural unconscious.

In China there are two kinds of theater: the traditional "opera" with around three hundred local varieties, of which Peking opera (*jingju*) is the best known and kunju the oldest and, some would say, most sophisticated. There is the so-called "spoken drama" (huaju), the term itself marking the distinction between them, drawing on the newly discovered Western drama. Modernization was not just a matter of a technological catching up. This negotiation with modernity seemed to necessitate the adoption of Western forms and to involve cultural transformation and self-denial.

In the first decades of this century the realist or naturalist Western theater, addressing immediate social problems, made a strong impact on the powerless Chinese intellectuals in the coastal cities as they watched the decline of their culture. In Ba Jin's novel *Family* the impact of *A Doll's House* is obvious. But where, asked Lu Xun, could Nora go in China, once she has left home?[12] There was no available social space. In the process, the play and "Ibsen," as its author, are read in terms of China's lack. This has the effect of fixing that play, or any other, both as a function of this lack and of a conventionalized reading through which it became visible in the first place. Comparative studies of Ibsen and Chinese culture often deal positivistically with such topics. They are more concerned with aspects of Ibsenism, not with really rereading the plays, which must surely be the starting point for more searching cultural comparisons.[13]

Brief descriptions of two productions in Beijing in 1993 illustrate some of the problems of developing spoken theater in the different cultural and political environment of contemporary China. The first, *Thunderstorm*, by Cao Yu, widely regarded as one of the best exponents of this form, was warmed-up Ibsen, a derivative classic, skeletons in the bourgeois Confucian cupboard in which, as in Ibsen's *Ghosts,* a half-brother's and -sister's love is frustrated when the servant girl and the young master learn they have the same father.[14] The set had an upended grandfather clock and overturned furniture right at the front of the stage and cavelike spaces created out of black crepe paper that bunched up like lowering thunderclouds, and classical domestic furniture in the center. The curtain parted onto darkness as a clock struck twelve and the characters standing in separate alcoves lit candles in front of their faces. Reality as a bad dream. History as nightmare. They then turned it into a cultural melodrama, playing to the emotional highpoints in an excruciating style, perhaps best described as naturalist presentational, like Peking opera without the externalizing subtleties, savoring each new and ghastly turn of fate. The ultimate climax came in a universal freeze, with all the characters' hands in the air, gesticulating in various directions.

The other place, Guo Shixing's *Birdmen* (*Niaoren*), more interesting and topical, the talk of the town, was sold out for weeks.[15] There is a story but no plot in a Western sense. Rather the play is a series of *Stimmungsbilder*—evocations of mood—in scenes that caricature and hence easily defeat outside ideas threatening to question inside culture, only it is expounded as that which differentiates the native from the foreign, or as traditional Chinese values. *Birdmen* takes place in a Beijing park among bird fanciers, who meet to parade their precious captives and exchange views about the passing scene. Some of the men have retired, but this is also a way of dropping out of modernizing China. There is a strong old man, an irascible old man, an irrepressible young man, and a number of hangers-on, making up the ubiquitous group. The curtain parted inch by inch onto a supernaturalistic recreation of a park in front of a large dark red wall, suggesting what is left of the old imperial palace, known in the West as the Forbidden City, and doubtless symbolizing the might of Chinese history, the lighting designer assiduously painting sunrise while the loudspeakers trillered out a dawn chorus. After this *son-et-lumière* spectacle, the birdmen make their appearance.

They argue about the virtues of their protegés. The young man tries to join in but is suspiciously received. He has a Tianjin accent, which allows the audience to see the clannish narrowness at work. After a while he persuades them that he knows more than some of them about caged birds, which can stand for traditional Chinese culture or national values. The irascible old man returns after an interlude to find his pet bird imitating somebody else's. He becomes so enraged at this display (of independence?) that he stamps on the cage, kills the bird, and then evidently collapses with a heart attack.

Three further outsiders have meanwhile interrupted this ambiguous idyll. One, a psychologist, has studied abroad and, now returned, wants to try out his foreign knowledge. He has decided to psychoanalyze the birdmen and their strange ways in order to probe the mystery of the Chinese cultural psyche. They turn the tables on him. The second intruder, an ornithologist, walks around the set holding a large magnifying glass and explaining that birds are a proper object of scientific study and should be liberated from their cages. He too gets his comeuppance.

## Macbeth in Kunju Opera

Intruder number three is an American environmentalist who leans on both his cane and his Chinese wife. He determines to buy the park and ban the birdmen who are then temporarily evicted by an officious policeman. They ask the woman why she married a foreigner. She replies she is only going to stay with him for a few months. I began to recall the *Eight Model Revolutionary Operas* during the Cultural Revolution, which caricatured foreigners in this kind of way. The only difference, apart from a now credible temporary marriage, was the color of their hair: now black instead of red.

After observing the birdmen, the psychologist unsurprisingly decides that they like birds more than people, that one of them harbors murderous thoughts that he is likely to put into practice, and that all of them suffer, but especially the powerful old man, from sexual dysfunction. One of their sidelines is Peking opera, and so they convene an opera trial in order to investigate the foreign-trained expert. He is made to prostrate himself, is then vigorously beaten, threatened with execution and finally released, in mock terror of his life. The old man's prowess, both cultural and sexual, which has to be defended against this foreign Freudian assault, is triumphantly reasserted. At the end, a line of middle-aged female *yangge* dancers slowly glide among the trees. This is the folk dance from Shanxi that the Communist Party encountered in Yenan during the Japanese invasion and the Civil War. It was later popularized throughout China, so that it evokes officially sanctioned cultural-national values. The ornithologist, chiding the birdmen for keeping the creatures in cages, is ridiculed since he is looking for a unique specimen in order to stuff and display it in the museum.

There were many local jokes I didn't understand about keeping birds. The audience loved the play. It had the easy popularity of local accent comedy. Yet the main message seemed to me a fascinating but regressive, chauvinistic, sexist display of cultural insecurities, pseudosolutions for the problems real life is not resolving. A fine line often exists between critique and approbation, so that one could read this cultural chauvinism as unmasked, rather than self-defensively savored, were it not for the evident need to triumph in this stage battle with foreign modernity by representing it with straw figures. Although this can also be the price you must sometimes pay in order to represent them in the first place within a culture where public representations are always potentially part of a political discourse. It would be nice to be able to laugh them off, but that is not going to work. Hence this place encapsulated many of the problems, as well as some of the opportunities, in this development of a Western-style "spoken drama" and its Chinese cultural content.

## III

The kunju *Macbeth* takes another, far more difficult and challenging possibility of presenting Shakespeare: not as straight translation in an imitated Western style like the transplanted Ibsen, nor as nativized cultural psychology employing a "Western" dramatic form, but by radically transforming the play through adapting it to a traditional Chinese performance style. Most productions of Shakespeare take the other route, and perform according, or close to, Western conventions.[16] From the perspective of traditional Chinese aesthetic style, the difference between performing Shakespeare or Arthur Miller may not seem so great. Yet Western realist conventions are only invisible because the participants have naturalized them. It is possible to find them as "arbitrary" as the symbolic conventions of Chinese traditional theater. Even the most denotative or psychologizing naturalist style always contains this possibility of undermining its representational presuppositions.

Erika Fischer-Lichte explains how a "primary" sign outside the theater, apparently replicated by a realist style, always becomes a "secondary" sign on the stage.[17] Such secondary signs no longer encode meaning unequivocally. They are always placed between quotation marks. If the semantic range of codes is potentially endless, then in the theater there is always this additional dimension or equivocation or qualification: the code employed is a code about a code, a sign about a sign, because it stands in relation to, is in some sense produced by or through, a figure embodied by an actor. In the theater, signs are also polyfunctional. They are not natural; they can stand for anything else. Everything is placed between quotation marks; all signs are denaturalized. Nothing is directly represented. Everything is distanced by its representation. Western realism contains as much artifice as Chinese conventionalized style. The artifice merely looks different.[18]

Shakespeare is reimagined in a traditional Chinese style because the

## Macbeth in Kunju Opera

practitioners can test and extend its conventions. The fixed system of signification in Chinese theater, which can appear rigid if uncreatively automatized, is jolted in this production, and the predominant musical structure is dislocated in order to recapture a forgotten dramatic potential within the traditional form. For a Western observer, juxtaposing the "familiar" Shakespearean play with Chinese performance style naturally, and initially, underscores the fundamental visual and dramaturgic differences. The linguistic code can be important in East Asian theater, although the most important passages in Chinese theater are always sung, hence transformed by the musical code. Yet the main difference from Western theater lies in the relative importance of the lyrical musical and the proxemic or gestural code. Words move more quickly than gestures, although music perhaps moves more deeply on a somatic level. Nothing can replace the rapidity of the linguistic code. The visual codes move more slowly, but they are probably more memorable. A theater that privileges them must concentrate on carefully selected episodes.

This *Macbeth* is divided into eight scenes. The kunju musical structure is organized around a dramatic core in a stark departure from conventionalized form. This version has done away with virtually all the subsidiary speaking parts. The first five scenes—the Witches; the Plotting Scene; the Murder of Duncan; the Murder of Banquo; the Banquet Scene—tell the essentials of the story up to the end of act III. The three scenes after the interval—the Cauldron Scene; the Sleepwalking Scene; Bloody Hands Avenged—correspond to IV.i, V.i, and the final battle. While the externalizing, spectacular style slows the play down and can appear diffuse if you are not accustomed to the medium, this episodic concentration upon the essentials has the effect of intensifying the plot. Where the spectacular visual effects operate as another level of intensification, this theater can create extraordinary effects.

I find the kunju musical style more interesting than jingju where the pentatonic scale and the isomorphic rhythmical reiteration produces melismatic repetition of musical phrase, too much for my taste. Kunju uses harmonic effects unavailable to jingju, whose instruments exchange the same melodic line. Kunju also uses lyrical folk melodies. Its leading instrument is not the nasal two-stringed erhu, but instead the flute with its gentler tones. The orchestra is also noticeably different. It contains a small bamboo organ and a wider range of instruments—lutes, zithers, and trumpets—as well as the percussive instruments for the acrobatic and dramatic moments. There is also greater rhythmical variation. In sum, the music is more developed.

Characteristically, the Chinese title, *Story of the Bloody Hands* (Xue shou ji), focuses on the vivid visual metaphor of guilt. As the play begins, one person stands at the center and back of the darkened stage. It is a man. He is a witch. On both sides narrow ramps slope upward into the wings. He walks rapidly up one of them and then down to the center, then up the other and down to the center again. He is wearing a long black cloak that sweeps open and closes with the rhythm of his movements. He makes a sudden movement and shakes a figure out of one side of the still billowing cloak. Another witch, a midget, tumbles onto the stage. Then from the other half of the cloak, the same thing happens. Both are played by men with legs bent double. They sway or roll around the stage like balls. Everything here is fluid, in movement, incapable of staying still. Nothing will stay in place. And when they turn their heads, all three witches display grotesque facial masks with grinning teeth or red outstretched tongues under protuberant eyeballs fixed to the back of their heads. Right from the start, they create a stunning, dislocating, and particular visual effect that certainly does not occur in traditional Chinese theater. It produces an intellectual and emotional shock and will do so in both cultures. Nothing that will follow, you realize, can be like anything you have ever seen before. (See figures 7, 8, and 9.)

I happily accept this spectacular visual effect in exchange for Shakespeare's witches' reptilian soup, which was intended, presumably, to invoke moral disgust over a black and fallen nature, incapable of regeneration, but which in fact almost sounds, at least up to "fillet of a fenny snake," or "toe of frog" and "tongue of dog," like a recipe for a style of Cantonese cooking (IV.i). Here nature is not a moral emetic but healthily edible. There is even a suggestion of shark's fin.

In place of Shakespeare's ideological potpourri that demonizes nature, we gain something much more interesting and contemporary, although expressed through values available in traditional Chinese culture: an objective apprehension of the distance between these witches and Ma Pai (Macbeth) who sees only half of their faces and will seize on their predictions and destroy himself. They survive him, returning, as they do not in Shakespeare, at the end of the play. They incorporate forces indifferent to his fate, which they have enabled. He sees their smiling faces, not the grotesque masks behind their heads. One side of their heads encourages his desire, the other side evaluates it. They are visibly "double," like the linguistic metaphors in Shakespeare's play. The dwarf witches anticipate the ideologically necessary judgment at the end of Shakespeare's play:

> Now does he feel his title
> Hang loose about him, like a giant's robe
> Upon a dwarfish thief. (V.ii.20)

Western theater verbalizes; East Asian theater visualizes. The Western actor speaks the words; the East Asian actor embodies the codes. How we respond to the production turns on what we see in the performance. We can distinguish between obviously spectacular effects, and the externalization of states of mind, of the character's unconscious, which corresponds to that fluidity in the Shakespearean text while transferring it to another code. To the Western audience virtually everything appears visually astonishing. The face masks, headdress, and costumes appear exceptionally spectacular, gratuitously fabulous, although we know they constitute a rigorous and explicit codification and, thus, represent to some extent the opposite of the fabulous, namely, a form of denotative precision.

The company's brochure asserts, "Spectacle replaces Shakespeare's penetrating characterization." This raises a question about the nature of spectacle and the visual code. Hence we should distinguish between the spectacular acrobatic effects in kunju and the externalizing codes that suggest gradations in states of mind. We need to decide the status of these codes, how they operate, whether they signify preestablished and conventional attitudes, or whether they might indeed relate, in a more complex way, to that "penetrating characterization" that this adaptation of the play is supposed to have replaced with spectacle. But does "spectacle" not relocate and reinforce "characterization," rather than replace it. If so, how might this relate to Shakespeare's text? We step into territory where East Asian and Western theater engage with the emotions and demarcate differences in representation.

An English critic, Lois Potter, observed of the production, "Whereas Shakespeare's play stages the supernatural and the process of introspection but keeps most 'real' events offstage, Kunju is almost pure spectacle.

7 Ji Zhenghua as Ma Pai (Macbeth) and Zhang Jingxian as Tie Shi (Lady Macbeth) in the kunju *Macbeth* *(photo courtesy of Huang Zuolin)*.

8 Macbeth inspects his bloody hands *(photo courtesy of Huang Zuolin)*.

## Macbeth in Kunju Opera

9  Macbeth sees Banquo's ghost *(photo courtesy of Huang Zuolin)*.

It shows everything except the murder of Duncan and even that is so audible that the royal physician rushes off to tell the heir-apparent to escape. Encounters with the supernatural take the form of whirling dance movements. In the banquet scene, Macbeth's courtiers flatter him by pretending to see the ghost and encourage him in his spectacular attempts to kill it."[19] She wondered if Pepys's seventeenth-century *Macbeth* was perhaps not like this, whether it was not like nineteenth-century Western theater "with its striking poses, sharp contrasts, and use of sound effects to reinforce emotion. We are not asked to assume an ultimate reality behind what we see." Potter also remarked the unfamiliar sign system made it difficult to know whether she should read it in terms of tragedy, comedy, melodrama, burlesque, or even circus. Her conclusion is interesting: "The more effectively the actor struts and frets his hour upon the stage, the more he emphasizes the power of the illusions to which he has succumbed.... It would seem that the problem of *Macbeth* can best be solved by embracing its spectacular theatrical possibilities rather than regarding them as a distraction from its true meaning."[20]

This astute critic is uncertain about the style, wanting to place it correctly and find an appropriate response. She also senses that what seems an exaggerated, Grand Guignol spectacularity, which we might expect should somehow come from a level below the capacity of Shakespeare's text as a "distraction from its true meaning," may after all add to its understanding. We need to analyze "spectacle." Western critics are understandably uncertain about it.

Yet it hardly requires a deep knowledge of kunju to see what the performance accomplished. Philip Brockbank saw performances during the 1986 Shakespeare Festival in China and remarked on the connection between movement and emotion, both in the etymological and metaphorical senses.[21] Instead of worrying whether we are seeing the right thing, we need such a freshness of perception. We may then defamiliarize assumptions about this style. If that proves possible, there is much to learn. Perhaps we ought to ask whether Shakespeare's vividly metaphorical text is not visually encoded in the kunju performance in ways not immediately apparent, if we think of "spectacle" simply in terms of physically vigorous effects.

Is there indeed "no ultimate reality behind what we see" in the kunju performance? If so, would this diminish something vital to Shakespeare's text, or confirm it in another dimension? Has kunju visualized Shakespeare's metaphors? "Characterization" might then not have been disregarded but differently envisaged.

A plot about ambition, disloyalty, and the galloping, self-engulfing curse of murder that once begun can only feed upon itself, *Macbeth* uncovers the repressed underside of the feudal game of power. For a hierarchically structured society based upon mutual obligations, disloyalty is the most grievous crime. Of course this makes the plot eminently suited to the politics of traditional China and Japan. Disloyalty breaks the chain of command, synonymous with social order. Things fall apart. Shakespeare's text is fraught with the historical tensions working their way through English society and encodes them in relation to the political formations of his day and their ideologies. We can see what these tensions produced, how they were created, and how the language grapples with intractibilities.

This dark tale, providentially set in remote times and in the dubious cultural borderlands, takes up a theme that jars on the nerves of the culture and goes to the roots of its insecurities and self-understanding. Often this is revealed on the edges of the text in remarks that do not seem central and that therefore beg to be interrogated. One such example, in the battle description right at the beginning of the play, uses the

## Macbeth in Kunju Opera

unusual words "kerns and gallowglasses" to refer to what the Riverside edition explains as "light- and heavy-armed foot soldiers" (I.ii.13). Later there is mention of the "skipping kerns" from the opposing army, sent skipping, driven into flight. But these are by no means neutral terms, since they refer specifically to Irish soldiers and so to a permanent threat of insurrection from that rebellious island that must be contained. This problem was about to be "solved" by the settlement of Ulster on land dispossessed from the just defeated Irish under their chieftain-kings O'Neill and O'Donnell. The Stuart James VI of Scotland had just taken the throne of England. The English state was not secure. We need to watch how Shakespeare shows these insecurities.

Shakespeare's play neither culminates nor begins with the murder of the lawful king, although it occurs relatively early on. The play imagines the illegal possession of power, the seizing of it by the only available means, murder, and the impossibility of trying to hold onto power so won. But it is not concerned with investigating political power and barely describes the mechanics of its employment. It only describes an illicit will to power and how this works upon the mind, but upon a mind or minds expressly constructed to produce a particular response. These minds do not preexist, or exist apart from, the codes that enable us to place them. There can be no question of wishing Macbeth would only behave otherwise "for the sake of humanity" or anything else. Shakespeare's play is about dissemblance and self-deception, about the gulf between showing and being. It must therefore imagine ways of embodying the invisible repressed.

Shakespeare's "character" Macbeth is demarcated by the other figures in the play, and then all of them depend upon how the plot functions within its culture, as we interpret these interrelationships. But on the level of character-reading *within* the play, he is placed between extremes, that of his hyperdetermined wife and of the saintly Edward, who not only heals the body politic but the physically sick as well. Macbeth's conscience apparently negotiates his repressions as he grapples with the consequences of his actions. Since language is his primary mode of communication, Shakespeare's linguistic code verbalizes this repressed. In kunju the proxemic code is primary, and other means are used to indicate its presence.

Shakespeare's figures harp on the deceptive nature of appearance. They fall victim to it, like Duncan, or worry about it, like Malcolm at

Edward's court, or attempt, like Macbeth and Lady Macbeth, to negotiate the disproportion between seeming and being to their own advantage. Unmasked to their unsettled selves, they grow ever more preoccupied with concealment, with masking what emerges and, especially in the case of Macbeth, with the problem of living and dealing with the inadmissible. They become obsessed by what the eye may see and what can be concealed from it. This ranges from simple precautions for determining what can and cannot be physically seen, through to perceptions that threaten to reach right into and expose the repressed.

Macbeth plans Banquo's murder and warns the murderers of the need for: "Masking the business from the common eye . . ." (III.i.124), and later tells Lady Macbeth:

> we must . . .
> . . . make our faces vizards to our hearts,
> Disguising what they are. (III.ii.34)

Duncan therefore could not anticipate the treachery of Cawdor: "There's no art / To find the mind's construction in the face" (I.iv.11). Yet Macbeth also wants to mask his desire not just from others but from himself as well:

> Stars, hide your fires,
> Let not light see my black and deep desires;
> The eye wink at the hand; yet let that be
> Which the eye fears, when it is done, to see. (I.iv.50)

As he gets deeper in, the figure of Macbeth becomes ever more the focus of contradictions and begins to learn things he only half knew about "himself." These are presented as deceptions of the senses and, as in no other play by Shakespeare, appear as externalizations before him—the famous dagger, visions, illusions, ghosts, apparitions—until it becomes hard to tell what is external and internal, what is real or unreal:

> Mine eyes are made the fools o' th' other senses . . .
> . . . and wither'd Murther
> . . . towards his design
>     Moves like a ghost. (II.i.44ff.)

## Macbeth in Kunju Opera

Until finally what for Macbeth "seem'd corporal, melted / As breath into the wind" (I.iii.81).

His fantasies are realized, as his metaphors reach deeper into the driving impulses and eroticize political power:

> Two truths are told,
> As happy prologues to the swelling act
> Of the imperial theme. (I.iii.127)[22]

But driven by these impulses, he is shown as losing touch with what is solid and what is not, with what is sanctionable and ultimately sustainable and what is not, as Fortune helps to uncork the fantasies he had kept in check:

> Present fears
> Are less than horrible imaginings:
> My thought, whose murther yet is but fantastical,
> Shakes so my single state of man that function
> Is smother'd in surmise, and nothing is,
> But what is not. (I.iii.137)

When he can no longer turn back, when fantasy can no longer be controlled as fantasy, when it has become brute fact, the mind begins to spin ahead of itself: "These deeds must not be thought / After these ways; so, it will make us mad" (II.ii.30).

How does kunju engage with this metaphorical strategy? Does it find correspondences on another plane of signification, in another code? Is there indeed in the kunju version, "no ultimate reality behind what we see?" If so, would that interfere with, or perhaps help and extend, our understanding of "Shakespeare"?

### IV

I do not want to get into detailed questions about the Chinese text or how the performance is "read" from within its own culture.[23] That would be another perspective, another study, and deal with the interrelationship of the codes, musical, visual / proxemic, and linguistic. I have never seen this adequately described for Chinese opera. The importance of such an enterprise was defined for me once and for all, when I saw an astonishing film of Mei Lanfang performing in Moscow in 1935. For the first time I fully understood why Brecht was fascinated by his artistry. But our topic now is how the Chinese performance might relocate and reread Shakespeare, how the proxemic code transposes the linguistic code and the consequences of these possibilities.[24]

When those witches turn their heads to show the comic-gruesome masks that belie their smiling faces, this externalizing gesture undoes, has from the start already undone, the strategy of dissemblance that spreads and deepens as it takes hold of Macbeth, as duplicity seeps into his being, and that he will therefore be ever more desperate to sustain. These externalizations have situated dissemblance from the beginning, before Macbeth knew anything about it and while, in Shakespeare's text, he is still fighting the old battles for his king. These defamiliarizing witches therefore externalized his unconscious; they anticipate what lies ahead. But they also stand, even as they survive him, for an agency that can read and place it. To recognize this in no way diminishes the increasing tension as the play probes his state of mind, yet the witches signal these unfolding dimensions in advance. They are not those fog-begotten, filthy females, let alone Polanski's terrified male fantasy of powerful, superannuated hags whose superstitious incantations reek of degradation. The kunju alignments are more psychological, political, and cultural, and much less transcendental, in both directions, than in conventional readings of Shakespeare. This, of course, constitutes a reading, a very productive one, of his text.

Right from the start, this shift in the plane of signification alerts the audience of the need to look for, literally to watch, what happens later with an attention that is unaccustomed, and not possible in most Western theater. Such a presaging device, fundamental to East Asian theater, was much admired by Meyerhold and Brecht. Meyerhold called his version of it "preacting," an equivalent of the Japanese *mie* in the Kabuki theater, an externalizing moment of arrestation. In Brecht's plays too we have alluded to moments when especially important contradictions are strikingly externalized, when everything comes to a halt, and the present moment, set in aesthetic time outside the confines of the imagined action in the play, pulls the future into itself, even as it also incorporates the past. Such moments externalize what is essential to the plot. These visualizations are unforgettable. They do not dull our curiosity by blandly showing us what is to come. If anything, they heighten our alarm, because they make us aware of how complex and vicious the forces are that construct the characters as the plot unfolds and crushes them.

The witches both externalize and evaluate, they grotesquely represent Macbeth's repressed. His delusions, and Lady Macbeth's later madness, are made as palpable for us as for them, because we see in this performance what they must undergo. Seeing really is believing in a play where insight and blindness overlap. In Western theater ghosts and apparitions are a perpetual embarrassment. How can they be shown? Either not at all, or as if they were not really there. In *The Family Reunion,* Eliot's decorous afternoon tea party Furies are a naturalist High Church joke. Ghosts and apparitions in Shakespeare still trip up performance. Sometimes they are shown as a compromise between the imagined and the empirical, doubtful in status and uncertainly presented. There is a plethora of ghosts at the end of *Richard III,* and I have never seen them acted except as if they were somehow not supposed to be there.

But there is no mistaking the presence of the ghosts in the kunju *Macbeth.* They appear in the full panoply of their rank, bristling with the dignity of which they have been robbed and striking terror into those that see them. Banquo's ghost, and Macbeth's delusion, are also so much more palpable, although only he perceives it, when the courtiers point to the strutting, multicolored figure that they cannot see, and therefore ingratiatingly indulge Macbeth who seeks to dispatch it with his sword.

The loss of control or "madness" preceding Lady Macbeth's death is internalized in Shakespeare and expressed through the linguistic code. The actress will try to wash the invisible blood off her hands, and does this naked in Polanski's Playboy *Macbeth,* and although sleep-walking externalizes the unconscious.[25] In the kunju version this scene is turned into an elaborate and extraordinary event that, once again, both externalizes and evaluates from beyond any presumed subjectivity of the "character." In Shakespeare, Lady Macbeth refers to the deaths of Duncan, Lady Macduff, and Banquo, as her mind providentially collapses into its predestined abyss. In the Chinese version they literally appear before her eyes and torment her. She tries in vain to fight them out of her mind. But they close in upon her, and she collapses at the end of a long sequence of whirling movements that cut off all mental escape. The constriction is physically palpable. When she finally falls, they bend over her and, in the dark, breathe fire out of their mouths. You can literally see the flames. Two further figures participate in this torment, the ghost of her maidservant and another wholly unexpected externalization of her anxiety: a parrot belonging to the doctor. She had earlier broken its neck in a fit of pique. This parrot is dressed in a green feather costume and has a red, curved, retributive beak.

What does this wonderful invention stand for? It seems to parody the other ghosts, as the creatures of her aristocratic conscience, troubled by the slaughter of her feudal coequals, and so mocks her own gestures of self-defense. It both externalizes her torment and evaluates its by absolutizing it, thus shifting it into the comic-grotesque. Such palpable ghosts, indisputably creations of "the heat-oppressed brain," again raise that question of the relationship between "spectacle" and interiority, and hence the status of these externalizations.

Brockbank observes, rather patronizingly, that "Chinese theatre was apparently in need of the intimate attentiveness to life to be found in Shakespeare's plays."[26] In one sense, Shakespeare's texts probably are different, perhaps uniquely complex, and so maybe "all" theater can somehow learn from them. But behind such a judgment there surely lurks the double supposition that Shakespeare is uniquely different in his understanding, empathetic creation of "character" that Chinese theater largely lacks. Instead, it is solely concerned with reproducing elaborately codified traditional performance skills, savored as a kind of aesthetic athletics, that have therefore separated themselves from the troubling discontinuities of real human experience. Yet of course there was considerable "attentiveness to life" in Chinese theater, in the sense of response to the problems and dilemmas of Chinese society.

One could even argue the theater in China showed greater "attentiveness to life" than did Western theater, or at least that it did so just as much, although in a different way. It obviously had a political function. The bureaucracy was always nervous about its disruptive potential. There was always an underside to the process whereby it was supposed to inculcate those Confucian virtues. It was no accident that the Cultural Revolution was triggered by the performance of a play, an adaptation by Wu Han, the mayor of Beijing, of an old story about imperial highhandedness, *Hai Rui Dismissed from Office*, correctly perceived as an attack on the policies of Mao Zedong. Here the theater reached right into the formulation of political policy with extraordinary consequences.

## Macbeth in Kunju Opera

Chinese society evolved forms of social behavior less tolerant of overt social or familial dissent than was permitted in the West. Traditional Chinese society lost its capacity to renew and change itself. Finally it stagnated. In that society, avoiding overt altercation became something like an unquestioned rule, and this behavioral model still characterizes East Asian neofeudal or post-Confucian and protodemocratic societies. The loss of social face, of the internalized, and ultimately feudal sense of order, was and perhaps remains the intolerable embarrassment, an unforgivable social sin. This naturally led and leads to massive and endemic repression, to the formation of that social unconscious, in proportion to the force of the demands of social character. The theater, as public performance in social space, functioned as a mechanism for dealing with this fact, for enacting surrogate derepression. In this sense too, it was indeed "attentive to life," but in a manner necessitated by the different cultural value system. The persuasiveness of the styles in Chinese theater depended on the fact that such repressions were only showable when they were so distanced from actuality, as if projected onto the dramatic characters.

For this reason, the analogy with melodrama is not so helpful. In the West, melodrama emerged as a crudification of sophisticated forms and serviced with its restricted range the limited cultural needs of a petit-bourgeois class. It concentrated on an exaggerated and hence simplistic portrayal of undifferentiated emotions. It really constitutes the opposite of Chinese theater or, at any rate, the sophisticated forms like kunju. For here the exemplary plots, often focusing on moments of emotional strength, explored these moments instead of simplifying them. Through such performance, the audience could engage with, rather than crudely indulge, the repressed of its own culture. If the plots seemed narrower in range, compared with Western theater, their treatment was particularly intense.

"Attentiveness to life" in the Chinese theater takes the form of attention to gradations in the exploration of culturally constructed repressions and emotional states. Such gradations can be finely separated and brilliantly externalized in a sophisticated elaboration of visual codes. Watching these codes unfold, the audience constructs its reading of the play.

Brockbank also observed that the more Chinese the performance is, the more Shakespearean it seems, for the Chinese theater can enrich

Shakespeare's plays by "the energies and styles of an exotic, simultaneously courtly and popular tradition."[27] Zheng Shifeng, the author of the Chinese translation/adaptation points to the many analogies between Shakespeare's and traditional Chinese society, both of which articulated feudal values.[28] They therefore thematized feudal loyalty. Performance, in theory at least and sometimes also in practice, took place before the whole social range of an audience unified by feudal society. But in spite of some similarities in performance conditions that produced analogous forms, and in spite of the significance of the text for some Chinese opera, the major difference remains that Shakespeare's metaphors in the linguistic code are transposed into gestural metaphor. Signification occurs on another plane.

The energy of Shakespeare's linguistic code accrues from the fact that it was produced during a period of explosive and traumatic social and cultural change, at a time when a major shift in cultural models was underway in a process that the participants could not themselves comprehend. In comparison, Chinese society appeared far more stable and integrative and developed uniquely efficient ways of inhibiting cultural change. Instead of extending the range of human experience as a consequence of discovering the world, Chinese theater explored in depth experiences available to that culture. But the emotional life that it investigated constituted a contestable field of social perception. To explore this was to enable the audience to negotiate, or come to terms with, potential or actual traumata in their own lives. The bureaucracy would not have been wary of the theater, if it had not also suggested the possibility of perceptual change.

In a society that depended on the acceptance of imposed or internalized and unquestioned mutual obligations, egocentricity is intolerably destabilizing. In the kunju version of *Macbeth* the witches, who also reappear at the end of the play, and the presence of the comic-grotesque parrot, locate a social and psychological reality beyond what Macbeth and Lady Macbeth can see. By such devices the unconscious of the character is suggested. But the social unconscious of the interpreting audience in which everything is embedded, which produces them, is also made accessible. Yet nothing of this is located in an invisible and transcendant reality. There is no transcendental access or refuge. There is, in this sense, no "ultimate reality behind what we see."

Finally, I would argue, the intercultural kunju *Macbeth* enlivens Shakespeare not just because of the feudal analogies, whose evocation implies orientalist associations, since it pins the production to a superceded social formation, nor because of the vividness of its defamiliarizing style but, more interestingly, because it constitutes a disturbingly modern reading that departs from views of the play as constructed by traditional criticism. There are grounds for analogous readings in Renaissance humanist thought. Instead of any transcendental predication of the characters or the text, we encounter a network of psychological and social relations. Macbeth's "nothing is but what is not" then expresses the depth of an imagined personal psychosis that, because of his social position, amounts to a threat for his political culture. His is the pathology of a subsystem, as he unlawfully claims to incorporate the whole of governance within himself. This "nothing" is the reverse of a transcendentally secure universe and so undermines all its claims. The kunju witches do not grossly embody contaminated nature, do not represent an endemic, transcendentally projected "evil," but rather externalize the quotidian fears and forces that attract and impel Macbeth. A reading of the codes of this production must constitute a social semiosis.

V

The supposition that stylized, typified, painted-face figures in Chinese opera function in a way that is incompatible with the individualized Shakespearean characters is not true. We have seen how those Shakespearean "characters" are in fact sites for the passage of language, and the "stock" characters of Chinese opera are potentially fragile and as infinitely interpretable as the interplay of the codes produced by the actors who embody them.

Hsü Tao-Ching argues that the Chinese theater is close to Shakespeare's because its acting conventionalized, but I do not find in his book much about what really interests me in the Chinese forms: their capacity to reach into the repressed.[29] The Chinese theater does not reproduce or represent a predefined emotional life or interiority; it presents or symbolizes. What is shown is therefore distanced, even as it is brought close to us. There is always this doubleness in the mode of communication. Nothing is ever identical with itself. This separation in technique can also separate the observing interpreter from what he observes and from

## The Intercultural Sign

his observations. On this point Hsü makes an interesting comment that corroborates something often denied by commentators, who have perhaps an insufficiently differentiated view of the audience, but is important to my argument: "The sophisticated audience of the Chinese theatre remains emotionally aloof. They understand but do not share the passions of the characters in the drama. . . . They do not feel involved in the drama . . . (there is) always a psychological distance between drama . . . and audience."[30]

The nature of the form allows us to understand why the figures are so structured. Appreciation therefore does not simply and exclusively concentrate on revealing, enabling participation in, the emotional life of the characters, as is so often thought, but rather on showing its, and hence their, structuration. The supposedly purely aesthetic effects, savored by the discerning audience, actually constitute information about the complexity of that structuration, because the emotions are themselves culturally and socially constructed.

The effect of so exteriorizing the figures' structuration is that they are de-essentialized and can be seen as the function of the forces that sweep through them. They become the battleground of the discourses, rather than their producers. The mind is then not private to itself but displayed across the stage. The language of Shakespeare's text can also take that mind apart, but the Western conventions of representation have dulled our sense of how all discourse is culturally structured. It has come to appear identical with itself, which only means, of course, that we do not see the ideological position of our reading. Defamiliarizing or alienating performance codes enable us to "de-moralize" individuality and ethical choice and thus to understand them in terms of cultural possibilities.

When Macbeth is separated from "himself" by means of externalizing gesture, or collapsed back into the language that "he" only ever was, we can then begin to see what is at stake in our reading of these codes. We do not then identify with Macbeth, as Kermode evidently still does, measuring him against the morality that positions them both. Instead we can step back and gauge the skill of the whole "performance." We do not simply condemn "evil"; we understand what makes it seem intolerable, or why it may appear desirable. Then we can also place other readings of this work: those that see it in terms of Shakespeare's alleged nostalgia for feudal order, as a result of insight into the disruptive consequences of an incipient bourgeois individualism, where bourgeois en-

## Macbeth in Kunju Opera

ergy and self-aggrandizement will and must appear as "evil," precisely because such egocentricity is about to be revalued as necessary and hence as virtuous; or in terms of obeisance to James I's authority, where it is interesting to note how Shakespeare changed Holinshed's successful monarch Macbeth into a doomed usurper; or those who read it as punishment for the stronger and rebellious woman, as a political display of contested patriarchal power.

We can see why the "nothing" that life signifies to Macbeth is taken as absolute, and then read out of the play in terms of radical stoicism; or read into the character's moral collapse, as rebellious fustian that has been properly reduced to nothing. We have seen how that "nothing" can be read as a Nietzschean or as a Derridean and poststructuralist refutation that life, and this text, might be interpreted in terms of a restricting and fixed "something."

I have suggested that what may look like an unflinchingly contemporary reading, one that denies the authority of any fixed "something" can be related to an important Buddhist sense of "emptiness," which does not signify "nothing" either, but rather an unsettling, intellectually and emotionally rebellious multiplicity of meanings. This furnishes the foundation for the relationalism that, for example, so attracted Brecht to Chinese painting and thought. The Buddhist concept of nirvana conventionally connotes escape from samsara, or illusion, which means "being underway." We have seen that Brecht used Nietzsche's phrase, "the stream of happening," in his defining poem, *The Doubter*.[31] A metaphor resonates elsewhere in the texts: "The flow of things."[32] In philosophical Buddhism, especially as formulated in the Madhyamika tradition of Nagarjuna, nirvana embraces samsara, for there is no nothing.

This suggests that life consists of relations continuously in process, where nothing can ever stand still, and from which there is no escape. Hence we can understand the opposition within such thinking to a determinate order imposed through language and to the tyranny of absolute terms and rectifying names. This can clearly be related to Renaissance conventionalism. In a Chinese context, this could then be read in terms of a Daoist or Buddhist resistance to Confucian concepts of social and linguistic order.[33]

Here we can probably make a distinction between the kunju version of *Macbeth* and Kurosawa's *Throne of Blood*. It would be along the lines of a distinction between Chinese and Japanese cultural expectations and between Buddhist religion and Buddhist philosophy. In Kurosawa's film, everything has disappeared in the end, the Spider's Nest Forest and the Spider's Nest Castle, which was not Macbeth's "own" castle, but the seat of all authority, precariously and temporarily placed on volcanic ground. Nothing is left but the mark of the castle's site and the graves with which the film began, which therefore tells its narrative from the perspective of that ending. This is a figuration of that Buddhist maya, which equates the world with illusion or absence, in the context of a longing to escape from the wheel of karma. It is not the philosophical nothing, or emptiness, that de-essentializes experience in terms of always changing relations.

Ninagawa's *Macbeth* can also be read in terms of Buddhist religious values, expressing a desire for escape from the inconstant and ephemeral world:

> Ninagawa also had the boldness to frame the whole stage inside what is called a Butsudan, a Buddhist altar which can (or used to) be found in most Japanese houses and are the religious centres of daily life where the spirits of ancestors are supposed to dwell. And Ninagawa put a couple of old women on both sides of this huge Butsudan on stage, squatting, eating, knitting, and doing various everyday jobs during the performance of *Macbeth*. This scenic device made the whole action of *Macbeth* look like a play within a play and when the play ends, the old women, who look like Bedouins, close the doors of the Butsudan, which suggests that the tragedy has taken place inside that altar, inside the collective memory of the nation. And so the play acquires a religious dimension unknown in the original.[34]

Perhaps we encounter here an aspect of that distinction within but also between Japanese and Chinese sensibilities that is marked by a more passive and "religious" or a more active and "philosophical" reading of Buddhist thought. In any event, there clearly exists a distinction between, in the Japanese case, a more culturally disciplined, self-sacrificial acceptance of transience, exemplified by the unquestioning fealty and obedience of the samurai, than the anarchic and more materialist Chinese culture could so easily countenance, a difference which could be expressed in terms of a more isolationist or a more moralist approach to the problems of psychosocial identity, hence of the models found useful in thinking about them.[35] We can probably assume that Buddhism in China

## Macbeth in Kunju Opera

and Japan was affected by "nativist" or culturally developed strains of thinking and, respectively, by Confucianism and Shintoism, leading to different nuances in the direction of thought and representation.

Japanese culture was, as is well known, strongly influenced, even partly shaped, by Chinese cultural behavior. If, for example, you can read the characters of the Chinese script, you will never get lost in Tokyo. That such influences, as well as the noticeable differences, reach way back into expressions of traditional culture can perhaps be corroborated by the following illustration. Before his execution in 687 CE, the Japanese Prince Otsu wrote two poems: one in a more philosophical and measured Chinese style, the other in Japanese style that presents the feeling of transience directly through poignant imagery:

> The golden crow lights on the western hut;
> Evening drums beat out the shortness of life.
> There are no inns on the road to the grave—
> Where is the house I go to tonight?
>
> Today, taking my last sight of the mallards
> Drying on the pond of Iware.
> Must I vanish into the clouds![36]

Perhaps the differences of emphasis could be encapsulated and partly explained as follows: in Japanese aesthetic and political sensibility, identity disperses into transience as a homology for the expression of an absolute social demand on personal fealty and automatic self-sacrifice from which escape is finally inconceivable. However in China Buddhist and Daoist thought, turning away from the exigencies of bureaucratized social and familial relations, recourse to another form of reticularity that does not constitute a simple refutation of Confucian concepts of social order but rather represents a subversive, "horizontal" reimagining of an otherwise hierarchical or "vertical" assertion of interconnectedness.[37] The Japanese Imperial house traces its lineage back to the Sun Goddess. In China the dynasties were changed by rebellion.

Huang Zuolin, the artistic director, has himself explained what he wanted to achieve with his kunju version of *Macbeth*, yet does so in terms that need situating. He uses the vocabulary of an idealist aesthetics in order to define a position incompatible with what such terminology normally connotes. He wishes to capture the "spirit or essence" of beauty that is "synonymous" with "poetic feeling." He also observes that Western drama and its "picture-frame stage ... presents individual, realistic, static, little worlds of their own." Later in this essay he remarks, "However, Chinese drama often emphasizes the subjective rather than the essence. This, to me, is a defect which can be remedied or cured by Brecht."[38]

The most interesting reading of these remarks seems to me that the theater has to externalize the subjective into the range of its relations. They are what is essential because they are essential in the construction of subjectivity. The theater must help us catch a glimpse of the totality or complexity of constructed relations that are always in process, as Brecht also tried to do, instead of constantly holding them down and collapsing the subjective beyond redress into an objective and hierarchical dependency. The "poetic" feeling, the aesthetic effect, depends on a sense of the accuracy of the presentation and the inclusiveness of our understanding, producing that moment of cathartic self-transcendence that Koestler also detected in his analysis of laughter. We then look into the movement of a performance text and understand how culture constructs the totality of these processes, even as the texts of a culture appear to assign the space of individual experience.

# EPILOGUE

Living in political times, Adorno observed the most radical critique is always aesthetic. We could argue for an objective, although maybe not subjectively deliberate, anticipation of this principle in the apparently so unpolitical forms of Japanese culture. Social content is apparently turned into pure form, an extraordinary, seemingly self-absorbed and self-referential aesthetic language. Form is not thereby subverted, but rather refined to the point where its properties begin to deconstruct themselves, and the aesthetic becomes the highest expression of the political.

We can differentiate this assertion through an inflection of Nietzsche, if the world can only be justified, or comprehended, or represented, as an aesthetic phenomenon. In the 1873 essay, *On Truth and Lies in an Extra-Moral Sense* he spoke of an "aesthetic relationship" between subject and object. The subject cannot correctly describe the object, but attempts a "tentative translation, a stammering rendition into a quite alien language."[1] Hence the world is not justified *only* as an aesthetic phenomenon; it cannot otherwise exist for us. This was, of course, read in a trivializing art for art's sake sense, which Wilde parodied, implying the right to impose your taste or power. But it can be seen as an extension of the Kantian *transcendental aesthetic*.[2] It is more productive to extend this view of "reality" as an "aesthetic phenomenon" to the shape or structure we impose upon reality through language, even as we think to derive it directly from reality itself. This is, in part, why I reformulated Clifford Geertz's phrase to say that "the imaginary is as real as the political."[3]

Referring specially to the plays of the Noh theater, Earle Ernst argues in his excellent study of Kabuki that Japanese theater is more inclined to farce than comedy.[4] He relates this both to the absence of a Western concept of character and to the structures of Confucian ideology. The

# Epilogue

rigid hierarchization, for which Confucianism furnished the necessary moral ideology, created social behavior that depended on sustaining considerable repression. We might say, the greater the repression, the more elaborate the etiquette, and vice versa. This is really the outward expression of an internalized, culturally specific formalization of social relations, perceived as unchangeable or not needing change. A society that so fetishizes etiquette or the appearance of formal order will have no mechanism for negotiating change and will always risk sudden collapse in upon itself, like the red giant that glows outwardly but has consumed its own substance, as happened in Tokugawa Japan and, more drastically, in Qing dynasty China or, for that matter, to the Soviet Union. Traditional societies devised aesthetic experiences that enabled audiences to work in the imagination through crushingly real situations, deflected in the theater, when the inevitable personal conflicts, engendered by so rigid a system, become intolerable.

Ernst makes a careful argument, anxious to balance out the positions. Like Miner, whose views were discussed in chapter 2, he takes certain criteria as absolute in their Western context, which in fact depend upon assumptions about character representation and that must themselves be relativized within a reading of Western culture. He finds these criteria more productive than those that operate within Japanese culture, although not wishing to impose them upon it. Hence Japanese farce is found less compelling than Western comedy. I have earlier questioned such "Western" criteria and what they actually sustain. Ernst's assumptions about representation apply equally to tragedy and comedy. I disagree with them, but a sympathetic account might assume the following presuppositions.

Where time is innovative, not cyclical and eternally recurring, individuals embody the conflicts produced by historical change. The basis for choice must be moral preference, a desire to shape the future. Tragedy shows the price of change is often personal failure, as the character shoulders the burden of choice. Comedy sometimes suggests it is possible to change the world if characters can adjust to a developing social norm.

The obligations put upon a character cannot be absolute, because then there is no choice, no moral problem, and no tragic flaw. A complex inner life, and so an evolving character, is only possible where cultural obligations are fundamentally negotiable. Where they are not, where

# Epilogue

society refuses this personal space, drama can only envisage typifications, repetitions of the recurring conflicts, but without the opportunity of individual refusal and of new resolutions. In such cultures there can be no tragedy in the Western sense, only victimization by fate, and no comedy of character either, only a form of farce that laughs at the absurdly typical.

An alternative to such presuppositions and to the traditional Western hierarchization of genres, whereby tragedy is the most and farce the least elevating, is to recognize that the concept of "character," on which everything rests, is itself ideological, shaped by forces we do not well understand. Farce, as the logic of the unconscious, sharpening our focus on the nature of character, helps to uncover the constraints. That is the first step to understanding anything and then, perhaps, to changing something. Seen in this light, farce is the wider category and the comedy of character a stage in the development of bourgeois culture, which both offered the prospect of a real space for individual choice and the illusion that such space was an absolute moral demand made on behalf of all humanity, the recognition of an undeniable universal freedom and an inherent right.

Growing out of Carnival performance, commedia dell'arte drew on many sources. Its performances were unscripted, based on scenarios around which the actors would improvise. The characters consisted of types, whose roles were signified by the mask. Improvisation and typification complement each other. The actors brought this scenario to life through improvisation. They could do this because the types or "masks" they embodied were fixed by convention. Where such conventions are understood, improvisation can produce strong effects, probably related to Carnival's *social* improvisation.

There are obvious connections between this form and the traditional Chinese and Japanese theaters, in which a set of conventions governing performance style and behavioral expectations was devised to distinguish a number of character types. In the Chinese theater, the names of the individual characters change, but they are absorbed into the types or roles that they represent and that have their own separate designations. The actors specialized in playing certain types; the name of the character was almost immaterial. Society creates or permits certain roles, and individuality consists in performing within the constraints, exploring the space determined by these roles.

## Epilogue

Part of the pleasure of watching a performance, as in the Chinese or Japanese traditional theaters, depended on the fact that you knew what was going to happen but not exactly how it was going to happen. The actors had so completely internalized the types they represented that they could concentrate on reinventing them for each performance, and since there were no scripts this is precisely what they had to do.[5] A refinement of this relationship between actor, character, and type can be seen in the Japanese theater, where not only do the types continue through a range of plays, although the characters may have different names, but the actors who embody these types are known by a traditional family actor's name. The individual actor loses his ordinary name and assumes the name of the famous actor who plays the type.

Since farce is invariably associated with physicality, absurd improprieties, and gross motor jokes, "philosophical farce" may first appear a contradiction in terms, although Plautus's *Menaechmi* shows how intellectually complex identity misrecognition can become. That suspension of three-dimensional physical and social gravity, which physical farce appears to defy, is replicated in language and ideas, so that anything appears possible and the limits of the absurd are immeasurably extended. Instead of hands, fists, and bodies, ideas smack into each other and produce comic mayhem or appear so inconsequentially connected, no matter how seriously taken, as to be almost physically risible. The tempo and collisions of physical farce must be somehow replicated by conceptual equivalents. Anarchic farce does not necessarily entail fast physical movement, but it does depend on radically challenging cultural decorum and the laws that organize us, and through which we explain the world to ourselves.

Philosophical farce can destroy the basis for a *particular* position since it calls all positions into question. This may of course imply everything requires rethinking, so it should by no means be equated with philosophical nihilism.[6] Physical farce, however, seems more immediately associated with social incoherence, and less with universal meaninglessness, loss of hope, or intellectual incomprehensibility, for the energy of physical farce is animating.

In *Accidental Death of an Anarchist*, Dario Fo produces a sequence of dazzling and farcical impersonations of authority figures. Just like the Maniac's body that falls apart, which consists of false, false legs, the

Epilogue

figures he impersonates are false, false figures, impersonations of proven impersonators who do not embody what they are supposed to, the moral and intellectual qualities expected of their professions. The presence of false, false legs and false, false identities links the intellectual-political and physical farce. Because of all this anarchic interweaving, one form of normality reversal reinforcing the other, the façade of moral authority is undermined and, if it really is a façade, it will eventually collapse. In Fo's play, Identity collapses. Knock it on the back and a glass eye, the false, false eye, the unseeing, morally cold eye of the corrupted expert, shoots out of its head. That is an example of physicalizing metaphor. Impersonated identity is shown to be wholly spurious. It literally comes apart on the stage.

The comic kyogen plays of the Noh theater, essentially elaborate and sophisticated jokes, compress the obsessions of comedy—the problems of identity, power, fear, and representation—into a *non plus ultra* of formal concentration, without really appearing to reduce them. Of course they function within the parameters of their culture and are characterized by specific expressive restraints. As so often, these apparent "limitations" can be turned into advantages. Like the Zen koans, which are at once riddle, joke, dramatic encounter, and enigmatic gesture in need of interpretation, these plays unsettle our certainties. They are comic meditations on the effects of reality created by representation and language, which are then taken for reality itself and by means of which people structure their subjectivities.

Buddhist dialectics are the starting point for an enquiry into the nature of subjectivity, for Zen contemplation of the self. Brecht called Hegel one of the world's great humorists, because in his system nothing ever stayed still, everything was continuously turning into its opposite. A comic catharsis through self-transcendence, the ability to be taken out of "yourself," is available through Zen as well and can therefore become the basis of a clarified pragmatics, once you have seen the absolute relativity of your position. Zen seems to offer a more radical, but also a more rational, pragmatics, if we understand why it is absolutely possible for us to be "descended," not from a god and trailing clouds of glory, but through transmigration, from a frog, since our destiny is linked to his. We have no claim to any special privilege. To explore such relationships may not occasion that explosive laugh that signals an immediate release

# Epilogue

from a directly felt repression. But this comic form has perhaps the capacity to provoke the longest laugh of all.

What makes the play I now present a fitting conclusion to this intercultural study is its sophisticated combination of the apparently contradictory demands of physical and philosophical farce, a special characteristic of the kyogen plays. They work as a kind of slow-motion slapstick, all the funnier for moving so slowly. The physical confusion becomes philosophically more interesting and comic, because the whole process is specially charged, moving onto another plane, another stage, where body and mind, representing and reading, are thrown into each other, challenging us to seize the opportunity and make sense of what is happening. This is not how these plays are normally described in critical writing, but what they show us none the less.

*Fumi Yamadachi, Literate Highwaymen,* like most kyogen has the structure of an elaborate joke and hence, perhaps, that capacity to produce the transformative consequences Koestler anticipated in such epigrammatic drama.[7]

> *Fumi Yamadachi*
> Characters: Gendayu, Chobei.
> Gendayu: (*As if in fright, he walks backward and shouts*): Get him! Get him! Don't you dare to let him go through here!
> Chobei: Let's go! Let's go! Hey you there! Why didn't you get in action?
> G: Because you shouted, "Let's go! Let's go!" I thought the fellow was either your friend or relative, and let him go unharmed.
> C: I said, "Let us go!" Don't you know the password of highwaymen? It means the fellow is rich and we should rob him.
> G: If that was what you meant, why didn't you say so? Look! How fast the fellow flees!
> C: Who would not? But alas! This all comes from your being so cowardly. My bad luck began when I became your ally. No more of this. (*So saying, he throws his spear on the ground.*)
> G: If you do not want to be with me, that's all right. But why did you throw your spear?
> C: I did it purposely. If you do not know what I meant, I will tell you: "Out with you!"
> G: Hum! You dared, did you? (*He throws his bow and arrow.*)

# Epilogue

C: Hey! Why did you throw your bow and arrow?
G: To trample you under.
C: I am a man. I am not going to be trampled under. (*They begin to fight.*)
G: Stop! Don't push me so hard. There is a bramble bush behind me.
C: What of a bramble bush to one who is to die in a few minutes?
G: All right.
C: Wait! Wait for a moment.
G: What?
C: Don't push me so. I shall fall off a precipice.
G: What of a precipice to you who is to be killed?
C: Say!
G: What?
C: The way we are grappling with each other must be a wonderful sight.
G: Ah indeed. I should like to show it to all the manly men.
C: If we should die now, no one will see this heroic scene. Moreover, who is going to notify our wives and children of our tragic end? Our dying is utterly wasted, I fear.
G: What you say is very true. No one will let our families know about it.
C: We might leave a note of farewell. What do you think?
G: That is an excellent idea. But our arms are locked tightly. There is no way of unlocking them.
C: That's simple. Let's say, "One, two, three," and at "three" we'll both unlock them.
G: Very well.
Both: One! Two!
C: The last one, and I am not going to be beaten.
G: Look here! We no longer are fighting. Let us withdraw our arms peacefully.
C: Very well. By the by, have you a brush and ink?
G: No, I have not.
C: I have. I brought them in case we get many valuables and have to make out a list.
G: You are a clever fellow.
C: You compose a note and I will write it.
G: Very well. But what shall we say?

C: Indeed, what shall we say?

G: "At this auspicious occasion of the New Year . . ." How about that?

C: When we are about to die, we can hardly call the occasion auspicious.

G: What you say is true enough, but how shall we begin?

C: I wonder.

G: How about, "I beg your pardon to write a few lines?"

C: No, no! The occasion is much too acute for that sort of rhetoric. Never mind. I will compose a fitting message.

G: Please do so. Oh, how he writes! The top of his brush is actually dancing.

C: Here! I have finished it!

G: What did you say?

C: I started out, "To get back to the very beginning . . ."

G: That's good.

C (*reading*): "To get back to the very beginning, by a strange mishap I ran away from my family and became a highwayman who robbed innocent travelers and priests. But alas, I had quarreled with my fellow highwayman, and after a long and hard grappling, I grabbed my sword . . ."

G: (*jumping up*): Oh, you betrayer!

C: What is the matter?

G: You said, "Grab hold of my sword," and I thought you were going to attack me.

C: That was only a sentence.

G: Oh, only a sentence! Why didn't you tell me? I nearly fainted with fright.

C: I am sorry. Then let us read this together.

Both: "I grabbed my sword. But wait! Should I die here without witness, people may think I was killed by unworthy fellows. But, my dear wife, I want you to remember my story, and honor and narrate correctly my tragic fate. Alas, when I think of my wife and children whom I leave behind, I cannot keep back my tears . . ." (*They both cry.*)

C: What a tragic affair this is!

G: It is.

C: How about postponing our dying for a little while?

G: Five days?

C: That seems too short. A little longer perhaps?

Epilogue

> G: How about a year or two?
> C: A year or two pass away in a dream. Really, come to think of it, no one has seen our altercation, and if we two agree, we can give up this idea entirely. How about it?
> G: What you say is very true. Let's be friends again.
> C: This certainly is felicitous. Let us chant the adventure of the day and return home together.
> G: Excellent.
> C: Realizing that to die is utter waste . . .
> Both: Hand in hand the two highwaymen
>       Wend their way to their home.
> C: Listen, my friend!
> G: What is it?
> C: You and I shall live five hundred eighty years.
> G: Ah, indeed! To the end of seven incarnations.
> Both: Oh, happy day! Happy day!

We encounter a pair of comically timorous bandits, two inseparable incompetents, so a version of the comic duo in Beckett's plays where each questions the other's existence yet must define himself in terms of it. One of them, Chobei, is brighter than the other or there would be no dynamic. Their problem is they question the relationship between language and meaning and then confuse narrative and reality. A robber must be able to act decisively. These ones cannot even agree about the meaning of words.

This is philosophical slapstick. The hapless couple get so locked in combat with each other that they have great difficulty untangling their arms and extricating themselves. They need to do this in order to write about what is happening to them. This comic matrix clash is implied in the title. The audience / reader watches the actors as characters deny the "reality" of actual events because, although their incompetent attempts at robbing may have taken place, they have not yet been "narrated," they have not yet been composed and organized by memory, and therefore do not properly exist. This, of course, reminds us how we construct versions of ourselves, of our past behavior, by a careful, selective, and mostly unconscious arranging of events into a suitable narrative in accordance with the internalized narratives of our culture. But if the narrative has not yet been properly composed, then neither have the characters.

It appears these bandits are highly self-conscious. Not only afraid of brambles when fighting for their lives, they fear they can only truly exist in the knowledge of other people. They can only see themselves in terms of figuration, as heroically figured, not as heroes. They do not exist except as the object of interpretation. These characters in a play also wish to incorporate within themselves, as participants in a spectacular encounter, an aesthetics of representation. Indeed, they cannot conceive of themselves except as the embodiment of such an aesthetic or the object of interpretation. They cannot, therefore, properly exist unless they are mediated by language. Constructing their narrative then produces for them an effect of reality that was previously lacking and that confuses the slower one because he takes it for reality itself—he is told it is "only a sentence"—but that finally absolves them of the necessity of completing the narrative they set out to tell.

Reality is an effect of narrative, of recollection, not of a direct experience. At the very least this is true for reality in the theater. They can exist as figures in a narrative but only if it is being interpreted: "Two characters in search of an audience." But if they could find one, which they must in order to come properly into existence, then, for the sake of their honor, they would have to die. Yet since they cannot find anyone who would be able, or constrained, to "narrate correctly my tragic fate," they can avoid it and live forever. They set about constructing a myth of their own behavior, of their own existence, according to the prescribed cultural expectations. This, however, then enables them to reject the behavior necessitated by that guiding cultural narrative or myth. Only the creation of the narrative can lead to an alteration of the behavior it was supposed to explain and justify. They only perceive their "comedy" through the parody of a "tragic" myth. They have transformed themselves through the power of reflection. They have unwritten and rewritten themselves; they have written their way to happiness.

Such awareness of the mediation or structuring of the cultural conventions in the narratives of myth and literature enables a self-transcendence when it offers the reader the opportunity of escaping from the trap of its own artifice. The highwaymen do not "see" this; after all they are characters in a play. They simply do it. They are at the same time the actors, writers, and readers of their own self-absorbed narrative. And of course the readers or audience whose absence they first regret, but then turn to their own advantage, are watching their every move in the theater and

## Epilogue

this demonstration of the deconstruction of mimesis that consequentially and simultaneously enables them to reinvent themselves.

The whole story shows the potential for a form of self-transcendence, for escaping from a "self" that has been trapped by language, by narrative, or by convention, because that self has acquiesced in its own apparently inescapable structuration by these binding cultural mediations. Zen Buddhism was virtually invented to deal with this problem. That is why it dispensed with theology and with grand philosophical narratives, preferring jokes, riddles, and any form of communication that fractured the stereotype, smashed the Buddha, and questioned the reliability of all convention.

This is the Japanese equivalent for that suspicion of mimetic doctrines and their constraining political and intellectual implications, which has structured so much of the best Western dramatic writing. The radical aesthetics of the cleverly constructed Japanese play also relates to that aspect of deconstruction that, in refusing points of rest or metalanguage, reminds us of the changing and relational nature of all experience. The effect, as in Buddhist dialectics, is to undo the purchase of universalizing ideologies, just as the rejection of the ultimate absolute, nirvana, in Madhyamika philosophy, returns us to an ever-changing samsara. In respect to historicizing that also involves culturalizing, we might say that where social control is unquestionable, the critique of absolutes occurs on a philosophical level and through probing the aesthetics of representation. Here we connect with the antimimetic countercurrent in Brecht's writing that draws on East Asian art and thought and that, because it seeks escape from ontological fixations, whether philosophical, metaphysical, or political, consistently figures relationalism. This is the point of contact with Derrida, and with the dynamic concept of sunyata, or emptiness, which intrigued Heidegger whom Derrida admired.[8] It also connects with that view of (post-)Marxist thinking that informs recent writing, attacking vestiges of a materialist foundationalism or essentialism that Brecht, in his own way, resisted through those dissenting representations. This is, as I understand it, what Laclau and Mouffe imply when they write, "As the social is permeated by negativity—that is, by antagonism—it does not attain the status of transparency, of full presence, and the objectivity of its identities is permanently subverted."[9]

I take this to be cognate with that dialectic of the Dao, which undoes

# Epilogue

the hegemonic by virtue of its antagonism to any form of absolutizing.[10] Poststructuralism and post-Marxism both de-essentialize the subject. Their antimetaphysical relationalism is compatible with East Asian forms of thought. But instead of an ahistorical and abstract, endlessly splitting identity, the focus of much poststructuralist criticism, it is imperative to historicize these processes.[11] If socially organized identity is subject to splitting, such proliferation is never abstract, but rather is produced by historical pressures that must be situated. If the positivities always deconstruct themselves, it is because all terms are inescapably relational. Disintegrating unification and hierarchical centerings, dispersal is regularly figured as loss, whether in Freedman's poststructuralist psychoanalytical model, or as Lacanian lack, or as a weak deconstructionist ceaseless postponement of meaning. The alternative to disintegrated hierarchies is not a theoretical anomie, but a horizontal and democratic, rather than vertical and hierarchical concept of integration. When hierarchies have been deconstructed, there is a need for relational reintegration. Nothing can exist in isolation, not even the practice of perpetual deferment.

We may seem to have come a long way from the Shakespearean texts, but their "positivities" are also beset by unsettling relativities as, for example, when their plots' social conclusions are suddenly questioned or undercut by their epilogues, or when the contradictions they embody are what we remember, even if they appear enclosed by the social and philosophical expectations of his culture. Shakespeare's genius consists in always letting us see or sense the other side of what can be thought and felt.

In conclusion I quote three characteristic responses to encounters signified by the intercultural sign. Juxtaposing Shakespeare and traditional Japanese theater, one critic appreciates the force of psychoanalytic readings within Western culture but understands externalization in Japanese theater simply as a manifestation of "beauty."[12] Such a position endorses an internalized ideological need and turns aside the opportunity of rereading.

Another critic, remarking how a production of *The Good Person of Szechwan* as Sichuan opera regained from Brecht what he had earlier appropriated from Chinese style and enabled a reinvigorating extension of the capacity of Chinese "opera," refers accurately and amusingly to "Reaping the interest on our loan."[13] Here we see acknowledged what I

Epilogue

have called the dialectics of acculturation. Chinese opera style profits from this impulse from outside that has reworked its own dormant capacities. These return, transformed, because there is a sense of their potential to free the form from its inherent repressions and provoke new developments.[14]

Finally, yet another critic ascertains that Shakespeare has perhaps been "assimilated into the Japanese repertoire." This has not, however, produced an increased understanding of his work through what is specifically Japanese. He nevertheless then observes that the effect of these differently visualized productions enables him to envisage a more poetic and less literal Shakespeare than heretofore, to see fresh possibilities both of performance and for offering the audience a greater role.[15]

Do we not in this final example encounter a response from the aesthetic unconscious? The experiences are untheorized and remain unconnected, but they are addressed, even if separately and ambivalently. This is how the process begins. While rejecting the possibility of intellectual or critical insights into Shakespeare from Japanese culture, a suppressed aesthetic potential is nevertheless acknowledged and implications suggested. But what does that then entail for such an automatic, naturalized, hence somehow unconscious separation of thinking and seeing, of the critical and poetic categories? Where might investigating such implications then lead us?

# NOTES

## Prologue

1 Lévi-Strauss mentions the Chinese opera troupe he watched for hours in New York in 1941, probably the same one that also intrigued Bertolt Brecht.
2 See Antony Tatlow, "'Those Savages—That's Us': Textual Anthropology" (inaugural lecture), supplement to *The Gazette,* University of Hong Kong, 40, no. 1 (Feb. 15, 1993).
3 Philip Goodchild, *Deleuze and Guattari: An Introduction to the Politics of Desire* (London: Sage, 1996), 5.
4 The première of Erich Engel's production of *Coriolanus* took place on Feb. 27, 1926, in the Lessing Theatre, Berlin. See Wilhelm Hortmann, *Shakespeare on the German Stage* (Cambridge: Cambridge University Press, 1998), 84; for Brecht's opinion, see Werner Hecht, *Brecht Chronik* (Frankfurt: Suhrkamp, 1997), 181; for Brecht's use of the term "dialectical theatre" in the later context, see the last entry in Bertolt Brecht, *Arbeitsjournal* (Frankfurt: Suhrkamp, 1973), 1022; or Bertolt Brecht, *Journals 1934–1955* (London: Methuen, 1993), 460.

## 1 Reading the Intercultural

1 "Intercultural angst" is invoked by J. R. Mulryne in "The Perils and Profits of Interculturalism and the Theatre Art of Tadashi Suzuki," in *Shakespeare and the Japanese Stage,* ed. Tadashi Sasayama, J. R. Mulryne, Margaret Shrewing (Cambridge: Cambridge University Press, 1998), 73. I discuss some of these anxieties in later chapters
2 Otherwise we tend to insularize our own culture. Comparative literature constituted itself as a discipline in order to escape this trap but, even when not universalizing, often concentrated on formal and microcultural variations, although such investigation is naturally justified as a

stage of discovery, instead of addressing macrocultural challenges. I criticize the neglect of anthropologically focused difference in my study *The Mask of Evil* (Berne: Peter Lang, 1976). Although greatly changed in recent years, Anglo-American Shakespeare studies long inhabited a world unto itself and developed its own culture of reading.

3 In his assault on what he sees as the debilitating consequences for criticism of a misunderstood Saussurean linguistics that have reached through to Foucault and Derrida, Brian Vickers takes Lévi-Strauss to task for his mentalistic constructions, as if reality could be reduced to a schema of falsely constructed oppositions based on spurious language theory. Vickers does not appreciate the range of Lévi-Strauss, or that such constructions were only the starting point for arranging otherwise verifiable material, or how Lévi-Strauss, like Brecht, drew on East Asian models of thinking, or how his descriptions can be brought to bear on Shakespeare's (and Brecht's) texts. See Brian Vickers, *Appropriating Shakespeare: Contemporary Critical Quarrels* (New Haven, Conn.: Yale University Press, 1993), especially 3–91.

4 Shakespeare is not on the "political" agenda in the United States or in most English-speaking countries, but is in England. Because of the different cultural and social circumstances, academic discussion in the United States, often intensely focused, sometimes underestimates the extent of its social isolation, equating the state of academic debate with the totality of social discourse on the topic. See David Lister, "Was Shakespeare a Tory?" in *The Independent on Sunday*, Jan. 3, 1993. Lister draws attention to the continuing influence of this wider, neoconservative debate on the practice of Shakespeare interpretation in the classroom.

5 Michael Bristol makes these points from the perspective of the United States. He argues for the need to get beyond "the frame of the play." This, of course, is precisely what happens in intercultural performance. Bristol reads *Coriolanus* as a Bakhtinian and Rabelaisian battle between Carnival and Lent: the grotesque plebeian body versus the private body of Coriolanus, the lower body asserting itself against the head. Seeking to escape a conventionally attributed authorial mimesis, this marks a dissatisfaction with earlier conservative political readings. The text, however, eludes that mimesis through its own complexity, which is in fact the focus of Brecht's interest. See Michael D. Bristol, "Lenten Butchery: Legitimation Crisis in *Coriolanus*," in *Shakespeare Reproduced: The Text in History and Ideology*, ed. Jean E. Howard and Marion E. O'Connor (London: Methuen, 1987), 207–24.

6 Jean Marsden observes of Shakespeare criticism, "It is only recently that any consistent attempt has been made to view his works as part of a historical context." Brecht was doing this in the 1920s, but nobody no-

Notes to Chapter 1

ticed in the English-speaking world. I can well remember when raising such questions produced consternation or incomprehension among scholars. Discussion was virtually impossible. See Jean I. Marsden's introduction to the volume she edited, *The Appropriation of Shakespeare: Post-Renaissance Reconstructions of the Works and the Myth* (Hemel Hempstead: Harvester Wheatsheaf, 1991).

7 Stanley Cavell, "'Who Does the Wolf Love?' Coriolanus and the Interpretation of Politics," in *Shakespeare and the Question of Theory*, ed. Patricia Parker and Geoffrey Hartman (London: Methuen, 1985), 245–72. These, Cavell observes, "are necessarily shadowy matters" (256).

8 Cavell, "Who Does," 246. Jan Kott contrasts Brecht's "didactic" with Shakespeare's "anti-didactic" *Coriolanus*, in *Shakespeare Our Contemporary* (New York: W. W. Norton, 1964), 179, 191. I later juxtapose their readings of Shakespeare and find more common ground than one might suppose.

9 Cavell, "Who Does," 247.

10 Terence Hawkes, *Meaning by Shakespeare* (London: Routledge, 1995), 55. Reading the subsequent 1960s Berliner Ensemble production "as a denunciation of Fascism" (45), Hawkes refers to the play by Grass, *The Plebeians Rehearse the Uprising*, which sets Brecht's rehearsal of *Coriolanus* in the context of the 1953 workers' protest in Berlin, thereby containing in the theater what was actually happening on the streets outside. Grass could not and Hawkes does not know of the record of Brecht's discussion of that projected production with his assistants, subsequently published.

11 Friedrich Nietzsche, *The Birth of Tragedy*, trans. Francis Golffing (New York: Doubleday, 1956); *Die Geburt der Tragödie, Sämtliche Werke*, Kritische Studienausgabe, vol. 1 (München: Deutscher Taschenbuch Verlag / de Gruyter, 1988). Page numbers and quotations from the German text are enclosed in brackets. This text was first published in 1872 as *Die Geburt der Tragödie aus dem Geiste der Musik*, and republished in 1886 as *Die Geburt der Tragödie: Griechenthum und Pessimismus. Neue Ausgabe mit dem Versuch einer Selbstkritik*. A pioneering text on Brecht is Reinhold Grimm, *Brecht und Nietzsche. Geständnisse eines Dichters* (Frankfurt: Suhrkamp, 1979).

12 F. Nietzsche, *Ecce Homo*, Sämtliche Werke, Kritische Studienausgabe (München: Deutscher Taschenbuch Verlag, 1988), 6: 323, 316.

13 Nietzsche, *Birth*, 78f. [84].

14 Bertolt Brecht, *Diaries 1920–1922* (London: Methuen, 1979), 98.

15 See Fred Dallmayr, *Beyond Orientalism: Essays on Cross-Cultural Encounter* (Albany: State University of New York Press, 1996), 187.

16 "Der Fluß des Geschehens," see especially, *Die fröhliche Wissenschaft*, book 3, ch. 112, in Friedrich Nietzsche, *Sämtliche Werke: Kritische Studienausgabe* (München: Deutscher Taschenbuch Verlag, 1988), 3: 472f. Nietzsche problematizes the relationship between cause and effect, argu-

Notes to Chapter 1

ing we cannot explain but only describe, and that we create the illusion of scientific understanding and control by ignoring the perspectival and segmental nature of our knowledge that is shaped by the categories we apply to the continuum of reality. Bertolt Brecht, *Poems 1913–1956* (London: Methuen, 1979), 270f.; also *Gesammelte Werke* (Frankfurt: Suhrkamp, 1967), 587. For a discussion of this poem, see my essay, "Alienation and the Dialectics of Acculturation: Brecht and the Aesthetics of Chinese Painting," in Andrew Gerstle and Anthony Milner, eds., *Recovering the Orient, Artists, Scholars, Appropriations: Studies in Anthropology and History* (Chur, Switzerland: Harwood Academic Publishers, 1994), 83–107; also Antony Tatlow, *Brechts Ost Asien* (Berlin: Parthas Verlag, 1998), 13–16.

17 For a discussion of ghosts in Brecht and Derrida, see Tatlow, *Brechts Ost Asien*, 79–95.

18 For a discussion of the philosophical significance of this poem's metaphors, see Tatlow, *Brechts Ost Asien*, 8f. For a fuller English version, see Antony Tatlow, *Repression and Figuration: From Totem to Utopia* (Hong Kong: Department of Comparative Literature, University of Hong Kong, 1990), 112–17. The best translation of this poem is by John Willett, in Bertolt Brecht, *Poems and Songs from the Plays* (London: Methuen, 1990), 71.

19 In *Me-ti, Book of Changes*, or *Book of Twists and Turns*, passages sometimes in "Chinese" disguise and occasionally related to Chinese thought, see Bertolt Brecht, *Werke: Große Berliner Ausgabe* (Berlin: Aufbau und Suhrkamp, 1988–), 18:73. The obsession with death is often given a psychobiographical reading, but it can, as here, be understood as a rejection of conceptual fetishization in the name of dialectics, as acceptance of inevitable change in what may seem rock solid and unalterable. For the textual comparison with Zhuangzi, see Tatlow, *Brechts Ost Asien*, 60.

20 Brecht, *Gesammelte Werke*, 17:992.

21 Jacques Derrida, *Specters of Marx: The State of the Debt, the Work of Mourning, and the New International* (New York: Routledge, 1994), 51. Heiner Müller maintained that to play Brecht without changing him was a betrayal. He believed the texts only came alive again when opened up, separated from the classical patina that has smothered them. In this context, see "Ein Gespräch zwischen Wolfgang Heise und Heiner Müller," in Wolfgang Heise, ed., *Brecht 88: Anregungen zum Dialog über die Vernunft am Jahrtausendende* (Berlin: Henschelverlag, 1987), 189–208; also "Das Vaterbild ist das Verhängnis: Heiner Müller im Gespräch mit Werner Heinitz," *Theater Heute* Heft 1 (1998): 61f.

22 Walter Benjamin, *Illuminations* (London: Fontana, 1972), 256.

23 Derrida, *Specters*, 59.

24 Brecht, *Poems 1913–1956*, 270f.

25 Derrida, *Specters*, 74.

Notes to Chapter 1

26 My translation of *Bargan läßt es sein*, in Bertolt Brecht, *Short Stories 1921–1946* (London: Methuen, 1983), 1–15.
27 Derrida, *Specters*, 156, 155, 156, 174.
28 Michel Foucault, *The Order of Things: An Archaeology of the Human Sciences* (New York: Vintage Books, 1973), 383.
29 I discuss Fromm's theories below. Foucault once observed that he would have saved himself much time, had he been aware of the work of the Frankfurt school.
30 For a fuller description, see Tatlow, *Brechts Ost Asien*, 65–75; on Nietzsche in this context, see also Graham Parkes, *Nietzsche and Asian Thought* (Chicago: University of Chicago Press, 1991).
31 Claude Lévi-Strauss, *The Savage Mind* (London: Weidenfeld and Nicolson, 1966), 50.
32 Bertolt Brecht, *Collected Plays*, vol. 1 (London: Methuen, 1970), 56.
33 Claude Lévi-Strauss, *Structural Anthropology* (London: Penguin, 1993), 200.
34 Brecht, *Werke*, 1:478.
35 Brecht, *Poems 1913–1956*, 439–45.
36 Lévi-Strauss, *Structural Anthropology*, 206–31, esp. 219–27.
37 See the chapter, "Das Schweigen des Buddha," in Tatlow, *Brechts Ost Asien*, 37–44; the starting point for that discussion is Brecht's poem, *Gleichnis des Buddhas vom brennenden Haus*, in Brecht, *Werke*, 12:36.
38 "Der Fluß der Dinge," an expression Brecht employs many times in *Me-ti, Buch der Wendungen* for the interconnected and ceaseless dialectic that is part of a strain or strategy of metaphor that runs from the beginning through to the end of the whole work, connoting the irresistible and permanent processes of change.
39 In *Of Grammatology*, which consists of an extended argument with Lévi-Strauss about Rousseau, Derrida finds Lévi-Strauss's inclusion of Marxism within the wider category Buddhism incomprehensible. I have discussed these readings of and by Lévi-Strauss more fully in Tatlow, *Brechts Ost Asien*, 65–75.
40 Fredric Jameson, *The Political Unconscious: Narrative as a Socially Symbolic Act* (Ithaca, N.Y.: Cornell University Press, 1981), 69–74. Jameson also draws attention to a significant aspect of Frye's thought, evident in the formulation that "desire is the social form" of the emotions (71). For Northrop Frye, the *anagogic* is the highest phase, corresponding to the mythical mode. The monad contains the whole world within itself. Here literature is conceived "as existing within its own universe, no longer a commentary on life and reality, but containing life and reality in a system of verbal relationships." The myth or informing narrative *mythos* has become, as *dianoia* or meaning, the logos. The absolute horizon is here

Notes to Chapter 1

no longer mythical but mystical as well, and it guarantees the spiritual meaning of reality. See Northrop Frye, *Anatomy of Criticism: Four Essays* (Princeton, N.J.: Princeton University Press, 1957), 121f.

41 On the links between Brecht's "Buddhism," Wittgenstein, and theories of language, see Tatlow, *Brechts Ost Asien*, 37–44; see also W. F. Haug, *Philosophieren mit Brecht und Gramsci* (Hamburg: Argument Verlag, 1996), 69; also Chris Gudmunsen, *Wittgenstein and Buddhism* (London: Macmillan, 1977).

42 It is significant that otherwise helpful recent studies of Shakespeare and Japan do not really probe the compatibilities between Buddhist philosophy and poststructuralist theories in relation to their potential contribution to rereading the texts of Shakespeare and Brecht and to understanding what underlies all these relationships.

43 Lévi-Strauss has been severely criticized by literary scholars in this regard. In his analysis, the trickster, for example, is criticized as a "structuralist cog" in a "vast intellectual machine of mediations." See Robert D. Pelton, *The Trickster in West Africa: A Study of Mythic Irony and Sacred Delight* (Berkeley: University of California Press, 1980), 236. Pelton is quoted in Richard Hillman, *Shakespearean Subversions: The Trickster and the Play-text* (London: Routledge, 1992), 10.

44 Hillman, *Shakespearean Subversions*, 66.

45 Frye, *Anatomy of Criticism*, 106. Also quoted in Rajiva Verma, *Myth, Ritual, and Shakespeare: A Study of Critical Theory and Practice* (New Delhi: Spantech Publishers, 1990), 154.

46 Verma, *Myth, Ritual and Shakespeare*, 78; See Jane Harrison, *Prologmena to the Study of Greek Religion* (Cambridge: Cambridge University Press, 1922), esp. 567ff., on the relationship of ritual and drama.

47 Verma, *Myth, Ritual and Shakespeare*, 77; Jane Harrison, *Themis: A Study of the Social Origins of Greek Religion* (Cambridge: Cambridge University Press, 1927), 44.

48 Hillman, *Shakespearean Subversions*, 17.

49 Hillman, *Shakespearean Subversions*, 18. See also William C. Carroll, *The Metamorphoses of Shakespearean Comedy* (Princeton: Princeton University Press, 1985), 25.

50 Hillman, *Shakespearean Subversions*, 8.

51 Brecht, *Werke*, 8:191.

52 Hillman, *Shakespearean Subversions*, 60.

53 See the entry for Sept. 5, 1944, in his *Journals 1934–1955* (London: Methuen, 1993), 327. Charles Laughton reawakened Brecht's interest with his carefully prepared private readings.

54 Quoted in Verma, *Myth, Ritual, and Shakespeare*, 154.

55 "Jene gewisse Unlogik der Vorgänge, jener immer wieder gestörte Ab-

lauf eines tragischen Geschehnisses ist unserem Theater nicht eigen, er ist nur dem Leben eigen" (Brecht, *Gesammelte Werke*, 15:117).

56 Izumi Momose traces some loosely assembled parallels between Shakespeare and the Noh, attending to formal correspondences and to the concept of nothingness in both theaters, in an article "Shakespearean Drama and the Noh: *theatrum mundi* and Nothingness," in Sasayama et al., *Shakespeare and the Japanese Stage*, 176–85. In an interesting comparison of ghosts in Shakespeare and Japanese theater, Peggy Muñoz Simonds points out that the Shakespearean ghosts were already appearing ridiculous to sixteenth-century spectators, whereas the Noh ghosts are wholly credible. Shakespeare's ghosts are emanations of conscience, creations of the superego. See her article, "Shakespeare's Ghosts and the Phantasms of Japanese Noh Plays: A Matter of Theatrical Technique," in *Shakespeare East and West*, ed. Minoru Fujita and Leonard Pronko, Japan Library (Surrey, Eng.: Richmond, 1996), 115–33. I see the Japanese ghosts as externalizing unconscious obsessions, hence as the consequence and the revenge of what transcends our understanding yet shapes us nonetheless. Brecht's work is permeated by ghosts. See Tatlow, *Brechts Ost Asien*, 86ff.

57 These plays are the two versions of *He Who Says Yes, He Who Says No* and *The Measures Taken*. I have discussed the relationship of these plots to Japanese ritual theater in Tatlow, *The Mask of Evil*, 180–203, and more recently in an article, "Eine Maßanalyse aus anthropologischer Sicht," in Inge Gellert, Gerd Koch, and Florian Vaßen, eds., *Massnehmen: Bertolt Brecht / Hanns Eislers Lehrstück Die Maßnahme*, Theater der Zeit, Recherchen 1 (1999): 165–73.

58 Masao Miyoshi, "Against the Native Grain: Reading the Japanese Novel in America" (paper delivered at the Occident and Orient conference in the Humanities Research Centre of the Australian National University, Aug. 1987).

59 Werner Schulze-Reimpel, in *Rheinischer Merkur / Christ und Welt*, July 12, 1991. See *The German Tribune*, no. 1447, July 28, 1991, 10f. I discuss the critique of Mnouchkine in the next chapter.

60 Clifford Geertz, *Negara: The Theatre State in Nineteenth Century Bali* (Princeton, N.J.: Princeton University Press, 1980), 136.

61 Dennis Kennedy and J. Thomas Rimer, "Koreya Senda and Political Shakespeare," in Sasayama et al., *Shakespeare and the Japanese Stage*, 53–70. Although this is a standard critical move, I doubt if Kott's absurdist and Brecht's politically committed, appropriating readings of Shakespeare are as opposed as is argued here. I return to this topic in the following chapter. Relevant here is also the chronology of Senda's directing history compiled by Darko Suvin, in Marc Silberman, Renate Voris, Antony

Tatlow, Carl Weber, *The Other Brecht 1: The Brecht Yearbook* (Madison, Wis.: The International Brecht Society, 1992), 19:297–321.

62 Kennedy and Rimer, 66.
63 Kennedy and Rimer, 68.
64 Senda Koreya, "Greetings from Japan," in John Fuegi et al., *Brecht in Asia and Africa, The Brecht Yearbook*, 14:6.

## 2 Intercultural Signs

1 Patrice Pavis, *The Intercultural Performance Reader* (London: Routledge, 1996), 1; Erika Fischer-Lichte, Josephine Riley, and Michael Gissenwehrer, *The Dramatic Touch of Difference: Theatre, Own and Foreign* (Tübingen: Gunther Narr Verlag, 1990), 284.

2 In the sixties Jan Kott was objecting that the "enormous" influence of East Asian theater on the Western avant-garde was "underestimated." In my opinion it is still not really accounted for in recent discussions. See Jan Kott, *Theatre of Essences and Other Essays* (Evanston, Ill.: Northwestern University Press, 1984), 132.

3 Patrice Pavis, *Theatre at the Crossroads of Culture* (London: Routledge, 1992), 2. These crossroads indicate a parting of the ways, perhaps a moment of choice, certainly a movement out of familiar theoretical territory onto much less certain ground.

4 "Theory had its hour of glory with Brechtianism" (Pavis, *Theatre*, 93).

5 Pavis, *Theatre*, 153. In my opinion such views are unhelpful for reading Brecht but are common enough. Pavis evidently still holds them, as we can see from this contribution to a publication marking Brecht's centennial in which he observes that in *Mother Courage*, Brecht offers "an undifferentiated concept in respect of gender," because that play is "exclusively concerned with the mimetic representation of social relations." These quotations are contained in *driveb*, published by *Theater der Zeit* and the *Brecht Yearbook*, 23:45.

6 In the introduction to Pavis's edited volume, *Intercultural Performance Reader*, 5ff. In this move away from earlier paradigms, he also quotes Clifford Geertz on culture's "system of significations" as a means of engaging with new material. See Geertz, *The Interpretation of Cultures* (New York: Basic Books, 1973), 130.

7 Pavis, *Theatre*, 13. In *Intercultural Performance Reader*, Pavis suspects that universality may be a "construction of the dominant West" (17). I would agree. Perhaps this is just another grand narrative.

8 Pavis, *Reader*, 2. "Every intercultural project obeys the constraints and

the needs tied specifically to the target culture that produces it" (Pavis, *Reader*, 16).

9 Pavis, *Theatre*, 12.
10 Pavis, *Theatre*, 202, 210.
11 See Tatlow, "'Those Savages—That's Us.'" Also Antony Tatlow, "Visions and Illusions in East-West Literary Relations," in *The Force of Vision 3: Powers of Narration*, ed. Will van Peer and Elrud Ibsch (Proceedings of the XIIIth Congress of the International Comparative Literature Association, Tokyo 1991), 397–406. See Foucault, *Order of Things*, 379.
12 Dennis Kennedy, ed., *Foreign Shakespeare: Contemporary Performance* (Cambridge: Cambridge University Press, 1993), 294. In the afterword Kennedy lists other texts on intercultural theater, noting they have little to say about Shakespeare. Neither do they address my interest in the interactive nature of intercultural theater or its relationship to a cultural unconscious. See also the further discussion in Dennis Kennedy, "Shakespeare and the Global Spectator," *Shakespeare-Jahrbuch* 131 (1995): 50–64.
13 This is certainly as much the case as the fact, in spite of what critics often assume, that such processes do not necessarily result from careful study of the relevant source material or even from conscious, clarified decisions to explore its possibilities. The activities are both more haphazard and more interesting.
14 Kennedy, *Foreign Shakespeare*, 300f. John Russell Brown draws attention to another type of answer that complements but is quite different from my own, because it looks at the economics of large-scale directorial theater with the power to impose its interpretations, compared with underfunded smaller companies. My interest lies in asking what interpretive capacity such intercultural performance liberates and why this comes about. In his article "Shakespeare and the Global Spectator," Kennedy reads the intercultural sign, following Fredric Jameson, as "signs of 'late monopoly capitalism' in the way that successful theater works at this time. Like Coca-Cola and McDonalds' hamburgers, this mode of production 'works by transcending national borders and creating attractive images of its material products designed to make their consumption inevitable.'" See John Russell Brown, "Shakespeare, Theatre Production, and Cultural Politics," in *Shakespeare Survey*, ed. Stanley Wells (Cambridge: Cambridge University Press, 1995), 48:15.
15 Earl Miner, *Comparative Poetics: An Intercultural Essay on Theories of Literature* (Princeton: Princeton University Press, 1990), published when he was president of the International Comparative Literature Association and awarded a prize in Japan.
16 Aristotle is equated with that mimetic naturalism that trusts in effica-

cious representation. Insufficient account is taken of conventionalist language theory, also traceable to Aristotle, or of the validation in Aristotelian mimesis of the creative process, of the fictional as not grounded in a preposited "reality," or of the reason for Ricoeur's hermeneutic recuperation of mimesis through a series of engagements between the prefiguration of a socially negotiated preunderstanding, the configuration of the text, and the transfiguration through reading. Ricoeur, of course, wished to rescue mimesis from its presumed poststructuralist dissolution. See his essay, "Mimesis and Representation," in *A Ricoeur Reader: Reflection and Imagination,* ed. Mario J. Valdés (Hemel Hempstead: Harvester Wheatsheaf, 1991), 137–55. Derrida returns to the concept in "Economimesis," in *Diacritics* 11 (June 1981): 3–25, to discuss the hierarchical forces that operate through the concept. For a fuller historical account of mimesis in its widest sense and in relation to power, see Gunter Gebauer and Christoph Wulf, *Mimesis: Kultur, Kunst, Gesellschaft* (Reinbek bei Hamburg: Rowohlt, 1992).

17 "It is striking that the affective-expressive and the mimetic poetics do share what may be termed a prior presumption. Both have traditionally held to the philosophically realist ground that the world is real and knowable" (Miner, *Comparative,* 25). The proposition that philosophical realism grounds East Asian art is doubtful.

18 Miner, *Comparative,* 40.

19 Miner also disapproves of eating chocolates when watching Shakespeare.

20 Mimesis is here identified with a theatrical style influential in film and television (Miner, *Comparative,* 48).

21 It seems surprising to call on Brecht's anti-Aristotelian theater to witness Aristotelian mimesis, since he suspected psychological verisimilitude aroused superficial emotions and wished to get beyond it. Imitation of the surface conceals deeper structures of feeling, covers up the workings of the unconscious, and so fails to uncover the complex social and cultural structuring of subjectivity. This less conventional view, for which I offer evidence later, links Brecht's theater with an East Asian aesthetic.

22 Pavis, *Reader,* 2.

23 Miner, *Comparative,* 101f.

24 Quite an impressive opposing team.

25 See the essay *Engagement,* in Theodor Wiesengrund Adorno, *Noten zur Literatur* (Frankfurt: Suhrkamp, 1958), 3:109–35.

26 See Keir Elam, *Shakespeare's Universe of Discourse: Language Games in the Comedies* (Cambridge: Cambridge University Press, 1984).

27 Craig's *Übermarionette* remained a fantasy until Mnouchkine, which is not to say she realized his intentions. In all four, mimesis is uniquely

## Notes to Chapter 2

tested, transformed into methods that reveal what its conventions cannot countenance.

28 Jan Kott, *Shakespeare Our Contemporary* (New York: W. W. Norton, 1974), 45.

29 See his version of Hamlet in Heiner Müller, *Shakespeare Factory 2* (Berlin: Rotbuch Verlag, 1989), 7–123; also Carl Weber's translation and excellent introduction to Müller's *Hamletmachine*, in Heiner Müller, *Hamletmachine and Other Texts for the Stage* (New York: Performing Arts Journal Publications, 1984). See also Maik Hamburger, "Shakespeare on the Stage of the German Democratic Republic," esp. "1989–1990: Hamlet at World's End: Heiner Müller's Production in East Berlin," in Hortmann, *Shakespeare on the German Stage*, 428–34. For Brecht's further views on Hamlet, see Brecht, *Werke*, 22:611, 753, 840ff.

30 Kott, *Shakespeare Our Contemporary*, 66f. See also John Elsom, *Is Shakespeare Still Our Contemporary?* (London: Routledge, 1989), 14. Kott observes *Mother Courage* was one of the "five greatest theatrical experiences of my life" (*Shakespeare Our Contemporary*, 353). There are other signs of compatibilities, for example the very Brechtian sentence in the same text: "Weak bushes are bowed down to the earth, while tall trees fall uprooted" (Kott, *Shakespeare Our Contemporary*, 48).

31 "The point of departure of Polish productions of Hamlet in 1956 and 1959 was very similar, however they may have differed from Brecht's concepts" (Kott, *Shakespeare Our Contemporary*, 48). Also Kott, *Shakespeare Our Contemporary*, 196. Kott's respect for Brecht is evident. Concluding his *Theater of Essence* he observes of *Mother Courage*, played as a Jewish mother during the holocaust: "If there is a theater of essence, then this is it."

32 Kott, *Shakespeare Our Contemporary*, 210.

33 See Kott's exceptional autobiography, *Still Alive: An Autobiographical Essay* (New Haven, Conn.: Yale University Press, 1994). In one passage Kott observes dryly that he is probably the only Shakespeare critic to have his execution postponed due to ill-health, something that happens in *Measure for Measure*.

34 Elsom, *Is Shakespeare*, 15.

35 Elsom, *Is Shakespeare*, 15f.

36 Brecht, *Gesammelte Werke*, 15:188f., in a conversation entitled *Dialog über Schauspielkunst*, dated Feb. 17, 1929.

37 Brecht, *Gesammelte Werke*, 9:794.

38 Bertolt Brecht, *Schriften zum Theater* (Frankfurt: Suhrkamp, 1964), 6:124.

39 A recent argument for universality is offered by Patrick Colm Hogan, "Shakespeare, Eastern Theatre, and Literary Universality: Drama in the

Context of Cognitive Science," in Fujita and Pronko, *Shakespeare East and West*, 164–80.

40. For a fuller intercultural discussion of these issues, see Tatlow, *Brechts Ost Asien*.

41. Fenollosa, hired to teach economics in Japan, which was rushing toward Westernization, then equated with modernization, persuaded the Japanese that their traditional culture was worth preserving. Recognizing that Brecht worked with ideas from traditional Chinese philosophy persuaded some Chinese intellectuals to take it more seriously, as I have personally experienced.

42. If we consider the origins of Noh and how it was later socially institutionalized for the samurai class as their exclusive cultural property, we are reminded of Yeats's rhetoric and of his admiration for this very exclusivity. There is also perhaps something troubling in the parallel between his Neoplatonizing desire to escape the triviality of comedy, with its socially disruptive unsettling of identity, and the paradoxical Japanese location of identity in evanescence. The pragmatic psychotherapy of a popular shamanistic practice, banned perhaps for that reason, for which the pine tree depicted at the back of the stage was the conduit for the gods, was refunctioned as elaborate performance ritual, developing a remarkable aestheticisation of symbolic forms, which contained or exorcised the social unconscious as the samurai were enjoined to accept and identify with their allotted social role. Were Yeats's plays to realize his intentions, they might achieve an analogous exorcising or further repression of the social unconscious, hence an affirmation of socially required and therefore ideologically congenial identity. We can, of course, read these plays against the grain of such Neoplatonic assumptions, and then a play like *Purgatory* is most revealing, just as the Noh theater can offer exceptional insight into levels of the psyche.

43. Bertolt Brecht, *Briefe* (Frankfurt: Suhrkamp, 1981), 1:221f.

44. Brecht, *Gesammelte Werke*, 18:278.

45. Brecht, *Gesammelte Werke*, 12:463. Brecht possessed the translation by Alfred Forke, *Me Ti* (Berlin: Kommissionsverlag der Vereinigung Wissenschaftlicher Verleger, 1922).

46. Such art figures the interfiliation of processes, the psychosocial interdependencies that must be otherwise addressed in aesthetic and philosophical theory even if, as is the case with Zen Buddhism, the means of apprehension do not easily agree with Western presuppositions about the nature of meaningful discourse. The early, prebourgeois cultures developed a lively sense for the fragility of natural relations. We can find examples of this in many parts of the world. These early cultures were by no means simply resigned to a passive tolerance of what the natural

Notes to Chapter 2

world put upon them. Anthropological study has shown how they searched for ways, and hence sought to develop the necessary social relations, that would enable humankind to exist with nature and protect not only one's own tribe or community but others as well. Such methods of thinking enabled, for example, the Australian Aborigines to survive. They held the land on which they lived in trust for neighboring tribes. They could not dispose of it as they wished. There are parallels with the Buddhist and Daoist consciousness of a world of interdependencies, and the nature of its representation in their developed cultures, the superb forms through which such thought is figured and through which repressions are addressed, must give us pause.

47 I discuss some of the intricacies of Brecht's response to Chinese theater in *Brechts Ost Asien*, and present detailed arguments concerning both manuscripts and published comments in *The Mask of Evil*, esp. 153–346.

48 Homi Bhabha's *The Location of Culture* (London: Routledge, 1994) is a crucial modern critical text that engages with the hybridity of contemporary culture, although risking in its innovative theorizing what might be called, in a punning modification of Adorno's criticism of Heidegger, the "jargon of inauthenticity," rerunning a similar risk of eliding a political critique.

49 Relevant texts include Johannes Fabian, *Time and the Other: How Anthropology Makes its Object* (New York: Columbia University Press, 1983); George E. Marcus and Michael M. J. Fischer, *Anthropology as Cultural Critique* (Chicago: University of Chicago Press, 1986); Victor W. Turner and Edward M. Bruner, eds., *The Anthropology of Experience* (Urbana: University of Illinois Press, 1986); Thomas C. Heller et al., eds., *Reconstructing Individualism: Autonomy, Individuality, and the Self in Western Thought* (Stanford: Stanford University Press, 1986); Clifford Geertz, *Works and Lives: The Anthropologist as Author* (Stanford: Polity Press, 1988); James Clifford and George E. Marcus, eds., *Writing Culture: The Poetics and Politics of Ethnography* (Berkeley: University of California Press, 1988).

50 Clifford Geertz uses this phrase as a marker of authentic anthropological presence (*Works and Lives*, 97).

51 For different opinions, see David Bradby and David Williams, *Director's Theatre* (London: Macmillan, 1988), esp. 98ff. For a view of Mnouchkine and Orientalism, see Kennedy, "Shakespeare and the Global Spectator," 54ff.

52 See Richard Halpern, *Shakespeare among the Moderns* (Ithaca, N.Y.: Cornell University Press, 1997), esp. 24ff., 34ff.

53 See Simone Seym, *Das Théâtre du Soleil: Ariane Mnouchkines Ästhetik des Theaters* (Stuttgart: Metzler, 1992), 151. This critical text is informative on the development of Mnouchkine's theater in the context of French popu-

lar theater, but it follows the standard view of Brecht's theory and practice.

54 The Berliner Ensemble brought *Mother Courage* to the Paris theater festival in 1954 and created a sensation. The evidence of Brecht's success in combining a politically focused social critique and a powerful, aesthetically innovative theatrical performance made a decisive impact on French intellectual life. The most discerning critiques came from Roland Barthes. Sartre, who sought a decisionist, existentialist, action-centered, and language-focused theater, both praised and distanced himself from Brecht. He liked *Life of Galileo* and criticized *The Caucasian Chalk Circle*, whose characters appeared abstract, insectlike, not in control of themselves. He accuses Brecht of an inadequate Marxism, granting his characters insufficient subjectivity, overly objectifying them. I would say Brecht shows the clash between historical forces and the social unconscious without offering easy solutions. What Sartre disliked here, the epic theater's objectivizing, which actually uncovers the constructions of subjectivity, as well as the obvious response to East Asian dramaturgy and style, almost describes the direction Mnouchkine would later take.

55 She has pertinent observation on Copeau, Seami, and Brecht who, "tout original et idéologue qu'il peut être, dans ses moments les moins législateurs, redécouvre des choses tout à fait traditionnelles du théâtre orientale" (Josette Féral, *Rencontres avec Ariane Mnouchkine: Dresser un monument à l'éphémère* [Montréal: XYZ éditeur, 1995], 40).

56 "Je ne mettrais pas Artaud et Brecht sur le même plan. Artaud est plus proche du fondamentale que Brecht. Brecht a donné des lois d'un certain type de théâtre, dont certaines se retrouvent dans tous les types de théâtre. Je crois qu'Artaud a envisagé la fonction, la mission de l'acteur de façon plus profonde . . . moins politique et plus métaphysique" (Féral, *Rencontres*, 40).

57 "Il a dit qu'il ne faut pas tromper" (Féral, *Rencontres*, 47).

58 Putting aside the sociopolitical analysis in which I ground it, my interpretation is perhaps congruent with an observation from Peter von Becker who, when interviewing Mnouchkine, remarked that this scene suggested Hal, in killing Percy, was excising part of himself. Mnouchkine agreed, although she added that this was not a conscious interpretive intention. Perhaps we encounter here, on the level of dramaturgical practice, a variation of what Foucault called the "positive unconscious of knowledge." See Peter von Becker: "Die Theaterreise zu Shakespeare: Aufbruch in das ferne, fremde Land, das wir selbst sind. Ein Gespräch mit Ariane Mnouchkine nach Abschluß ihres Shakespeare-Zyklus," in *Theater Heute 1984, Jahrbuch der Zeitschrift*, 13–19.

59 Kennedy, *Foreign Shakespeare*, 296f.

Notes to Chapter 2

60 I have discussed these questions concerning the immediate or mediate social and political function of art and aesthetic experience in relation to readings of Picasso and Brecht in my book, *Repression and Figuration: From Totem to Utopia*, Cultural Studies Series no. 1, Department of Comparative Literature (Hong Kong: University of Hong Kong, 1990), esp. 11–29.

61 For a Japanese critical response from the author of this version, see Yasunari Takahashi, "Kyogenizing Shakespeare / Shakespeareanizing Kyogen: Some Notes on *The Braggart Samurai*," in Sasayama et al., eds. *Shakespeare and the Japanese Stage*, 214–25 (the English text of this version is now available on 226–40). Takahashi's account concludes with what is for me its most interesting observation: the actors "told me that in no single Kyogen play had they ever been able to make such a full use of their traditional skills." This corroborates the response of the Chinese performers in the kunju version of *Macbeth*, creatively challenged when developing their own form, and it underscores how a passage through the foreign culture can lead to a rediscovery of neglected possibilities in one's own. This is, however, a very different matter from "the imitation and borrowing" from outside in order to "affirm and stabilize" the "target" culture; see the discussion of Pavis's model at the beginning of this chapter.

62 Tadashi Suzuki, *The Way of Acting: The Theatre Writings of Tadashi Suzuki*, trans. J. Thomas Rimer (New York: Theatre Communications Group Inc., 1985), 123.

63 Eugenio Barba, "Theatre Anthropology," *The Drama Review* 26, no. 2 (1982): 6.

64 Bertolt Brecht, *Me-ti: Buch der Wendungen*, in *Gesammelte Werke*, 12:493.

65 With respect to Yeats and Japan, I refer to Hiro Ishibashi, *Yeats and the Noh: Types of Japanese Beauty and Their Reflection in Yeats's Plays* (Dublin: Dolmen Press, 1965), and to my discussion of Pound, Yeats, and Japanese poetry and theater in *The Mask of Evil*. See also K. P. S. Jochum, *W. B. Yeats: A Classified Bibliography of Criticism* (Urbana: University of Illinois, 1978), 380–82.

66 Barba, "Theatre Anthropology," 18.

67 Antonin Artaud, *The Theatre and its Double* (London: John Calder, 1977).

68 In Book I, chapter 31 of *The City of God*, Augustine describes theater as a plague of the mind, worse than the plague of the body for which affliction it was supposedly offered as a distraction.

69 A recent example of such a production, a working through the body of Brecht's *The Good Person of Szechwan* by students of the Hochschule für Schauspielkunst Ernst Busch in Berlin, is described in my article, "Analysis and Transference," in Silberman et al., *Brecht Yearbook*, 17:133.

70 Arguing from a Japanese perspective on Western theater, Yasunari Taka-

hashi corroborates my view of what is happening in these productions. He observes that in their performances of Shakespeare, Ninagawa and Suzuki "created their own styles, in their efforts to go beyond modern psychological realism, by drawing upon the traditions of noh and kabuki. Neither of them, however, is a 'traditionalist' if the term means preserving traditions. Rather than obeying the existing forms of traditional theatre, they sought to tap the primeval energy which must have produced these forms originally." Takahashi also remarks that they "keep creative tension vis-à-vis native tradition . . . in achieving a certain universality, or an archetypal dramatic experience." The question is, what is meant by terms like "primeval energy" or "universality" or "archetypal dramatic experience" in relation to what I term the "intercultural sign"? Takahashi leaves us with an expression of belief in the existence of such experiences, but without any explanation of their cause or of what they accomplish. See Yasunari Takahashi, "Hamlet and the Anxiety of Modern Japan," in Wells, ed., *Shakespeare Survey*, 109.

71 This problem is also touched on in an article by Zha Peide and Tian Jia, "Shakespeare in Traditional Chinese Operas," *Shakespeare Quarterly* 39, no. 2 (summer 1988): 205f.

72 One that has yet to be sufficiently realized, but such developments take time. See also "Speaking about China's Spoken Drama: A Roundtable with Chinese Directors and Playwrights," *The Drama Review* 33, no. 2 (1989): 87–103, esp. 97f.

73 Discussing the possibilities of drawing on the repertoire of traditional forms, Chen Rong observed: "The West is paying attention to us, but we are not paying attention to ourselves—and that is not a rational attitude." She can point to herself and to Lin Zhaohua and others who hoped to innovate. The subsequent kunju *Macbeth* is one consequence of these expectations. See "Speaking about China's Spoken Drama," 95ff.

74 Dennis Kennedy has collected some of the reviews in his *Foreign Shakespeare*, 32–43. Yasunari Takahashi also reports on this production in J. Elsom, *Is Shakespeare*, 86f. A photograph of Kurihara as Lady Macbeth is found in *Shakespeare and the Japanese Stage* (and also used on its dust cover).

75 Leonard C. Pronko, "Approaching Shakespeare through Kabuki," in Fujita and Pronko, *Shakespeare East and West*, 36.

76 Pronko, "Approaching," 39.

77 Detailed evidence of these encounters, of critical reaction, and of some consequences for Brecht's theater is contained in Tatlow, *The Mask of Evil*, 235–40, and further discussed in Tatlow, *Brechts Ost Asien*, 21f.

78 Likewise, it is interesting to observe how upsetting the films of Zhang Yimou and Li Ang have proven to many Chinese who accuse them of pan-

Notes to Chapter 3

dering to "Western" perspectives that are visible in representational methods that challenge the conventions of "Chinese" self-understanding.

79 Kennedy also communicates direct evidence of this production's effect upon the expectations brought to Noh performance whose aesthetic Ninagawa adapted and that corroborates my argument about acculturation. A critic wrote, "The spectators, rather than getting lost in the beauty and phantasy of the drama itself, are rather made to observe the play with a clear-headed alertness." That sounds like an appropriately Brechtian consequence. See Kennedy, "Shakespeare and the Global Spectator," 60.

80 Discussed further in Tatlow, *Repression and Figuration*, 129–36.

## 3 Desire, Laughter, and the Social Unconscious

1 In his essay on Racine, which set the wildcat of imagination among the pigeons of philology, Barthes remarked that, instead of Racine's characters, it was perhaps time to psychoanalyze the university.

2 Gary Waller, ed., *Shakespeare's Comedies* (London: Longman, 1991), 11.

3 A great deal has been written on psychoanalysis and representation. The discussion of film has been particularly productive. There is a good bibliography, with entries up to 1992, in *The Johns Hopkins Guide to Literary Theory and Criticism*, 595–605. Texts I have found useful include Elizabeth Wright, *Psychoanalytic Criticism: Theory in Practice* (London: Methuen, 1984); Elizabeth Wright, ed., *Feminism and Psychoanalysis: A Critical Dictionary* (Oxford: Blackwell, 1990); Sonu Shandasani and Michael Münchow, eds., *Speculation after Freud: Psychoanalysis, Philosophy and Culture* (London: Routledge, 1994); Linda Ruth Williams, *Critical Desire: Psychoanalysis and the Literary Subject* (London: Edward Arnold, 1995); Peter Brooks, *Psychoanalysis and Storytelling* (Oxford: Blackwell, 1994), esp. the chapter "The Idea of a Psychoanalytic Criticism," 20–45; Stephen Frosh, *The Politics of Psychoanalysis: An Introduction to Freudian and Post-Freudian Theory* (London: Macmillan, 1987). I cite later and separately the texts I find most interesting and relatively neglected.

4 Norman H. Holland et al., eds., *Shakespeare's Personality* (Berkeley: University of California Press, 1989), 1–15.

5 Holland draws on other essays in his volume, esp. "Shakespeare in the Rising Middle Class," by C. L. Barber and Richard P. Wheeler, 17–40.

6 Elizabeth Wright, "The Good Person of Szechwan: Discourse of a Masquerade," in *The Cambridge Companion to Brecht*, ed. Peter Thomson and Gladys Sacks (Cambridge: Cambridge University Press, 1994), 117–27.

7 See Joan Rivière, "Womanliness as Masquerade," in *Formations of Fantasy*,

ed. Victor Burgin, James Donald, and Cora Kaplan (London: Methuen, 1986), 35–44. This essay was first published in 1929.
8. Brecht, *Arbeitsjournal*, entry for June 20, 1940.
9. This play has received the worst and the best productions of Brecht that I have seen.
10. Like much of his dramatic work, this play was also written in collaboration with a woman, in this case both with Margarete Steffin and Ruth Berlau.
11. Quotation in Wright, *Feminism and Psychoanalysis*, 165.
12. Pierre Macherey, *A Theory of Literary Production* (London: Routledge, 1978). Sherlock Holmes's forensic intelligence creates the illusion of control over what threatens English culture, displacements of late Victorian alarm over the working class and the exotic infections of imperialism. See in this context *The Speckled Band* whose plot turns on an impossibility. The deadly Indian swamp adder, used to kill the woman, could not respond to a recalling whistle from another room, since snakes cannot hear. This "mistake" reveals the unconscious of that story.
13. I quote from August Strindberg, *The Father* (London: Methuen, 1986).
14. Strindberg described his imagined relationship to his mother as incest of the soul.
15. On the mother's desire, see Juliet Mitchell, *Psychoanalysis and Feminism* (London: Allen Lane, 1974); Nancy Chodorow, *The Reproduction of Mothering: Psychoanalysis and the Sociology of Gender* (Berkeley: University of California Press, 1978); also Klaus Theweleit, *Male Fantasies* (Cambridge: Polity Press, 1987–1989).
16. I would read the relationship between Laura and the Captain not as caused by an endemic war of the sexes, although Laura so explains it, nor as illustrating a perennial death wish that the Captain appears to embody, but rather as a clash resulting from an incompatibility between personality structure and social stereotyping. Laura has "male" strength; the Captain displays a "female" hysterical personality. Both are equally unable to fulfill the requirements of social character. The writing does not ask us to take sides. It shows us a catastrophe caused by cultural expectations. They are not anthropologically constant, no matter what the author may have thought.
17. In chapter 4, I allude to Thomas MacCary's psychoanalytic readings based on a theory of narcissism or search for self, equated with wholeness, therefore presupposing straight identification with the dramatic character. In various publications Carl Pietzcker offers a symptomology of the Brechtian texts in relation to neuroses attributed to the author. We then discover the underlying heart condition, which apparently provokes

the work and forms the basis for the analysis, is also experienced by the critic. See Antony Tatlow, *Gab es denn überhaupt einen Bertolt Brecht? Anthropologie eines Irrtums* (Berlin: Literaturforum im Brecht-Haus, 1995).

18. See Norman H. Holland, "Hermia's Dream," in Waller, *Shakespeare's Comedies*, 75–92, here 78, 82.

19. Another example of such a procedure would be a study that explains Brecht, with a weak father and a lost mother, as a homoerotic mother searcher, placing him in the company of Proust, Rilke, Thomas Mann, Hemingway, and Karl May. See Hans A. Hartmann, "Von der Freundlichkeit der Weiten oder Auf der Suche nach der verlorenen Mutter. Der junge Brecht," in *Bertolt Brecht—Aspekte seines Werkes, Spuren seiner Wirkung*, ed. Helmut Koopman and Theo Stammen (München: Ernst Vögel Verlag, 1983), 31–83, esp. 76.

20. Foucault, *Order of Things*, xi. Foucault had earlier criticized Freud's fixed interpretation of dreams, finding them more an indication of the strength of the imaginative life. Freud saw only the "semantic function" and not the "morphological and syntactic structures" (from Foucault's introduction to a French edition of Ludwig Binswanger, *Le rêve et l'existence* [Bruges: Desclée de Brouwer, 1954], 19). In other words, Freud gave a one-dimensional interpretation of the dream material. In the earlier studies Foucault remarks on the direct social consequences of such views: "Psychoanalysis psychologizes the real in order to derealize it: it forces the subject to regard his conflict as the disordered law of his own heart, in order to avoid seeing there the contradictions of the order of the world" (Michel Foucault, *Maladie mentale et personnalité* [Paris: Presses universitaires de France, 1954], 109). But Foucault moves from a contemporary, direct-cause type of sociological explanation for mental illness to an historical account of the conception of madness, the crucial step for his later systematic work. Foucault saw that madness is defined by a *discourse*, not by empirical observation of a medical or psychiatric condition.

21. In *Order of Things*, Foucault rejects a "psychoanalytic anthropology" (379) because, as always within his terminology, that would mean establishing universal and uniformly valid rules and a common human nature. Ethnology is sometimes understood as an anthropology of the contemporary. Here I use the terms interchangeably.

22. Giacomo Oreglia, *The Commedia dell' arte* (London: Methuen, 1968), 43–55.

23. See the article by Peter Gay, "The Father's Revenge," in the interesting collection edited by Jonathan Miller, *The Don Giovanni Book: Myths of Seduction and Betrayal* (London: Faber and Faber, 1990), 70. For a reading of Don Giovanni's libertinism as "radical ethical stance" in relation to

Kant's "radical evil" and in the wider context of his Lacanian position, see Slavoj Zizek, "A Hair of the Dog that Bit You," in *The Zizek Reader*, ed. Elizabeth Wright and Edmond Wright (Oxford: Blackwell, 1999), 272ff.

24 Peter Conrad, "The Libertine's Progress," in *The Don Giovanni Book*, 85.

25 Sigmund Freud, *Jokes and their Relation to the Unconscious* (Harmondsworth, Eng.: Penguin Freud Library, 1991), 6:196.

26 Freud, *Jokes*, 161.

27 "What is the definition of a sadist"—"A sadist is someone who is kind to a masochist." Most readings of this joke dwell on its surface, as if the sadist emerged the victor. But sadist and masochist live within a double bind and consequently destroy the logic to each other's position, since depriving a masochist of pleasurable pain is to be the cause of pain and hence of pleasure.

28 Bergson's essay *Le Rire*, first published in 1900, is available in Wylie Sypher, ed., *Comedy: "An Essay on Comedy" by George Meredith and "Laughter" by Henri Bergson* (Baltimore, Md.: Johns Hopkins University Press, 1980).

29 Erich Fromm, *The Erich Fromm Reader*, readings selected and edited by Rainer Funk (Atlantic Highlands, N.J.: Humanities Press, 1994), 9. Originally in Erich Fromm, *The Crisis of Psychoanalysis* (New York: Henry Holt, 1955).

30 The essay is contained in Erich Fromm, *Beyond the Chains of Illusion* (London: Abacus, 1962). Page references in the text refer to the 1962 edition.

31 Gilles Deleuze and Felix Guattari, *The Anti-Oedipus*, (New York: Viking, 1977), 109. In this context, see also Jameson, *The Political Unconscious*, esp. 22, 71f. Jameson quotes Northrop Frye for whom desire is the "social aspect" of emotion.

32 Arthur Koestler, *The Act of Creation* (London: Arkana, 1989).

33 During a course of lectures in 1809–1811: "Träumerische Sorglosigkeit," unfortunately translated as "visionary carelessness" in *The Readers' Encyclopaedia of Shakespeare*, Oscar J. Campbell, ed. (New York: Thomas Y. Crowell, 1966), 46f.

34 A. W. Schlegel, *Courses of Lectures on Dramatic Art and Literature*, trans. John Black (New York: AMS Press Inc., 1973), 391f. Here is Schlegel's own text: "Durch dies ganze Gemälde hat der Dichter zeigen wollen, daß es nichts bedarf, um die der Natur und dem menschlichen Geiste innewohnende Poesie hervorzurufen, als mit Abwerfung des angekünstelten Zwanges beide der angeborenen Freiheit zurückzugeben. In dem Ganze des Schauspiels selbst ist die träumerische Sorglosigkeit eines solchen Daseins ausgedrückt: sogar durch den Titel hat Shakespeare dies ange-

Notes to Chapter 3

deutet" (in *Vorlesungen über dramatische Kunst und Literatur* [Stuttgart: W. Kohlhammer Verlag, 1967], 2:157).

35 In an essay, "*As You Like It* and *Twelfth Night*: Shakespeare's 'sense of an ending,' " Anne Barton refers to the characters who are "transformed" by "the extraordinary," hence to "that 'new society' which makes its way back to the normal world at the end of the play." Furthermore, "Rosalind in her boy's disguise is the central consciousness of it all: a heroine both involved and dispassionate who seems largely responsible for that new social order which leaves Arden so hopefully at the end." This essay first appeared in 1972, but my point is that it has been republished. It represents an audible, if criticized, position within English Shakespeare studies. Anne Barton, *Essays, Mainly Shakespearean* (Cambridge: Cambridge University Press, 1994), 92.

36 Historicizing both concepts of identity and the text, McLuskie observes that comedy is pervaded by sexism that is not particularly funny (98). Quoting Raymond Williams that tragedy presupposes "a permanent, universal and essentially unchanging human nature," she also points out that the "aesthetic satisfactions of tragedy" depend upon a view of human nature that is "most often explicitly male" (98). I am interested in her related, apparently commonplace, ungrudging assumption that "a much more difficult pleasure to deny is the emotional, moral and aesthetic satisfaction afforded by tragedy" (98). Underneath her critique one can detect the belief that tragedy somehow is more universal than comedy, that it reaches deeper into the heart, so that in contemplating the end of Lear, "the most stony-hearted feminist could not withhold her pity even though it is called forth at the expense of her resistance to the patriarchal relations which it endorses" (102). Identification with the figure depends on the force of the realist style: "The psychological realism of the dramatic writing and the manipulation of the point of view, forges the bonds between Lear as a complex character and the sympathies of the audience" (100). This is reinforced when "the realism of Lear's struggle closes off any responses other than complete engagement with the characters' emotions" (101). This argument is itself caught up within a Western understanding of theater that Brecht, who so admired the East Asian theatrical aesthetic, did his best to counteract. Brecht, many years ago, argued for a new way of reading the Shakespearean text that both distances the characters, so that we cannot simply identify with them, and simultaneously intensifies their emotions—since they have been historicized, we can understand them better. There is no temptation to withhold pity in order to deny assent, or anguish at being unable to do so. You need do neither, because we can sympathize with the human tragedy without necessarily

endorsing the values or the social character that once seemed to make it inevitable. We feel pity for the character caught in such a world. This accompanies a crucial interpretive shift out of the mimetic. Behind any privileging of tragedy over comedy, making the former more humanly persuasive, reaching more deeply into the substantial, and hence more difficult to resist, lie two assumptions: Tragedy not only deals with more universal questions, but also is itself a more universal form than comedy. Yet neither supposition is true. The issues of tragedy are not more universal than those of comedy, because they are the same issues, at least within the realm of farce. Hence we can envisage a comic catharsis as a usually temporary transcendence or loss of the self through mitigating the limitations "reality" imposes upon identity; these universal issues are just differently treated. Furthermore, it is an illusion, particular to Western culture, that tragedy is more universally shared. Of the two, comedy is the more "universal" form since, to take just one example, the concept of "tragedy" is, strictly speaking, unknown in East Asian culture. See Kathleen McLuskie, "The Patriarchal Bard: Feminist Criticism and Shakespeare: *King Lear* and *Measure for Measure*," in *Political Shakespeare: New Essays in Cultural Materialism*, ed. Jonathan Dollimore and Alan Sinfield (Manchester: Manchester University Press, 1985), 88–108.

37 This is well described in Keir Elam, *Shakespeare's Universe of Discourse: Language Games in the Comedies* (Cambridge: Cambridge University Press, 1984). Elam offers abundant evidence for reading them in terms of incompatible and therefore clashing contemporary theories of language. This helps us align various characters with a conflicting politics of meaning "inside" the text. Yet his view of the function of theater itself as representational form appears to side with one of the two fundamentally opposed positions. Discussing *Love's Labor's Lost*, he states, "Navarre's belief in a world-conquering textuality is the hope that the dramatist, at his most optimistic, invests in his art" (166). This really does seem to align the writing or representing with certain views that have been represented or written, and the qualification in his sentence actually reinforces, even if it seems at first to relativize, this belief. This is nothing less than a version of Orphic naturalism or what he calls "semiotic animism" (165). Orphic naturalism proposed a mystical or magical theory of the sign, based on misreadings of Plato's *Cratylus*, much favored in Renaissance Platonism, whereby linguistic signs naturally nominate and cohere with their meanings. This implies in the social sphere the power to nominate and control or stabilize essences, the power to decide the truth of something because others must defer to your superior use of language. It is therefore not surprising when he argues that actors embody charac-

Notes to Chapter 3

ters as words embody meanings, and that both together "do indeed embody, for the duration of the spectacle, the properties of another sphere" (166). This untroubled supposition must be related to the fact that speech act theory, the basis for his semiotics of discourse, does not really give a voice to the unconscious.

38 Foucault, *Order of Things*, 34ff. Foucault, however, does not consider the conventionalist alternative within Renaissance language theory that resists the Orphic assumption that words resemble things. Conventionalism recognizes that such an assumption encourages the imposition of an inimical power structure and probably derives from the need to sustain it.

39 Orphic naturalism, so important in Shakespeare's texts because of the prevalence of Neoplatonic theory in his culture, imposes a meaning on nature and on society. Both naturalism and mimesis, which on one level appear opposed to each other, starting with and stressing either the representation or the represented, on another level both assume an untroubled correspondence between representation and represented or reality. The one accurately creates it, the other accurately reflects it.

40 The Confucian rectification of names, *zheng ming*, based social control on a moralized naturalist theory of language that had merely to be properly realized in behavior to ensure proper stability to the state: let the prince be a prince, the father a father, and so on. Ezra Pound seized on this theory as indicating the superior clarity of trickle-down Confucian moral thought.

41 Tasmin Spargo, "Gender and Literature: Feminist Criticism," in *Introducing Literary Studies*, ed. Richard Bradford (London: Prentice Hall/Harvester Wheatsheaf, 1996), 651.

42 The reason these Greek maenads were so mad was they had no vote, something that was available, of course, to male citizens of Athens. I allude here to the abundant evidence of female frustration in Greek culture and to the consequent surrogate practices, forms of bonding that, unsurprisingly, were often directed against male authority figures. For a view of the role of laughter in a specifically female festival that excluded male participation, see John J. Winkler, "The Laughter of the Oppressed: Demeter and the Gardens of Adonis," in *The Constraints of Desire: The Anthropology of Sex and Gender in Ancient Greece* (London: Routledge, 1990). See also David M. Halperin, John J. Winkler, and Fromma I. Zeitlin, eds., *Before Sexuality: The Construction of Erotic Experience in the Ancient Greek World* (Princeton: Princeton University Press, 1990). Unquestionably, these stories and their myths had an edgy resonance in Elizabethan England.

43 Catherine Belsey, "Peter Quince's Ballad: Shakespeare, Psychoanalysis,

History," in *Shakespearean Criticism: Yearbook 1994*, ed. Michael Magoulias (New York: Gale Research, 1994), 19.
44  Kott, *Shakespeare Our Contemporary*, 236.
45  Kenneth Muir found the behavior of the lovers "completely irrational," part of a sequence in which "Shakespeare presents Titania's infatuation with Bottom—Beauty's love for the Beast—as only an extreme example of love's irrationality" (Kenneth Muir, *Shakespeare's Comic Sequence* [Liverpool: Liverpool University Press, 1979], 44 and 46).
46  Edited by R. A. Foakes, 1984, 12–21.
47  Foakes in *The New Cambridge Shakespeare* edition, 32. Foakes, of course, embodies an earlier critical tradition. Although he indicates other possible readings, he sees the passions and transformations mitigated by "stylistic control" and "aesthetic distancing" that "ensures the promise of a genial outcome." We hear echoes of Spitzer's classical dampening.
48  Jan Kott, "Der versetzte Zettel," *Theater Heute* Heft 8 (August 1981): 32–41, and Heft 9 (September 1981): 46–49. These two stimulating articles were translated from the Polish manuscript by Peter Lachmann.
49  Pictured in a beautiful study by Lys de Bray, *Fantastic Garlands: An Anthology of Flowers and Plants from Shakespeare* (Poole, Dorset: Blandford Press, 1982), 107.
50  Bray, *Fantastic Garlands*, 107.
51  Thomas Laqueur, *Making Sex: Body and Gender from the Greeks to Freud* (Cambridge, Mass.: Harvard University Press, 1990).
52  Louis Montrose, "'In Mirrours More than One': Elizabethan Ideology and the Spenserian Text," in *Literature and Anthropology*, ed. Jonathan Hall and Ackbar Abbas (Hong Kong: Hong Kong University Press, 1986), 12–51. In another interesting essay, "'Shaping Fantasies': Figurations of Gender and Power in Elizabethan Culture," in *Representations* 1, no. 2 (spring 1983): 61–94, Montrose discusses the sexual nature of the images in the play but does not explore the metaphoric implications of "love-in-idleness" in relation to male anxieties and contemporary biophysiological beliefs.

## 4  Historicizing the Unconscious in Plautine and Shakespearean Farce

1  Maccius derives from *maccus*, meaning "clown," and suggests a theatrical nickname. Plautus, say the Latin authorities, implies "flat-footed" and metaphorical comedy. Little is known about him but there are lots of stories: that he came from a poor family, that he worked on a treadmill in a granary, was perhaps himself a slave, that he became a performer who

## Notes to Chapter 4

made and lost a lot of money. The status of the texts, the extent to which it is at all possible to arrive at a reliable original text, as well as the degree to which they draw on or simply translate Greek models and sources are all matters of some dispute among classical scholars. Apart from texts cited below, see the introductory discussion in Otto Zwierlein, *Zur Kritik und Exegese des Plautus I: Poenulus und Curculio*, Akademie der Wissenschaften und der Literatur, Franz Steiner (Mainz: Verlag, 1990); and Plautus, *Menaechmi*, ed. A. S. Gratwick (Cambridge: Cambridge University Press, 1993).

2 This first exploration of an expressive style suited to a developing individualist ideology will encourage the development of instrumental technologies that later produce that epitome of bourgeois music, the pianoforte, offering a hitherto unavailable combination of melodic expressivity and structured harmonic control, all placed in the hands of a single performer. The great nineteenth-century piano concertos, duels between piano and orchestra as equal antagonists, represent the culmination of this expressive ideology.

3 Margarete Bieber, *The History of the Greek and Roman Theatre* (Princeton: Princeton University Press, 1961), 181.

4 T. S. Dorsch in the introduction to *The Comedy of Errors*, New Cambridge Shakespeare (Cambridge: Cambridge University Press, 1988), 8, 14. The Bible helped Shakespeare "to refine the atmosphere he wanted to evoke in his Ephesus and he avoided the coarse and immoral aspects of Plautus's Epidamnus, and it encouraged him to impart more feeling to his comedy—an important addition to what he found in his sources" (Dorsch, Intro., 10). Anne Barton observes that, compared with Shakespeare, Plautus concentrates "almost entirely upon plot mistakings." The characters in the *Menaechmi* are "simple," that is to say, "mere types," whereas in Shakespeare we encounter a "serious confrontation with mortality, violence and time," as Egeon awaits execution while the play unfolds. See her introduction to the play in *The Riverside Shakespeare*, ed. G. Blakemore Evans (Boston: Houghton Mifflin Co., 1974), 79–82. It is wholly symptomatic that two recent school editions communicate in their short introductions absolutely no sense of the complexity of the figures in either play. They are simply twins who create scenes of mistaken identity. Academic critics often consider such pedagogic texts below their horizons, but they should nevertheless acknowledge their existence and counteract their influence. See Richard Andrew, ed., *The Comedy of Errors*, Cambridge School Shakespeare (Cambridge: Cambridge University Press, 1992); *The Comedy of Errors* (Ware, Hertfordshire: Wordsworth Editions, 1995).

5 Michael Mangan, *A Preface to Shakespeare's Comedies 1594–1603* (London: Longman, 1996), 149. The play also remains undiscussed in an interesting

Notes to Chapter 4

volume that specifically addresses the politics of reading Shakespeare, especially in the context of the United States: Ivo Kamps, ed., *Shakespeare Left and Right* (New York: Routledge, 1991).

6 Such distinctions echo and may well have been influenced by Bergson's essay *Le Rire*, in which he differentiates "comedy" from "drama." In drama we encounter characters capable of change and, as I observed in the previous chapter, come "face to face with reality itself," whereas comedy, standing here for "farce," only offers a second-level insight into what is essentially immobile. Henri Bergson, *Laughter*, in Sypher, *Comedy: "An Essay on Comedy" by George Meredith and "Laughter" by Henri Bergson*, 162.

7 See the conclusion in T. G. A. Nelson, *Comedy: An Introduction to Comedy in Literature, Drama, and Cinema* (Oxford: Oxford University Press, 1990).

8 The date is uncertain but 1592–1594 was assumed. Barton, Introduction to the Riverside edition of the play, 79.

9 Barton, Intro., 79.

10 Leah Scragg, *Shakespeare's Mouldy Tales: Recurrent Plot Motifs in Shakespearian Drama* (London: Longman, 1992), 74f.

11 But the effect has often been to compound the problems rather than clarifying the issues. Gary Taylor takes Barton and others to task for reducing Plautus, when discussing Shakespeare's assumed "singularity." However, he does not provide any analysis of the difference, or similarities, beyond metaphorically speaking, with Bevington, although now approvingly, of the "hardness" in Plautus, compared with what he terms the less satisfactory "wholesomeness" in Shakespeare. Such "wholesomeness" hardly does justice to the raciness or the complexity of Shakespeare's texts. What is needed is not a simple reversal of conventional criticism, but rather a historicization of the various positions. See Gary Taylor, *Reinventing Shakespeare: A Cultural History from the Restoration to the Present* (London: Hogarth Press, 1990), 395–98, 400–2.

12 In W. D. Howarth, ed., *Comic Drama: The European Heritage* (London: Methuen, 1978), 22–39, 37, 33f.

13 E. F. Watling in his introduction to the translation in Plautus, *The Pot of Gold and Other Plays* (Harmondsworth, Eng.: Penguin, 1965), 99.

14 Watling, Intro., 99.

15 Thomas van Laan, *Roleplaying in Shakespeare* (Toronto: University of Toronto Press, 1978), 21. Van Laan discusses forms of self-misrepresentation and how "identity consists of the various functions a character acquires through participating in a number of social relationships." He describes a name as "a label designating the point of intersection where a number of separate identities converge, although not without the possibility of colli-

Notes to Chapter 4

sion" (25). But there is no explanation of why this happens or of what actually collides.

16 Thomas MacCary, "'The Comedy of Errors': A Different Kind of Comedy," in Waller, *Shakespeare's Comedies*, 36. Centered on S. Antipholus, this reading rests on "identification between audience and protagonist . . . and must be based on common experience, actual or fantasized" (37). Hence, the "plight of the protagonist is felt almost physically, his yearning for his double accepted as natural and inevitable" (32).

17 Erich Segal, *Roman Laughter: The Comedy of Plautus* (Oxford: Oxford University Press, 1987), 40f.

18 Segal, *Roman Laughter*, 69.

19 Robert Miola, *Shakespeare and Classic Comedy: The Influence of Plautus and Terence* (Oxford: Clarendon Press, 1994), 18. He also holds that "Plautus plays the resolution of errors, the *cognito*, for laughs" (53), whereas Shakespeare moves "the farce of complication towards a comedy of identity and deliverance" (28).

20 Wolfgang Riehle, *Shakespeare, Plautus and the Humanist Tradition* (Cambridge: D. S. Brewer, 1990), 2f.

21 Erasmus is quoted in corroboration.

22 The labyrinth is the place of self-encounter. See Tatlow, *Repression and Figuration*, 5–50.

23 Riehle registers—an exception in this critical discourse—that the wife is an *uxor dotata*, but because *Menaechmi* "is a turbulent comedy, social criticism . . . is not brought into focus" (54). This begs an important question as to how such "social criticism" is figured.

24 What is still perhaps the best account of farce, also reading it in terms of Freud's analysis of laughter, does not take the argument through to my formulation. The unconscious is not formally on its agenda. Although the study moves through history from Plato to Chaplin, nothing is thereby historicized, an essential analytical step since the (social) unconscious is historically and culturally constructed. See Eric R. Bentley, *The Life of the Drama* (London: Methuen, 1965), esp. 219–56.

25 Barbara Freedman, *Staging the Gaze: Postmodernism, Psychoanalysis, and Shakespearean Comedy* (Ithaca: Cornell University Press, 1991), 103.

26 For an account of the sources of *The Comedy of Errors* and some views on the relationships between them, see Geoffrey Bullough, ed., *Narrative and Dramatic Sources of Shakespeare* (London: Routledge and Kegan Paul, 1961), 1:12–39; and Kenneth Muir, *The Sources of Shakespeare's Plays* (London: Methuen, 1977), 14–17. Perhaps the figurines and illustrations from Roman and Greek comedy that appear crude, when uninterpreted, reinforce this presupposition of later sophistication. Those enlarged phal-

luses did not, however, celebrate, but rather signified wastage of male sexual heat, which is what made them comical.

27  There is disagreement about the sequence of the early plays.
28  *Epistle to the Ephesians* 4:22–24.
29  This information comes from Frankie Rubinstein, *A Dictionary of Shakespeare's Sexual Puns and their Significance* 2d ed. (London: Macmillan, 1989). Corroboration for these readings and the pervasive importance of sexual metaphor can be found in the earlier and better-known book by Eric Partridge, *Shakespeare's Bawdy* (London: Routledge and Kegan Paul, 1968). I stress this bawdy because it undermines idealizations of Shakespeare's text.
30  I base these comments on Thomas Laqueur's fascinating recent study, *Making Sex: Body and Gender from the Greeks to Freud* (Cambridge, Mass.: Harvard University Press, 1990), 64ff.
31  Scragg, *Shakespeare's Mouldy Tales*, 34.
32  Dated 186 BCE. The Greek "original" is supposed written one hundred years before.
33  The Argument of the play, not in the Penguin text, is advanced in ten acrostic lines, whose initial letters, read vertically, spell "Menaechmei."
34  The Latin text does not contain the question. It simply says the day is dead down to the umbilical cord, or navel.
35  *Plautus*, vol. II (Cambridge, Mass.: Harvard University Press, 1951), 382.
36  Confarreatio refers to an ancient, solemn, ritual, and expensive form of marriage, conducted by the High Priest, in which a special corn cake (farreum) was used. The husband and wife shared the ritual food, an act that signified the "indissoluble relationship" (Dionysius Halicarnassensis, quoted in my source for all this information, Otto Kiefer, *Sexual Life in Ancient Rome* [London: Abbey Library, 1934], 15). Coemptio, a more mundane contract, originally a plebeian form of marriage, because the aristocratic confarreatio was not permitted to them, was concluded by a symbolic or mock purchase, and caveat emptor. Usus, meaning custom or practical experience, was the least formal bond, which included the important escape clause known as *trinoctium*, which I will explain.
37  Kiefer, *Sexual Life*, 17.
38  *Menaechmi*, 110.
39  *Furtum, scortum, prandium.*
40  *Hoc animo decet animatos esse animatores probos.*
41  Threshold or border, *Limen*.
42  *Periisti, si intrassis intra limen.*
43  Even though it is a lively translation, William Warner's Elizabethan text evades the disturbing directness of psychological transvestitism and excises all references to the smell of the female that so animates and unset-

Notes to Chapter 5

tles the unhappy husband in Plautus, in other words, the contemporary socioeconomic and cultural agenda requires different dispositions. Warner's text is reprinted in Bullough, *Narrative*, 12–39.
44 Scragg, *Shakespeare's Mouldy Tales*, 13.
45 Scragg makes these arguments in praise of Shakespeare over Plautus, but she shows no appreciation of the financial, emotional, and cultural costs.

## 5 *Coriolanus* and the Historical Text

1 There are several accounts of Brecht's engagement with Shakespeare, although none really get into the complex interrelationships between readings of history and of literary text, into the textual anthropology that allows us to glimpse the historical unconscious, attempted here. The following investigations are useful: Friedrich Dieckmann, "Die Tragödie des Coriolan. Shakespeare im Brecht-Theater," *Sinn und Form* (1965), 17:463–89; Robert Weimann, *Shakespeare and the Popular Tradition in the Theatre: Studies in the Social Dimension of Dramatic Form and Function* (Baltimore, Md.: Johns Hopkins University Press, 1979) (a translation of his *Shakespeare und die Tradition des Volkstheaters* [Berlin: Aufbau, 1967]); Rodney Symington, *Brecht and Shakespeare* (Bonn: Bouvier, 1970); Dirk Grathoff, "Dichtung versus Politik: Brechts 'Coriolan' aus Günter Grassens Sicht," in *Brecht Heute—Brecht Today, Jahrbuch der internationalen Brecht-Gesellschaft* Bd. 1 (1971): 168–87; Arrigo Subiotto, *Bertolt Brecht's Adaptations for the Berliner Ensemble* (London: Modern Humanities Research Association, 1975); John Rouse, "Shakespeare and Brecht: The Perils and Pleasures of Inheritance," *Comparative Drama* 17 (1983): 266–80; Margot Heinemann, "How Brecht Read Shakespeare," in Dollimore and Sinfield, *Political Shakespeare*, 202–30; Lawrence Gunther, "Brecht and Beyond: Shakespeare on the East German Stage," in Kennedy, *Foreign Shakespeare*, 109–39; Nancy C. Michael, "The Affinities of Adaptation: The Artistic Relationship between Brecht's Coriolan and Shakespeare's Coriolanus," in J. Fuegi et al., eds., *The Brecht Yearbook*, 13:145–54; Paula K. Kamenish, "Brecht's Coriolan: The Tragedy of Rome," *Communications from the International Brecht Society* 20, nos. 1–2 (1991): 53–69; Hortmann, *Shakespeare on the German Stage*.
2 Michael Bogdanov and Michael Pennington, *The English Shakespeare Company: The Story of The Wars of the Roses 1986–1989* (London: Nick Hern Books, 1990), 26.
3 John Barton's *The Wars of the Roses*, produced by Peter Hall with the Royal Shakespeare Company in 1963, turned the *Henry VI* plays and *Richard III* into three plays, entitled *Henry VI, Edward IV, Richard III*,

containing about half of the originals and around 1,400 lines written by Barton. Hall's production was influenced by Kott and the contemporary applicability of conventional assumptions about order, decorum, and the Elizabethan World Picture—"Revolution . . . leads to destructive anarchy." See Alan Sinfield, "Royal Shakespeare: theatre and the making of ideology," in Dollimore and Sinfield, *Political Shakespeare*, 160f.

4  Bogdanov and Pennington, *English Shakespeare*, 83. Let's assume he meant Marxist readings that are dubious.

5  Bogdanov and Pennington, *English Shakespeare*, 50. "Something about Shakespeare," Bogdanov remarked on another occasion, "always brings out the worst in people" (55).

6  It is remarkable how frequently these suppositions return in evaluating Brecht's use of Shakespeare. Fixated by some simplifications, scholars often miss Brecht's complicating, or replication on his own terms, of Shakespeare's complex text. Lawrence Gunther, for example, believes Wekwerth and Tenschert's later production of Brecht's *Coriolanus* improved on the simplicities of the earlier text: "In this production, the representatives of the lower orders were no longer Brecht's idealized replacement for the deposed Roman nobility but were shown as initially undecided, hesitant, and also responsible for making Coriolanus into the hero and despot he was to become" (Kennedy, *Foreign Shakespeare*, 112). Someone has forgotten that it was Brecht who objected to his assistant's earlier idealizations of the working class, insisting they were divided among themselves. I discuss this later.

Likewise John Rouse, in an otherwise interesting article, maintains, "I need hardly mention that Brecht saw the plebian-patrician division in Shakespeare's play in terms of a class war, or that the sympathies of his interpretation went to the plebians—a direct reversal of Shakespeare" ("Shakespeare," 275). I do not believe the issues are so clear-cut. Rouse also states, "Brecht had idealized his plebs into a class-conscious proletariat that is already politically mature at the very beginning of the play" (277). This is flatly contradicted by the evidence I will present. Inga-Stina Ewbank, who believes "any translator worth his/her salt takes the supremacy of the original text for granted," also simplifies the complexities by reducing Brecht's version to a "leading idea" that Coriolanus "must not become the tragedy of an 'unersätzlich' (sic)—'indispensable' or 'irreplaceable'—individual." This results in "playing Coriolanus down and the Roman people up." But this traduces Brecht's text in which the tragedy, both for the individual and the society that has produced him, consists precisely in the inescapable fact that he has become indispensable. He ought not to have been, but he was. That is the enduring

Notes to Chapter 5

problem. See Inga-Stina Ewbank, "Shakespeare Translation as Cultural Exchange," in *Shakespeare Survey*, 48:4, 8.

7 Kott, *Shakespeare Our Contemporary*. In his contribution to Elsom, *Is Shakespeare*, Kott himself makes plain how much he was affected by Brecht's positions, even if these are sometimes given an unjustifiably reductive reading.

8 See Brecht's *A Short Organum for the Theatre* Nr. 36, in John Willett, ed., *Brecht on Theatre* (New York: Hill and Wang, 1964), 190.

9 Brecht, *Gesammelte Werke*, 16:848.

10 Maik Hamburger gives a highly interesting account of continuing resistance in the German Democratic Republic to any attempt at developing Brecht's approach to Shakespearean texts by drawing on what Hamburger felicitously terms his "performative" language with its capacity to upset the settled and ideologically necessary view of a clarified and self-perfecting system. See Maik Hamburger, "'Are You a Party in this Business?' Consolidation and Subversion in East German Shakespeare Productions," in *Shakespeare Survey*, 48:171–84. He is, however, mistaken in thinking it was Wekwerth and Tenschert, the directors of *Coriolanus* in 1964, who advanced the idea that he was invaluable to Rome. This can be traced to Brecht's correction of their earlier and simpler condemnation of the "heroic" figure (see Hamburger, "Are You," 175, 178).

11 Brian Vickers, ed., *Shakespeare: The Critical Heritage* (London: Routledge and Kegan Paul, 1974), 1:387.

12 This passage was part of an address to the British Academy delivered in 1912 and printed in A. C. Bradley, *A Miscellany* (London: Macmillan, 1929). See Campbell, *Reader's Encyclopaedia of Shakespeare*, 149. For Granville-Barker, Coriolanus "cannot be ranked with the greatest of the tragedies. It lacks their transcendent vitality and metaphysical power" (149). Writing in 1950, Willard Farnham describes the pride of Coriolanus as both bad and good, but sees it in terms of a benefit or defect of character, not in relation to the social ground and political life of any time (149). In these judgments we encounter the familiar preoccupation with an outstanding individual from whose transcending perspective alone the play is lost or won and that guided the productions to which Brecht objected.

13 Reuben A. Brower, *Hero and Saint: Shakespeare and the Graeco-Roman Tradition* (Oxford: Clarendon, 1971), 371.

14 In his introduction to the play in *The Riverside Shakespeare*, 1393. Fifty years after Brecht's innovative readings English Shakespeare criticism still stressed his lamentations over the disappearing feudal values.

15 John Elsom, *Is Shakespeare*, 145–52.

16 Margot Heinemann communicates a hilarious interview in which Nigel

Lawson, then chancellor of the Exchequer, explains why "Shakespeare was a Tory, without any doubt" (see Dollimore and Sinfield, *Political Shakespeare*, 203).

17 He had admired it for a long time, calling *Coriolanus*, in a letter of June 8, 1917, "wonderful" (Brecht, *Briefe*, 1:15) and in 1929, "one of Shakespeare's finest works" (*Gesammelte Werke*, 15:181).

18 In Willett, *Brecht*, 252–65, and in the notes to the Vintage edition of the *Collected Plays* (New York: Vintage, 1973), 9:378–94.

19 In Willett's translation, "Building up a Part: Laughton's Galileo" (*Brecht*, 165ff.).

20 A characteristic misunderstanding of the function of the visual and of design can be found in the supposition that Brecht's theater was defined by "the distressed clothing" evident in the production of Mother Courage. See, Kennedy, *Foreign Shakespeare*, 14. Brecht stressed the importance of gracefulness and aesthetic pleasure in his plays, something he admired in the Chinese theater and sought to emulate. The Berliner Ensemble's production of *Coriolanus* also embodied these qualities. Some sense of the appearance of that production is communicated by Gunther in Kennedy, *Foreign Shakespeare*, 111–13.

21 In 1927, Brecht, *Gesammelte Werke*, 15:119, 149. In this passage from the *Kölner Rundfunkgespräch* (the Cologne Radio Discussion) in April 1928, which exists in the form of Brecht's subsequent account, he identifies the quality of the dramatic form in Shakespeare that displays the energies of the outstanding individual and that needs to be criticized and restrained by his developing epic theater form. What interests me here is the obvious admiration for the complexity in Shakespeare that Brecht appreciated better when working on *Coriolanus*. "As rich as life" is quoted by Heinemann, in Dollimore and Sinfield, *Political Shakespeare*, 219. Discussing Shakespeare in the light of his own drama, Brecht writes in 1927: "A good play needs many depths, unfathomable passages, a lot of gravel and an astonishing amount of absurdity [*Unvernunft*], and it must be alive before it can be anything else" (*Gesammelte Werke*, 15:121).

22 Brecht, *Gesammelte Werke*, 15:118f.

23 Willett, *Brecht*, 252; Vintage ed. 379.

24 Bertolt Brecht, *The Messingkauf Dialogues*, trans. John Willett (London: Methuen, 1965), 63. Peter Brook has a similar comment: "What he wrote is not interpretation: it is the thing itself." See Ralph Berry, *On Directing Shakespeare* (London: Croom Helm, 1977), 115.

25 See the account of this production of Christof Nel by Hubert Spiegel, "Der ferngesteuerte Held," *Frankfurter Allgemeine Zeitung*, Sept. 19, 1990.

26 See Karl Heinz Bohrer's excellent account, "Der Kult des theatralischen

Helden: Shakespeares Coriolan gegen die römische Republik: Ein konservativer Stil in Stratford," *Frankfurter Allgemeine Zeitung*, Dec. 8, 1977. This evaluation is corroborated in Ralph Berry, *Changing Styles in Shakespeare* (London: Allen and Unwin, 1981), 33.

27. See Michael Grant, *History of Rome* (London: Weidenfeld and Nicolson, 1978), 62ff.
28. See John Walter and Keith Wrightson, "Dearth and the Social Order in Early Modern England," in *Rebellion, Popular Protest and the Social Order in Early Modern England*, Paul Slack, ed. (Cambridge: Cambridge University Press, 1984), 108–28.
29. Walter and Wrightson, "Dearth," 111.
30. Public Record Office SP 14/34/4, qtd. in Slack, *Rebellion*, 116.
31. Quoted in Paul Slack, *The Impact of Plague in Tudor and Stuart England* (London: Routledge, 1985), 309.
32. Plutarch's dates are 50–125 CE; Livy's 59 BCE–17 CE.
33. There was a term for such removal of service and literal physical departure, *secessio*. See Grant, *History*, 63.
34. Livy, II.36. Plutarch has a more elaborate version.
35. Plutarch's *Lives of Coriolanus, Caesar, Brutus and Antonius*, trans. Thomas North, ed. R. H. Carr (Oxford: Clarendon, 1906), 15f.
36. In the second decade of the sixteenth century.
37. Niccolò Machiavelli, *The Discourses*, ed. Bernard Crick (Harmondsworth, Eng.: Penguin, 1974), 124f. In his account of Coriolanus, Plutarch (*Lives*, 20) narrates this incident in considerable detail, which Shakespeare elaborates (III.i), and comments on the "lawful process in law" that it implied. Shakespeare's dramatization necessarily withholds narrative evaluation, but the distribution of voices at this point perhaps implies a positional shift.
38. The contemporary theoretical arguments are quoted at some length in an informative study by Robin Headlam Wells, *Shakespeare, Politics and the State* (London: Macmillan, 1986). Aquinas cites the Romans' rebellion against Tarquin the Proud in *On Kingship: To the King of Cyprus* (1266), see Wells, *Shakespeare*, 91ff.
39. Wells, *Shakespeare*, 95ff.
40. Robert Parsons, "A Conference about the next Succession to the Crown of England," excerpted in Wells, *Shakespeare*.
41. Quoted by W. Gordon Zeeveld, "Coriolanus and Jacobean Politics," *Modern Language Review* 57, no. 3 (July 1962): 321–34, 323.
42. Adrian Poole, ed., *Coriolanus: Harvester New Critical Introductions to Shakespeare* (Hempstead, Eng.: Hemel, 1988), 75.
43. According to the *Oxford English Dictionary*, this is the first documented

Notes to Chapter 5

use of the word "lonely." Coriolanus is isolated by his singularity, and the analogy with the bourgeois claim for an individual economic identity and independence is unmistakable.

44 In this context, and with regard to the metaphorical strategy of this particular play, it is instructive to notice the metaphors editors use when discussing, for example, "the problems that plague Shakespeare's texts" (G. Blakemore Evans, "Shakespeare's Text," in *The Riverside Shakespeare*, 28). The textual editor seeks to establish the "authority" of a particular text, which is threatened by "corruption" and "disease," by seeking the "remedies" that will enable him to "recover" the "true text" from that which threatens it (27). This implies the editorial, and perhaps also the interpretive, goal of a univocal wholeness, purged of its debilitating or life-threatening imperfections.

45 Willett, *Brecht*, 255; Vintage ed., 9:382.

46 Willett, *Brecht*, 252f., 256f.; Vintage ed., 379f., 384f. In-text citations that follow indicate both versions.

47 The German says, "Können wir den Shakespeare ändern?"—"Ich denke, wir können Shakespeare ändern, wenn wir ihn ändern können" (Brecht, *Gesammelte Werke*, 16:879). This in effect means, "Are we permitted to change Shakespeare?"—"We may, if we are able to."

48 Willett, *Brecht*, 264; Vintage ed., 394: "Herausgelesen und hineingelesen"—"Read out of it and read into it." In a late conversation, Brecht observed of Shakespeare, "Of course you can't play him word for word. This is 1956. . . . But if I were putting him on today, it is only small changes I would have to make in the production, changes of emphasis" (see Ronald Hayman, "A Last Interview with Brecht," *London Magazine*, 3, no. 11 [Nov. 1956]: 47–52, 50).

49 I therefore think Rouse misses the point when he observes, "It might have been more accurate to provide a copy of Shakespeare's original, with Brecht's cuts indicated and translations of his additions and replacements in italics. Such an approach might at least have restrained Manheim from rendering into a brutish English that does not even bother to be iambic several passages where Brecht's text itself is simply a faithful German translation of the Shakespearean original" ("Shakespeare," 276f.). "Faithful" is here too credulous.

50 Brecht, *Collected Plays*, Vintage ed. 60. Brecht's text (*Gesammelte Werke*, 6:2399) says, "zugrunde richten," which means "ruin" or "destroy."

51 Here is Brecht's German:

Freunde, glaubt mir, erstaunlich liebevoll
Sorgt für euch der Senat. Was euer Hungern
In dieser Zeit der Teurung angeht, könnt ihr

## Notes to Chapter 5

      Grad so dem Himmel drohn mit euren Knüppeln
      Als dem Senat; denn solche Teurung wird
      Von Göttern über uns verhängt und nicht
      Von Menschen. Ach, euer Elend führt euch
      Dorthin, wo größeres Elend euch erwartet.
      So beißt der Säugling in die leere Brust
      Der unglücklichen Mutter. Ach, ihr scheltet
      Wie eine Feindin Rom, das für euch sorgt. (6.2399)

52. I refer here to my analysis of this interesting, and not often discussed, topic in the context of their response to Chinese poetry: "Stalking the Dragon: Pound, Waley and Brecht," in *Comparative Literature* 25, 3 (1973): 193–211.
53. "... wie sie jetzt ist, würde sie nur einen vergnügten Abend ruinieren" (*Gesammelte Werke*, 6.2409).
54. "Und / Strebend nach Selbstherrschaft" (*Gesammelte Werke*, 6.2473).
55. Brecht, however, uses the more literal translation, "Handwerk" (*Gesammelte Werke*, 6.2476). In rewriting Shakespeare's passage, Brecht draws on other terms of disparagement for the plebs used elsewhere in Shakespeare.
56. "... Jetzt könnt ihr eure vielgeliebten
    Verbrieften Rechte in paar Mauselöcher
    Der Altstadt stopfen" (*Gesammelte Werke*, 6.2476).
57. "Müßt' ich sie nochmals geben—doch meint'halb" (*Gesammelte Werke*, 6.2439).
58. Sic: Angeklagt
    Seid Ihr hier des Versuchs, die Volkstribunen
    Zu stürzen und tyrannische Gewalt
    Euch anzueignen, also des Verrats
    Am Volk.
    Cor: Verrats?
    Men: Faßt Euch!
    Com: Ihr habt versprochen—
    Cor: Der Hölle tiefster Schlund verschling das Volk!
    Sic: Hört ihr's?
    Cor: Verräter nennst du mich? Du Hund
    Von einem Tribun und du Tribun von Hunden!
    Du Dreck des Drecks! Lump, dessen Augen hungern
    Nach meinem Tod und dessen Schlund erstickt
    Von dicken Lügen! (*Gesammelte Werke*, 6.2457)
59. Brecht also remarked that the rebellion in East Germany at least brought the government into hitherto lacking contact with the people, even if it

was only the contact of the fist. Rodney Livingston justifiably explores the differences between "Brecht's' and Shakespeare's text but within perspectives closer to prevailing ideologies," in his study, *Brecht and Shakespeare* (Bonn: Bouvier, 1970). One justification for the changes in the 1964 stage version was to counteract a perceived "idealization" in Brecht's portrayal of the people (Manfred Wekwerth, *Notate. Über die Arbeit des Berliner Ensembles 1956–1966* [Frankfurt: Suhrkamp, 1967], 111). We have seen that Brecht in fact did not idealize them. His text, however, does idealize the tribunes (or the party), something that could not be critiqued in 1964. Such idealization stresses, once again, the weakness of the people who must rely on other seemingly indispensible figures.

60 Terry Eagleton, *William Shakespeare* (Oxford: Blackwell, 1986), 73.

## 6 *Macbeth* in Kunju Opera

1 His father sent him from Shanghai to Birmingham in the 1920s to learn economics, but he neglected those studies and became fascinated by the theater, working with Granville Barker. In China he was instrumental in introducing Western theater to the public. In 1956 he gave a celebrated six-hour lecture on Brecht and directed *Mother Courage* in Shanghai. Like so many artists, he suffered during the Cultural Revolution, whose cultural policies were determined by the Shanghai members of the Gang of Four. I have already referred to his remarkable production of Brecht's *Life of Galileo* in 1979. Huang Zuolin died in 1996. For further information, see his chapter, "Mei Lanfang, Stanislavsky, Brecht—A Study in Contrasts," in Wu Zuguang, Huang Zuolin, and Mei Shaowu, *Peking Opera and Mei Lanfang* (Beijing: New World Press, 1981), 14–29; also Antony Tatlow and Tak-Wai Wong, eds., *Brecht and East Asian Theatre* (Hong Kong: Hong Kong University Press, 1982).

2 For example, Li Jiayao has been quoted as stating, "We don't just adopt the plot of the original play but try to catch its spirit, that is, Shakespeare's humanistic ideal" (see Zha Peide, "Shakespeare in Traditional Chinese Operas," *Shakespeare Quarterly* 39, no. 2 [1988]: 205). Li here replicates the conventional East European views that for decades represented official cultural policies and exercised influence in China. In the early 1960s Robert Weimann objected that one should not so easily equate "Renaissance values and modern evaluations" (quoted by Gunther, in Kennedy, *Foreign Shakespeare*, 109) because he resisted the simplifications implied in the march of history argument that both swept all aesthetic expression into line as exemplifying this untroubled, Hegelian legitimization of the past, and justified present policy as its culmination. Wei-

Notes to Chapter 6

mann's research was inspired by Brecht's *The Caucasian Chalk Circle*, which proposed a more complicated view of the workings of history. Likewise, we should not pin the director of the kunju *Macbeth* or his production to this habit of official speech, but rather observe what they do with the play. Senda's Brechtian path to Shakespeare is analogous.

3 Campbell, *Reader's Encyclopedia of Shakespeare*. In *The Riverside Shakespeare*, the introductions to the tragedies are all written by Frank Kermode. Muir, *The Arden Shakespeare: Macbeth* (London: Arden, 1984). (The Arden is the most recent, updated edition.)

4 I mention as symptomatic critical texts relevant to my discussion of *Macbeth*: Germaine Greer, *Shakespeare* (Oxford: Oxford University Press, 1986); Terence Hawkes, *That Shakespeherian Rag: Essays on a Critical Process* (London: Methuen, 1986); Jonathan Dollimore, *Radical Tragedy Religion, Ideology and Power in the Drama of Shakespeare and his Contemporaries* (Brighton, Eng.: Harvester, 1984); Leonhard Tennenhouse, *Power on Display: The Politics of Shakespeare's Genres* (London: Methuen, 1986); Malcolm Evans, *Signifying Nothing: Truth's True Contents in Shakespeare's Text* (Brighton, Eng.: Harvester, 1986); Eagleton, *William Shakespeare*. The different focus in contemporary Shakespeare studies and the perspectival change in the whole language of criticism can be seen clearly by comparing Eagleton's idiosyncratically impressive book and his earlier *Shakespeare and Society: Critical Studies in Shakespearian Drama* (London: Chatto and Windus, 1967). The previously written book reveals the late- or post-Leavisite, existentialist critical framework of the day in phrases like "the gratuitousness of Lady Macbeth's commitment," or Macbeth's search for "authentic living."

5 R. S. Crane, *The Languages of Criticism and the Structures of Poetry*, the Alexander Lectures (Toronto: University of Toronto Press, 1953), 171. Although Crane does differentiate Chicago neo-Aristotelianism with the claim for a pluralistic and instrumental view of criticism—see his introduction to the volume he edited, *Critics and Criticism: Ancient and Modern* (Chicago: University of Chicago Press, 1952)—he also argues for the moral worth of the arguments within the text of the play, which deals with a "moral universal" (172), hence "identifies" with the characters instead of situating them, because he accepts the formal boundaries of Aristotelian mimetics.

6 Campbell, *Encyclopaedia*, 485.
7 In Kermode's introduction to the Riverside edition, 1307ff.
8 Muir, *Arden Macbeth*, xxvii.
9 Greer, *Shakespeare*, 67.
10 Perry Anderson, *Considerations on Western Marxism* (London: New Left Books, 1979), 59–67; see also Dollimore, *Radical Tragedy*, 154.

Notes to Chapter 6

11  Malcolm Evans argues this in his book.
12  In his 1923 lecture, "What happens after Nora leaves home?" Lu Xun: *Selected Works*, trans. Yang Lianxi and Gladys Yang (Beijing: Foreign Language Press, 1957), 2:85–92. Ba Jin's female characters in the novel *Family* (*Jia*) dream of imitating her. Lu Xun said Nora could not have then survived, alone and independent, in Chinese society because she would have nowhere to go.
13  Elisabeth Eide, *China's Ibsen: From Ibsen to Ibsenism*, Scandanavian Institute of Asian Studies Monograph Series, no. 55 (London: Curzon, 1987); Tam Kwok Kan, *Ibsen in China: Reception and Influence* (University Microfims International, 1984). A more recent article, whose title is self-explanatory, attributes what is understood as the continuing impossibility of emulating Nora in China to the traditional emphasis on harmony, concluding: "The Chinese Nora in the post–1949 drama, after winning her fight for her rights and equality, therefore stays with her Torvald happily ever after. Unlike the pre–1949 drama, China's post–1949 drama on women's issues demonstrates a deep moral and cultural conservatism" (see Constantine Tung, "Why Doesn't the Chinese Nora Leave Her Husband?: Women's Emancipation in Post–1949 Chinese Drama," *Modern Drama* 38, no. 3 [fall 1995]: 298–307).
14  Directed by Wang Xiaoying in the China Youth Arts Theatre, one of the few theaters in Beijing where, for example, Brecht's *Life of Galileo* was so successfully performed in 1979, now symptomatically demolished to make way for commercial redevelopment.
15  At the Capital Theatre and directed by Lin Zhaohua, who also directed an outstanding version of Brecht's *Schweyk in the Second World War* in a Beijing production, a film of which was shown at the Seventh International Symposium of the International Brecht Society in Hong Kong in 1986. Playing the young birdman was Liang Guanhua, whose Schweyk was an extraordinarily impressive performance. I watched him rehearsing *Schweyk* in 1985, working out how to do the scene with the dog on the way to Stalingrad in the snowstorm, a fascinating exercise in intellectual mime. That play caused cultural-political difficulties for Lin after 1989. A great rope net, hanging like a transparent tent over the whole set, signified an intransigent, all-enmeshing, suffocating bureaucracy. Liang, a fine character actor, had no real scope in the later play.
16  See Philip Brockbank's report mentioned below. For the most recent account of Shakespeare productions in China, see Zhang Ning, *L'Appropriation par la Chine du Théâtre occidental. Un autre sens de l'Occident* (Paris: L'Harmattan, 1998), esp. 135–65; also Li Ruru, "Chinese Traditional Theatre and Shakespeare," *Asian Theatre Journal* 5, no. 1 (1988): 38–48; Fan

Shen, "Shakespeare in China: *The Merchant of Venice*," *Asian Theatre Journal* 5, no. 1 (1988): 23–37.

17 I refer to the analytical model in three useful volumes by Erika Fischer-Lichte, *Semiotik des Theaters* (Tübingen: Günther Narr, 1983).

18 Questioning such artifice, Magritte constructed his art. Brecht explored what he first noticed in Chinese performance and was alien to prevalent Western conventions: a separation between person and personification, between the actor and the act, between the gesture and its meaning, between the audience and its self-understanding.

19 "The Spectacle of Macbeth," *Times Literary Supplement*, Nov. 13, 1987.

20 The "problem" she mentions is the falling away of dramatic tension after Lady Macbeth's death.

21 J. Philip Brockbank, "Shakespeare Renaissance in China," *Shakespeare Quarterly* 39, no. 2 (summer 1988): 196.

22 The witches correctly identify him as Thane of Glamis and of Cawdor. He anticipates the fulfillment of their third prediction.

23 Zhang Ning, *L'Appropriation*, has some illustrations.

24 I did not therefore see the English subtitles used in the performance before an English-speaking audience either as a guide or a hindrance to appreciation. I was not disturbed by sentences like: "Three cheers, let's drink to dynastic tradition."

25 Polanski's film was financed by Playboy Productions.

26 Brockbank, "Shakespeare," 195.

27 Brockbank, "Shakespeare," 195.

28 In the Souvenir Programme of the Shanghai Kunju Theatre Macbeth production.

29 Hsü Tao-Ching, *The Chinese Conception of the Theatre* (Seattle: University of Washington Press, 1985). Wei Shu-chu also refers to Hsü in her essay "English Renaissance Acting: With Reference to Peking Opera," in Luk Yun-Tong, ed., *Studies in Chinese-Western Comparative Drama* (Hong Kong: Chinese University Press, 1990), 115–34. She also points to the similar performance conditions but has nothing to say about how the methods of Chinese acting are structured or about the presuppositions that led to the particular structuration. The relationship between the conventions of Chinese theater and its obvious representation of the social unconscious, and of the personally repressed, for an audience that could not otherwise engage with it, which is especially a problem for women, is an underdiscussed, even undiscussed topic. It is, for example, not on the agenda of a fascinating and detailed recent study that persuasively argues for the connections between Chinese theater and cultural cosmology, exorcising rituals and mortuary rites, but explains it

Notes to Chapter 6

exclusively in terms of these relations. Here the spectator's perspective and the real social world of performance are discounted. See Jo Riley, *Chinese Theatre and the Actor in Performance* (Cambridge: Cambridge University Press, 1997).

30  Hsü Tao-Ching, *Chinese Conception of the Theatre*, 104.
31  "Der Fluß des Geschehens," see *Die fröhliche Wissenschaft*, Drittes Buch, Kapitel 112, in Friedrich Nietzsche, *Sämtliche Werke, Kritische Studienausgabe* (München: Deutscher Taschenbuch Verlag, 1988), 3:472f. See Brecht, *Poems 1913–1956*, 270f. The German original of this key poem, *Der Zweifler*, is best consulted in *Gesammelte Werke*, 9:587f., since the editors of the later *Werke: Große Berliner und Frankfurter Ausgabe*, modify the ending in a way that cannot be justified from the manuscript. I refer to these connections above, in chapter 1.
32  "Der Fluß der Dinge," an expression Brecht employs many times in *Me-ti, Buch der Wendungen* for the interconnected and ceaseless dialectic and that is part of a strain or strategy of metaphor that runs from the beginning through to the end of the whole work, connoting the irresistible and permanent processes of change.
33  I refer to the possibility of a "materialist" interpretation of the Buddhist concept of "emptiness" (*kong* or *sunyata*) in Chinese painting and in Brecht's response to it in two other studies, see Tatlow, *Repression and Figuration*, 118–23; *Brechts Ost Asien*, 37–44.
34  Yasunari Takahashi, in Elsom, *Is Shakespeare*, 87.
35  This is both a vast topic and a theoretical and cultural minefield where almost any abstraction provokes its opposite generalization that also seems to apply. I have discussed some cultural differences in the treatment of similar themes in Japanese and Chinese poetry in my study, *The Mask of Evil*, 31ff., 66ff.
36  Donald Keene, trans. *Anthology of Japanese Literature* (London: G. Allen & Unwin, 1956), 21.
37  Brecht's remarkable response to Chinese painting suggests perspectives that relate to these speculations about reticular models in East Asian culture; see Tatlow, *Repression and Figuration*, 112–36; also Tatlow, *Brechts Ost Asien*, passim.
38  All quotations from Huang Zuolin's essay, "Kunju Macbeth," *Cowrie: A Chinese Journal of Comparative Literature* 1, no. 5 (Nanning 1988): 34–44.

Epilogue

1  ". . . denn zwischen zwei absolut verschiedenen Sphären wie zwischen Subjekt und Objekt giebt es keine Causalität, keine Richtigkeit, keinen

Notes to Epilogue

Ausdruck, sondern höchstens ein ästhetisches Verhalten, ich meine eine andeutende Übertragung, eine nachstammelnde Übersetzung in eine ganz fremde Sprache" (Nietzsche, "Über Wahrheit und Lüge im außermoralischen Sinne," *Sämtliche Werke: Kritische Studienausgabe* [Munich: Deutscher Taschenbuch-Verlag, 1988], 1:884).

2 Kant had taken the original meaning of the Greek word "aesthetic," namely, "sense perception," and used it to show how what we see as the direct perception of our senses, the basis of knowledge for Lockean empiricism, is in fact structured for us, therefore as referring to the means whereby perception is always perspectival, even if it seems to apply equally to everybody, like the categories of time and space.

3 To quote from chapter 1 of this book: "The dramatic text only speaks in the context of its whole cultural performance, exploring the cultural unconscious as a symbolic exploration of the psychologically repressed, the culturally meaningful, and socially apposite, which cannot be read from the surface of a literary text. A poetics that reads from this surface cannot explore the formal unconscious and can be nothing but superficial."

4 Earle Ernst, *The Kabuki Theatre* (New York: Oxford University Press, 1956), 222.

5 The so-called stars in cinema became "stars" because they are fixed, always playing the same character. John Wayne could only play one role, but that is all he needed to do. The reverse is the position of the "character" actor, like Alec Guinness, who no longer knew if he had a personality of his own.

6 Beckett's plays move through series of repetitions. The first line of *Endgame* encapsulates this whole strategy: "Finished, it's finished, nearly finished, it must be nearly finished." The cultural echoes are still audible in this existential wasteland, even if their efficacy appears impossibly diminished, as the sparse phrases are stretched to the limits of communicability. But "it" is apparently not yet quite finished, even as each phrase explaining that it must be is longer than the previous one. There is also the teasing thought that these famous last words here echoed were not subsequently taken as pronouncing finality, but as promising hope and a resurrection of thought.

7 It is to be found in *Japanese Folk-Plays: The Ink-Smeared Lady and Other Kyogen*, trans. Shio Sakanishi (Tokyo: Tuttle, 1960), 90–94. In the pinyin transcription of Chinese the title is *Wen shan zei*.

8 See the exposition of these issues in Dallmayr, *Beyond Orientalism*, 188ff. Heidegger's preoccupation with death, discussed by Dallmayr in relation to Buddhist concepts of nothingness, has an equivalent in Brecht. Both figure a positive sense of negation as disruptive of any point of rest in

Notes to Epilogue

negation itself. Beckett's version seems markedly less benign in the remarks, also connectable with the Japanese play, prefacing *Film:* "*Esse est percipi*. All extraneous perception suppressed, animal, human, divine, self-perception maintains in being. Search of non-being in flight from extraneous perception breaking down in inescapability of self-perception." See Martin Esslin, *Meditations: Essays on Brecht, Beckett, and the Media* (London: Methuen, 1980), 77. For various readings of sunyata, see Tatlow, *Brechts Ost Asien*, 43.

9  Ernesto Laclau and Chantal Mouffe, *Hegemony and Socialist Strategy: Towards a Radical Democratic Politics* (London: Verso, 1985), 129. See also Wolfgang Fritz Haug, *Philosophieren mit Brecht und Gramsci* (Hamburg: Argument Verlag, 1996); Antony Tatlow, "¿Existen nuevos caminos hacia el viejo Brecht?" *La Gaceta de Cuba* (Union de Escritores y Artistas de Cuba, Feb. 1999), 9–13; "Gibt es neue Wege zum alten Brecht?" *Dreigroschenheft* 3 (2000): 13–25.

10 For a recent exposition of some of these topics in relation to Brecht, see Fredric Jameson, *Brecht and Method* (London: Verso, 1998).

11 We can observe such a process of abstraction in the interesting study I cited in the discussion of Plautine and Shakespearean farce by Barbara Freedman, *Staging the Gaze*.

12 Toshiro Date, "Shakespeare and the Traditional Theatre of Japan," in Fujita and Pronko, *Shakespeare East and West*, 80.

13 Used as a section heading in Ding Yangzhong: "On the Insatiable Appetite and Longevity of Theatre," in Fischer-Lichte et al., eds. *Dramatic Touch of Difference*, 169–77.

14 We have seen a variation of this process in the kunju theater. Kunju aesthetics are traditionally organized by its lyrical and musical structure, which softened or displaced an originally dramatic, and potentially disruptive, effect of the plot. Zhang Ning argues that the adaptation of *Macbeth* led to a rediscovery of neglected dramatic properties "au sein du kunju" (Zhang Ning, *L'appropriation*, 158).

15 Robert Hapgood, "A Playgoer's Journey: From Shakespeare to Japanese Classical Theatre and Back," in Sasayama et al., eds. *Shakespeare and the Japanese Stage*, 251, 254.

# WORKS CITED

Adorno, Theodor Wiesengrund. *Noten zur Literatur.* Frankfurt: Suhrkamp, 1958.
Anderson, Perry. *Considerations on Western Marxism.* London: New Left Books, 1979.
Artaud, Antonin. *The Theatre and its Double.* London: John Calder, 1977.
Augustine, Saint. *City of God against the Pagans.* London: Heinemann, 1972.
Barba, Eugenio. "Theatre Antropology." *The Drama Review* 26, no. 2 (1982): 5–32.
Barton, Anne. *Essays, Mainly Shakespearean.* Cambridge: Cambridge University Press, 1994.
Benjamin, Walter. *Illuminations.* London: Fontana, 1972.
Bentley, Eric R. *The Life of the Drama.* London: Methuen, 1965.
Berry, Ralph. *Changing Styles in Shakespeare.* London: Allen and Unwin, 1981.
———. *On Directing Shakespeare.* London: Croom Helm, 1977.
Bhabha, Homi. *The Location of Culture.* London: Routledge, 1994.
Bieber, Margarete. *The History of the Greek and Roman Theatre.* Princeton, N.J.: Princeton University Press, 1961.
Binswanger, Ludwig. *Le rêve et l'existence.* Bruges: Desclée de Brouwer, 1954.
Bogdanov, Michael, and Michael Pennington. *The English Shakespeare Company: The Story of The Wars of the Roses 1986–1989.* London: Nick Hern Books, 1990.
Bohrer, Karl Heinz. "Der Kult des theatralischen Helden: Shakespeare's Coriolan gegen die römische Republik: Ein konservativer Stil in Stratford." *Frankfurter Allgemeine Zeiting,* Dec. 8, 1977.
Bradby, David, and David Williams. *Director's Theatre.* London: Macmillan, 1988.
Bradford, Richard, ed. *Introducing Literary Studies.* London: Prentice Hall / Harvester Wheatsheaf, 1996.
Bradley, A. C. *A Miscellany.* London: Macmillan, 1929.
Bray, Lys de. *Fantastic Garlands: An Anthology of Flowers and Plants from Shakespeare.* Poole, Dorset, Eng.: Blandford Press, 1982.

*Brecht in Asia and Africa. The Brecht Yearbook*, vol. 14. Hong Kong: International Brecht Society, 1989.

Brecht, Bertolt: *Arbeitsjournal*. Frankfurt: Suhrkamp, 1973.

———. *Briefe*. Frankfurt: Suhrkamp, 1981.

———. *Collected Plays*. New York: Vintage, 1973.

———. *Collected Plays*. Vol. 1. London: Methuen, 1970.

———. *Diaries 1920–1922*. London: Methuen, 1979.

———. *Gesammelte Werke*. Frankfurt: Suhrkamp, 1967.

———. *Journals 1934–1955*. London: Methuen, 1993.

———. *Poems 1913–1956*. London: Methuen, 1976.

———. *Poems and Songs from the Plays*. London: Methuen, 1990.

———. *Schriften zum Theater*. Frankfurt: Suhrkamp, 1964.

———. *Short Stories 1921–1946*. London: Methuen, 1983.

———. *The Messingkauf Dialogues*. Trans. John Willett. London: Methuen, 1965.

———. *Werke. Große Berliner Ausgabe*. Berlin: Aufbau and Suhrkamp, 1988–.

*Brecht Performance. The Brecht Yearbook*, vol. 13. Detroit: Wayne State University Press, 1987.

Brockbank, Philip J. "Shakespeare Renaissance in China." *Shakespeare Quarterly* 39, no. 2 (summer 1988): 195–204.

Brooks, Peter. *Psychoanalysis and Storytelling*. Oxford: Blackwell, 1994.

Brower, Reuben A. *Hero and Saint: Shakespeare and the Graeco-Roman Tradition*. Oxford: Clarendon, 1971.

Brown, John Russell. "Shakespeare, Theatre Production, and Cultural Politics." In *Shakespeare Survey*, ed. Stanley Wells, vol. 48 (Cambridge: Cambridge University Press, 1995): 13–21.

Bullough, Geoffrey, ed. *Narrative and Dramatic Sources of Shakespeare*. London: Routledge and Kegan Paul, 1961.

Burgin, Victor, James Donald, and Cora Kaplan, eds. *Formations of Fantasy*. London: Methuen, 1986.

Campbell, Oscar J., ed. *The Readers' Encyclopaedia of Shakespeare*. New York: Thomas Y. Crowell, 1966.

Carroll, William C. *The Metamorphoses of Shakespearean Comedy*. Princeton, N.J.: Princeton University Press, 1985.

Chodorow, Nancy. *The Reproduction of Mothering: Psychoanalysis and the Sociology of Gender*. Berkeley: University of California Press, 1978.

Clifford, James, and George E. Marcus, eds. *Writing Culture: The Poetics and Politics of Ethnography*. Berkeley: University of California Press, 1988.

Conrad, Peter. "The Libertine's Progress." In *The Don Giovanni Book: Myths of Seduction and Betrayal*, ed. Jonathan Miller. London: Faber and Faber, 1990.

# Works Cited

Crane, R. S. *Critics and Criticism: Ancient and Modern.* Chicago: University of Chicago Press, 1952.

——. *The Languages of Criticism and the Structures of Poetry.* The Alexander Lectures. Toronto: University of Toronto Press, 1953.

Dallmayr, Fred. *Beyond Orientalism: Essays on Cross-Cultural Encounter.* Albany: State University of New York Press, 1996.

Deleuze, Gilles, and Felix Guattari. *The Anti-Oedipus.* New York: Viking, 1977.

Derrida, Jacques. "Economimesis." *Diacritics* 11 (June 1981): 3–25.

——. *Of Grammatology.* Baltimore, Md.: Johns Hopkins University Press, 1998.

——. *Specters of Marx: The State of the Debt, The Work of Mourning, and the New International.* New York: Routledge, 1994.

Dieckmann, Friedrich. "Die Tragodie der *Coriolan.* Shakespeare in Brecht-Theater." In *Sinn und Form,* ed. Akademie der Kunste, vol. 17. Berlin: Rutten and Loening, 1965.

Dollimore, Jonathan. *Radical Tragedy: Religion, Ideology and Power in the Drama of Shakespeare and his Contemporaries.* Brighton, Eng.: Harvester, 1984.

Dollimore, Jonathan, and Alan Sinfield, eds. *Political Shakespeare: New Essays in Cultural Materialism.* Manchester, Eng.: Manchester University Press, 1985.

*driveb: The Brecht Yearbook,* vol. 23. Berlin: Theater der Zeit / International Brecht Society / Berliner Ensemble, 1997.

Eagleton, Terry. *Shakespeare and Society: Critical Studies in Shakespearian Drama.* London: Chatto and Windus, 1967.

——. *William Shakespeare.* Oxford: Blackwell, 1986.

Eide, Elisabeth. *China's Ibsen: From Ibsen to Ibsenism.* Scandanavian Institute of Asian Studies Monograph Series, no. 55. London: Curzon, 1987.

Elam, Keir. *The Semiotics of Theatre and Drama.* London: Methuen, 1980.

——. *Shakespeare's Universe of Discourse: Language-Games in the Comedies.* Cambridge: Cambridge University Press, 1984.

Elsom, John. *Is Shakespeare Still Our Contemporary?* London: Routledge, 1989.

Ernst, Earle. *The Kabuki Theatre.* New York: Oxford University Press, 1956.

Esslin, Martin. *Meditations: Essays on Brecht, Beckett, and the Media.* London: Methuen, 1980.

Evans, G. Blakemore, ed. *The Riverside Shakespeare.* Boston: Houghton Mifflin Co., 1974.

Evans, Malcom. *Signifying Nothing: Truth's True Contents in Shakespeare's Text.* Brighton, Eng.: Harvester, 1986.

Fabian, Johannes. *Time and the Other: How Anthropology Makes its Object*. New York: Columbia University Press, 1983.

Fan Shen. "Shakespeare in China: *The Merchant of Venice*." *Asian Theatre Journal* 5, no. 1 (1988): 23–37.

Féral, Josette: *Rencontres avec Ariane Mnouchkine. Dresser un monument à l'éphémère*. Montréal: XYZ éditeur, 1995.

Fischer-Lichte, Erika. *Semiotik des Theaters*. Tübingen: Günther Narr, 1983.

Fischer-Lichte, Erika, Josephine Riley, and Michael Gissenwehrer. *The Dramatic Touch of Difference: Theatre, Own and Foreign*. Tübingen: Gunther Narr Verlag, 1990.

Foakes, R. A., ed. *A Midsummer Night's Dream*. Cambridge: Cambridge University Press, 1984.

*Focus Margarete Steffin. The Brecht Yearbook*, vol. 19. Madison, Wis.: International Brecht Society, 1994.

Foucault, Michel. *Maladie mentale et personnalité*. Paris: Presses universitaires de France, 1954.

——. *The Order of Things, An Archaeology of the Human Sciences*. New York: Vintage Books, 1973.

Freedman, Barbara. *Staging the Gaze: Postmodernism, Psychoanalysis, and Shakespearean Comedy*. Ithaca, N.Y.: Cornell University Press, 1991.

Freud, Sigmund. *Jokes and their Relation to the Unconscious*. Penguin Freud Library. Vol. 6. Harmondsworth, Eng.: Penguin, 1991.

Fromm, Erich. *Beyond the Chains of Illusion*. London: Abacus, 1962.

——. *The Crisis of Psychoanalysis*. New York: Henry Holt, 1955.

——. *The Erich Fromm Reader*. Readings selected and edited by Rainer Funk. Atlantic Highlands, N.J.: Humanities Press, 1994.

Frosh, Stephen. *The Politics of Psychoanalysis: An Introduction to Freudian and Post-Freudian Theory*. London: Macmillan, 1987.

Frye, Northrop. *Anatomy of Criticism: Four Essays*. Princeton, N.J.: Princeton University Press, 1957.

Fujita, Minoru, and Leonard Pronko, eds. *Shakespeare East and West*. Japan Library. Surrey, Eng.: Richmond, 1996.

Gebauer, Gunther, and Christoph Wulf. *Mimesis: Kultur, Kunst, Gesellschaft*. Reinbek bei Hamburg: Rowohlt, 1992.

Geertz, Clifford. *The Interpretation of Cultures*. New York: Basic Books, 1973.

——. *Negara: The Theatre State in Nineteenth Century Bali*. Princeton, N.J.: Princeton University Press, 1980.

——. *Works and Lives: The Anthropologist as Author*. Stanford, Calif.: Polity Press, 1988.

Gellert, Inge, Gerd Koch, and Florian Vaßen, eds. *Massnehmen: Bertolt Brecht / Hanns Eislers Lehrstück Die Maßnahme*. Theater der Zeit, Recherchen 1, 1999.

Works Cited

Gerstle, Andrew, and Anthony Milner, eds. *Recovering the Orient, Artists, Scholars, Appropriations: Studies in Anthropology and History.* Chur, Switzerland: Harwood Academic Publishers, 1994.

Goodchild, Philip. *Deleuze and Guattari: An Introduction to the Politics of Desire.* London: Sage, 1996.

Grant, Michael. *History of Rome.* London: Weidenfeld and Nicolson, 1978.

Grathoff, Dirk. "Dichtung versus Politik: Brechts 'Coriolan' aus Günter Grassens Sicht." *Brecht Heute—Brecht Today, Jahrbuch der internationalen Brecht-Gesellschaft* Bd. 1 (1971): 168–87.

Greer, Germaine. *Shakespeare.* Past Masters series. Oxford: Oxford University Press, 1986.

Grimm, Reinhold. *Brecht und Nietzsche: Geständnisse eines Dichters.* Frankfurt: Suhrkamp, 1979.

Gudmunsen, Chris. *Wittgenstein and Buddhism.* London: Macmillan, 1977.

Hall, Jonathan, and Ackbar Abbas, eds. *Literature and Anthropology.* Hong Kong: Hong Kong University Press, 1986.

Halperin, David M., John J. Winkler, and Fromma I. Zeitlin, eds. *Before Sexuality: The Construction of Erotic Experience in the Ancient Greek World.* Princeton, N.J.: Princeton University Press, 1990.

Halpern, Richard. *Shakespeare among the Moderns.* Ithaca, N.Y.: Cornell University Press, 1997.

Harrison, Jane. *Prologmena to the Study of Greek Religion.* Cambridge: Cambridge University Press, 1922.

———. *Themis: A Study of the Social Origins of Greek Religion.* Cambridge: Cambridge University Press, 1927.

Haug, Wolfgang Fritz. *Philosophieren mit Brecht und Gramsci.* Hamburg: Argument Verlag, 1996.

Hayman, Ronald. "A Last Interview with Brecht." *London Magazine* 3, no. 11 (1956): 47–52.

Hawkes, Terence. *Meaning by Shakespeare.* London: Routledge, 1992.

———. *That Shakespeherian Rag: Essays on a Critical Process.* London: Methuen, 1986.

Hecht, Werner. *Brecht Chronik.* Frankfurt: Suhrkamp, 1997.

Heise, Wolfgang, ed. *Brecht 88: Anregungen zum Dialog über die Vernunft am Jahrtausendende.* Berlin: Henschelverlag, 1987.

Heller, T. C., ed. *Reconstructing Individualism: Autonomy, Individuality and the Self in Western Thought.* Stanford, Calif.: Stanford University Press, 1986.

Hillman, Richard. *Shakespearean Subversions: The Trickster and the Play-Text.* London: Routledge, 1992.

Holland, Norman H. et al., eds. *Shakespeare's Personality.* Berkeley: University of California Press, 1989.

Hortmann, Wilhelm. *Shakespeare on the German Stage: The Twentieth Century.* Cambridge: Cambridge University Press, 1998.

Howard, Jean E., and Marion E. O'Connor, eds. *Shakespeare Reproduced: The Text in History and Ideology.* London: Methuen, 1987.

Howarth, W. D., ed. *Comic Drama: The European Heritage.* London: Methuen, 1978.

Hsü Tao-Ching. *The Chinese Conception of Theatre.* Seattle: University of Washington, 1985.

Huang Zuolin. "Kunju Macbeth." *Cowrie: A Chinese Journal of Comparative Literature* 1, no. 5 (Nanning 1988): 34–44.

Ishibashi, Hiro. *Yeats and the Noh: Types of Japanese Beauty and Their Reflection in Yeats's Plays.* Dublin: Dolmen Press, 1965.

Jameson, Fredric. *Brecht and Method.* London: Verso, 1998.

———. *The Political Unconscious: Narrative as a Socially Symbolic Act.* Ithaca: Cornell University Press, 1981.

*Japanese Folk-Plays: The Ink-Smeared Lady and Other Kyogen.* Trans. Shio Sakanishi. Tokyo: Tuttle, 1960.

Jochum, K. P. S. *W. B. Yeats: A Classified Bibliography of Criticism.* Urbana: University of Illinois Press, 1978.

Kamenish, Paula K. "Brecht's Coriolan: The Tragedy of Rome." *Communications from the International Brecht Society* 20, nos. 1–2 (1991): 53–69.

Kamps, Ivo, ed. *Shakespeare Left and Right.* New York: Routledge, 1991.

Keene, Donald. *Anthology of Japanese Literature.* London: G. Allen and Unwin, 1956.

Kennedy, Dennis, ed. *Foreign Shakespeare: Contemporary Performance.* Cambridge: Cambridge University Press, 1993.

———. "Shakespeare and the Global Spectator." *Shakespeare-Jahrbuch* 131 (1995): 50–64.

Kiefer, Otto. *Sexual Life in Ancient Rome.* London: Abbey Library, 1934.

Koestler, Arthur. *The Act of Creation.* London: Arkana, 1989.

Koopman, Helmut, and Theo Stammen, eds. *Bertolt Brecht—Aspekte seines Werkes, Spuren seiner Wirkung.* München: Ernst Vögel Verlag, 1983.

Kott, Jan. "Der versetzte Zettel." *Theater Heute* Heft 8–9 (1981): 32–41; 46–49.

———. *Shakespeare Our Contemporary.* New York: W. W. Norton, 1974.

———. *Still Alive: An Autobiographical Essay.* New Haven, Conn.: Yale University Press, 1994.

———. *Theatre of Essences and Other Essays.* Evanston, Ill.: Northwestern University Press, 1984.

Laan, Thomas, van. *Roleplaying in Shakespeare.* Toronto: University of Toronto Press, 1978.

Works Cited

Laclau, Ernesto, and Chantal Mouffe. *Hegemony and Socialist Strategy: Towards a Radical Democratic Politics.* London: Verso, 1985.

Laqueur, Thomas. *Making Sex: Body and Gender from the Greeks to Freud.* Cambridge, Mass.: Harvard University Press, 1990.

Lévi-Strauss, Claude. *The Savage Mind.* London: Weidenfeld and Nicolson, 1966.

——. *Structural Anthropology.* London: Penguin, 1993.

——. *The View from Afar.* Oxford: Blackwell, 1985.

Lévi-Strauss, Claude, and Eribon Didier. *Conversations with Claude Lévi-Strauss.* Trans. Paula Wissing. Chicago: University of Chicago Press, 1991.

Li Ruru. "Chinese Traditional Theatre and Shakespeare." *Asian Theatre Journal* 5, no. 1 (1988): 38–48.

Lister, David. "Was Shakespeare a Tory?" *The Independent on Sunday*, Jan. 3, 1993.

Livingston, Rodney. *Brecht and Shakespeare.* Bonn: Bouvier, 1970.

Lu Xun. *Selected Works.* Trans. Yang Lianxi and Gladys Yang. Beijing: Foreign Language Press, 1957.

Luk, Yun-Tong, ed. *Studies in Chinese-Western Comparative Drama.* Hong Kong: Chinese University Press, 1990.

Macherey, Pierre. *A Theory of Literary Production.* London: Routledge, 1978.

Machiavelli, Niccolò. *The Discourses.* Ed. Bernard Crick. Harmondsworth, Eng.: Penguin, 1974.

Magonliao, Michael. *Shakespearean Criticism: Yearbook 1996.* vol. 28. New York: Gale, 1996.

Mangan, Michael. *A Preface to Shakespeare's Comedies 1594–1603.* London: Longman, 1996.

Marcus, George E., and Michael M. J. Fischer. *Anthropology as Cultural Critique.* Chicago: University of Chicago Press, 1986.

Marsden, Jean I., ed. *The Appropriation of Shakespeare: Post-Renaissance Reconstructions of the Works and the Myth.* Hemel Hempstead, Eng.: Harvester Wheatsheaf, 1991.

Me Ti (Mozi). *Me Ti.* Trans and ed. Alfred Forke. Berlin, Kommissionsverlag der Vereinigung wissenschaftlicher Verleger, 1922.

Miller, Jonathan. *The Don Giovanni Book: Myths of Seduction and Betrayal.* London: Faber and Faber, 1990.

Miner, Earl. *Comparative Poetics: An Intercultural Essay on Theories of Literature.* Princeton, N.J.: Princeton University Press, 1990.

Miola, Robert. *Shakespeare and Classic Comedy: The Influence of Plautus and Terence.* Oxford: Clarendon Press, 1994.

Miyoshi, Masao. "Against the Native Grain: Reading the Japanese Novel in

America." Paper delivered at the Occident and Orient conference in the Humanities Research Centre of the Australian National University. Aug. 1987.

Mitchell, Juliet. *Psychoanalysis and Feminism*. London: Allen Lane, 1974.

Muir, Kenneth, ed. *Macbeth*. London: Routledge, 1984.

——. *Shakespeare's Comic Sequence*. Liverpool: Liverpool University Press, 1979.

——. *The Sources of Shakespeare's Plays*. London: Methuen, 1977.

Müller, Heiner. *Hamletmachine and Other Texts for the Stage*. New York: Performing Arts Journal Publications, 1984.

——. *Shakespeare Factory 2*. Berlin: Rotbuch Verlag, 1989.

Nelson, T. G. A. *Comedy: An Introduction to Comedy in Literature, Drama, and Cinema*. Oxford: Oxford University Press, 1990.

Neuschäfer, Anne, and Frédéric Serror. *Le Théâtre du Soleil. Shakespeare: Richard II / Henry IV / Was Ihr wollt*. Köln: Prometh Verlag, 1984.

Nietzsche, Friedrich. *The Birth of Tragedy*. Trans. Francis Golffing. New York: Doubleday, 1956. (*Die Geburt der Tragödie*. de Gruyter / dtv, Kritische Studienausgabe vol. 1, München, 1988).

——. *Sämtliche Werke: Kritische Studienausgabe*. München: Deutscher Taschenbuch Verlag, 1988.

Oreglia, Giacomo. *The Commedia dell' arte*. London: Methuen, 1968.

*The Other Brecht I. The Brecht Yearbook*, vol. 17. Madison, Wis.: International Brecht Society, 1992.

Parker, Patricia, and Geoffrey Hartman, eds. *Shakespeare and the Question of Theory*. London: Methuen, 1985.

Parkes, Graham. *Nietzsche and Asian Thought*. Chicago: University of Chicago Press, 1991.

Partridge, Eric. *Shakespeare's Bawdy*. London: Routledge and Kegan Paul, 1968.

Pavis, Patrice. *The Intercultural Performance Reader*. London: Routledge, 1996.

——. *Theatre at the Crossroads of Culture*. London: Routledge, 1992.

Pelton, Robert D. *The Trickster in West Africa: A Study of Mythic Irony and Sacred Delight*. Berkeley: University of California Press, 1980.

Plautus. *Menaechmi*. Ed. A. S. Gratwick. Cambridge: Cambridge University Press, 1993.

——. *The Pot of Gold and Other Plays*. Harmondsworth, Eng.: Penguin, 1965.

Plautus, T. Maccius. *Plautus*. Vol. II. Cambridge, Mass.: Harvard University Press, 1951.

Plutarch. *Lives of Coriolanus, Caesar, Brutus, and Antonius*. Trans. Thomas North; ed. R. H. Carr. Oxford: Clarendon, 1906.

Works Cited

Poole, Adrian, ed. *Coriolanus*. Harvester New Critical Introductions to Shakespeare. Hemel Hempstead, Eng.: Harvester, 1988.

Rouse, John. "Shakespeare and Brecht: The Perils and Pleasures of Inheritance." *Comparative Drama* 17 (1983): 266–80.

Riehle, Wolfgang. *Shakespeare, Plautus and the Humanist Tradition*. Cambridge: D. S. Brewer, 1990.

Riley, Jo. *Chinese Theatre and the Actor in Performance*. Cambridge: Cambridge University Press, 1997.

Rubinstein, Frankie. *A Dictionary of Shakespeare's Sexual Puns and their Significance*. 2d ed. London: Macmillan, 1989.

Sasayama, Tadashi, J. R. Mulryne, and Margaret Shrewing, eds. *Shakespeare and the Japanese Stage*. Cambridge: Cambridge University Press, 1998.

Schlegel, August Wilhelm. *Courses of Lectures on Dramatic Art and Literature*. Trans. John Black. New York: AMS Press Inc., 1973.

———. *Vorlesungen über dramatische Kunst und Literatur*. Vol. 2. Stuttgart: W. Kohlhammer Verlag, 1967.

Schulze-Reimpel, Werner. *Rheinischer Merkur / Christ und Welt*. July 12, 1991.

Scragg, Leah. *Shakespeare's Mouldy Tales. Recurrent Plot Motifs in Shakespearian Drama*. London: Longman, 1992.

Segal, Erich. *Roman Laughter: The Comedy of Plautus*. Oxford: Oxford University Press, 1987.

Seym, Simone. *Das Théâtre du Soleil: Ariane Mnouchkines Ästhetik des Theaters*. Stuttgart: Metzler, 1992.

Shakespeare, William. *The Riverside Shakespeare*. Boston: Houghton Mifflin Co., 1974.

Shandasani, Sonu, and Michael Münchow, eds. *Speculation after Freud: Psychoanalysis, Philosophy and Culture*. London: Routledge, 1994.

Slack, Paul. *The Impact of Plague in Tudor and Stuart England*. London: Routledge, 1985.

———, ed. *Rebellion, Popular Protest and the Social Order in Early Modern England*. Cambridge: Cambridge University Press, 1984.

Spiegel, Hubert. "Der Ferngesteuerte Held." *Frankfurter Allgemeine Zeitung*, Sept. 19, 1990.

Strindberg, August. *The Father*. London: Methuen, 1986.

Subiotto, Arrigo. *Bertolt Brecht's Adaptations for the Berliner Ensemble*. London: Modern Humanities Research Association, 1975.

Suzuki, Tadashi. *The Way of Acting: The Theatre Writings of Tadashi Suzuki*. Trans. J. Thomas Rimer. New York: Theatre Communications Group Inc., 1985.

Symington, Rodney. *Brecht and Shakespeare*. Bonn: Bouvier, 1970.

Sypher, Wylie, ed. *Comedy: "An Essay on Comedy" by George Meredith and*

"Laughter" by Henri Bergson. Baltimore, Md.: Johns Hopkins University Press, 1980.

Tam, Kwok Kan. *Ibsen in China: Reception and Influence.* University Microfilm International, 1984.

Takahashi, Yasunari. "*Hamlet* and the Anxiety of Modern Japan." In *Shakespeare Survey,* ed. Stanley Wells. vol. 46. Cambridge: Cambridge University Press, 1995.

Tatlow, Antony. *Brechts Ost Asien.* Berlin: Parthas Verlag, 1998.

———. "¿Existen nuevos caminos hacia el viejo Brecht?" *La Gaceta de Cuba.* Union de Escritores y Artistas de Cuba. (February 1999).

———. *Gab es denn überhaupt einen Bertolt Brecht?: Anthropologie eines Irrtums.* Berlin: Literaturforum im Brecht-Haus, 1995.

———. *The Mask of Evil.* Berne: Peter Lang, 1977.

———. *Repression and Figuration: From Totem to Utopia.* Cultural Studies Series no. 1, Department of Comparative Literature. Hong Kong: University of Hong Kong, 1990.

———. "*Those Savages—That's Us*": *Textual Anthropology.* Inaugural Lecture. Supplement to *The Gazette.* Hong Kong: University of Hong Kong, 40 no. 1 (Feb. 15, 1993).

Tatlow, Antony, and Tak-Wai Wong, eds. *Brecht and East Asian Theatre.* Hong Kong: Hong Kong University Press, 1982.

Taylor, Gary. *Reinventing Shakespeare: A Cultural History from the Restoration to the Present.* London: Hogarth Press, 1990.

Tennenhouse, Leonard. *Power on Display: The Politics of Shakespeare's Genres.* London: Methuen, 1986.

Theweleit, Klaus. *Male Fantasies.* Cambridge: Polity Press, 1987–1989.

Thomson, Peter, and Gladys Sacks, eds. *The Cambridge Companion to Brecht.* Cambridge: Cambridge University Press, 1994.

Tung, Constantine. "Why Doesn't the Chinese Nora Leave her Husband?: Women's Emancipation in Post–1949 Chinese Drama." *Modern Drama* 38, no. 3 (fall 1995): 298–307.

Turner, Victor W., and Edward M. Bruner, eds. *The Anthropology of Experience.* Urbana: University of Illinois Press, 1986.

Valdés, Marió J., ed. *A Ricoeur Reader: Reflection and Imagination.* Hemel Hempstead, Eng.: Harvester Wheatsheaf, 1991.

Van Peer, Will, and Elrud Ibsch, eds. *The Force of Vision 3: Powers of Narration.* Proceedings of the 13th Congress of the International Comparative Literature Association. Tokyo, 1991.

Verma, Rajiva. *Myth, Ritual, and Shakespeare: A Study of Critical Theory and Practice.* New Delhi: Spantech Publishers, 1990.

Works Cited

Vickers, Brian. *Appropriating Shakespeare: Contemporary Critical Quarrels.* New Haven, Conn.: Yale University Press, 1993.

———, ed. *Shakespeare: The Critical Heritage.* London: Routledge and Kegan Paul, 1974.

Waller, Gary, ed. *Shakespeare's Comedies.* London: Longman, 1991.

Weimann, Robert. *Shakespeare and the Popular Tradition in the Theatre: Studies in the Social Dimension of Dramatic Form and Function.* Baltimore, Md.: Johns Hopkins University Press, 1979.

———. *Shakespeare und die Tradition des Volkstheaters.* Berlin: Aufbau, 1967.

Wekwerth, Manfred. *Notate: Über die Arbeit des Berliner Ensembles 1956–1966.* Frankfurt: Suhrkamp, 1967.

Wells, Robin Headlam. *Shakespeare, Politics and the State.* London: Macmillan, 1986.

Wells, Stanley, ed. *Shakespeare Survey: An Annual Survey of Shakespeare Studies and Production.* Vol. 48. Cambridge: Cambridge University Press, 1995.

Willett, John, ed. *Brecht on Theatre.* New York: Hill and Wang, 1964.

Williams, Linda Ruth. *Critical Desire: Psychoanalysis and the Literary Subject.* London: Edward Arnold, 1995.

Winkler, John J. *The Constraints of Desire: The Anthropology of Sex and Gender in Ancient Greece.* London: Routledge, 1990.

Wright, Elizabeth. *Psychoanalytic Criticism: Theory in Practice.* London: Methuen, 1984.

———, ed. *Feminism and Psychoanalysis: A Critical Dictionary.* Oxford: Blackwell, 1990.

Wu Zuguang, Huang Zuolin, and Mei Shaowu. *Peking Opera and Mei Lanfang.* Beijing: New World Press, 1981.

Zeeveld, W. Gordon. "Coriolanus and Jacobean Politics." *Modern Language Review* 57, no. 3 (July 1962): 321–34.

Zha, Piede, and Tian Jia. "Shakespeare in Traditional Chinese Operas." *Shakespeare Quarterly* 39, no. 2 (summer 1988): 204–16.

Zhang Ning. *L'Appropriation par la Chine du Théâtre occidental: Un autre sens de l'Occident.* Paris: L'Harmattan, 1998.

Zizek, Slavoj. *The Zizek Reader,* ed. Elizabeth Wright and Edmond Wright, Oxford: Blackwell, 1999.

Zwierlein, Otto. *Zur Kritik und Exegese des Plautus I: Poenulus und Curculio.* Akademie der Wissenschaften und der Literatur. Mainz: Franz Steiner Verlag, 1990.

# INDEX

Acculturation, 29, 47–48, 77, 249n. 79. *See also* Dialectics of acculturation
Acting, 30, 37–39, 42, 46, 49, 54–55, 57, 66–67, 71, 73, 75, 77, 208, 213; Western and East Asian compared, 70–74, 76–78, 198–99, 201. *See also* Body; Mimesis
Adorno, T. W., 41, 219, 245n. 48
Aesthetic, 83; Brecht's later, 50; in Chinese painting, 52; in Chinese theater, 198, 210; as cognitive act, 65, 214, 218–20; consciousness, 93; conventions, 65, 68, 90; East Asian and Western compared, 49, 53–54; formalist, 27, 155; historicized, 120–21; ideology, 117; Japanese, 29–30, 40; lack, 29, 78; license, 145; perception, 102, 155, 219, 228; of performance, 61, 65, 77; and philosophical realism, 39; pleasure, 27, 38, 41, 47, 64, 264n. 20; power, 12, 28; realist, 49, 52, 62–63, 161; and repressed, 76, 78; and social experience, 33–34, 64, 217, 219; unconscious, 7, 29, 231
Alienation, 14–15, 18, 22, 36, 61, 78, 84, 159, 179
Althusser, Louis, 193
Anderson, Michael, 125
Anderson, Perry, 193
Anthropology, 1, 3, 6, 32, 55, 60, 80, 87–89, 245n. 46. *See also* Textual anthropology

Aristophanes, 41–42, 116–17, 119–20; *Wealth*, 116
Aristotle, 36, 39, 46, 110; fear and pity, 46. *See also* Brecht, Bertolt
Artaud, Antonin, 46, 62–63, 69–70, 72–73, 78
Auden, W. H., 55
Augustine, Saint, 72; *The City of God*, 247n. 68
Author function, 81
Authoritarian personality, 187

Bachelard, Gaston, 87
Bacon, Francis, 193
Ba Jin, 195; *Family*, 195
Bakhtin, Michail, 23, 234n. 5
Balinese theater, 72–73
Barba, Eugenio, 69–71
Barber, C. L., 126
Barthes, Roland, 246n. 54, 249n. 1
Barton, Anne, 122–23, 253n. 35, 257n. 4, 258n. 11
Barton, John, 261n. 3
Bawdy, 124, 130–31, 135–38
Becker, Peter von, 63, 246n. 58
Beckett, Samuel, 4, 40–41, 90, 227, 273n. 8; *Endgame*, 41–42, 90, 97, 273n. 6; *Film*, 273n. 8; *Waiting for Godot*, 40
Beijing opera, 54. *See also* Peking opera
Belsey, Catherine, 108, 256n. 43
Benjamin, Walter, 3; *Theses on the Philosophy of History*, 14

Berghaus, Ruth, 159
Bergson, Henri, 96–98, 117, 122, 258n. 6
Berlau, Ruth, 250n. 10
Berliner Ensemble, 159, 235n. 10, 246n. 54
Berry, Ralph, 265n. 26
Bevington, David, 258n. 11
Bhabha, Homi, 245n. 48
Billington, Michael, 151–52
Binary oppositions, 75, 82
Body, 28, 66–73, 78, 105, 114, 130, 136, 173, 192–93, 222–23; politic, 163–64, 173, 205
Bogdanov, Michael, 151–52
Bohrer, Karl Heinz, 264n. 26
Bradby, David, 61
Bradley, A. C., 157, 194
Brecht, Bertolt: aesthetics of daily life, 51–52; "amending" Shakespeare, 178–79; anti-Aristotelianism, 38, 242n. 21; and Artaud, 46, 62–63, 69–73; and Buddhism, 20, 23, 215, 223; Chinese and Japanese Shakespeare mediated, 5, 29, 190, 215; and Chinese opera, 2, 28, 208, 231; and Chinese painting, 50–54, 215; Chinese poetry, response to, 267n. 52; and Chinese theater, 16, 56–57, 74; deconstructing Marxist ontology, 13; and Derrida, 13–15, 229; dialectical theater, 2, 233n. 4; and East Asia, 3–5, 8, 26, 28–30, 34, 38–39, 46–47, 49, 54–56, 61–62, 74–76, 208, 229–31; epic theater, 2, 14; and French theater, 62; and horror, 45–47; intercultural practices, 5, 34, 47, 53; interventionary thought, 14; and Japanese theater, 27–30; and Kott, 43–45, 235n. 8; and Laughton, 159–60; and Lévi-Strauss, 1–2, 16–21, 23; literarization of the theater, 14; and Mei Lanfang, 208; and Nietzsche, 2, 10–13, 19, 22, 215; rereading drama, 8–10, 16, 109, 152–56, 170, 192; and Shakespeare, 2, 8, 20–26, 35, 43–45, 61, 151–56, 158–61, 166, 174–88; simplified reading of, 10, 32–33, 47, 53, 57, 63, 75–76, 81–82, 153, 155; on spectating (Zuschaukunst), 62; and unconscious, 13–19, 22, 39, 47, 55–56, 73, 75–76, 82, 153, 160, 242n. 21, 261n. 1. Works by: Antigone, 46; Aufstieg und Fall der Stadt Mahagonny, 13; Baal, 15, 17, 19; Bargan Gives Up (Bargan läßt es sein), 15; Buckow Elegies, 19; The Caucasian Chalk Circle, 21–26, 30, 55, 246n. 54, 268n. 2; Coriolanus, 13, 151–53, 158–62, 175–88, 262n. 6; The Doubter, 13, 15, 19, 215; Drums in the Night, 15–16; The Good Person of Szechwan, 12, 30, 74–75, 80–82, 230; In the Jungle of Cities, 16, 18–19; Life of Galileo, 26, 77, 102, 159, 246n. 54, 270n. 14; The Lovers (Terzinen über die Liebe), 13; Man equals Man, 24, 26, 42, 75; Me-ti, Buch der Wendungen, 13, 52, 70; Mother Courage, 19, 46–47, 98, 240n. 5, 243n. 31, 246n. 54, 264n. 20, 268n. 1; Schweyk in the Second World War, 270n. 15; The Threepenny Opera, 46, 72; Work Journal, 82. See also Distancing; Flow of things
Bristol, Michael, 234n. 5
British materialist criticism, 192–93
Britten, Benjamin, 109
Brockbank, Philip, 204, 210–11, 270n. 16
Brook, Peter, 32, 45, 48, 70
Brown, J. R., 241n. 14
Buddha, the, 19
Buddhist dialectics, 223, 229
Buddhist philosophy, 3, 7, 16, 19–20, 23, 28, 74, 194, 215–16, 223, 229, 238n. 42, 245n. 46, 273n. 8; Chinese and Japanese compared, 215–17; and Marxism, 19. See also Koan; Kong (emptiness); Zen Buddhism

Index

Buddhist religion, 215–16
Bullough, Geoffrey, 259n. 26
Bunraku, 38
Burton, Robert, 193

Campbell, Oscar, 190
Cao Yu, 195; *Thunderstorm (Leiyu)*, 195–96
Carnival, 23, 221, 234n. 5
Carroll, Lewis, 40
Carroll, William, 23
Cato (the Elder), 141, 143
Cavell, Stanley, 9
Chaplin, Charlie, 259n. 24
Charles I, 177
Chen Rong, 248n. 73
Chinese opera, 2, 27–28, 54–56, 72, 189–90, 194, 213, 230, 233n. 1. See also Chinese theater; Peking opera
Chinese painting, 50–55; perspective in, 50–52; and Western aesthetic, 51–52, 215
Chinese theater, 16, 54, 159, 194–98, 221, 264n. 20, 271n. 29; signification in, 198–204. See also Spoken drama
Cicero, 127
Coleridge, S. T., 122
Comedy, 4, 39, 97, 101–7, 116–17, 119, 121–23, 126–29, 134–35, 139–40, 145, 181, 197, 203, 219–21, 223, 228, 244n. 42, 253n. 36
Commedia dell'arte, 66, 221
Conan Doyle, Arthur, 83; *The Speckled Band*, 250n. 12
Confucianism, 7, 23, 215, 217, 219; *The Great Learning*, 70
Conrad, Peter, 95
Conventionalism, 3, 115, 215, 255n. 38
Copeau, Jacques, 246n. 55
Coppola, Francis, 76
Countertransference. *See* Transference
Crane, R. S., 190
Craig, Edward Gordon, 242n. 27

Cultural revolution, 57, 197, 210, 268n. 1
Cultural unconscious, 29, 33–34, 42, 78, 83, 88–89, 103, 140, 194, 227, 241n. 12, 259n. 24

Dallmayr, Fred, 235n. 15, 273n. 8
Dante, 20
*Daodejing*, 18–19, 24, 98
Daoism, 52, 70, 215, 217, 230, 245n. 46. See also *Daodejing*; Zhuangzi (Chuang Tse)
Dearth, 162–63
Deconstruction, 13–14, 36, 128, 229–30
Defamiliarization, 3, 5–6, 34, 49, 64, 214. See also Alienation; Distancing
Degas, Edgar, 49
Delacroix, Eugène, 12
Deleuze, Gilles, 2, 101
Derrida, Jacques, 3, 19, 108, 215, 229, 234n. 3; and Brecht compared, 13–15; *Of Grammatology*, 19; *Specters of Marx*, 14–15; views on Marxism, 14–15
de Sade, Marquis, 90–91; *Justine*, 91; *Philosophy in the Bedroom*, 91; *Yet another effort, Frenchmen, if you would become Republicans*, 91
Desire, 2, 7, 15, 22, 24–25, 29, 40, 53, 78, 80, 84–85, 91–94, 99, 101, 107–8, 114, 121, 133, 137, 149, 188, 201, 220
Dialectic, 12–13, 22, 43, 50, 60, 97, 152, 230. See also Buddhist dialectics; Dialectics of acculturation
Dialectics of acculturation, 4, 29, 47–50, 55, 57, 60–62, 74, 77–79, 199, 231
Dian's bud (flower), 112–14
Ding Yangzhong, 274n. 13
Distancing, 1, 22, 37, 41, 54–55, 92, 95, 152, 155, 166, 186, 198, 211, 213, 253n. 36
Dollimore, Jonathan, 193
*Don Quixote*, 90

Dorsch, T. S., 257n. 4
Double bind, 96–98, 101–2

Eagleton, Terry, 187, 269n. 4
East Asian theater, 24, 49, 53, 75; and Western theater compared, 3, 28, 30, 34, 46, 49, 54–57, 63–64, 68, 70–78, 190, 201, 210, 218, 220–23, 230–31, 240n. 2, 253n. 36. See also Intercultural poetics
Egopsychology, 37, 72–76, 160
Eight model revolutionary operas, 197
Eisler, Hanns, 11
Elam, Keir, 254n. 37
Eliot, T. S., 61, 209; *The Family Reunion*, 209
Elizabeth I, 114, 168, 177
Elizabethan world picture, 193, 262n. 3
Emotions, 12–13, 22, 31, 36, 44–46, 53–56, 62, 72–74, 87, 94, 100–101, 106, 133, 149–50, 155, 184, 189, 200–201, 204, 211–15, 253n. 36; in East Asian and Western theater, 54–56, 211
Emptiness, Buddhist concept of, 19, 194, 215, 272n. 23. See also Nothing (concept of)
Engel, Erich, 2
Erasmus, 259n. 21
Ernst, Earle, 219–20
Essentialism, 29, 82, 103, 123, 170, 191, 193, 229
Esslin, Martin, 274n. 8
Ethnology, 16, 87–89
Euripides, 10, 22
Ewbank, Inga-Stena, 262n. 6
Externalization, 3, 19, 46, 75, 206, 208, 214, 218, 230

Farce, 3, 101, 116–19, 121–22, 125, 127–29, 131, 139, 181, 219–22, 254n. 36, 259n. 24; as comedy of the unconscious, 127. See also Philosophical farce
Farnham, Willard, 263n. 12

Faust, 92–93
Fenollosa, Ernst, 49
Fetish, 140, 144–47, 149
Feudalism, 44, 57, 64, 104, 114, 142, 152, 158, 163, 168, 171–72, 204, 210–12, 214
First World, 27, 53
Fischer-Lichte, Erika, 31, 198
Flow of things, 3, 13, 19, 215
Fo, Dario, 101, 222; *Accidental Death of an Anarchist*, 222–23
Foucault, Michel, 2, 16, 28, 33, 35, 82, 87–91, 94, 100, 104, 234n. 3, 246n. 58; psychoanalytic anthropology, 89
Freedman, Barbara, 128, 230
Freud, Sigmund, 16, 80–81, 85, 93–99, 101–2, 109, 197, 251n. 20, 259n. 24
Fromm, Erich, 2, 16, 79, 98–101
Frye, Northrop, 22, 26, 126, 237n. 40
Fulbecke, William, 168, 173
*Fumi Yamadachi* (Literate Highwaymen), 224–29

Gay, Peter, 251n. 23
Geertz, Clifford, 28, 80, 219, 245n. 50
Gender roles, 82, 106, 108, 135, 148, 240n. 5
German Democratic Republic, 25, 45, 160–61, 263n. 10
Gestural aesthetic, 156. See also Gestural language
Gestural code, 69, 199. See also Proxemic code
Gestural language, 181–86, 212
Gesture, 21–22, 30, 46–47, 50, 54, 62–64, 66–67, 69, 72–73, 76–78, 199, 208, 214, 223. See also Gestural language; Gestus
Gestus, 19
Ghosts, 19; in Shakespeare and Japanese theater, 239n. 56
Globalization, 48, 53, 60
Goethe, Johann Wolfgang, 105, 153; *Ilmenau*, 105

Index

Grand Guignol, 203
Granville Barker, Harley, 263n. 12, 268n. 1
Grass, Günter, 9, 187; *The Plebeians Rehearse the Uprising*, 235n. 10
Greer, Germaine, 192
Grosz, Georg, 50
Grotowski, Jerzy, 70
Guattari, Félix, 2
Guinness, Alec, 273n. 5
Gunther, Lawrence, 262n. 6
Guo Shixing, 196; *Birdmen* (Niaoren), 196–98

*Hagoromo* (The Feather Cloak), 71
Haiyuza theater, 75
Hall, Peter, 109, 260n. 3
Halpern, Richard, 61
Hamburger, Maik, 263n. 10
Handel, G. F., 69
Hands, Terry, 162
Hapgood, Robert, 274n. 15
Harrison, Jane, 22
Hartmann, Hans A., 251n. 19
Hauptmann, Elizabeth, 27
Hawkes, Terence, 9
Hegel, G. F. W., 15, 70, 101, 223
Heidegger, Martin, 15, 229, 245n. 48
Heinemann, Margot, 263n. 16, 264n. 21
Hillman, Richard, 21, 23, 25
Hindu philosophy, 19, 23
Historical unconscious, 78, 94, 153
Historicism, 152
Historicity, 88–89
Historicizing, 7, 16, 20, 43–44, 61–62, 89, 96, 103, 115–16, 120–21, 125, 152, 180, 186, 229, 253n. 36; the unconscious, 16, 89, 116
Hitler, Adolf, 163
Hoffmann, E. T. A., 93; *Don Juan*, 93
Hogan, P. C., 243n. 39
Holinshed, Raphael, 215
Holland, Norman, 80, 85–86

Hong Kong International Brecht Festival, 75
Horror, 28, 45–46
Hsü Tao-Ching, 213–14
Huaju. *See* Spoken drama
Huang Zuolin, 190, 217–18
Humanism, 100, 117

Ibsen, Henrik, 83, 195, 198; *A Doll's House*, 195; *Ghosts*, 195
Identity, 4, 26, 30, 42, 60, 64, 81, 86–87, 94–95, 100, 122, 124, 126–29, 134, 137–39, 145–48, 153, 217, 222–23, 230; fear of loss of unity, 84, 86–87, 93, 128
Identity theory, 86
Ikebana, 69, 71
Intercultural angst, 6
Intercultural hermeneutics. *See* Intercultural reading
Intercultural performance, 6, 7, 31, 35, 68, 74, 78, 234n. 5, 241n. 14, 270n. 15
Intercultural poetics, 35–43
Intercultural reading, 5–6, 35, 53, 66, 68, 70, 77, 224
Intercultural sign, 2–7, 9, 31, 39, 41–42, 61, 74, 77–79, 151, 194, 230, 248n. 70
Intercultural theater, 3, 5, 31–33, 45, 47, 74, 87, 212

James I (James VI of Scotland), 164, 174, 191, 205, 215
Jameson, Fredric, 20, 241n. 14, 252n. 31, 274n. 10
Japanese theater, 26–30, 49, 56, 69, 76, 219, 221–22, 230. *See also Fumi Yamadachi* (Literate Highwaymen); Mansaku, Namura; Ninigawa, Yukio; Senda, Koreya; Suzuki, Tadashi
Jingju (Peking opera), 194, 199
Johnson, Paul, 162
Joke, 70, 95–98, 101–2, 106, 110, 125, 131, 134, 136–38, 148, 197, 209, 222–24, 229; Buddhist, 101, 224–27

291

Joruri, 38
Jung, Carl Gustav, 48, 87

Kabuki, 45, 61, 75, 208, 219, 248n. 70
Kant, Immanuel, 219
Karma, 216
Kennedy, Dennis, 30, 33, 35, 64, 77
Kermode, Frank, 158, 191, 214
Kiefer, Otto, 260n. 36
Kierkegaard, Søren, 93; *Either/Or*, 93
Kleist, Heinrich von, 40
Koan, 223
Koestler, Arthur, 101, 106, 218, 224
Kong (emptiness), 272n. 33
Kott, Jan, 33, 43–45, 61, 65, 73, 76, 105, 111, 155, 235n. 8, 240n. 2, 262n. 3; *Shakespeare Our Contemporary*, 111; *Theater of Essence*, 243n. 31
Kunju, 39, 74, 189–90, 194, 198–204, 274n. 14
Kurihara, Komaki, 74–75
Kurosawa, Akira, 45, 76, 215–16; *King Lear (Ran)*, 45; *The Throne of Blood*, 45, 76, 215–16
Kyogen, 77, 101, 223–29, 247n. 61

Lacan, Jacques, 2, 81–82, 85
Laclau, Ernesto, 229
Laqueur, Thomas, 114
Laughter, 3, 72, 75, 94–98, 101–2, 106–7, 121–22, 147, 218, 255n. 42, 259n. 24
Laughton, Charles, 159–60
Lévi-Strauss, Claude, 1–3, 16–23, 80, 234 n. 3; *The Savage Mind*, 16–17; *The Structural Study of Myth*, 19; *The View from Afar*, 1
Lewis, P. Wyndham, 61
Li Ang, 248n. 78
Li Jiayao, 190, 268n. 2
Liang Guanhua, 270n. 15
Libertarianism, 94
Libertinism, 94
Libido, 84, 92, 99
Linguistic code, 67–68, 78, 199, 205, 207–8, 212

Lin Zhaohua, 248n. 73, 270n. 15
Lister, David, 234n. 4
Livingston, Rodney, 267n. 59
Livy, 143, 164–67
Lorre, Peter, 75
Love-in-idleness (flower), 112–14
Lu Xun, 195
Luxemburg, Rosa, 25

MacCary, Thomas, 126, 250n. 17
Macherey, Pierre, 83
Machiavelli, Niccolò, 166–67, 193; *Discourses on the First Ten Books of Titus Livius*, 166–67; *The Prince*, 166
Madhyamika Buddhism, 215, 229
Magic, 21, 23–26, 123
Magritte, René, 271n. 18
Malinowski, Bronislav, 80
Manheim, Ralph, 179, 266n. 49
Mansaku, Namura, 66; *The Braggart Samurai (Kyogen Falstaff)*, 66–68
Mao Zedong, 178, 210; *On Contradiction*, 178
Marlowe, Christopher, 156; *Life of Edward II*, 156
Marsden, Jean, 234n. 6
Marx Brothers, 72
Marx, Karl, 15, 99–100, 177
Marxism, 13–15, 19, 30–31, 53, 81–82, 151–52, 187. See also Post-Marxism
Mayakovsky, Vladimir, 25
McLuskie, Kathleen, 103
Mead, Margaret, 80
Mei Lanfang, 208
Meier-Graefe, Julius, 12
Melodrama, 195, 203, 211
Menander, 116, 122
Mendelssohn, Felix Bartholdy, 109
Meyerhold, Vsevolod, 208
Michaelis, Karen, 50
Miller, Arthur, 198
Mimesis, 3, 7, 36–37, 39–42, 131, 145, 193, 229, 234n. 5, 242nn. 16, 20, 21, 27, 255n. 39. See also Mimetic reading; Mimetic realism

# Index

Mimetic reading, 3, 7, 78, 102–3, 115, 124–25, 144–45
Mimetic realism, 37–42, 63–64, 70, 73, 76–77, 103–4, 115, 125, 229
Miner, Earl, 35–42, 220; on narrative, 38; and security of subject position, 38, 40
Minotaur, 111
Miola, Robert, 126
Misrecognition, 138, 144–48, 222
Miyoshi, Masao, 27–28
Mnouchkine, Ariane, 28, 33–35, 45, 49, 57–65, 68, 72–76, 78, 242n. 17; compares Artaud and Brecht, 62–63; and East Asian style, 61–65; 1789, 62; German reaction to, 49, 57–60; L'âge d'or, 62
Molière, Jean-Baptiste P., 92, 117; Don Juan, or The Statue at the Feast, 92
Molina, Tirso de, 92
Momose, Izume, 239n. 56
Montaigne, Michel de, 8, 193
Montrose, Louis, 114, 256n. 52
Mörike, Eduard, 94; Mozart auf der Reise nach Prag, 94
Mouffe, Chantal, 229
Mozart, Wolfgang Amadeus, 80, 91–94; Don Giovanni, 80, 91–94, 104
Mozi, 52
Muir, Kenneth, 192, 256n. 45
Müller, Heiner, 14, 43
Myth, 16–19, 22, 26, 92, 192, 228; and psychoanalysis, 18
Mythemes, 21–25
Mythical thought, 17–19

Nagarjuna, 20, 215
Nel, Christof, 264n. 25
Nelson, T. G. A., 122
Neoplatonism, 8, 17, 104, 244n. 42
New Comedy, 116, 126
New Historicism, 192
Nietzsche, Friedrich, 2, 10–13, 16, 19, 22, 93, 117, 215, 219; active nihilism, 13; Apollonian form, 10, 12; disdain for anti-Semitism, 11; disgust with German nationalism, 11; and East Asian culture, 13; on Euripidean drama, 11–12, 22; on falsity of the economy, 11; as immoralist, 11; in relation to Brecht, 11–13, 22; and Will, 10, 93; *The Birth of Tragedy*, 10–12; *Ecce Homo*, 12; *On Truth and Lies in an Extra-Moral Sense*, 219
Ninagawa, Yukio, 35, 68–69, 73–74, 76–77, 216, 248n. 70, 249n. 79; *Macbeth*, 68, 73, 216; *Medea*, 68–69; *The Tempest*, 68, 77
Nirvana, 3, 19, 23, 215, 229
Noh theater, 1, 4, 7, 27–29, 40–41, 66, 71–72, 76, 106, 219, 223, 244n. 42, 248n. 70; *Hagoromo*, 71; social function of, 27–28; and Western theater compared, 27–28. See also Kyogen
North, Thomas, 165–66
Nothing(ness), 3, 19, 194–95, 213, 215–16, 273n. 8

Olivier, Laurence, 157
Opera serie, 94
Order, 7, 20, 23, 25, 42, 51–52, 57, 81–82, 85, 114, 124, 142, 163, 168, 193, 204, 211, 214–15, 217, 220. See also Feudalism; Rectification of names
Orientalism, 33–35, 61, 213, 245n. 51. See also Orientalizing
Orientalizing, 6, 27–28, 63–64
Orphic naturalism, 254n. 37, 255n. 39

Palitzsch, Peter, 158, 177
Pannwitz, Rudolph, 48
Paris Theater Festival, 246n. 54
Parsons, Robert, 168
Partridge, Eric, 260n. 29
Pastoral, 36, 105
Patriarchy, 81–82, 106, 143–44, 182, 215, 253n. 36
Patrician, 9, 141–42, 161, 164–65, 172–73, 175–76, 181–82, 186–87. See also Plebeian

293

Paul, Saint, 123, 132, 169; *Epistle to the Ephesians*, 123, 132
Pavis, Patrice, 31–33, 35
Peking opera, 189, 195, 197; and kunju compared, 189, 199–200. *See also* Chinese opera; Jingju (Peking opera)
Peloponnesian Wars, 119
Pensée sauvage, 17
Pepys, Samuel, 203
Performative interpretation, 14, 157, 263n. 10
Peron, Juan, 163
Personality structure, 80–81, 85, 107, 250n. 16
Phenomenalism, 105
Philosophical farce, 4, 222–29
Philosophical realism, 36–37, 39, 242n. 17
Picasso, Pablo, 247n. 60
Pietzcker, Carl, 250n. 17
Pingtan, 38
Pirandello, Luigi, 42; *Six Characters in Search of an Author*, 42
Plague, 162–64, 172, 266n. 44
Plato, 254n. 37, 259n. 37; *Cratylus*, 254n. 37
Platonism, 7, 37, 104–5, 111, 130, 137, 193, 254n. 37. *See also* Neoplatonism
Plautus, T. M., 21, 42, 116–30, 139–42, 222; *Amphitryon*, 129; *Menaechmi*, 3, 21, 42, 120–22, 129, 139–40, 144–50, 222, 257n. 4; *Miles Gloriosus*, 122, 145
Plebeian, 9, 41, 156, 161–63, 171–72, 175–76, 180, 182, 184, 186–87, 260n. 36, 262n. 6, 267n. 55
Plutarch, 158, 161–67, 171–74, 178; class distinctions, 172
Polanski, Roman, 208–9
Politics of the sign, 7–8, 234n. 4
Positive unconscious of knowledge, 2, 87, 100, 246n. 58
Post-Marxism, 3, 16, 27, 194, 229–30

Postcolonial, 60–61
Postmodern, 6, 31–33, 36, 60–61, 74
Poststructuralism, 3, 8, 16, 193–94, 230, 238n. 42
Potter, Lois, 201, 203
Pound, Ezra, 49, 71, 183, 255n. 40; and Brecht compared, 183
Prince Otsu, 217
Pronko, Leonard, 74
Proxemic code, 31, 65, 68–69, 73, 199, 205, 207–8
Psychoanalysis, 2, 16, 18, 33, 80, 84–89, 94, 108, 196, 251n. 20. *See also* Psychoanalytic readings; Shaman; Transference
Psychoanalytic readings, 3, 9, 80–87, 92, 121, 126–28, 192, 230, 250n. 17
Psychologizing, 35, 43, 48, 54, 72, 75–76, 127, 170, 198. *See also* Egopsychology
Psychomythology, 16–17
Psychosocial, 56–57, 139, 147, 198, 213, 216. *See also* Fromm, Erich; Social character; Social unconscious
Punic Wars, 119, 140–42

Rabelais, François, 40, 234n. 5
Racine, Jean, 249n. 1
Rectification of names, 3, 104–5, 255n. 40
Relationalism, 3, 19–20, 52, 55–56, 80, 102, 215, 229–30, 245n. 46
Renaissance language theory, 193, 255n. 39. *See also* Conventionalism
Repression, 4, 6–7, 42, 47, 51, 65, 73–75, 79, 82, 87, 89, 97, 99, 102, 106–8, 128–29, 133, 138, 204–5, 211, 213, 220, 224, 231; aesthetic, 76, 78, 231; critical, 3, 30, 49, 109, 127; cultural, 3–4, 6, 29, 42, 47, 53, 76–78, 89, 108, 128, 138, 211; and depression, 7, 97–99, 102, 106–7, 211, 224; and double identity, 79, 82, 126–27, 129, 144, 147; externalized, 42, 46, 74–75, 92, 209, 213, 245n. 46; and female

Index

social unconscious, 106, 110, 115, 271n. 29; and social character, 99, 103; socially constructed, 65, 99–100, 106, 109, 115, 128, 133, 138, 149, 204–5, 220; and social unconscious, 7, 73. *See also* Social character; Social unconscious
Ricoeur, Paul, 242n. 16
Riehle, Wolfgang, 126
Riley, Jo, 271n. 29
Rimer, Thomas, 30
Ritual, 16–18, 22, 26–27, 29, 46–47, 69, 73, 77, 118, 126, 239n. 57, 244n. 42, 260n. 36, 271n. 29
Rivière, Joan, 82
Roman Republic, 119, 140, 162, 164–65, 176, 182; economic relations compared with Shakespeare's England, 142, 148–50, 162–63; and Greek city-state compared, 119–20; Lex Oppia, 142–43; Lex Voconia, 142; Ordo matronarum (women's assembly), 142; position of women, 140–44, 149–50; property rights, 140–41, 148; *secessio*, 265n. 33; social change, 140–42; marriage, 141–42; relations of production, 142. *See also* Patrician; Plebeian; Slaves
Romance, 22–25, 90, 127, 131–32
Rouse, John, 262n. 6, 266n. 49
Royal Shakespeare Company, 109, 162
Rubinstein, Frankie, 260n. 29
Rülicke-Weiler, Käthe, 158

Samsara, 3, 19, 23, 215, 229
Sartre, Jean-Paul, 246n. 54
Schlegel, August Wilhelm, 103
Schlegel-Tieck translations, 153–54, 158, 179, 183
Schopenhauer, Arthur, 84, 93; and "will," 84
Scragg, Leah, 123–25, 138, 149
Seami. *See* Zeami

Segal, Erich, 126
Self-transcendence, 101, 106, 218, 223, 228–29
Semantic naturalism, 3, 41, 193
Semiotic animism. *See* Orphic naturalism
Senda, Koreya, 29–30, 75, 269n. 2
Sexual punning, 135–39
Seym, Simone, 245n. 53
Shakespeare, William: Chinese Brechtian, 190; in Chinese theater, 189–90, 194, 198–204, 207–18; essential assumption for reading, 171; German translation, 153–54; in Japanese theater, 29–30, 66–68, 73, 75, 77, 216, 231, 233n. 1, 239n. 56, 248n. 70; Marxist reading, 151–52; and Noh theater compared, 239n. 56; personality of, 81; and Plautus, 117. Works by: *As You Like It*, 103, 105–6; *The Comedy of Errors*, 3, 21, 121–24, 126–39, 142; *Coriolanus*, 2, 9–10, 43–45, 156–58, 160, 162–75, 234n. 5, 235n. 7; *Hamlet*, 20, 30, 41–43, 154, 243n. 31; *Henry IV, Part 1*, 63–64, 151; *Henry V*, 151–52, 157, 162, 192; *Henry VI*, 151, 263n. 3; *King Lear*, 43, 45, 253n. 36; *Love's Labor's Lost*, 95, 102, 104, 254n. 37; *Macbeth*, 39, 68, 73–74, 135, 189–94, 198–218, 274n. 14; *A Midsummer Night's Dream*, 39, 85–86, 107–15; *The Merry Wives of Windsor*, 66; *Othello*, 155, 160; *Richard II*, 75, 151; *Richard III*, 151, 209, 262n. 3; *Romeo and Juliet*, 108; "Sonnet 135," 84; "Sonnet 143," 84; *The Tempest*, 21–24, 26, 77; *Twelfth Night*, 33, 104, 138. *See also* Transformation
Shaman, 18, 23, 26, 244n. 42
Shanghai Kunju Theater, 189
Shintoism, 217
Simonds, Peggy Muñoz, 239n. 56
Slaves, 120, 122, 142, 144–45, 147–48, 164; and identity, 120

Social change, 93, 140, 158, 163, 211–12, 220
Social character, 75, 77, 79, 99–100, 211, 250n. 16, 254n. 36
Social unconscious, 2, 7, 13, 16, 21–22, 28, 52, 55–56, 73, 76–78, 80, 82, 87, 92, 94–95, 97, 99–101, 103–8, 110, 112, 115, 121, 144, 149, 164, 174, 211–12, 244n. 42
Socialist realism, 51
Socrates, 10–11
Source / target model, 32, 34, 47
Spargo, Tasmin, 106
Spectacle, 201, 203–4, 210
Speech act theory, 102, 255n. 37
Spenser, Benjamin, 163
Spiegel, Hubert, 264n. 25
Spielberg, Steven, 76
Spinoza, Baruch, 99, 193
Spitzer, Leo, 256n. 47
Spoken drama (huaju), 57, 74, 194–98
Stalin, Josef, 25, 44, 161–62, 177
Stanislavsky, Konstantin, 160
Steffin, Margarete, 250n. 10
*Story of the Bloody Hands (Xue shou ji)*, 200
Strauss, Richard, 94; *Don Juan*, 94
Strindberg, August, 83; *The Father*, 83–85
Sudden glory, 102
Sunyata, 272n. 33, 274n. 8
Surrogate action, 96–97, 101–2, 106, 133, 211
Suzuki, Tadashi, 68–69, 73, 76, 78, 248n. 70; on gesture, 69; *Clytemnestra*, 68; *The Bacchae*, 68; *The Trojan Women*, 68
Swift, Jonathan, 40
Symbolic action, 101–2, 106

Takahashi, Yasunari, 247n. 70, 248n. 74
*Taniko*, 27
Tate, Nahum, 156–57; *The Ingratitude of a Common-Wealth*, 156–57

Taylor, Gary, 258n. 11
Tennenhouse, Leonard, 192
Tenschert, Klaus, 262n. 6, 263n. 10
Terence, 116, 126
Textual anthropology, 2–3, 33, 35, 79, 129, 261n. 1
Third World, 27, 35, 53, 62
Totemic thought, 16–17
Tragedy, 2, 10–11, 36, 56, 97–98, 101, 157, 203, 216, 220–21, 253n. 36
Transference, 80, 83, 87, 128
Transformation, 134–37
Trickster, 19–25
Tudor ideology, 167–69
Tung, Constantine, 270n. 13
Type, 121, 221–22

Unconscious, 2, 47, 61, 65, 75, 80, 87–88, 99, 102, 108, 125, 160; of the character 7, 47, 56, 64, 75, 83, 85, 93, 108, 201, 208–9, 212; Elizabethan, 3, 108–15, 129, 131–38; externalized, 64, 75, 93, 107, 208–9, 239n. 56, 242n. 21; and farce, 3, 127–28, 221; historicized, 2, 16, 78, 89–90, 92, 94, 96, 116, 129, 153, 259n. 24, 261n. 1; of reader, 86, 90, 94, 155, 193; Roman, 3, 119, 122, 129, 144–48; socially constructed, 2; of the text, 7, 83, 88, 131, 133, 250n. 12; of theory, 15. *See also* Aesthetic; Author function; Cultural unconscious; Desire; Freud; Fromm; Koestler; Laughter; Joke; Positive unconscious of knowledge; Social unconscious
Unified self. *See* Identity
Universals, 48, 124–25, 155, 243n. 39

van Laan, Thomas, 126, 258n. 15
Verisimilitude, 129, 145, 242n.21
Verma, Rajiva, 22
Vickers, Brian, 234n. 3
Visual code, 54, 65–66, 156, 159, 199, 200–203, 207, 211
Voltaire, F. M. A. de, 11

Index

Wagner, Richard, 12; *Tristan and Isolde*, 12
Waley, Arthur, 26–27
Waller, Gary, 80
Wang Xiaoying, 270n. 14
Warner, William, 149
*The Wars of the Roses*, 151
Watling, E. F., 258n. 13
Wayne, John, 273n. 5
Weigel, Helene, 46
Weill, Kurt, 11
Weimann, Robert, 126, 268n. 2
Wei Shu-chu, 271n. 29
Wekwerth, Manfred, 158, 178, 262n. 6, 263n. 10, 268n. 59
Wells, Robin Headlam, 265n. 38
Whistler, James, 49
Wilde, Oscar, 219
"Will," 10, 84, 93. *See also* Desire; Libido
Willett, John, 178
Williams, David, 61
Williams, Raymond, 253n. 36
Wilson, Richard, 158
Winkler, John J., 255n. 42
Witchcraft, 123, 133–35, 148, 191, 200, 208, 212–13
Wright, Elizabeth, 81–82
Wu Han, 210; *Hai Rui Dismissed from Office*, 210

Yangge, 197
Yeats, William Butler, 49, 71; *Purgatory*, 244n. 42

Zeami (Seami), 1, 246n. 55
Zeeveld, W. Gordon, 168
Zen Buddhism, 101, 106, 223, 229, 244n. 46
Zhang Ning, 270n. 16, 271n. 23, 274n. 14
Zhang Yimou, 248n. 78
Zheng ming. *See* Rectification of names
Zheng Shifeng, 212
Zhuangzi (Chuang Tse), 13
Žižek, Slavoj, 252n. 23
Zwierlein, Otto, 257n. 1

Antony Tatlow is Professor of Comparative Literature at the University of
Dublin. He was President of the International Brecht Society from 1982–1990,
and founding head of the Department of Comparative Literature at the University of Hong Kong from 1987–1996. He has been Consultant to the Central
Academy of Drama, Beijing from 1986, and a Member of Academia Europaea
from 1999.

He is the author of *Brechts Ost Asien: ein Parallog* (1998), *Benwen Renleixue*
[*Textual Anthropology: A Practice of Reading*] (1996), *Shakespeare in Comparison: A Politics of the Sign* (1995), *Repression and Figuration—From Totem to Utopia*
(1990), *The Mask of Evil: Brecht's Response to the Poetry, Theatre, and Thought of
China and Japan* (1977), and *Brecht's Chinesische Gedichte* (1973).


Library of Congress Cataloging-in-Publication Data

Tatlow, Antony.

Shakespeare, Brecht, and the intercultural sign / Antony Tatlow.

p. cm. — (Post-contemporary interventions)

Includes bibliographical references and index.

ISBN 0-8223-2753-8 (cloth : alk. paper)

ISBN 0-8223-2763-5 (pbk. : alk. paper)

1. Shakespeare, William, 1564–1616—Adaptations—History and criticism.

2. Brecht, Bertolt, 1898–1956—Adaptations—History and criticism.

3. Shakespeare, William, 1564–1616—Appreciation—Asia. 4. Brecht, Bertolt,
1898–1956—Appreciation—Asia. 5. Intercultural communication in literature.
6. Intercultural communication. 7. Theater—Asia—History. I. Title. II. Series.
PR2880.A1 T37 2001

822.3'3—dc21         2001023233

www.ingramcontent.com/pod-product-compliance
Lightning Source LLC
Chambersburg PA
CBHW070753230426
43665CB00017B/2347